BIG CRIME AND BIG POLICING

All about Big Money?

Edited by Tonita Murray, Elizabeth Kirley, and Stephen Schneider

Following money over national borders, banking systems, casinos, and free trade zones, as well as the world of the corrupt elites, *Big Crime and Big Policing* brings new scholarly and practical insights into our understanding of the interplay of money, crime, and policing on the grand scale.

In this wide-ranging volume, a mixed group of scholars and practitioners aim to show how money dictates the scope and nature of financial and corporate crimes, and the impact of these crimes on national economies, social institutions, and communal well-being alike. The book examines how the combined efforts of governments and international organizations fail to stop financial crime at its source and, despite apparently generous human and financial resources, police and law enforcement efforts ultimately fall short of defeating big crime and of meeting public safety needs. International in scope, *Big Crime and Big Policing* provides fresh reflection on a significant problem of our age, one that demands greater attention from governments and the public.

TONITA MURRAY is an independent researcher and police reform consultant.

ELIZABETH KIRLEY is a professor in the Professional LLM program at Osgoode Hall Law School and called to the Ontario bar.

STEPHEN SCHNEIDER is a professor in the Department of Criminology at Saint Mary's University.

Big Crime and Big Policing

All about Big Money?

EDITED BY TONITA MURRAY, ELIZABETH KIRLEY, AND STEPHEN SCHNEIDER

UNIVERSITY OF TORONTO PRESS
Toronto Buffalo London

© University of Toronto Press 2024
Toronto Buffalo London
utorontopress.com
Printed and bound by CPI Group (UK) Ltd, Croydon, CR0 4YY

ISBN 978-1-4875-5373-9 (cloth)   ISBN 978-1-4875-5377-7 (EPUB)
ISBN 978-1-4875-5376-0 (paper)   ISBN 978-1-4875-5378-4 (PDF)

Library and Archives Canada Cataloguing in Publication

Title: Big crime and big policing : all about big money? / edited by
   Tonita Murray, Elizabeth Kirley, and Stephen Schneider.
Names: Murray, Tonita, 1939– editor. | Kirley, Elizabeth Anne, editor. |
   Schneider, Stephen, 1963– editor.
Description: Includes bibliographical references and index.
Identifiers: Canadiana (print) 20230552757 | Canadiana (ebook)
   20230552781 | ISBN 9781487553739 (cloth) | ISBN 9781487553760 (paper) |
   ISBN 9781487553777 (EPUB) | ISBN 9781487553784 (PDF)
Subjects: LCSH: Commercial crimes. | LCSH: Police.
Classification: LCC HV6768 .B54 2024 | DDC 364.16/8 – dc23

Cover design: Epsilon Dvlpmnt and John Beadle
Cover images: Wirestock Creators/Shutterstock.com; Karolina Grabowska/Pexels;
Impact Photography/Shutterstock.com; Mehaniq/Shutterstock.com

Photo credits for Leonardo da Vinci, *Salvator Mundi*: *(left)* Pre-treatment photograph of the painting, May 2005 © 2011 Salvator Mundi LLC, Photograph Robert Simon; *(middle)* Cleaned or "stripped state" photograph of the painting © 2011 Salvator Mundi LLC, Photograph courtesy Dianne Modestini; *(right)* After-treatment photograph, February 2011 © 2011 Salvator Mundi LLC, Photograph Tim Nighswander/Imaging4Art

We wish to acknowledge the land on which the University of Toronto Press operates. This land is the traditional territory of the Wendat, the Anishnaabeg, the Haudenosaunee, the Métis, and the Mississaugas of the Credit First Nation.

University of Toronto Press acknowledges the financial support of the Government of Canada, the Canada Council for the Arts, and the Ontario Arts Council, an agency of the Government of Ontario, for its publishing activities.

Funded by the   Financé par le
Government   gouvernement   Canada
of Canada   du Canada

Contents

Foreword vii
RICHARD G. MOSLEY

Tribute to Professor Margaret E. Beare xi
ANDREW GOLDSMITH

Introduction   1

Section One: Global Money Systems and Financial Crimes: Limitations of State Regulation

1 Policing and the Money System   15
   JAMES SHEPTYCKI

2 Big Banks, Big Money, and Big Crimes in the Era of "Too Big to Fail"   35
   STEPHEN SCHNEIDER

3 Locating the Centre: State, Capital, and the Political Economy of Money Laundering in Canada   59
   SANAA AHMED

4 Policing Financial Crime – Do We Care?   83
   PETER M. GERMAN

Section Two: Beyond Reach: Crimes of the Entrepreneurial Elites

5 Opportunistic Prosecution? Huawei and the Role of Banking Regulation in China's Trade War with the United States   105
   STEPHEN WILKS

6 From Brushstrokes to Keystrokes: Policing Entrepreneurial
  Art Crime   121
  ELIZABETH A. KIRLEY

7 Big Money, Small Tax: The Normalization of Tax Evasion   149
  LAUREEN SNIDER

Section Three: Big Police: If We Can't Live with Them Can We Live without Them?

8 Reform of the Police   171
  PETER K. MANNING

9 Inquiring into Public Policing   187
  MARGARET E. BEARE

10 Nowhere to Turn for Survivors of Gender-Based Violence: Misogyny in
   Policing   207
   ANNA WILLATS

11 Offloading, Upstreaming, Defunding, and Costing: Re-thinking
   Calls to Police for Absconding Social Work and Mental Health
   Clients   229
   LAURA HUEY AND LORNA FERGUSON

12 Engaging Evil? Conducting Research with and on Policing
   Organizations   249
   KEVIN D. HAGGERTY, SANDRA M. BUCERIUS,
   AND DANIEL J. JONES

13 Big Policing and Defunding: What's at Stake?   265
   TONITA MURRAY

Contributors   293

Index   297

Foreword

It is a privilege for me to write a foreword to this collection of essays in honour of Dr. Margaret Beare. I know that the topics addressed in this book were important to Margaret and she would be grateful to the contributors, editors, and publishers for making it happen after the planned colloquium in March 2020 could not proceed due to the pandemic.

Margaret and I began to work for the federal government in Ottawa at roughly the same time in early 1982. Margaret joined the Ministry of the Solicitor General as a Senior Research Officer in policing policy. I was seconded from the Ontario Attorney General to work on criminal law amendments with the Department of Justice. We were both assigned to, among other things, the "Federal-Provincial-Territorial Working Group on Enterprise Crime." This project was prompted by a study conducted for the Attorney General of British Columbia, entitled "The Business of Crime," on the American Racketeer Influenced and Corrupt Organizations Statute (RICO). Our task was to examine the US experience with RICO and report to Ministers on whether it could be adapted to Canadian law and practice. The focus was on the seizure and forfeiture of the profits generated by drug trafficking, prostitution, gambling, and other traditional gang-related crimes. This is what we saw as "big crime" at the time.

Margaret had a great deal more knowledge of the subject than I based on her studies and work in the United States. I had courtroom experience as an Assistant Crown Attorney in Ontario and involvement with the Law Reform Commission of Canada representing the interests of the Canadian Association of Crown Counsel. But research-driven policy development was only a vague concept to me. RICO seemed to be a good idea, I thought, so why don't we give it a try? Margaret proceeded to school me in the many pitfalls and traps that lay in the path of the "let's give it a try" approach to public policy.

We did ultimately report to Ministers, and that work led to what became the Proceeds of Crime amendments to the Criminal Code in the mid-1980s and funding for integrated task forces led by the RCMP. We also worked on a great many other proposals for legislative and program changes with colleagues from other departments and agencies. Concerted action was required to deal with transnational organized crime and money laundering. Among other things, this work contributed to the creation of the Financial Transactions Reporting Agency (FINTRAC), international bodies such as the Financial Action Task Force (FATF), and Canada's mutual assistance legislation and treaties.

Many of the same issues, with the addition of terrorist financing, remain of concern to the international community, as was noted in the 2016 FATF assessment of Canada's measures and the 2021 follow-up report. As the introduction to this book states, the globalization of markets and looser controls on the money system have facilitated the movement and conversion of the proceeds of crime within legitimate commercial and financial structures. This was reflected in the Report of the Commission of Inquiry into Money Laundering in British Columbia in June 2022. New players have entered the field that were not contemplated forty years ago when "The Business of Crime" was written, such as virtual asset service providers. Moreover, the global threat landscape has changed considerably with the growth of terrorism and the financial systems that fund it.

The other theme of this book is "big policing." My sense is that the resources required to fund the police in Canada and their influence on public policy have grown considerably over the past forty years. When Margaret and I appeared on the Federal scene, the Canadian Association of Chiefs of Police had a history of being consulted on changes to law and policy that could have an impact on their operations. We attended their meetings for that purpose. The Canadian Police Association, representing other ranks, was only then beginning to have a national presence but is now a major voice on policing and public safety.

Margaret and I had vigorous debates, especially over what powers the police required to deal with money laundering and gang violence. But even when she derided my ideas, her sense of humour was always just below the surface. "But, but, Mosley" she would sputter before launching a cascade of arguments ending in gales of laughter. I couldn't help but join in.

At meetings with police organizations, Margaret had a unique ability to deliver a tough message without offending her audience, which I greatly admired. They too would laugh with her while reluctantly accepting that what they were asking for would simply not fly in Ottawa and the provincial capitals.

The misuse of police powers by individual officers was the focus of much of the work on criminal justice in government in the 1980s, as it was in the Law Reform Commission's Research Programme. There was less attention to questions of police management given the notion, inherited from the United Kingdom, that their internal operations were independent of government. But the larger picture of problems with police governance and accountability was always on Margaret's radar, and her work contributed to the understanding of those issues. As we have seen from recent events, Canada is not immune from the type of policing problems which occur in the United States. But it is not clear how those problems can be resolved. Do we ask too much of the police? What is it exactly that we expect them to do? And should funding be diverted from enforcement to social services? These are some of the questions which will be addressed in this book.

During our work together, Margaret and I became good friends. At the outset, neither of us had any intention of remaining in the federal government. Margaret's natural home was academia where she could conduct independent research and express her views freely. Which she could not do in the bureaucracy. While she remained in a management capacity for ten years, she found this stifling and her intent was always to get back to what she loved best. This she did by escaping first to Queen's and then to York and Osgoode. For my part, I agreed to manage the criminal law policy shop in Justice "for just a few months" and remained for two decades before I too returned to where I started, in the courts.

In later years, when I was in Toronto, we would often get together for meals and catch up on our lives and views of current events. Sometimes, dinners were at Margaret's home on Major Street with others of her wide collection of friends. I remember stimulating conversations fuelled with copious amounts of red wine and punctuated by Margaret's infectious laughter as she commented on the follies of public policies and personalities. We didn't always agree, but I never left those evenings without being better informed.

As Andrew Goldsmith says in his wonderful tribute, I was just one of the many who was fortunate to share time, food, wine, ideas, and laughter with Margaret over her eventful and meaningful life. For that I will always be grateful, as I am to those who have made this book possible.

Hon. Richard G. Mosley
Federal Court, Ottawa

Margaret Evelyn Beare

A Personal and Professional Tribute

My first memory of Margaret was as a graduate student at the Centre of Criminology, University of Toronto. It was the summer of 1981, and I was filling in over lunchtime at the Centre's reception desk, one of my side hustles to cover my living expenses. This informally dressed, friendly, auburn-haired woman approached the desk, announcing to me that she was a new visiting fellow at the Centre and that she believed she had a desk space arranged for her. On hearing my Antipodean accent, she soon asked where I was from and what was I doing in Toronto. It didn't take long for her to reveal that she had spent some time in Australia, in the early 1970s, tutoring in anthropology at the (then) Western Australian Institute of Technology in Perth. Forty years ago, to have been an Australian graduate student in Toronto was relatively uncommon; as one of that discrete group, for me to encounter a Canadian who had visited Australia, let alone to have lived there for any period, was almost unprecedented. While Canadians and Australians at the time (and since) found it easy to relate to each other given commonalities of history and cultural traditions, I was well-used to Canadian friends saying how much they would like to visit Australia but adding that it was "so far away." So Margaret very early on distinguished herself in my eyes by not only being interested in Australia but by showing a familiarity and fondness for the place and its people.

Over the coming weeks and months, we realized that we were also pursuing similar research interests and had much to talk about on that front. Both of us were looking at policing in Ontario, Margaret's was focusing on media representation work undertaken by the Metropolitan Toronto police, while I was looking at police unionism across the province of Ontario (a strange topic perhaps for someone from Adelaide, South Australia). We consequently had many stimulating, sometimes robust, conversations about what was going on at that time. Questions of police governance and accountability became interests of ongoing interest to Margaret for the rest of her life. The early 1980s was a fascinating time to be interested in policing in Toronto. In an increasingly diverse community, problems of police dealings with community members were coming to public attention, resulting in protests and demands for new ways of moderating police–community relationships. The local civil liberties association was prominent in demands for improved ways of handling public complaints about police behaviours. A trial public complaints mechanism was put in place in 1981 at the city level, that subsequently was expanded to the provincial level, and that became a model for similar innovations in Manitoba and other provinces in a relatively quick time. However, as Margaret and others associated with the Centre of Criminology at the time (including Philip Stenning) were to find, there were always going to be difficulties reconciling police actions with community expectations, providing a source of ongoing research opportunities as well as prompts for community activism. Margaret became friendly with the late Alan Borovoy, general counsel in those days for the Canadian Civil Liberties Association in Toronto, because of their shared interest and engagement in this area. Through visiting her in the Annex, I met Alan once or twice.

Early on, I came to realize that spending time with Margaret was never dull; her passionate positions on various topics combined with her empathy and concern for others, including those she was engaging with in discussion, made her a stimulating professional colleague as well as friend. At that time, Margaret was working to complete her dissertation at Columbia University, New York, and had taken an apartment near the University on Spadina Avenue in the Annex district. This was only a few blocks from my room at Massey College, and even closer to the blues music venues located around the University of Toronto. Her apartment was only a few hundred metres from the renowned El Mocambo club, where famously Margaret Trudeau had been spotted a few years earlier in the company of members of the Rolling Stones. I went there with Margaret once or twice, once to see a touring band from my home city of Adelaide, but never encountered any celebrities of Margaret Trudeau's stature. Our shared love of music provided numerous occasions through the early 1980s to visit various clubs around Toronto. Another favourite of mine, Alberts Hall on Spadina, sponsored a number of visiting Chicago blues acts. I recall seeing such legendary artists as Buddy Guy, Matt (Guitar) Murphy, and Hubert Sumlin there, often in the company of Margaret. During this time, Margaret drove a red MG sports car, usually with the top off if the weather permitted. She cut quite a dash in that car, driving around the city, reflecting her sense of style and adventure. Not having a car myself, I found myself a passenger in that car from time to time. We once drove from Ottawa out to her family cottage where I met her sisters and her father (her mother had passed away by then). We were both, of course, young enough then to spring in and out of such a low car with ease. Later on, she graduated to a Volkswagen Golf – a convertible model, of course!

Our paths separated around 1984. Margaret had moved to Ottawa a year or so earlier to take up a public service job in the Solicitor-General's Secretariat. I visited her a few times in the early years. She had the misfortune on one occasion in midwinter of trying to teach me to skate on the Rideau Canal. She was naturally more gifted in the skating stakes. After a respectable interval, we called it a day and retired to somewhere drier and warmer (me with agonizingly painful ankles), in my case, never to repeat the experience. I moved to the United Kingdom in 1984, but we stayed in touch. Another thing I shared with Margaret was an appetite for travel, including long-distance travel. This enabled me to visit Toronto from time to time up to the time of her death. As well as seeing her in Ottawa, I visited her later during her time teaching at Queen's University in Kingston, Ontario. She shared an apartment there at one point with several other academics. After a late night out, I woke up one morning in the apartment, and went in search of something to drink and eat. By the time Margaret arose, I had been through the contents of the refrigerator and cupboards in order to find myself some breakfast. She emerged when I was halfway through downing some kind of fruit juice I'd found in the fridge. "I'm not sure how long that's been there," she said to me. I hesitated and reached for the juice bottle. The expiry date indicated it was indeed past its "use by" period, three years past! I learned a couple of lessons; always check the dates in future before consuming, especially if found in the fridge of a shared house or apartment; and (having survived the experience) never underestimate the longevity of Canadian supermarket fruit juice products. Another reliable way of meeting up with Margaret, despite the fact of living on different continents, was through her longstanding commitment to attending the annual American Society of Criminology conferences wherever they occurred. She attended as often as she was able and was a frequent contributor to the panels on organized crime. When in Vancouver, she could often be found staying at the Sylvia Hotel. She also loved attending the Economic Crime conferences held in Cambridge, England, each year, and caught up with many colleagues and friends on those occasions.

As many of her friends from out of town or country can attest, Margaret was always a wonderful, welcoming host. In addition to invitations to come to dinner, there was for many of us the offer of a bedroom if we were visiting Toronto. When she moved to Major Street, there was always the option of the room at the top of the stairs, with its own bathroom. Many prominent and/or colourful figures stayed there over the years, including Peter Manning, the US policing scholar; Freddy Martens, former Executive Director of the Pennsylvania Crime Commission; and Nigel Hadgkiss, one of Australia's top anti-corruption fighters. Many of her visitors would travel up to York University to speak to or meet with her students in Sociology and, later, Law. Her friendship networks were, as one can see, both extensive and strong, with many of us staying with her on multiple occasions. She expected little in return, other than one's company. Inevitably there would be delicious dinners and generous quantities of red wine, with often six or more persons present. And always, so many books!

Margaret loved literature of all kinds. These visits were occasions to be relished and are now memories to be treasured.

An important moment in Margaret's life, of course, was her adoption of her daughter, Nhai, around 1999 or the beginning of 2000. In August of 2000, I brought my young family to Toronto to take up a five-month visiting sabbatical position at Osgoode Hall Law School. During this time, I was attached to the Nathanson Centre, which Margaret then headed. I had been drawn to her Centre in part by my growing interest in transnational crime and policing, which were key themes of the Centre. My family set up in a small rental house in the Bloor/Jane area of west Toronto, near the Humber ravine. Margaret had been invited to a crime conference in Italy, which she was keen to attend (no surprises there), there was just the issue of who would look after young Nhai, who was four at the time. Jane, my wife, was there and we already had sons aged eleven, nine, and one with us in the house, as well as my five-year-old daughter visiting us from western Canada. When Margaret mentioned her difficulty, Jane offered to take Nhai as well for the duration of Margaret's absence. Margaret duly flew off to Italy, and we juggled five children. I can recall some of that time vividly, some of it not at all now. Jane tells me that I don't remember now because I was away myself overseas for part of that time, doing research in Colombia. However, I do remember some rivalry emerging between Nhai and Katyana, my daughter, that added to the challenges of five young children under the same roof. After Margaret's multiple acts of kindness over many years, we were happy to help out, and Nhai was a delightful child.

In the years that followed, Margaret managed to visit Australia on a couple of occasions. I recall her visit to Alice Springs in 2011 as a keynote speaker at the Australian and New Zealand Society of Criminology annual conference. She was presenting on two of her favourite themes, organized crime and money laundering. She had travelled to Australia business class, and aside from cursing her national airline for its substandard service on the flight over, was intensely conscious of how much her hosts had paid for her airfare. She asked me to look over her PowerPoint presentation before her keynote address. I was flabbergasted to find that she had nearly one hundred slides prepared for a forty-five-minute presentation. Showing her stubborn streak, she pushed back on my suggestion that she cut the number of slides down to a more manageable number. She firmly retorted that she'd come all this way business class, and felt she had to give them value back. Needless to say, she delivered her customary warm and engaging lecture despite the tsunami of slides. As an aside, I reviewed one of her lectures from 2014, archived on YouTube, in preparation for writing this tribute. I was reminded that her fondness for PowerPoint lived on, with something like a modest ninety slides for that particular lecture.

I have touched a couple of times already on Margaret's passion. It was particularly evident in her scholarship in the areas of policing, organized crime, and money laundering as well as in her intense loyalty and commitment to friends and family. Many prominent figures and institutions would find themselves the targets of "friendly fire" in her writings and public lectures in the form of critiques of instances of unjust enrichment, corruption, police misconduct, and other moral shortcomings, delivered in that firm but humorous manner. While never vicious in her criticism, she could be gently scathing of those she disapproved of or who had acted badly. As a longstanding friend, I was aware that though she was not religious, she had Mennonite roots and influences on her mother's side. This bestowed upon her, aside from acute memories of being expected to wear uncomfortable old-style undergarments as a young girl, a strong sense of the importance of personal integrity and a concern for righting the wrongs committed on behalf of public institutions as well as by private entities such as organized crime groups. The problems of "big policing" then, as indeed the problems of "big crime," the twin themes of this volume, lay at the heart of her most significant scholarship. As a researcher interested in organized crime, her work (including her notable book) in the area of criminal conspiracies reflected a complex view of the world in which there were frequently no bright lines between the "good" and the "bad" actors, but also that often bad things occurred on the "official" side of public affairs. She was right to bring these matters to public attention, and to impress upon the many students she taught the importance of looking critically at those who hold and exercise power of any kind.

Her scholarly commitment was as long as it was deep. Her ongoing care and concern for her students was palpable. She continued to work right up to the last months of her life, supervising students towards completion of their degrees. I was hoping to see her in Toronto in June 2019, and she'd indicated before my arrival that she looked forward to catching up, though there was the matter of her medical treatment that might affect when, and for how long, we might meet. Unfortunately, the meeting was not to happen. She'd been put back in Mount Sinai Hospital at the time of my visit and was taking no visitors. In my last couple of communications with her, she always managed to talk down her own problems and to continue to show interest in the lives of others. I had called her a few months earlier, having had word that she was quite unwell, only to be greeted by her on her home phone expressing surprise that I'd called her "all the way from Australia" and inquiring when I would next be visiting Toronto. Her selflessness, lack of self-pity, and residual sense of humour, despite everything, was striking.

I was just one of many of those fortunate to share time, food, wine, ideas, and laughter with Margaret over her eventful and meaningful life. Such friendships are rare. Those who knew her professionally or personally were lucky indeed.

(With thanks to Philip Stenning and Fred Martens for sharing memories and prompting mine.)

Andrew Goldsmith
Emeritus Professor
Flinders University

Introduction

The theme running through this book is money in all its forms. It underpins both crime and policing and is the major factor in making them both big. Crime becomes big when money in different forms is acquired and multiplied into vast wealth by a variety of illegitimate means, which we categorize as financial, white-collar, corporate, and organized crime and their overlapping forms. Policing becomes big in part from the large amounts of money governments spend to control big crime. In the simplest of terms, money flows as a credit to big crime perpetrators but flows out as a debit on the public purse for policing and law enforcement services. This suggests that society pays twice for the activities of big crime: once in having financial resources diverted from the legitimate economic system and second from the high cost of regulating and monitoring legitimate business systems to prevent malfeasance or to investigate and prosecute offences when they occur. There is an opportunity cost to governments in apportioning scarce public resources to preventing and suppressing big crimes that could be spent on education or health care programs rather than protecting the integrity of business and the economy. Nor is it just a case of choices between expenditures on health care or financial crime control, but that resources within the regulatory and policing systems of a country may have to be disproportionately divided between activities aimed at the well-being of society or the containment of the depredations of big crime.

We use the term "big crime" in this book to refer to illegal activities in the financial and business worlds. Until comparatively recently, big crime was regarded mainly as organized criminal activities, such as drug trafficking or gambling, which yield large profits from selling illegal commodities or services. Although still a problem, changes in social attitudes and laws have decriminalized some former organized criminal activities while globalization of markets and looser controls on the money system have focused attention on the financial proceeds of crime. The new focus has given insight into how illegal proceeds can be moved, changed, and reinvested for greater returns, and sheds light on a range of crimes yielding enormous gains that can be committed within the legitimate commercial and financial structures by seemingly trustworthy business practitioners. The prospect of financial gain can also lead those in positions of either public or private trust to collude in illegal transactions, so corruption is also an element of big crime. The activity often crosses the boundaries of enterprises, sectors, and even countries, creating a threat to legitimate financial systems and even to the economies and stability of nations. Added to this danger is the development and application of information technology to business and financial processes. Such innovations as the internet or information management and communications technologies have led to greater efficiencies and profitability but have also enabled the growth of big crime activity and rendered legitimate enterprises more vulnerable to criminal infiltration or direct attack. Present day big crime is thus more extensive, complex, profitable, and threatening to the social and economic fabric than earlier manifestations of organized and white-collar crime, or even street-level crime.

"Big policing" is a term coined for this volume to signify the monolithic nature of policing. It can refer at one moment to large individual national and municipal police organizations with budgets ranging from a few millions to billions of dollars, and in another to policing as a specific activity spanning continents which, despite political and cultural diversity around the world, is surprisingly uniform in its structure and standard practices. Particularly in relation to big crime, "big policing" can also include many regulatory or law enforcement agencies, such as those regulating financial institutions, or customs and taxation. At a stretch, it can even include the self-policing of institutions and corporations, who invest in the security protection of their financial or data systems. And big policing for ordinary people is the ubiquitous presence and power of an authorized force, which can be reassuring or menacing depending on one's position and behaviour in society.

Big policing is the result of expanding responsibilities, budgets, and personnel numbers to deal with the problems of a diverse and complex modern society. But the multitasking of police leads to tension between different responsibilities, such as their responsibility for keeping the peace at the community level and their responsibility for investigating big crime. This is the tension that exists between "high" and "low" policing. High policing is concerned with the security of the nation, and low policing is the routine keeping of the peace performed by mainly uniformed agents.[1] In this volume Sheptycki places big crime in the high policing category. The tension extends into setting relative priorities between each and in allocating resources; because of the different nature of the problems, a tension also exists between the different legal, training, or time requirements needed for responding to public order incidents or to financial crimes. There have also been many contradictory developments in policing, perhaps as a result of conflicting demands for police responses. Social order problems, for example, might elicit a community policing solution on the one hand or a militarized response on the other, while a known corporate crime might languish without attention. Police are seen to get it wrong on many occasions, and when they get it right it is usually taken for granted because they are mandated and expected to get it right. The result is that big policing is often regarded as a problem in itself rather than a solution, and the issue of financing and accountability of the police remains a burning topic. Those who regard the police as richly resourced, unaccountable, and biased against racialized people are calling for defunding of the police. But others consider the police under-resourced for effective control of big crime.

Using money as a starting point for understanding big crime has been a fruitful avenue for scholars[2] and for police investigators alike. Using money as a starting point for understanding the police has not been so common. While there has been some government and scholarly attention in recent years in the United Kingdom, the United States, and Canada to police and public finances, it has concentrated mainly on the costs of policing and achieving efficiencies and economies of scale.[3] Money as the dynamic, central factor in the policing response to complex crime and social order problems has received little scholarly treatment, although short analyses and articles are beginning to appear in the United States on defunding the police and the reasons why.[4] Some are also regarding defunding of police as a key to social change. While this could well launch both social and police reform if it were to occur, without careful management it could also lead to the baby being thrown out with the bathwater, since defunding would almost certainly lead to some adverse impact on the control of big crime and community policing alike. Therefore, knowing how money links policing, crime, and social order is important for evidence-based decision-making. The analyses in this volume help to fill the gap in knowledge.

While the book contributors are in agreement that big crime, big policing, and big money are linked and are of concern, from there on their topics and their conclusions diverge and even conflict. Scholars have contributed most of the chapters, but practitioners and community activists are also represented. All are acknowledged experts in the matters they discuss. Some chapters are theoretical or research-based, others are case studies or personal accounts, while some take a particular political stance. The heterogeneity of topics, approaches, and conclusions reflects the ambiguity, dispute, and contrary interpretations that exist in general when it comes to gauging the threat of either big police to individual or collective rights of society, or big crime to the integrity of the money system, business, or the general economy.

The chapters in the first section of the book are concerned with institutional and corporate crime. The opening chapter by James Sheptycki provides a framework for all the other chapters in the book. In an overview of the interplay between big money, big crime, and big policing, he traces the evolution of both the global money and the global policing systems from their beginnings to the present. He argues that the money system is a massive opportunity structure for crime that enables a global capitalist class to exist out of reach of national policing and regulatory systems, while the policing system continues to reproduce an order that protects the interests of those who benefit most from the money system. With respect to Canada, the policing and regulatory apparatuses are too weak to contain the flood of dirty money that flows into the country.

The same themes are evident in the chapters by Stephen Schneider and Sanaa Ahmed. From his examination of large complex financial institutions such as HSBC and other banks offering global financial services, Schneider demonstrates how they facilitate an "emerging class of the global rich" in illegal activities ranging from tax evasion and money laundering to avoiding trade sanctions, while themselves engaging in criminal activity, such as manipulation of exchange and interest rates or irresponsible and reckless practices to maximize profits. Such activities sparked the 2007–8 global financial crisis. While the banks have collectively paid out billions of dollars in fines and penalties, their profits are in the hundreds of billions of dollars, and few have been put out of business. That they were bailed out by governments in 2008 because they were "too big to fail" yet have rebounded with little ill effect suggests that they can operate with impunity and governments are not prepared to hold them to account or inflict effective punishment. Ahmed's chapter concentrates on the Canadian situation, but her political economy analysis suggests a reason for apparent government reticence in penalizing big crime. She presents evidence that the Canadian economy lacks sufficient capital to support public infrastructure and programs and argues that money laundering in its widest sense brings in much-needed capital. This encourages the government to turn a blind eye to its sources and that where the interests of the state and big money converge there is the possibility of state crime. Peter German's description of the difficulties of the Canadian public police in curbing financial crime reinforces the point made throughout the section about their weakness in the face of powerful financial criminals. It also gives credence to the view that governments are culpable in allowing big crime to flourish. When governments have the power to change police structures and responsibilities to enable effective law enforcement but fail to do so, or when governments do not provide sufficient resources to be effective and then reduce even those, or when businesses are made responsible for their own policing but face few penalties for non-compliance, it could be the result of government incompetence or negligence. It could also be government reluctance to be too effective in suppressing big crime for the reasons discussed in this section; the power and impunity of the global capitalist class which invests proceeds in Canadian casinos or real estate, corruption in politics, or the intertwined interests of big money and the state may be reaching a point where they can no longer be controlled by one national government.

The second section of the book considers big crime from other angles. While some of the same characteristics found in financial and corporate crime are evident, the activities and the actors are more heterogeneous in the cases discussed in this section. The role of corrupt elites is more in evidence, but it is the influence of governments and their policies that often create the conditions for big crime that is most apparent.

Laureen Snider argues that government adoption of neoliberal policies that have led to privatized or downsized government services and reduced regulatory controls in favour of free markets, competitiveness, globalization, and maximization of profits has created an economic environment in which ethics and social responsibility take a backseat to entitlement, deception, and corruption. Using the examples of tax avoidance or evasion, her view is that rampant capitalism is criminogenic. The global rich make use of government mechanisms for attracting capital or encouraging trade to hide their assets in offshore tax havens, while international companies report revenues they earned in one country in another country with a lower tax rate.

In the chapter on Huawei, the global Chinese telecommunications company, Stephen Wilks shows how growing US government protectionism under the Trump administration and a trade war with China led to attempts to prosecute Meng Wanzhou, the chief financial officer of Huawei, on charges of breaching US economic sanctions against Iran. Wilks points out the futility of trying to criminalize a trade dispute, but in this particular case, inappropriate government use of the criminal extradition process resulted in two innocent Canadians spending nearly three years imprisoned in China as virtual hostages and the Huawei executive serving a similar length of house arrest in Canada. In this case there was a high level of politicization, big money, and police intervention in arresting and holding an executive for extradition, but the big crime seems to have been in appearance only. The case is thus remarkable for illustrating the complexity and murkiness of global business, which makes it difficult to identify whether criminality is present, and the ease with which social justice can be disregarded even by democratic governments when in pursuit of an economic goal.

As in the example of tax havens, the tendency of governments to follow two contradictory paths at the same time is also evident in the chapter by Elizabeth Kirley. She examines art crime in the digital age. In a capitalist global economy, art has become commodified and is regarded as a financial asset with a monetary value. The global art market provides opportunities for money laundering, tax evasion, and for selling forged works of art. The criminal activity in the art world is facilitated by the existence of government-approved freeports in various countries that promote global trade. They also provide a haven where works of art may be bought and sold many times over and used for money laundering without ever being moved or coming into the orbit of art experts, tax officials, or police investigators, showing once more how governments can inadvertently or otherwise abet big crime.

The final section of the book examines big policing from various angles. The chapters by Peter Manning, Margaret Beare, and Anna Willats view police with a sharply critical eye. They concentrate on the social responsibilities of the police, particularly where they fail in their responsibility to protect human rights and the well-being of society. In different ways they show how the many well-publicized reforms of the police in the last fifty years have left the original structure and culture virtually untouched, and more recent developments have resulted in police becoming more militarized and uncompromising in their management of public order. For Willats in particular, the failure of the police to deal sensitively with human crisis is a good reason to defund the institution and divert the savings to community agencies able to deal more humanely with victims of crime and vulnerable and racialized people. Collectively, the three chapters present evidence that police accountability to the public falls far short of what should be expected in a democracy.

The chapter by Laura Huey and Lorna Ferguson presents the results of their empirical research on a variety of health service organizations in one particular municipality. They found that the organizations offload community crisis responses to the police. The researchers concluded that the police generally handled such crises satisfactorily and absorbed the cost into their existing budgets. Kevin Haggerty, Sandra Bucerias, and Daniel Jones stimulate reflection on current negative attitudes towards the police in their examination of the dynamics underlying universities and researchers severing their research and study connections with the police because of recent incidents of police violence against racialized people. They suggest this is a short-sighted reaction that will not change the policing situation and in fact cuts off an avenue for contributing to police reform. The final chapter by Tonita Murray in some respects bookends the opening chapter of the book in examining the practical interplay of high and low policing functions, the tension between the two and their relationship to big money and big crime. The big money in this case is the public funds spent on maintaining big police, and she raises the question of whether it is well spent or if indeed police should be defunded. The chapters in the section suggest that there is no easy answer to the question.

The contention of the book is that big crime and big policing are indeed all about big money. The evidence presented here makes a strong case for the truth of the statement as well as for the accuracy of James Sheptycki's assertion that the money system is essentially criminogenic, a massive opportunity structure for crime. As a principle, it can be argued that the bigger the money system, the greater the risk of criminality. The principle challenges the long-running narrative that poverty correlates with crime. Greed may be a factor, but there are more opportunities for crime when there is more money at stake. Without more effective controls, the money system will continue to be exploited by those engaged in big crime. Severing big crime from big money, however, requires determined global government intervention. Some modest measures have been put in place and are described in the book. Governments would argue that it is a delicate balance to control the money system without adversely affecting the global economy and democratic freedoms. Critics would argue that it is not so much democracy as capitalism that governments are fearful of destabilizing by controlling big money. Added to this is Murray's argument that governments are willing to curb big spending on low policing while increasing it, albeit modestly, for high policing; but ultimately, they are not so ready to exercise their power to give firm and clear policy direction to either level of police or to hold them consistently to account for their activities or for their mistakes.

The chapters in this book do not consider the role of private policing in countering big crime, even though private policing numbers may well dwarf those of public policing and its activities frequently contribute to the public as well as the private good. Our concentration on state remedies for big crime is deliberate because the state has ultimate control of the money system, ultimate responsibility for policing in the public interest, and the ultimate duty to prevent crime. The obligations appear compatible but, in practice, government actions are often contradictory or equivocal. On the one hand they provide remedies for big crime, but on the other they promote policies and programs that encourage exploitation and manipulation and, despite the power of the various levels of government to control police through laws, budgets, and direction, either by design, neglect, or incompetence, many of them, particularly those at the municipal level, tend to abdicate responsibility and leave police organizations to decide their own direction. An alternative explanation based on political developments since the late twentieth century might be that the neoliberal agenda has whittled down the size and reach of the state to a point where it no longer has the capacity to regulate the private sector effectively. The two explanations are not mutually exclusive, but the state has not devolved its power for policing and law enforcement; it appears merely to be relaxing by default its responsibility to direct and hold the police to account. We cannot know without further examination, but it is possible that state weakness in setting clear and achievable expectations for the police and ensuring they are met are a greater impediment than resource issues to the defeat of big crime.

Although not examined directly, big government in all its manifestations is a shadowy presence running through all the contributions in the book. The collective evidence suggests that government together with its many proxy institutions is an integral part of the nexus of big money, big policing, and big crime. It is not within the scope of this volume to examine in detail the role government plays in perpetuating the existence of the problematic three, although the insights provided here might help to lay the groundwork. There is a need for a clearer and more comprehensive understanding of how government decision-making and action strengthen and perpetuate big money, big crime, or big policing before any effective action can be taken against the three.

This book is presented to honour the memory of Professor Margaret E. Beare who had a cross-appointment between the Sociology Department and Osgoode Hall Law School at York University in Toronto and was the first Director of the Jack & Mae Nathanson Centre on Transnational Human Rights, Crime and Security. Her areas of academic interest were financial and transnational crime, corruption, and the politics of policing, which in other words means big crime, big policing, and big money. Her most notable publication was *Criminal Conspiracies*.[5] Margaret died while still on faculty and while in the middle of writing another book provisionally entitled "Inquiring into Public Policing." An edited excerpt from her unfinished manuscript is included as a chapter in this book.

After her death two close colleagues, Professor James Sheptycki and Professor Emeritus Liora Salter of York University organized a colloquium in her honour for mid-March 2020. They obtained funding, organized the program, issued invitations to present papers, and dealt with the numerous obstacles that are always attendant on such events. Her daughter Nhai Nguyen Beare arranged a small gathering to be held immediately following the colloquium to celebrate her mother's life. The final arrangements were made as the COVID-19 epidemic gathered momentum. Two days before the colloquium the World Health Organization declared a global pandemic, and the next day the colloquium was cancelled. The undelivered papers are the basis for this book and form a delayed but still heartfelt tribute from the colleagues and friends of Professor Beare.

The volume is an eclectic mix organized around some strong themes. The authors are academics and practitioners with impeccable credentials as experts and with strong arguments and views about big crime, big policing, and big money. They are the sort of people Professor Beare made her friends. Although their discussions with her could be fiery, they had respect for her work on big crime and big policing, and affection for her and her inclusiveness and friendship. Professor Andrew Goldsmith's tribute to her at the beginning of this book captures perfectly the person she was and, for those who knew her, this book is suffused with her personality. For those who do not know her, the book is nonetheless a stimulating examination of the big crime, big policing, and big money that dominate much academic and public discussion today, when the topic of discussion is not the COVID-19 pandemic and its aftermath.

Professors James Sheptycki and Liona Salter merit special recognition for the genesis of the book. They organized the colloquium and had arranged for the presented papers to be published in book form. While neither was able to continue to the effort, they have remained engaged and provided advice and support to see the project to its conclusion. We thank them both most warmly for their support and encouragement in making the book a possibility.

NOTES

1 Jean-Paul Brodeur, "High and Low Policing: Remarks about the Policing of Political Activities," *Social Problems* 30, no 5 (1983): 507–20. https://doi.org/10.2307/800268; Jean-Paul Brodeur "High and Low Policing in Post-9/11 Times," *Policing* 1, no. 1 (2007): 25–37, https://doi:10.1093/policing/pam002.
2 James Sheptycki, "Policing the Virtual Launderette," in *Issues in Transnational Policing*, ed. James Sheptycki (Routledge, 2000); Margaret E. Beare, ed. *Critical Reflections on Transnational Organized Crime, Money Laundering and Corruption*, Toronto: University of Toronto Press, 2003; Margaret Beare and Stephen Schneider, *Money Laundering in Canada: Chasing Dirty and Dangerous Dollars*, University of Toronto Press, 2007.
3 Federation of Canadian Municipalities, Towards Equity and Efficiency in Policing; A Report on Policing Roles, Responsibilities and Resources in Canada (2008). https://studylib.net/doc/8796950/towards-equity-and-efficiency-in-policing; Tate Fegley and Lisa Growette Bostaph, "Is Bigger Better? An Analysis of Economies of Scale and Market Power in Police Departments," *Policing: An International Journal* 41, no. 5 (2018): 578–92, https://doi.org/10.1108/PIJPSM-08-2016-0135.
4 John Kleinig, "Reform, Don't Abolish, the NYPD," Gotham Philosophical Society, 2016, https://www.researchgate.net/publication/333634959_Reform_Don't_Abolish _the_NYPD; John A. Shjarback, David C. Pyrooz, Scott E. Wolfe & Scott H. Deckerd, "De-policing and Crime in the Wake of Ferguson: Racialized Changes in the Quantity and Quality of Policing among Missouri Police Departments," *Journal of Criminal Justice* 50, (2017): 42–52.
5 Margaret E. Beare, *Criminal Conspiracies: Organized Crime in Canada*, Second edition. Oxford, UK: Oxford University Press, 2015.

SECTION ONE

Global Money Systems and Financial Crimes: Limitations of State Regulation

In his "spectrum-based theory of enterprise," Dwight Smith analyses commercial activity using a continuum he calls the "spectrum of legitimacy." Smith places legal, profit-oriented companies and illegal (organized crime) enterprises at the opposite ends of the continuum, situating legal enterprises that periodically engage in criminal conduct somewhere in the middle.[1] The implication of this theory – that the boundaries between legal and illegal commercial enterprises are often blurred – resonates with many criminologists who have enumerated the abundant parallels between corporate crime and organized crime, including their financial motivation, their serious and harmful nature, the involvement of multiple offenders, and some form of rational organizational structure.[2] Von Lampe identifies another shared attribute between malfeasant corporations and organized crime groups: "that criminal activities and criminal structures can be found to be embedded in a subculture conducive to crime."[3]

In their example of how the "distinction between licit and illicit markets is often difficult to determine," Lyman and Potter draw a comparison between "loan-sharks who make high-interest loans and predatory cheque-cashing businesses that do the same, often targeting the most vulnerable in society."[4] The precedent for modern-day organized criminality was established by American's original business tycoons – John Jacob Astor, Leland Stanford, John D. Rockefeller, Cornelius Vanderbilt, and J. Pierpont Morgan – who collectively have been affixed with the inglorious label "robber barons" because they amassed their fortunes through the liberal use of intimidation, price-fixing, extortion, theft, violence, bribery, and fraud.[5] In the early part of the twentieth century, pharmaceutical producers and distributors in Europe, America, and Canada regularly diverted legal drugs like morphine to the black market. During the era of Prohibition, legally incorporated liquor producers in Canada, such as Seagram's, sold huge quantities of spirits to smugglers, bootleggers, and established crime groups in the United States.[6] These examples and more prompted Edwin Sutherland to coin the phrase that would become the title of his 1949 book: *White Collar Crime*. Sutherland "found that the criminality of the corporations, like that of professional thieves, was persistent, extensive, usually unpunished, most often deliberate, and involved the connivance of government officials or legislators. It was, in sum, organized."[7] More recently, investigations in the United States have shown how automobile manufacturers refused to reveal or even repair dangerous car defects despite their knowledge of resulting deaths,[8] while cigarette and firearm manufacturers hid research findings that revealed incontrovertibly the widespread mortality that resulted from their respective products.[9] Tobacco companies have also been implicated in illegal schemes that diverted legal products to the black market.[10] A chief culprit behind the ongoing opioid epidemic in the United States and Canada was Purdue Pharmaceuticals, a corporation that used predatory and corrupting tactics, including kickbacks to physicians, to market the highly addictive prescription drug OxyContin.[11]

In addition to the theoretical overlap between corporate and organized crime, criminal organizations are bound with corporations through the illegal process of money laundering – a common theme presented in the chapters in this section. As I discuss in my chapter, some of the largest banks and investment firms in the world have been repeatedly penalized for their complicity in the laundering of the proceeds of drug trafficking and other organized crimes. Sanaa Ahmed points out that casinos in British Columbia, operated by large corporations, have been implicated in massive money laundering schemes, an indication of "how deeply embedded money laundering practices" are in Canada. Peter German refers to "the attraction that Canada poses to domestic and international criminal organizations which seek to launder the proceeds of their nefarious activities." James Sheptycki places money laundering in the broader context of "the global money system," which is "a gigantic criminal opportunity structure."

Despite a common deviant subculture that exists at the locus of corporate and organized crime, state responses are widely divergent and unequal. Von Lampe writes that "corporate and other elite offenders are less likely to be investigated and apprehended. And if they are brought to justice, sanctions tend to be less severe. In fact, it may be the case that fines are set so low that corporate crimes remain profitable even if they are detected."[12] Margaret Beare speculates that one reason corporations typically do not qualify as criminal organizations is due to their power in society: "they have the financial backing to sue anyone who would try to extend a definition of serious, continuous, organized criminal activity to include their corporate business policies."[13] Corporations can also count on powerful politicians to protect them from criminal prosecution or lawsuits (the same politicians who actively solicit campaign donations from these corporations). Whether they are abetting in trafficking pharmaceutical drugs, tobacco smuggling, or money laundering, it is common to view "the alleged corporate criminals in these criminal processes as somehow still 'outside' organized crime – useful to organized crime but 'different' from it. However, the conduct that has been alleged, if proven in court, is organized crime activity."[14]

Similar conclusions are reached in the chapters in this section. My own research shows that few if any executives or directors have been criminally prosecuted for their corporations' highly unethical and illegal acts, including money laundering, fraud, circumventing US trade sanctions, facilitating tax evasion, manipulating interest and foreign exchange rates, or their role in the 2007–8 financial crisis.

Sheptycki maintains that "white-collar crime, corruption, and other crimes of the moneyed elite remain under-policed." German rationalizes this when he writes, "police cannot, nor can they be expected to deal with all aspects of financial crime" because the "sheer volume makes it impossible." Ahmed argues there are structural determinants to the lack of proceeds of crime enforcement – "the state also operates to protect and propagate its own institutional interests, which are often entwined with those of big money."

As the chapters in this section illuminate, the retrenchment of the RCMP and other law enforcement agencies in Canada in applying proceeds of crime laws in recent years are due to the complexity and resource-intensive nature of financial crimes investigations, the concomitant lack of expertise and resources within law enforcement agencies, as well as competition from other pressing enforcement priorities. While federal laws and regulations have essentially deputized corporations and professionals to combat the problem by reporting suspicious and large cash transactions, there is little incentive to do so. The Canadian government has shown it is uninterested in penalizing recalcitrant corporate entities, while the influx of illicit cash into the coffers of financial institutions does not exactly create a self-interested motivation to comply with federal reporting laws. Thus, both the federal government and corporate interests in Canada continue to create the necessary portals for dirty money into the legitimate economy. Much of the illicit funds circulating in the world's financial markets is not the product of drug trafficking but is generated from crimes and other unethical activity carried out by the "legitimate" corporate actors operating within the boundaries of a corrupt global financial system itself. The illicit proceeds of tax fraud, capital flight, accounting fraud, insider trading, market manipulation, and predatory product marketing – not to mention the negligence and unnecessary risk-taking by financial service providers that brought about the 2008 crisis – are generated from, laundered through, and then reinvested into the global financial system. In a 2015 report, Finance Canada notes the significant money laundering threat emanating from capital markets fraud, which is a "rich source of proceeds of crime." Most of the "large-scale securities frauds in Canada have been perpetrated by *criminalized professionals*, who have (or purport to have) professional credentials and financial expertise. Alongside the sophisticated fraudulent schemes, there are sophisticated ML schemes designed to integrate and legitimize the fraud-related proceeds into the financial system."[15] The frequency, scope, and impact of corporate crimes dictate that the offending corporations and professionals be situated as close as possible to the illegitimate extreme of Smith's spectrum and that law enforcement begin treating them as such.

NOTES

1 Dwight Smith, "Paragons, Pariahs and Pirates: A Spectrum-based Theory of Enterprise," *Crime and Delinquency* 26, no. 3 (1980).
2 Margaret Beare, ed., Critical Reflections on Transnational Organized Crime, Money Laundering, and Corruption (Toronto: University of Toronto Press, 2003).
3 Klaus von Lampe, Organized Crime: Analyzing Illegal Activities, Criminal Structures, and Extra-Legal Governance (Los Angeles: Sage Publications, 2016), 233.
4 Michael Lyman and Gary Potter, *Organized Crime*, 6th ed. (Boston: Pearson, 2014), 10.
5 Howard Abadinsky, *Organized Crime*, 10th ed. (Belmont, CA: Wadsworth, 2013), 10–20.
6 Stephen Schneider, *Iced: The Story of Organized Crime in Canada*, 2nd ed. (Toronto: HarperCollins, 2016), 197–205.
7 Michael Woodiwiss, "Transnational Organized Crime: The Strange Career of an American Concept," in *Critical Reflections on Transnational Organized Crime, Money Laundering, and Corruption*, ed. Margaret Beare (Toronto: University of Toronto Press, 2003), 14.
8 Adam Penenberg, Blood Highways: The True Story behind the Ford-Firestone Killing Machine (Eugene, OR: Wayzgoose Press, 2012).
9 Robert Proctor, Golden Holocaust: Origins of the Cigarette Catastrophe and the Case for Abolition (Berkeley: University of California Press, 2012).
10 Margaret Beare, "Organized Corporate Criminality: Corporate Complicity in Tobacco Smuggling," in *Critical Reflections on Transnational Organized Crime, Money Laundering, and Corruption*, ed. Margaret Beare (Toronto: University of Toronto Press, 2003).
11 Patrick Keefe, Empire of Pain: The Secret History of the Sackler Dynasty (Toronto: Bond Street Books, 2021).
12 Klaus von Lampe, Organized Crime: Analyzing Illegal Activities, Criminal Structures, and Extra-Legal Governance (Los Angeles: Sage Publications, 2016), 234.
13 Beare, "Organized Corporate Criminality," 184.
14 Beare, "Organized Corporate Criminality," 201.
15 Finance Canada, Assessment of Inherent Risks in Money Laundering and Terrorist Financing in Canada (Ottawa: Department of Finance Canada, 2015), 20.

1 Policing and the Money System

JAMES SHEPTYCKI

We are at the beginning of a mass extinction, and all you can talk about is money and fairy tales of eternal economic growth. How dare you!
(Greta Thunberg, New York, UN General Assembly 23 September 2019)

Introduction

Perhaps more than any other Canadian scholar, Margaret Beare cast a critical light on the dark and nefarious world of policing and "dirty money."[1] Prior to the turn of the millennium researchers working on law enforcement practices involving money laundering were invariably concerned with specific predicate criminal offences, most often having to do with illicit markets in drugs and psychotropic substances from the Global South to the Global North.[2] In that time and context dirty money was supposedly clearly demarcated from financial flows more generally. Even then, the problem of money, its corruption of politics, and the consequent politics of corruption were evident to those who examined the situation carefully. Years later white-collar crime, corruption, and other crimes of the moneyed elite remain under-policed.[3] Following the attacks of 9/11 there was a brief period where the concern was to police both drug money and "terrorist financing," and after the financial crisis of 2007–8 criminologists began to argue all financial flows were complicit in, or somehow facilitative of, criminal harms.[4] In the aftermath of the pandemic panic of 2020 the global money system was torn by war and turmoil. Financial experts, business leaders, central bankers, economists, and lawyers opine about the vagaries of the money system, but what does an honest criminologist have to say?

The early criminological focus on dirty money was upturned by the disclosures of the so-called Panama Papers and the Paradise Papers. In these reports investigative journalists exposed the secretive global banking system and demonstrated that it was facilitative of innumerable illicit and criminal transactions on a very large scale.[5] Depicted as distant and inevitable, if saddening, in Steven Soderbergh's ironically loaded film *The Laundromat* (2019, starring Meryl Streep), the Moloch money system has become banal and culturally assumed. The global money system is a gigantic criminal opportunity structure. What is this pervasive process of global financial flows that so facilitates organized criminality and corrupts the very marrow of politics? And how is it related to the existing architecture of global policing? The answers to these two simple questions are complex and perplexing. This chapter aims to connect thinking about transnational policing and the global money system. It is seldom that these social institutions are thought about in conjunction, but doing so reveals striking features of the present-day scene. There is now almost nowhere in the world untouched by the ideas of policing and money. These institutions merge in a global nexus of information, surveillance, and communications technologies that are part and parcel of the technological foundations necessary for "surveillance capitalism," "behavioural governance," and "post-democracy."[6] The global money system is both stratified and pluralized, and it is tilted towards the advantage of the powerful few occupying positions at the commanding heights of major institutions.[7] Theorizing policing and the global money system opens an important window into the present.

This chapter proceeds in two parts. The first section considers the historical genesis of the present global money system and modern policing. Secondly, the chapter also explores these issues in the contemporary Canadian context, but overall the discussion aims at something more. The discussion casts light on the evolution of global class hierarchies and the politics of the global system that are of general interest to historical and political sociologists by interpreting some evidence concerning the economics and politics of crime and policing in Canada from this broader perspective.[8] Ultimately, these considerations are bracketed by the fact of ongoing criminal destruction of the ecosphere that hangs like the Sword of Damocles over human civilization.[9]

The Global Money System and Modern Policing

Writing at the end of the twentieth century, the historian of money Jack Weatherford said the world was on the threshold of "the third great mutation in money."[10] The first major step in the technological history of money began with the invention of the coin in the ancient Greek kingdom of Lydia c. 550 BCE. As a token of value, the coin transformed the trade and barter that humans had practised since pre-historic times into true commerce and created the world's first retail markets. Ideas entailed in the practices of buying and selling have spread around the world, becoming part of common understanding. Twenty-five centuries later, money is the world's most pervasive belief system. The spread of the money idea accelerated as the European conquest got under way at the end of the fifteenth century, especially after the invention of printing with movable type. This second phase in the history of money, during which commercial culture began to flourish and the European bourgeois and working classes began to consolidate, corresponded with the period of European state-building, colonialism, and imperialism. The money system of mercantile exchange that underpinned the colonizing project was accounted for in tallies on paper of gold and silver bullion. As the nation-state system consolidated, so too did the system of national currencies issued on paper backed by gold and, by the nineteenth century, capitalist relations of exchange were increasingly globally predominant. European domination of the money system was an important element of colonial and imperial power during the early modern period, domination ceded to the United States following the end of hostilities in 1945. Towards the end of the twentieth century the third revolutionary transformation in the money system began with the emergence of electronic money.

Richard Nixon took the American dollar off the "gold standard" in 1972, ending the Bretton Woods system of global state currency management at what was, in retrospect, the high point of the modern state system. Seeds of the historic shift to the age of electronic money were sown with the invention of the credit card in the 1950s, which, by the 1970s, had already attained widespread international presence in the economies of the Global North. Another important moment in the historical manifestation of the electronic money system was the so-called big bang of the London Stock Exchange, inaugurated under the Thatcher government in 1986, which ushered in the era of screen-based online financial trading.[11] In between these developments was the creation in 1977 of the Society for Worldwide Interbank Financial Telecommunication (SWIFT) to coordinate the cross-border movement of money. SWIFT is a secure international electronic communications network currently linking thousands of financial institutions in nearly two hundred countries in what is arguably the most critical electronic communications infrastructure in the world. After the abandonment of the gold standard and its replacement with a system of floating currencies in the so-called neoliberal age, the technological innovation of electronic money consolidated changes in the relationship between the global money system and nationally-based states in what was then described as the era of "mad money" and "casino capitalism."[12] A cloud of electronic money made up of innumerable digital transactions in cyberspace now shrouds the world, and it operates outside the control of any single state or combination of states.

Two characteristics of the contemporary money system need to be emphasized. The first is that the system is complicated by the plurality of *types* of money.[13] Alongside national currencies (differentiated into "hard" and "soft" currencies"), which are mostly electronically accounted for but are still circulating in the form of paper and coins, there are a plethora of other ways of storing, exchanging, and accounting for value. In some countries forms of "paramoney," such as food stamps, welfare vouchers, and other tokens of state provision, but also credits earned through consumer loyalty programs, are important supplements to the household economy of many people. Social media platforms and online consumption have given rise to cyber-payment systems that are also forms of paramoney. With the internet, multiple forms of cybercurrency and other digital items marked using blockchain technology (non-fungible digital tokens), also compete for market share in the imaginary world of money value. The collapse of a number of "crypto exchanges" in multiple jurisdictions in the early stages of the economic crisis that followed the pandemic panic of 2020 served to expose the significant fraud opportunities in the newly emerging world of un-regulated "cryptocurrency." For the wealthy investor wary of the fluctuating value of abstract currencies, high-value art and antiques can be used as media of exchange for the global movement of money, and at the lower end, expensive watches, jewellery, and other luxury items serve not only as symbolic displays of wealth but also as a method of moving value across borders and storing it for the longer term. The global financial system, including the central banks, private equity firms, and other multinational institutions, counts value in various types of exotic financial instruments, which are another species of money. This pluralized money system is highly variegated and fluid, and it acts as an autonomous variable affecting the actions of politicians and governments.

The second characteristic of this pluralized money system that needs to be emphasized is that it is socially *hierarchical*. At the top of the global money system, so to speak, are players dealing with complex financial instruments or who have access to sovereign wealth funds.[14] The commanding heights of the global money system are dominated by competing hedge fund managers, currency traders, and others who participate in the strategic management of the global financial service industries, but also private individuals and corrupt politicians, all of which collectively constitute the transnational capitalist class, red-in-tooth-and-claw, vying for influence and power. At the bottom of this hierarchy are those territorially confined in "cash ghettos" where people still primarily engage in market relations through the medium of paper currency and perhaps even barter exchange.[15] In between these two extremes operating at varying degrees of geography – local, national, regional, global, virtual – and using different kinds of money, is worked out a complex global hierarchy of social class. Class position is defined in relation to the pluralized, and still evolving, global money system. A key indicator is access to the legal tools facilitating private offshore banking because of the secretiveness it allows. This shapes the consciousness of rootless monetary elites so that, regardless of geographic location, "high net-worth" individuals and corporations tend to want to avoid the responsibility of public forms of state governance by paying taxes. Indeed, high-level participants in the global money system have interests that are quite antithetical to democratic state governance, especially if it impedes transnational currency flows. Deracinated monetary elites in the post-democratic countries of the West, who have benefited from surveillance capitalism and implemented techniques of behavioural governance from a transnational level, have also been responsible for the hollowing-out of the state at the domestic level. The evolution of money has transformed governance globally, and the results are revolutionary as well as criminogenic. From top to bottom, the global money system is the structural means for the organization of crime.[16]

When the Canadian cultural critic Naomi Klein articulated the "shock doctrine" in the wake of the 2003 US invasion of Iraq, the 2004 Indian Ocean tsunami and Hurricane Katrina's devastation of New Orleans in 2005, she followed the money and discovered the importance of the web of policing, security, and military personnel contracted to enforce the system worldwide.[17] Her book was a widely read popular account that resonates with this discussion. It was dismissed at the time by critics as being naïve and over-simplified, and for some even dishonest. However, the scholarly literature reviewed here supports theoretical discussion of the practical intertwining of policing and the money system and suggests that disaster capitalism is quite an apt description of what is going on.

The exchanges between Socrates and his various interlocutors throughout the Platonic dialogues illustrate the point that the politics of policing practice are as ancient as coinage. The *modern* police idea is a product of Enlightenment thinking that developed along with European state-making. In the eighteenth century "police science" encompassed the entire "art of government" and, for political economists like Adam Smith, the wealth of nations depended on it.[18] In addition to national currencies, the modern international state system that began to emerge after the American and French revolutions evolved the convention that each state's jurisdiction would have its own internal system of police, while its military "pointed outwards." Over the course of the nineteenth and twentieth centuries, as the international state system was gradually unfolded onto the world map, there emerged a patchwork quilt of national police systems, each with its own internally complex structural network. Decades of empirical research have revealed how the police in different countries formed a complex "policing web" with points of connection with military and security service apparatuses, as well as a variety of possible security providers in the private sector. The nation-state system of police reached its peak during the Cold War, when the world system was seemingly locked in a titanic two-sided struggle between capitalism in the West and communism in the East. During the transformative years of the 1990s, especially in Europe which was then unified by a single currency of the euro, but also more generally, there grew up a dense interlocking network of transnational policing with interconnections operating at local, national, inter-regional, and international levels globally.[19] This was when Francis Fukuyama famously concluded that the world had evolved to an end stage coming into being as a cosmopolitan, democratic, and capitalist order. In the wake of the attacks of 11 September 2001, research revealed how existing police networks quickly adapted into new, sophisticated hybrids of policing and security that extended globally.[20] Notwithstanding obvious geopolitical hostilities, by the early years of the new millennium there was a discernable global policing web.

Police the world over exhibit considerable differences and yet all maintain a certain family resemblance. That is because they all share a common occupational métier. The police *métier* involves people in the practical organization and application of an extensive surveillance and intelligence capacity, backed up with the ability to apply force (including fatal force), so as to maintain the existing social order, make crime into an institutional fact for the criminal justice system, manage institutional risks, and govern insecurity so that conditions remain conducive for existing relations of social power.[21] Although the cast of suitable foes and folk devils shifts from time to time and place to place, everywhere the modern police métier evolved it has been implicated in the political reproduction of the domestic and international social hierarchies of the money system. Policing is Janus faced. While policing often involves conflict and there is usually someone being policed against, theorists try to make an important distinction between "high policing" and "low policing." High policing is concerned to secure the particular interests of social, political, economic, and cultural elites, whereas low policing is concerned to secure the general social order that is of interest to all. Preventing street crime such as assault and robbery or ensuring road traffic safety are quintessential examples of low policing. Just as everyone is better off when the ecology is not subject to criminal despoliation on an industrial scale, if there is less fear of crime and traffic is not hazardous then life in public is generally improved. Protecting private corporate property interests and secretive state institutions are examples of high policing. High policing is concerned with the particular interests of a relative few who are the main beneficiaries of a highly unequal money system. The temperature of the politics of police and crime ultimately reflects the degree of hierarchical difference in the money system in the polity being policed. The greater the degree of economic privilege and exclusion, the more policing is preponderantly concerned with high policing matters and the higher the temperature. When the money system exhibits a greater degree of economic equality the polity is more concerned to focus on low policing issues of general concern. The more generally inclusive the society, the less need for police to enforce particular interests and the lower the temperature of the politics of crime and policing.

Over decades since at least the 1970s a number of identifiable and interrelated phenomena significantly shaped the organization of contemporary policing worldwide, among which the most important were developments in information, surveillance, and communications technologies. The resultant organizational convergence of the police and military in the recent past has been the subject of considerable research.[22] Here the analysis emphasizes parallel technological convergences that simultaneously revolutionized the money system, and it thereby points at the authoritarian drift into what Neil Postman called *technocracy*.[23] As central fixtures in a complex division of labour, police control the way populations relate within territories defined by geographical jurisdiction. Police function positively in order to facilitate the social and financial flows necessary to contemporary consumer capitalism and negatively in response to social conflict and disorder where it arises, and to enforce particular property and territorial interests. Whereas the police division of labour operating under state-based auspices is massively involved in the attempt to control migration and population movements, suppress political dissent, and criminalize poverty, it has not been so active undertaking surveillance control of financial flows relating to the nefarious activities of transnational elites, despite any appearances or claims to the contrary.

Those parts of the police division of labour operating under the auspices of private law are configured so as to privilege the interests and privacy of key actors, to protect those interests against things like fraud and intellectual property theft, and to facilitate the business of making money.[24] The end result of this is that the division of labour is generally well-equipped to police against anti-capitalism protesters, but it is ill-equipped to police against corporate malfeasance and white-collar crime.[25] Police surveillance is intended to facilitate crime control in the streets, but it is also viewed as a threat to financial privacy, so the perceived balance between the need for due process restrictions and the aims of crime control is tilted differently for crime in the suites.[26] In other words, the transnational police system is, from the global to the local level, a system for re-enforcing, as much as is organizationally possible, the existing (and highly unequal) cultural, economic, social, legal, and political order consolidated through the money system.

Signs of the Times – Policing and the Global Money System from the Canadian Perspective

Post-colonial, multi-cultural, open for business, technically sophisticated, and metropolitan, Canada is a country that has been shaped by the institutions of modern policing from the outset.[27] In the terminology just described, it is fair to say that Canada's First Nations people have been, on the whole, confined in the lowest echelons of the money system. There have been any number of confrontations that symbolize the situation. One of the most potent was the *Ipperwash Crisis* of 1995, during which a number of people from the Stony Point Ojibway First Nations band occupied land in a provincial park in Ontario. The situation led to a stand-off between police and the occupiers which became violent, and a protester named Dudley George was killed in a confrontation with members of the Ontario Provincial Police. This kindled a crisis of police accountability after an official judicial inquiry, launched in 2003, determined that pressure from top politicians in the provincial government had affected front-line policing of the occupation. Answering the question "who is calling the shots?" academic lawyers would answer describing the respective roles of the Canadian constitution and the courts, administrative processes, and the principle of the "rule of law" in democratic governance.[28] Answered this way, the question itself elides the more fundamental issue of Canada's First Nations placement in the global money system. This was at least tacitly acknowledged as the central issue when the land that had been occupied in 1995 was ceremoniously handed back to the Kettle and Stony Point First Nation by the Canadian Federal Government on 14 April 2016, along with a payment of $95 million. Now the practical question arises as to whether someone, or some group, moving higher in the money system does any overall good.

Research on policing and Indigenous rural communities is patchy. Policing resource extraction on the Canadian frontier continues to favour corporate interests over the health and safety of First Nations and other rural people.[29] According to empirical research, attempts to "responsibilize" First Nations for their own policing have been hamstrung by lack of funding and lack of organizational capacity in meeting the demands of high crime and anti-social behaviour in those communities that most need it. Other findings reveal the organizational failure of the Royal Canadian Mounted Police (RCMP) and a history of distrust between public police and First Nations people. The shortcomings of police operational activity, even including modest efforts at community capacity building, have directly contributed to processes of child welfare control, criminalization, and prisonization.[30] A symbolic *coup de grâce* in the de-legitimation of policing among First Nations peoples in Canada was the massive police organizational incompetence and indifference documented in an official national inquiry into missing and murdered Indigenous women.[31] The money system and the way it is policed provide the seedbed for low-level lifestyle criminality to emerge in rural areas and among Aboriginal peoples in Canada and is the ultimate cause of the epidemic of toxic drug deaths in Western Canada.[32] It is difficult to call this situation a hollowing-out of the state, since the state apparatus has never operated for the benefit of First Nations populations. Nevertheless, it is kindred to it because the demonstrated governmental lack of care is to the benefit of the transnational capitalist class. Under pressures generated in the global money system, policing on the Canadian frontiers away from the cities and towns looks like state failure, even while natural resource extraction of petroleum and minerals continues unabated.

Canada is a mostly urban country and approximately 80 per cent of public policing services are delivered through municipalities. Its cities are becoming ever more multicultural as well as more densely populated, increasing social conflict involving police and the criminal justice system.[33] Urban geographers have revealed growing social, political, and economic inequality in Canadian cities from the 1970s onward. Social class and ethnicity segment urban conurbations.[34] In 2019 Canada added approximately half a million new citizens through inward migration to an existing population base of about thirty-six million. In 2022 the figure was about one million. Urban development and inward migration are deemed essential to Canadian economic growth, but city expansion has generated intense political pressure at the municipal level concerning the cost of public services amid neoliberal, pro-market policies favouring businesses and the lowering of taxes. Whittling away at the cost and provision of public social, educational, health, and mental health services has been demonstrated to create more work for public police.[35] Alok Mukherjee, Chair of the Toronto Police Services Board from 2005 to 2015, reflected on the culture conflict between police and members of the Canadian public nearer the bottom of the money system, and suggested that the core function of public police would, without significant resistance, regrettably continue to focus narrowly on crime and public order, while privatization and national security concerns would continue to dominate the domain of community safety.[36] The "guns and gangs" crisis characteristic of crime in the cash ghettos of Canada should be read against this background of the ongoing pluralization of policing in a pluralized money system. Like the so-called housing crisis, mental health crisis, and toxic drugs crisis, it represents a failure of multilevel democratic governance under pressure of the global money system, and it erodes the legitimacy and effectiveness of Canadian municipal police and government more generally.[37] In the summer of 2020 erupted the politics of defunding the police in urban centres across the country. These demanded a new economics of policing, one that called for "divestment *and of investment*: a movement away from prisons and police and toward institutions and initiatives that protect, nurture and sustain living and all of the richness of human and ecological life."[38]

Criminological research reveals that, under conditions of neoliberalism favouring transnational flows of hot money, Canada has become a weak state. Empirical research has established an understanding of the extent of penetration of the fabric of Canadian society by transnational illicit flows of drugs, guns, and money.[39] Additionally, Margaret Beare's work revealing the collusion of Big Tobacco in the smuggling of illicit cigarettes in southern Ontario and Stephen Schneider's work on Canadian real estate markets and money laundering revealed that illicit money flows have not been restricted to the economy of "drugs and gangs."[40] In 2015 the official report of the Charbonneau commission in Quebec documented the corruption of the building and construction industry by organized crime. On the other side of the country, in British Columbia, the extent of white-collar criminality in the real-estate sector prompted an inquiry on behalf of the provincial government, which produced a best estimate of in excess of $40 billion of illicit money laundered through the Canadian financial system annually, or about 2.5 per cent of GDP. According to that report, the transnational inflows and outflows of massive amounts of illicit money into Canada required "serious attention of every senior government across the country."[41] As with the world money system of the early twenty-first century more generally, the Canadian financial sector – including the commercial, industrial, and residential property development industries – is awash in "hot" money, much of it of transnational origin.[42]

In 2018 a confidential report to the Attorney General of British Columbia by Peter German KC, a private consultant and former senior RCMP officer with thirty-one years of experience, revealed that there were essentially no police anti–money laundering investigative teams operating anywhere in Canada, other than on a piecemeal ad hoc basis. The report said that more than $100 million had been laundered through casinos licensed through the British Columbia Lottery Corporation (BCLC) system annually over previous years, citing the example of one casino which, in a one-month period, accepted some $13 million in twenty-dollar bills thought to be possible proceeds of crime.[43] Margaret Beare's work on anti–money laundering in Canada had already revealed that the system of suspicious transactions reporting (STR) to Canada's financial intelligence unit (FIU) the Financial Transactions and Reports Analysis Centre of Canada (FINTRAC) was not fit for its purpose.[44] The persistence of organized crime phenomena has been attributed to "due process safeguards" on Canadian system surveillance of illicit flows in the financial system.[45] However, the B.C. Civil Liberties Association has argued that the existing law is deficient in terms of due process safeguards and has raised objections concerning "repeated urgings for more invasive powers, broader disclosures of sensitive, highly prejudicial personal information, more onerous administrative burden on the private sector, and more resources for FINTRAC."[46]

In certain respects, policing the money system in Canada appears to be a failure in spite of institutional efforts. Over thirty thousand businesses must comply with legal obligations to report suspicious financial transactions, including all banks and credit unions, insurance companies, money services businesses, securities dealers, casinos, real estate brokers, and a number of others. In the recent past, these institutions filed more than 23 million STRs annually to FINTRAC, which then circulated analyses of these data as "intelligence products" to a network of eleven federal departments and police agencies, including the RCMP, but also the Canada Revenue Agency (CRA, i.e., the tax authority), the Canada Border Services Agency (CBSA), and the Canadian Security Intelligence Services (CSIS). One estimate is that all of this activity generated approximately fifty criminal convictions in a ten-year period. Conviction rates are not the gold standard of effectiveness in counter–money laundering, but other kinds of figures for these undertakings are murky and hard to come by. The available evidence suggests that financial system surveillance tends to reinforce the hierarchies embedded in the money system.[47] The report of the Rouleau Commission into the use of the Emergencies Act, which allowed Canadian authorities to remove all organizational and legal obstacles in responding to the occupation of Ottawa by the so-called Freedom Convoy in 2022, revealed the real, practical, technical capacity to police the money system. Among other things, use of the Act allowed authorities to freeze the assets of individual persons and groups associated with that "carnival of chaos."[48]

The licit money system creates criminal opportunities. Electronic money changes ordinary everyday banking. Consider how consumers have been encouraged to adopt and adapt self-service banking technologies (SSBT) such as automated teller machines (ATMs), online banking (OLB), and banking by phone (BBP).[49] Electronic money flows through the hands of middle-class consumers daily and the digital currents of the SSBT system create opportunities for crime. Such systems concentrate data, which itself is a target for crime. The centralization of financial data poses security threats and risks to privacy, raising questions about who is entitled to have access to information and how information is distributed and shared. Customers face cybersecurity risks like identity theft, while bank employees, IT specialists, and related professionals may become both security risks and threat targets. Once sensitive personal financial information is compromised it may be impossible to reverse the damage in terms of loss of trust and damage to institutional reputation. At the atomic level, so to speak, where ordinary people operate, the global money system is rife with criminal opportunities and seemingly remarkably absent capable guardians.

The digitization of money flows enables new variations on old crimes that are then hidden as systemic risks, for example, cheque fraud. Cheque deposit banking applications on mobile phones allow consumers to upload photos of cheques and other negotiable instruments to bank accounts. Evidently fraudsters have discovered ways of uploading images to multiple accounts, thereby doubling or tripling the value of a given cheque.[50] Lest this example seem trivial or mislead, electronic fraud in the banking system is endemic, highly organized, and transnational. Best estimates of the annual losses due to different types of bank-card fraud were in excess of US$4 billion in the recent past.[51] As ever, the costs of such frauds are absorbed by financial institutions and passed on to customers, and the best hopes are not put into developing deterrence-based approaches based on arrest and conviction, but rather into developing intelligent systems to manage the risks of cybercrime.[52]

The twenty-first-century money system in Canada is integrated globally, not least because major chartered banks maintain branches in overseas territories known for banking secrecy, particularly the Cayman Islands, the Turks and

Caicos Islands, and Barbados.[53] Like the clue of Sherlock Holmes's non-barking dog in Conan Doyle's mystery *Silver Blaze*, one of the principal findings deducible from the country report for Canada by the Financial Action Task Force (FATF) in 2016 was how it excluded consideration of dirty money in the hands of social and economic elites in making so-called organized crime groups and terrorist financiers the dramatic focus of attention.[54] Corporate criminality and elite criminality are invisible to the authorities in countries where neoliberal mentality has taken hold and legitimated almost any kind of money-making.[55] Canada and the United States are the two most lax jurisdictions in the world when it comes to rules for preventing the incorporation of anonymous shell companies, according to the World Bank and the Canadian Bar Association. The Panama Papers leak revealed that the Panamanian law firm Mossack Fonseca was advising international clients in 2010 that "Canada is a good place to create tax planning structures to minimize taxes like interest, dividends, capital gains, retirement income and rental income."[56] In other words, the licit money system is rigged to facilitate tax efficiencies and transnational flows of capital, into and out of Canada, and provide beneficial owners the secrecy behind the veils of interlocking corporate ownership. Investigative work by the *Tax Justice Network* reveals the upper echelons of the money system do not so much present opportunities for crime as they are almost criminal of themselves since the network of "tax havens" provides the necessary corruption interface between the licit and illicit economies the world over.[57] The money system is criminogenic. That is, it creates the motives for crime and it organizes crime. And the way it is policed distorts markets and increases economic inequality.

Security operations for the Toronto G20 Summit in June of 2010 have become emblematic of policing anti-capitalist globalization protest in Canada.[58] A multi-agency police operation drew on the continent-wide policing web in order to concentrate thousands of public police and private security guards, with military units waiting quietly in the wings and the security services maintaining vigilance. The operation resulted in the largest mass arrests in Canadian history to date and became a textbook example of over-policing in a public order context. Heavy-handed policing of peaceful protesters calling attention to the excesses of global capitalism was nothing new in Canada. For example, anti-capitalist protests at the 1997 APEC Summit, the 2001 Summit of the Americas in Quebec City, and the 2002 G8 meetings in Ottawa were all met with no-nonsense policing.[59] Symbolically the Canadian government uses public police to enforce against political protesters challenging the money system and the capitalist order of consumption. Similar tactics are used against other social movements like ecological and social justice protesters.[60] Ultimately, the mobilization of thousands of police officers across the country in response to the Trucker Convoy occupations of 2022 revealed the enormous capacity of networked policing in Canada to be able to respond and uphold the fundamental basis of the existing money system. Policing political protest in Canada shows the liberal ideal – that the democratic police are apolitical, autonomous, and accountable to the "rule of law" alone – is a mystification that discourages inquiry into the complex connections of power.

Policing everywhere in the global system was dramatically revealed during the pandemic panic that arose in the first months of the 2020 COVID crisis.[61] As Canada and other countries struggled with the public health and economic consequences of the virus, the People's Bank of China announced the launch of the world's first central bank digital currency, the e-RMB.[62] It is too soon to tell the outcome, but signs indicate that the conflict over Ukraine is part of a larger strategy to challenge US dominance of the money system due to its position as the preferred reserve currency. While Canada presents itself to the world as a relative haven of tranquillity and economic prosperity in a rapidly decaying world, this is largely an illusion. As the Canadian philosopher Andrew Potter observed, "below deck on the Western techno-consumerist pleasure cruise, all is not well."[63]

Conclusion

The previous considerations bring us back to thinking about how the evolution of money has transformed governance globally. This chapter has explored the broad contours of global policing and the money system by focusing on how things look from the particular jurisdiction of Canada. Although it is difficult to see, there is a global policing web which can be mapped as a complex police division of labour working to manage the flows of people and capital across territories defined by functional and geographical jurisdiction, and it is the *sine qua non* of the worldwide money system. Across the international patchwork of jurisdictions, police function to reproduce the hierarchy of money relations. Criminological considerations about policing in Canada allow glimpses of the global money system that reveal bigger transnational transformations, showing the apparatus of governance itself has been impoverished in this system. Monetary elites compete with each other on a transnational playing field they dominate, and which the existing institutions of governance and policing around the world are designated to uphold. Without necessarily being authoritarian, the organizational goals of policing in Canada are integral to these social hierarchies that are simultaneously local, transnational, and global. Currently the world system is entering the beginning of a new Great Power stand-off between what appears to be the rising financial power of the Peoples Republic of China and the declining economic power of the United States, and the conditions of crisis justify high policing measures in the particular interests of existing powerholders, while, in the pervasive logic of neoliberalism, the ability to undertake policing in the general social interest has to be justified in terms of economic costs and benefits that are seemingly unaffordable for the many.

These processes and conflicts could continue for some considerable time into the future because there is no discernable way to detach global governance from belief in the money system. Every conceivable solution to the present crisis has to contribute to economic growth. However, as the excoriating words of Greta Thunberg quoted at the beginning of this chapter indicate, this abstract belief system is creating unsustainable existential conditions. After examining present realities in Canada, imagining global democratic policing in the general interest is difficult precisely because of the collective failure to think outside of the belief system of money. If Canada is not to continue its decay from post-democracy to authoritarianism, along with the other countries of the Western alliance, its citizens need to be able to fulfil necessary low-policing functions grounded in social and ecological justice, against the practices of high policing for the protection of the interests of moneyed elites because money is, in any form, a mere token and has no intrinsic value whatsoever.

NOTES

1 Margaret E. Beare, Critical Reflections on Transnational Organized Crime, Money Laundering and Corruption (Toronto: University of Toronto Press, 2003); Margaret E. Beare and Tonita Murray, Police and Government Relations: Who's Calling the Shots? (Toronto: University of Toronto Press, 2007); Margaret E. Beare and Stephen Schneider, Money Laundering in Canada: Chasing Dirty and Dangerous Dollars (Toronto: University of Toronto Press, 2007); Margaret E. Beare, Nathalie des Rosiers, and Abigail C. Deshman, Putting the State on Trial: The Policing of Protest during the G20 Summit (Vancouver: University of British Columbia Press, 2015).
2 James Sheptycki, *Issues in Transnational Policing* (London: Routledge, 2000).
3 David Nelken and Michael Levi, "The Corruption of Politics and the Politics of Corruption: An Overview," *Journal of Law and Society* 23, no. 1 (March 1996): 1–17; Melissa L. Rorie, ed., *The Handbook of White-Collar Crime* (Oxford: John Wiley, 2019).
4 Alexandra V. Orlova and James W. Moore, "'Umbrellas' or 'Building Blocks'? Defining International Terrorism and Transnational Organized Crime in International Law," *Houston Journal of International Law* 27 (2005): 268–93; Vincenzo Ruggiero, *Crime and Markets: Essays in Anti-Criminology* (Oxford: Oxford University Press, 2000); Vincenzo Ruggiero, *The Crimes of the Economy: A Criminological Analysis of Economic Thought* (London: Routledge, 2013); Vincenzo Ruggiero, *Power and Crime* (London: Routledge, 2017); Toine Spapens et al., *Green Crimes and Dirty Money* (London: Routledge, 2018).
5 Jake Bernstein, *Secrecy World: Inside the Panama Papers Investigation of Illicit Money Networks and the Global Elite* (New York: Henry Holt and Co., 2017); Garfield Juliette, "Paradise Papers Leak Reveals Secrets of the World Elite's Hidden Wealth," *Guardian*, 5 November 2017.

6 Colin Crouch, Post-Democracy after the Crisis (Cambridge: Polity, 2020); Mark Whitehead et al., Neuroliberalism: Behavioural Government in the Twenty-First Century (London: Routledge, 2020); Shoshana Zuboff, The Age of Surveillance Capitalism: The Fight for a Human Future at the New Frontier of Power (New York: Public Affairs, 2018).
7 Richard W. Carney, Authoritarian Capitalism: Sovereign Wealth Funds and State-Owned Enterprises in East Asia and Beyond (Cambridge: Cambridge University Press, 2018); Thomas Piketty, Capital in the Twenty-First Century (Cambridge, MA: Belknap Press, 2014); Richard Wilkinson and Kate Pickett, The Spirit Level: Why More Equal Societies Almost Always Do Better (London: Allen Lane, 2009).
8 John A. Hall and Ralph Schroeder, *An Anatomy of Power: The Social Theory of Michael Mann* (Cambridge: Cambridge University Press, 2006); Leslie Sklair, "The Transnational Capitalist Class and the Discourse of Globalisation," *Cambridge Review of International Affairs* 14, no. 1 (2000): 67–85.
9 Rob White and Diane Heckenberg, Green Criminology: An Introduction to the Study of Environmental Harm (London: Taylor and Francis, 2014).
10 Jack Weatherford, *The History of Money: From Sandstone to Cyberspace* (New York: Three Rivers Press, 1997), xxi.
11 David Graeber, *Debt: The First 5,000 Years* (Brooklyn: Melville House, 2011).
12 Susan Strange, *Casino Capitalism* (Manchester: Manchester University Press, 1986); Susan Strange, *Mad Money* (Manchester: Manchester University Press, 1998).
13 Nigel Dodd, *The Social Life of Money* (Princeton, NJ: Princeton University Press, 2014).
14 Jeb Sprague, "Transnational Capitalist Class in the Global Financial Crisis: A Discussion with Leslie Sklair," *Globalizations* 6, no. 4 (2009): 499–507.
15 Weatherford, *History of Money*, 209.
16 Nicholas Shaxson, Treasure Islands: Tax Havens and the Men Who Stole the World (London: Palgrave MacMillan, 2011); Nicholas Shaxson, The Finance Curse: How Global Finance Is Making Us All Poorer (London: Bodley Head, 2018).
17 Naomi Klein, *The Shock Doctrine: The Rise of Disaster Capitalism* (Toronto: Random House, 2007).
18 Benjamin Bowling, Robert Reiner, and James Sheptycki, *The Politics of the Police*, 5th ed. (Oxford: Oxford University Press, 2019), 5; Jean-Paul Brodeur, *The Policing Web* (Oxford: Clarendon, 2010).
19 Malcolm Anderson et al., *Policing the European Union* (Oxford: Oxford University Press, 1995); Benjamin Bowling, *Policing the Caribbean* (Oxford: Clarendon, 2010); Benjamin Bowling and James Sheptycki, *Global Policing* (London: Sage, 2012); Ethan Nadelmann, *Cops across Borders: The Internationalization of U.S. Law Enforcement* (University Park: Pennsylvania State University Press, 1993); James Sheptycki, *In Search of Transnational Policing* (Aldershot, UK: Ashgate, 2003).
20 Peter Andreas and Ethan Nadelmann, *Policing the Globe: Criminalization and Crime Control in International Relations* (Oxford: Oxford University Press, 2008);

Mathieu Deflem, "Europol and the Policing of International Terrorism: Counter-Terrorism in Global Perspective," *Justice Quarterly* 23, no. 3 (2006): 336–59.
21 Bowling et al., *Politics of the Police*, 36–7.
22 Bowling et al., *Politics of the Police*, 93–4; Brodeur, *The Policing Web*, 310–22.
23 James Sheptycki, "Technopoly and Policing Practice," *European Law Enforcement Research Bulletin*, 4 SCE (2019): 133–9, https://bulletin.cepol.europa.eu/index.php/bulletin/article/view/362.
24 Bowling et al., Politics of the Police, 145–63; Blayne Haggart, Kathryn Henne, and Natasha Tusikov, Information, Technology and Control in a Changing World: Understanding Power Structures in the 21st Century (London: Palgrave MacMillan, 2019); Natasha Tusikov, Chokepoints: Global Private Regulation on the Internet (Los Angeles: University of California Press, 2016).
25 Benjamin Bowling and James Sheptycki, "Global Policing and Transnational Rule with Law," *Transnational Legal Theory* 6, no. 1 (2015): 141–73, https://doi.org/10.1080/20414005.2015.1042235.
26 Michael Levi, "Suite Revenge? The Shaping of Folk Devils and Moral Panics about White-Collar Crimes," *British Journal of Criminology* 49, no. 1 (2008): 48–67.
27 Greg Marquis, *The Vigilant Eye: Policing Canada from 1867 to 9-11* (Ocean Vista, NS: Fernwood Publishing, 2016).
28 Lorne Sossin, "The Oversight of Executive-Police Relations in Canada: The Constitution, the Courts, Administrative Processes, and Democratic Governance," in *Police and Government Relations: Who's Calling the Shots?*, eds. Margaret E. Beare and Tonita Murray (Toronto: University of Toronto Press, 2007), 96–146.
29 James Sheptycki, "Reflections on Hydrocarbon and Resource Extraction, Crime and Criminological Thinking," in *Environmental Crime in Transnational Context: Global Issues in Green Enforcement and Criminology*, eds. Toine Spapens, Rob White, and Wim Huisman (Aldershot, UK: Ashgate, 2016), 67–85.
30 John Kiedrowski, Nicholas A. Jones, and Rick Ruddell, "'Set Up to Fail? An Analysis of Self-administered Indigenous Police Services in Canada," *Police Practice and Research* 18, no. 6 (2017), https://doi.org/10.1080/15614263.2017.1363973; Curt Taylor Griffiths, "Policing and Community Safety in Northern Canadian Communities: Challenges and Opportunities for Crime Prevention," *Crime Prevention and Community Safety* 21, no. 3 (2019): 246–66; Robert Chrismas, *Canadian Policing in the 21st Century* (Montreal and Kingston: McGill-Queen's University Press, 2013); Murray J. Swastsky, Rick Ruddell, and Nicholas A. Jones, "A Quantitative Study of Prince Albert's Crime/Risk Reduction Approach to Community Safety," *Journal of Community Safety and Well-Being* 2, no. 1 (2017), http://dx.doi.org/10.35502/jcswb.38; Elizabeth Comack, "Corporate Colonialism and the 'Crimes of the Powerful' Committed against the Indigenous Peoples of Canada," *Critical Criminology* 26, no. 4 (2018): 455–71; Shiri Pasternak, "The Fiscal Body of Sovereignty: To 'Make Live' in Indian Country," *Settler Colonial Studies* 6, no. 4 (2016): 317–38.

31 National Inquiry into Missing and Murdered Indigenous Women and Girls, *Reclaiming Power and Place: The Final Report of the National Inquiry into Missing and Murdered Indigenous Women and Girls* (Vancouver: Privy Council Office, 2019), https://publications.gc.ca/site/eng/9.867037/publication.html.

32 Jane P. Preston, Sheila Carr-Stewart, and Charlene Bruno, "The Growth of Aboriginal Youth Gangs in Canada," *Canadian Journal of Native Studies* 32, no. 2 (2012): 193–207; James Michael Dixon, "The Political Economy of the Overdose Crisis in Western Canada: An Exploratory Case Study" (PhD diss., University of Saskatchewan, 2022), https://harvest.usask.ca/bitstream/handle/10388/13858/DIXON-DISSERTATION-2022.pdf?sequence=1.

33 Guy Ben-Porat, "Policing Multicultural States: Lessons from the Canadian Model," *Policing and Society* 18, no. 4 (2008): 411–25; Siu-Ming Kwok, "How Asian Youth Cope with the Criminal Justice System in Canada: A Grounded Theory Approach," *Asian Pacific Journal of Social Work and Development* 19, no. 2 (2009): 21–37.

34 J. David Hulchanski et al., *The Three Cities within Toronto: Income Polarization among Toronto's Neighbourhoods, 1970–2005* (Toronto: Cities Centre Press, University of Toronto, 2010), http://hdl.handle.net/1807/94665; R. Alan Walks and Larry S. Bourne, "Ghettos in Canada's Cities? Racial Segregation, Ethnic Enclaves and Poverty Concentration in Canadian Urban Areas," *The Canadian Geographer/Le Géographe canadien* 50, no. 3 (2017): 273–97.

35 Marquis, *The Vigilant Eye*, 222.

36 Alok Mukherjee and Tim Harper, *Excessive Force: Toronto's Fight to Reform City Policing* (Vancouver, BC: Douglas and McIntyre, 2018), 236–7.

37 James Sheptycki, "What Is Police Research Good For? Reflections on the Moral Economy and Police Research," *European Journal of Policing Studies* 5, no. 3 (2018): 16–35.

38 Robyn Maynard, "Police Abolition/Black Revolt," *TOPIA: Canadian Journal of Cultural Studies* 41 (2020): 70–8.

39 Alex Chung, *Chinese Criminal Entrepreneurs in Canada*, 2 vols. (London: Palgrave Macmillan, 2019); Fred Desroches, *The Crime That Pays: Drug Trafficking and Organized Crime in Canada* (Toronto: Canadian Scholars Press, 2005); Catherine Prowse, *Defining Street Gangs in the 21st Century: Fluid, Mobile and Transnational Networks* (New York: Springer-Verlag, 2013); Adam Edwards and James Sheptycki, eds., Special issue, *Guns, Crime and Social Order: Criminology and Criminal Justice* 9, no. 3 (2009).

40 Margaret E. Beare, "Organized Corporate Criminality: Corporate Complicity in Tobacco Smuggling," in *Critical Reflections on Transnational Organized Crime, Money Laundering, and Corruption*, ed. Margaret E. Beare (Toronto: Toronto University Press, 2003), 183–206; Stephen Schneider, "Organized Crime, Money Laundering and the Real Estate Market in Canada," *Journal of Property Research* 21, no. 2 (2004): 99–118.

41 Maureen Maloney, Tsur Somerville, and Brigitte Unger, *Combatting Money Laundering in BC Real Estate*, report of the Expert Panel on Money Laundering in BC Real Estate (Victoria, BC: Ministry of Finance, 2019), 48.
42 R.T. Naylor, *Hot Money and the Politics of Debt*, 3rd ed. (Montreal: McGill-Queen's University Press, 2004).
43 Rhianna Schmunk, "BC Casinos 'Unwittingly Served as Laundromats' for Proceeds of Crime," *CBC News*, 27 June 2018, https://www.cbc.ca/news/canada/british-columbia/bc-money-laundering-report-1.4723958.
44 Beare and Schneider, Money Laundering in Canada.
45 Kevin Comeau, "Why We Fail to Catch Money Launderers 99.9 Percent of the Time," E-brief (Toronto: C.D. Howe Institute, 2019), https://www.cdhowe.org/sites/default/files/attachments/research_papers/mixed/Final%20for%20release%20e-brief_291_web%20%28003%29.pdf.
46 Michael Vonn, "FINTRAC: The National Security Conversation That's Flying under the Radar," BC Civil Liberties Association, 2 May 2015, https://bccla.org/2015/05/fintrac-the-national-security-conversation-thats-flying-under-the-radar/.
47 Anthony Amicelle and Vanessa Iafolla, "Suspicion-in-the-Making: Surveillance and Denunciation in Financial Policing," *British Journal of Criminology* 58, no. 4 (2018): 845–63; Maloney et al., *Combatting Money Laundering in BC Real Estate*, 22.
48 Catharine Tunney, "Federal Government Met the Threshold to Invoke the Emergencies Act: Rouleau," *CBC News*, 17 February 2023, https://www.cbc.ca/news/politics/poec-report-released-friday-1.6750919.
49 James M. Curran and Matthew L. Meuter, "Self-service Technology Adoption: Comparing Three Technologies," *Journal of Services Marketing* 19, no. 2 (2005): 103–13.
50 Bradley Crawford, "Fraudulent Abuse of Remote Deposit Capture," *Banking and Finance Law Review* 32, no. 1 (2016): 145–9.
51 Michael Levi, "Assessing the Trends, Scale and Nature of Economic Cybercrime: Overview and Issues," *Crime, Law and Social Change* 67, no. 1 (2017): 3–20.
52 Michael Levi and Jim Handley, *Criminal Justice and the Future of Payment Card Fraud* (London: IPPR, 2002); Michael Levi et al., *The Implications of Economic Cyber Crime for Policing* (London: City of London Corporation and Cardiff University, 2015), 60–4.
53 Alain Deneault, Canada: A New Tax Haven: How the Country That Shaped Caribbean Tax Havens Is Becoming One Itself (Vancouver, BC: Talon Books, 2015).
54 Financial Action Task Force, Anti-Money Laundering and Counter-Terrorist Financing Measures Canada: Mutual Evaluation Report (Paris: FATF, 2016), 33–5, 48.
55 Laureen Snider, "The Sociology of Corporate Crime: An Obituary (Or: Whose Knowledge Claims Have Legs?)," *Theoretical Criminology* 4, no. 2 (2000): 169–206.
56 Robert Cribb and Marco Chown Oved, "Snow Washing: Canada Is the World's Newest Tax Haven," *The Star*, 25 January 2017, https://projects.thestar.com/panama-papers/canada-is-the-worlds-newest-tax-haven/.

57 Tax Justice Network (website), https://www.taxjustice.net/.
58 Beare, *Putting the State on Trial*; Marquis, *The Vigilant Eye*; Mukherjee and Harper, *Excessive Force*; Jeffery Monaghan and Kevin Walby, "They Attacked the City: Security Intelligence, the Sociology of Protest Policing and the Anarchist Threat at the 2010 G20 Summit," *Current Sociology* 60, no. 5 (2012): 653–71.
59 Richard V. Ericson and Aaron Doyle, "Globalization and the Policing of Protest: The Case of APEC 1997," *British Journal of Sociology* 50, no. 4 (1999): 589–608; Mike King and David Waddington, "Flashpoints Revisited: A Critical Application to Policing of Anti-Globalization Protest," *Policing and Society* 15, no. 3 (2006): 255–82.
60 Jeffery Monaghan and Kevin Walby, "Surveillance of Environmental Movements in Canada: Critical Infrastructure Protection and the Petro-security Apparatus," *Contemporary Justice Review* 20, no. 1 (2017): 51–70; Kevin Walby and Jeffrey Monaghan, "Private Eyes and Public Order: Policing and Surveillance in the Suppression of Animal Rights Activists in Canada," *Social Movement Studies* 10, no. 1 (2011): 21–37; Lesley Wood, *Crisis and Control: The Militarization of Protest Policing* (London: Pluto Press, 2014).
61 James Sheptycki, "The Politics of Policing a Pandemic Panic," *Australian and New Zealand Journal of Criminology* 53, no. 2 (2020): 157–73.
62 Helen Davidson, "China States Major Trial of State-Run Digital Currency," *Guardian*, 28 April 2020, https://www.theguardian.com/world/2020/apr/28/china-starts-major-trial-of-state-run-digital-currency; Kenneth Rogoff, "The US dollar's Hegemony Is Looking Fragile," *Guardian*, 2 April 2021, https://www.theguardian.com/business/2021/apr/02/the-us-dollars-hegemony-is-looking-fragile.
63 Andrew Potter, *On Decline* (Windsor, ON: Bibliosis, 2021), 27.

2 Big Banks, Big Money, and Big Crimes in the Era of "Too Big to Fail"

STEPHEN SCHNEIDER

At the end of 2012, the US Department of Justice announced that HSBC – one of the largest financial institutions in the world, and the single largest bank in Europe by market capitalization – had agreed to pay $1.9 billion in fines and other penalties. At the time, this was the largest monetary penalty ever imposed on a bank in the United States. The penalties resulted from a "four-count felony criminal information" that was filed in federal court in New York. According to a 2012 Justice Department press release, HSBC Bank USA violated the *Bank Secrecy Act* "by failing to maintain an effective anti-money laundering program and to conduct appropriate due diligence on its foreign correspondent account holders." But that was not the extent of the infractions committed by the bank. It had also violated the *International Emergency Economic Powers Act* and the *Trading with the Enemy Act* by deliberately circumventing US trade sanctions that had been imposed against numerous countries and individuals. If that was not enough, a further serious accusation levelled against HSBC was that it provided US correspondent accounts, as well as other banking services, to banks in Saudi Arabia and Bangladesh, despite evidence of their links to terrorist financing.[1] The US Senate Permanent Subcommittee on Investigations conducted its own inquiry into the allegations against HSBC, and in July of 2012 it issued a scathing 339-page report that identified numerous "regulatory failures" committed by the American subsidiary of HSBC, including anti–money laundering policy and program deficiencies, taking on high-risk affiliates, circumventing US trade sanctions, disregarding terrorist links of clients, and offering high-risk bearer share accounts that were used to evade taxes.[2]

This chapter details the numerous transgressions committed by HSBC and other Large Complex Financial Institutions (LCFIs) in recent years, which are broken down thematically using the following categories: (1) laundering billions of dollars generated from drug trafficking and other organized crimes (and in the process failing to comply with anti–money laundering laws), (2) circumventing US government trade sanctions (by doing business with clients in countries subject to such sanctions), (3) disregarding the links between correspondent banks and political extremist groups, (4) facilitating capital flight and tax evasion by clients, (5) unnecessary risk-taking with regard to investments and financial products (which led to the 2007–8 financial crisis), (6) the misleading marketing and sale of certain financial products, (7) manipulating the London Interbank Offered Rate (LIBOR), and (8) conspiring to manipulate foreign exchange rates.

The abbreviated length of this chapter impedes any thorough diagnosis of what drives the unethical, reckless, and illegal actions of LCFIs. With that said, by way of conclusion, this essay will briefly put forth the thesis that based on the research findings, LCFIs may be characterized by an organizational pathology – a "polluted culture"[3] – often driven by corporate directors, executives, and management, which may make global banks criminogenic.

Money Laundering and the Lack of Compliance with AML Laws and Regulations

HSBC has been at the centre of some of the largest and most egregious international money laundering scandals in recent memory. Its American and Mexican subsidiaries (referred to as HBUS and HBMX respectively) were accused of laundering "at least $881 million in drug trafficking proceeds" by Mexican and Colombia cocaine cartels.[4] Bulk cash was being moved from the United States to Mexico and hundreds of thousands of dollars in US currency was being deposited daily into HBMX accounts "with little or no oversight of the transactions" by bank managers or compliance units.[5] Some of the cash was recorded as the legal repatriation of money from Mexican landscapers working in the United States.[6] The Senate subcommittee investigating HSBC accused the bank of wilful blindness, noting that "Mexican and US authorities expressed repeated concern that HBMX's bulk cash shipments could reach that volume only if they included illegal drug proceeds. The concern was that drug traffickers unable to deposit large amounts of cash in US banks due to anti-money laundering (AML) controls were transporting US dollars to Mexico, arranging for bulk deposits there, and then using Mexican financial institutions to insert the cash back into the US financial system."[7]

HBUS was plagued by severe AML deficiencies that allowed money laundering to occur unfettered at the bank for years. This included problems that had already been detected and communicated to HBUS by government regulatory agencies, including the following:

- a dysfunctional AML system for monitoring account and wire transfer activity,
- ineffective policies and procedures for identifying large cash transactions and other suspicious activity (in particular, a failure to monitor $15 billion in bulk cash transactions between HBUS and correspondent banks in other

countries and a failure to monitor $60 trillion in annual wire transfer activity by customers in high-risk countries),
- a failure to identify and submit suspicious activity reports in a timely manner to US authorities (at one time there was a backlog of 17,000 suspicious transaction alerts that had not been reviewed by HBUS compliance personnel),
- inadequate due diligence to assess the money laundering risks of other countries, HSBC affiliates, and clients doing business with HBUS,
- a severe shortage of resources, leadership, and qualified staffing in its compliance departments and a high turnover of compliance and AML managers,
- deliberate attempts by HSBC personnel in the United States to circumvent AML laws and reporting requirements, and
- complicity of HSBC executives (the London-based parent company admitted to the US Justice Department it did not inform HBUS of the significant AML deficiencies at HBMX, despite full knowledge of these problems and how it could potentially contribute to the flow of drug money to HBUS).[8]

The high-profile case of HSBC was a harbinger of further international money laundering scandals that engulfed many of the world's other LCFIs. In September 2020, the International Consortium of Investigative Journalists (ICIJ) and BuzzFeed News made public records leaked from the US Financial Crimes Enforcement Centre (FINCEN). The records vividly display not only the predominant role played by LCFIs in facilitating money laundering worldwide, but their failure to heed AML compliance measures. In total, the so-called FINCEN files include 2,657 documents, of which 2,100 are suspicious activity reports (SARs) filed with FINCEN from banks and other private-sector entities that are obligated to report any transactions flagged as suspicious of money laundering, terrorist financing, or other financial crimes. The trove of evidence also includes 17,641 records obtained through Freedom of Information requests and other sources. In all, the records covered approximately 200,000 transactions involving $2 trillion conducted between 1999 and 2017.[9]

According to the ICIJ, the data show that some of the biggest financial service providers in the world – JPMorgan, HSBC, Standard Chartered Bank, Deutsche Bank, UBS, Bank of New York Mellon, ING – continued to take on suspicious clients, processed financial transactions for people or entities they couldn't identify, and failed to file SARs when presented with suspicious activity or repeatedly processed transactions they had reported as suspicious.[10] All of this occurred despite these financial institutions having committed to strengthening their AML compliance regimes following previous fines and other sanctions. As the ICIJ put it, the banks "defied money-laundering crackdowns by moving staggering sums of illicit cash for shadowy characters and criminal networks" and "kept profiting from powerful and dangerous players even after US authorities fined these financial institutions for earlier failures to stem flows of dirty money."[11]

The FINCEN files shine another unflattering spotlight on HSBC. One journalist reported that the HBUS compliance office "filed reports identifying more than $2 billion in transactions through the company's Hong Kong subsidiary that bore the hallmarks of possible criminal activity."[12] Another media article stated that between 2013 and 2017, the same compliance office filed reports on sixteen shell companies that had processed approximately 6,800 transactions worth $1.5 billion through HSBC's Hong Kong operations. "More than $900 million of that total involved shell companies linked to alleged criminal networks." Many of these reports were lacking crucial customer information such as "who owned the accounts, what countries the owners lived in, and where the money came from." In addition, the leaked FINCEN records indicate that HSBC "processed at least $31 million between 2014 and 2015 for companies later revealed to have moved stolen government funds from Brazil; and more than $292 million between 2010 and 2016 for a Panama-based organization branded by US authorities as a major money launderer for drug cartels."[13] HSBC was also blamed for laundering money generated by a Ponzi scheme that victimized investors out of at least US$65 million by transferring $15 million in illicit funds through its US business to HSBC accounts in Hong Kong, despite knowing the source of the funds.[14] By 2017, the HSBC Hong Kong office was embroiled in yet another international money laundering controversy, along with more than one hundred other global banks (including Bank of America, JP Morgan, Wells Fargo, Citibank, Deutsche Bank, Standard Chartered, and Barclays). As much as $80 billion in illicit funds linked to Russia's corrupt kleptocracy was transferred out of the country between 2010 and 2014, with HSBC being accused of processing US$545 million of the tainted Russian funds, primarily through its Hong Kong offices.[15]

Facilitating Capital Flight and Tax Evasion by Wealthy Clients

In 2012, brothers Judas and Nessim El-Maleh, executives with the Swiss HSBC private banking arm, were accused of simultaneously orchestrating a drug-money laundering operation and a tax evasion scheme. The alleged operation entailed exchanging the cash revenue from illegal marijuana sales in France for assets that were being secreted in undeclared Swiss bank accounts by French clients who were evading taxes and who wished to repatriate these assets to France. Cash from drug sales in France was reportedly handed over in heavy plastic bags to the French tax evasion clients and the equivalent amount was debited from their HSBC accounts in Geneva. The funds removed from the secret HSBC accounts were then sent on a complex route through shell companies the brothers set up in London and from there to four hundred trust accounts in Panama that were used to finance assets in Morocco, Dubai, or Spain for their marijuana trafficking clients.[16] The brothers may have laundered as much as €100 million annually while taking a commission of 8 per cent.[17] In 2015, HSBC agreed to pay 40 million francs in fines and other penalties to the Swiss government to settle the resulting allegations of money laundering at its private bank.[18]

According to the book *Secrecy World* by Jake Bernstein, HSBC's private Swiss banking operations were expressly geared towards helping the rich avoid paying taxes. "HSBC's executives saw an emerging class of global rich as the bank's path to prosperity. The super wealthy were increasingly stateless. They banked in Geneva. Lived in London and New York. Shopped in Paris and Milan. And they held their assets through offshore companies registered in places like the British Virgin Islands."[19] HSBC's foray into facilitating capital flight and tax evasion began when it purchased Safra Republic Holdings, which operated a Swiss private bank.

> Republic's thirty thousand high-net-worth clients included bagmen for corrupt African leaders, Chinese princelings, Middle Eastern royalty, the Russian mafia, crooked diamond merchants, and money launderers. Most wanted the secrecy afforded by offshore companies. Republic specialized in absolute discretion, minimal questions, and concierge service – the kind of hands-on tight-lipped Swiss banking caricatured in a thousand spy novels.[20]

Bernstein concludes, "HSBC changed little about the manner in which Republic operated"[21] and henceforth aggressively marketed services that helped wealthy European clients hide their assets in Swiss private bank accounts and offshore shell companies.[22] "There was next to no review of clients. Bankers were not only creating offshore companies for customers, but they were also serving as directors for them. The files for the highest-level clients, such as Middle Eastern royalty, were not in the system but were kept in a safe in the CEO's office."[23]

In 2008, a former HSBC private bank employee-turned-whistleblower disclosed information to the French government about the illegal operations of his employer. "The leaked documents, which mainly cover the years 2005 to 2007, relate to accounts worth $100 billion held by more than 100,000 people and legal entities from 200 countries, according to the Associated Press."[24] More than 4,000 accounts were established by HSBC in the tax haven Jersey alone.[25] A spokesperson for HSBC admitted that the bank was complicit in tax evasion, conceding it exercised "lax compliance standards that fell short of regulators' expectations and our expectations, and we are absolutely committed to remedying what went wrong and learning from it."[26]

HSBC offices in other countries have also been implicated in other tax evasion conspiracies. In 2012, the Argentinian government accused the bank's subsidiary in that country of helping clients evade taxes through the creation of an illegal scheme that used "phantom bank accounts" and falsified receipts to hide financial information from government authorities and laundered almost US$80 million for various companies and even a criminal organization. The director of the country's tax authority, Ricardo Echegaray, was quoted as saying, "It's clear to us that there was a conspiracy between HSBC and private companies."[27]

HSBC was far from the only bank helping clients avoid paying taxes. In a 2014 article, the *Wall Street Journal* reported, "about a dozen Swiss banks remain under criminal investigation in the US for aiding tax evasion" while "dozens of Swiss bankers and advisers" have already been charged "with helping Americans evade taxes."[28] One of those banks was Credit Suisse, which, in a plea agreement with the US Department of Justice, admitted it was guilty of operating "an illegal cross-border banking business that knowingly and willfully aided and assisted thousands of US clients in opening and maintaining undeclared accounts and concealing their offshore assets and income from the IRS."[29]

Circumventing US Government Trade Sanctions

In 2012, US authorities sanctioned HSBC for deliberately circumventing the country's trade sanctions by "illegally conducting transactions on behalf of customers in Cuba, Iran, Libya, Sudan and Burma – all countries that were subject to sanctions enforced by the Office of Foreign Assets Control (OFAC) at the time of the transactions."[30] According to the report from the Senate Permanent Subcommittee on Investigations, "An outside auditor hired by HBUS has so far identified, from 2001 to 2007, more than 28,000 undisclosed, OFAC sensitive transactions that were sent through HBUS involving $19.7 billion. Of those 28,000 transactions, nearly 25,000 involved Iran, while 3,000 involved other prohibited countries or persons." The other prohibited countries in which HSBC processed US dollar transactions included Cuba, Sudan, Burma, and North Korea.[31]

HSBC staff and directors deliberately concealed the bank's ongoing business with clients in countries on the OFAC sanctions list. They diligently omitted the names of these countries from American dollar payment messages sent to HBUS branches and other financial institutions in the United States, an obfuscating process known as "stripping" (as in stripping revealing information from payment messages). A Department of Justice press release stated the bank "also worked with at least one sanctioned entity to format payment messages, which prevented the bank's filters from blocking prohibited payments." In addition, HSBC branches outside the United States inserted cautionary notes in payment messages to HBUS that included: "care sanctioned country," "do not mention our name in NY," or "do not mention Iran."[32] Not only were HSBC branches in Europe and the Middle East intentionally circumventing US laws, but management at the bank's global headquarters in London apparently approved of these moves. The HSBC Group became aware of the improper practices of stripping in 2000, according to the US Department of Justice. In 2003, the Director of the Compliance Department at HSBC Group wrote in a memo that this practice "could provide the basis for an action against [HSBC] Group for breach of sanctions." However, as the Justice Department notes, "Notwithstanding instructions from HSBC Group Compliance to terminate this practice, HSBC Group affiliates were permitted to engage in the practice for an additional three years through the granting of dispensations to HSBC Group policy."[33]

HSBC was not the only LCFI to have circumvented American trade sanctions. Between 2005 and 2014, at least seven other major global banks were penalized for violating American laws by conducting business with entities in countries on the OFAC sanctions list. These banks include ABN Amro Holding,[34] Barclays,[35] Credit Suisse,[36] Deutsche Bank,[37] JPMorgan,[38] Standard Chartered, Commerzbank,[39] Royal Bank of Scotland,[40] and BNP Paribus.[41] All of these banks purposely concealed or altered information, using stripping and other methods, to hide the identities of the sanctioned entities. Most of the fines were hundreds of millions of dollars, while France's largest bank, BNP Paribus, paid a penalty of US$8.9 billion, which resulted from a felony criminal indictment for transferring billions of dollars through the US financial system on behalf of Sudanese, Iranian, and Cuban entities subject to American sanctions. "BNP ignored US sanctions laws and concealed its tracks. And when contacted by law enforcement it chose not to fully cooperate," a Department of Justice statement reads.[42] An assistant US district attorney concluded, "This conspiracy was known and condoned at the highest levels of BNP."[43] In August 2012, the New York State Department of Financial Services determined that Standard Chartered bank had "schemed with the Government of Iran" for almost a decade to "hide from regulators roughly 60,000 secret transactions, involving at least $250 billion, and reaping SCB hundreds of millions of dollars in fees." This "left the U.S. financial system vulnerable to terrorists, weapons dealers, drug kingpins and corrupt regimes, and deprived law enforcement investigators of crucial information used to track all manner of criminal activity."[44]

Disregarding the Links between Correspondent Banks and Political Extremist Groups

Another serious accusation levelled against HSBC was that it provided US correspondent accounts, as well as other banking services, to financial institutions in Saudi Arabia and Bangladesh, despite evidence that these banks were processing transactions for al-Qaida and other terrorist groups. As the Senate subcommittee report notes, HSBC was active in Saudi Arabia and conducted "substantial banking activities" with the largest private financial institution in the country, Al Rajhi

Bank. "After the 9/11 terrorist attack in 2001, evidence began to emerge that Al Rajhi Bank and some of its owners had links to financing organizations associated with terrorism, including evidence that the bank's key founder was an early financial benefactor of al Qaeda." HBUS also did business with two other banks, Islami Bank Bangladesh Ltd. and Social Islami Bank, "despite evidence of links to terrorist financing."[45] HSBC personnel were aware of the allegations linking the three banks to possible terrorist financing but approved or maintained US dollar accounts for the banks anyway, according to the Senate subcommittee report.[46]

Based on data from the FINCEN files, Buzzfeed News reported that the London-based Standard Chartered bank, which does extensive business in the Middle East, was also accused of moving money "on behalf of Al Zarooni Exchange, a Dubai-based firm that was later accused of laundering cash on behalf of the Taliban." Standard Chartered also helped the clients of the Jordanian financial institution Arab Bank "access the US financial system after regulators found deficiencies in Arab Bank's money laundering controls in 2005 and forced it to curtail money-transfer activities in the US." Standard Chartered continued its relationship with Arab Bank even after US government authorities put it on notice that it must stop processing transactions for suspicious clients.[47]

Manipulation of Foreign Exchange Rates

In January 2018, the US Justice Department ordered HSBC to pay a US$63.1 million criminal penalty and $38.4 million in disgorgement and victim restitution. The case involved charges that HSBC traders engaged in a scheme to defraud bank clients for the benefit of the traders by manipulating foreign exchange rates. A Justice Department press release summarized the contents of the plea agreement with HSBC on this matter:

> According to HSBC's admissions, on two separate occasions in 2010 and 2011, traders on its foreign exchange desk misused confidential information provided to them by clients that hired HSBC to execute multi-billion dollar foreign exchange transactions involving the British Pound Sterling. After executing confidentiality agreements with its clients that required the bank to keep the details of their planned transactions confidential, traders on HSBC's foreign exchange desk transacted in the Pound Sterling for the traders and HSBC's own benefit in their HSBC "proprietary" accounts. HSBC traders then caused the large transactions to be executed in a manner designed to drive the price of the Pound Sterling in a direction that benefited HSBC, and harmed their clients. HSBC also made misrepresentations to one of the clients, Cairn Energy, to conceal the self-serving nature of its actions. In total, HSBC admitted to making profits of approximately $38.4 million on the first transaction in March 2010, and approximately $8 million on the Cairn Energy transaction in December 2011.[48]

In 2015, Citigroup Inc., JPMorgan, Chase, Barclays, and the Royal Bank of Scotland pleaded guilty to federal criminal felony charges in the United States and were collectively fined $2.5 billion for conspiring with one another to fix rates on US dollars and euros traded in the global currencies market, otherwise known as the FX Spot Market.[49] The plea agreements acknowledge that between December 2007 and January 2013, traders with Citicorp, JPMorgan, Barclays, and the Royal Bank of Scotland engaged in "communications, including near daily conversations, some of which were in code, in an exclusive electronic chat room, which chat room participants, as well as others in the FX Spot Market, referred to as 'The Cartel' or 'The Mafia.'"[50] In one of many techniques used, the "cartel" members manipulated the euro–dollar exchange rate "by agreeing to withhold bids or offers for euros or dollars to avoid moving the exchange rate in a direction adverse to open positions held by co-conspirators."[51] In 2019, the *New York Times* reported that the European Union fined Barclays, Citigroup, JPMorgan Chase, the Mitsubishi UFJ Financial Group, and the Royal Bank of Scotland for their role in manipulating foreign exchange rates. "Although the traders were direct competitors, the commission's investigation found that they had exchanged trading plans, shared sensitive information – including details of their customers' orders and evidence of their identities – and even coordinated strategies during chats on Bloomberg terminals."[52]

The LIBOR Scandal

In 2012, numerous LCFIs were implicated in a conspiracy to manipulate the London Interbank Offered Rate (LIBOR) between 2005 and 2009 for their collective benefit. The LIBOR is an average interest rate derived from submissions of rates posted by major banks in London. Banks are expected to submit the actual interest rates they are paying (or would expect to pay) for borrowing from other banks. According to the *Wall Street Journal*,

> Libor plays a crucial role in the global financial system. Calculated every morning in London from information supplied by banks all over the world, it's a measure of the average interest rate at which banks make short-term loans to one another. Libor provides a key indicator of their health, rising when banks are in trouble. Its influence extends far beyond banking: The interest rates on trillions of dollars in corporate debt, home mortgages and financial contracts reset according to Libor.[53]

The LIBOR scandal arose when it was discovered that banks were falsely inflating or deflating their interest rate submissions to the LIBOR so as to either profit from trades in securities or to create the impression that they were more creditworthy than actuality (many banks were in danger of having their credit rating downgraded in the wake of the 2007–8 financial crisis). By 2010, there was growing evidence that numerous banks were submitting false rates to the LIBOR. In February 2012, the US Department of Justice announced it was conducting a criminal investigation into abuse of the LIBOR,[54] while government bodies in numerous other countries launched investigations into similar allegations with more than twenty multinational financial institutions coming under scrutiny.[55] By 2013, an estimated US$2.3 billion in fines were levied by government authorities in various countries against eight banks: Barclays, Lloyds, JPMorgan, Citigroup, Deutsche Bank, Société Générale, UBS, and the Royal Bank of Scotland.[56] In addition to these fines, numerous class action lawsuits have been filed by individual consumers and consumer groups.

The 2007–8 Financial Crisis

It is beyond the scope of this chapter to document in detail the complex and multifaceted factors that led to the financial crisis of 2007–8 and the worst economic collapse since the 1930s; this has been covered by thousands of media articles, books, and government reports.[57] By way of summary, the 2011 report of the National Commission on the Causes of the Financial and Economic Crisis in the United States contends that the crisis was created by "vulnerabilities" that were years in the making.

> [I]t was the collapse of the housing bubble – fueled by low interest rates, easy and available credit, scant regulation, and toxic mortgages – that was the spark that ignited a string of events, which led to a full-blown crisis in the fall of 2008. Trillions of dollars in risky mortgages had become embedded throughout the financial system, as mortgage-related securities were packaged, repackaged, and sold to investors around the world. When the bubble burst, hundreds of billions of dollars in losses in mortgages and mortgage-related securities shook markets as well as financial institutions that had significant exposures to those mortgages and had borrowed heavily against them. This happened not just in the United States but around the world. The losses were magnified by derivatives such as synthetic securities. The crisis reached seismic proportions in September 2008 with the failure of Lehman Brothers and the impending collapse of the insurance giant American International Group (AIG). Panic fanned by a lack of transparency of the balance sheets of major financial institutions, coupled with a tangle of interconnections among institutions perceived to be "too big to fail," caused the credit markets to seize up. Trading ground to a halt. The stock market plummeted. The economy plunged into a deep recession.[58]

One jarring conclusion of the National Commission is that the "financial crisis was avoidable."[59] LCFIs were a primary contributor to this avoidable collapse due to their unnecessary risk taking, poor corporate governance, and a profound lack of fiduciary responsibility to investors and customers (and society as a whole) that was long-standing and widespread. The National Commission notes that the LCFIs took on "greater and more diverse kinds of risks" and that the "captains of finance and the public stewards of our financial system ignored warnings and failed to question, understand, and manage evolving risks within a system essential to the well-being of the American public." The Commission's report itself notes it is "replete with evidence" of unnecessary risk taking and other "failures" by LCFIs. These financial institutions "made, bought, and sold mortgage securities they never examined, did not care to examine, or knew to be defective; firms depended on tens of billions of dollars of borrowing that had to be renewed each and every night, secured by subprime mortgage securities; and major firms and investors blindly relied on credit rating agencies as their arbiters of risk."[60] More to the point, the National Commission observed that:

> dramatic failures of corporate governance and risk management at many systemically important financial institutions were a key cause of this crisis … Too many of these institutions acted recklessly, taking on too much risk, with too little capital, and with too much dependence on short-term funding. In many respects, this reflected a fundamental change in these institutions, particularly the large investment banks and bank holding companies, which focused their activities increasingly on risky trading activities that produced hefty profits. They took on enormous exposures in acquiring and supporting subprime lenders and creating, packaging, repackaging, and selling trillions of dollars in mortgage-related securities, including synthetic financial products.[61]

The National Commission concluded that its "examination revealed stunning instances of governance breakdowns and irresponsibility" by LCFIs. This was accompanied by "systemic breakdown in accountability and ethics" among LCFIs that "exacerbated the financial crisis. This was not universal, but these breaches stretched from the ground level to the corporate suites."[62] Geiss tersely attributes the culpability of LCFIs as such: "the investment industry, driven by a lust for lucre, irresponsibly and stupidly – and at times criminally – had taken risks that placed them in serious financial jeopardy and forced them to seek help from the government (that is, taxpayers) to keep themselves solvent."[63]

In subsequent years, many LCFIs have been penalized by government authorities in various countries and/or have been the subject of civil lawsuits. As the *New York Times* noted in 2012, prosecutors, industry regulators, investors, and insurers have filed dozens of lawsuits against some of the country's largest financial institutions asserting that they sold more than $1 trillion in "shoddy mortgage securities that imploded during the financial crisis."[64] By 2016, the Securities and Exchange Commission (SEC) had charged 2,004 entities and individuals with numerous regulatory infractions as a result of "misconduct that led to or arose from the financial crisis." Among the businesses sanctioned by the SEC were Citigroup, Goldman Sachs, J.P. Morgan Securities, Merrill Lynch, Wachovia Capital Markets, Wells Fargo, UBS Securities, Bank of America, Countrywide, Credit Suisse Securities, RBS Securities, and TD Ameritrade. The infractions committed by these and other corporations include concealing from investors the risks, terms, and improper pricing of complex structured financial products; making misleading disclosures to investors about mortgage-related risks and exposure; and concealing the extent of risky mortgage-related and other investments in mutual funds and other financial products.[65] In the United States, the SEC has been joined by the Department of Justice, state attorneys general, as well as numerous federal and state regulators in penalizing LCFIs for their role in bringing about the financial crises. A partial list of monetary penalties incurred by LCFIs for their role in marketing toxic mortgage-backed securities include $2 billion by Barclay's,[66] $5 billion by Goldman Sachs,[67] $5.3 billion by Credit Suisse,[68] $7 billion by Citigroup,[69] $7.2 billion by Deutsche Bank,[70] $13 billion by JP Morgan Chase,[71] and $16.65 billion by Bank of America.[72]

The Misleading Marketing and Sale of Financial Products

LCFIs have also been accused of the misleading and predatory marketing of financial products outside of the financial crisis. This category of infractions includes the practice of selling products and services customers did not order (and sometimes without their knowledge) or misrepresenting the nature of the product or services.[73] Often these products and services came with an initial and annual (or monthly) fee. In April 2014, Bank of America agreed to pay US$772 million in fines and consumer refunds to settle "regulators' accusations that it misled customers who bought extra credit-card products and illegally charged others for credit monitoring and reporting services they didn't receive," according to the Associated Press. The federal Consumer Financial Protection Bureau had already sanctioned four other major banks in the country for the misleading marketing and sale of the so-called credit card add-ons. This included JP Morgan Chase & Co., which agreed to pay $80 million in fines and about $309 million in consumer refunds for allegedly billing customers for ID theft protection they never received. The federal bureau also reached settlements with American Express Co., Discover Financial Services, and Capital One Financial Corp., the Associated Press reported.[74]

Perhaps the most egregious example of fraudulent and predatory sales practices by a bank concerns Wells Fargo and its creation of millions of savings and chequing accounts on behalf of the bank's clients without their knowledge or consent. Approximately 3.5 million fake accounts were created, and, in many cases, the accounts were accompanied by overdraft fees and other unauthorized charges. In addition, the bank violated federal and state consumer protection laws by selling credit cards to pre-approved customers without their permission (with sales staff creating phony e-mail addresses or using their own contact information to prevent customers from finding out). It also referred customers for enrolment in life insurance policies without their authorization, charging more than 850,000 auto finance customers for unnecessary insurance policies, and failing to ensure customers received refunds of unearned premiums on certain optional auto finance products. In late 2016, various regulatory bodies, including the Consumer Financial Protection Bureau, forced Wells Fargo to pay US$185 million in fines and victim restitution. In a 2020 settlement with the Department of Justice, the bank agreed to pay another US$3 billion to settle criminal and civil investigations.[75]

Conclusion

The pervasive, widespread, and ongoing nature of HSBC's unlawful actions establishes the bank as a textbook case study for an analysis of LCFI deviance. Yet, HSBC is not an outlier in this regard, as should be abundantly clear by now; numerous other LCFIs have been implicated in similar unethical, irresponsible, harmful, and unlawful behaviour. Like HSBC, many of these banks are repeat offenders, having been accused and penalized for multiple infractions. Between 2008 and 2016, Deutsche Bank paid close to $9 billion in fines and settlements for a wide range of transgressions: marketing toxic mortgages that contributed to the 2008–9 financial crisis; evading US-imposed trade sanctions by moving billions of dollars on behalf of financial institutions in Iran, Libya, Syria, Sudan, and Myanmar; conspiring with other banks to manipulate lending and foreign exchange rates; conspiring to manipulate the price of gold and silver; helping clients evade taxes; facilitating money laundering by turning a blind eye to suspicious transactions; and failing to put in place sufficient risk management and AML compliance policies. Based on leaked FINCEN documents, it has been reported that $1.3 trillion in suspicious transactions were processed by Deutsche Bank between 1999 and 2017. The bank was also fined $150 million by the New York Department of Financial Services for "significant compliance failures" in its relationship with Jeffrey Epstein and has also come under scrutiny for lending Donald Trump hundreds of millions of dollars despite his history of bankruptcy and loan defaults.[76]

In 2015, the Huffington Post reported that JPMorgan, another repeat offender, had been penalized more than $23 billion by US authorities "in recent years settling allegations that included conspiring to manipulate foreign-currency rates, allowing its 'London Whale' trader to exceed risk limits, failing to flag transactions related to Bernard Madoff's Ponzi scheme and misrepresenting the value of mortgage-backed securities."[77] For its role in aiding Madoff, the bank paid monetary penalties of $2.6 billion, and in 2011 it forfeited $88.3 million to settle claims it violated trade sanctions against Iran and other countries subject to US embargoes.[78] In 2013, JPMorgan was issued a "consent order" by the US Treasury Department for "systemic deficiencies in its transaction monitoring systems, due diligence processes, risk management, and quality assurance programs." The order noted that JPMorgan "failed to identify significant volumes of suspicious activity and file the required SARs concerning suspicious customer activities."[79] In October 2020, the US Commodity Futures Trading Commission announced the investment bank would pay $290 million in penalties and restitution for manipulating the precious metals and US Treasury futures markets that "significantly benefited JPM and harmed other market participants." It was the largest penalty ever imposed by the CFTC.[80]

As detailed throughout this chapter, HSBC, Deutsche Bank, and JPMorgan are just the tip of the iceberg when it comes to the penalties paid by LCFIs for their malfeasance. In 2015, the *Financial Post* quoted Don Coxe, a global portfolio strategist for BMO in Chicago, who estimated that, overall, banks around the world had paid US$350 billion in fines "for all the frauds they are admitting to since 2008."[81] Since the time of this comment, billions more in penalties have been levied against numerous LCFIs in various countries.

Following the US savings and loan crisis of the 1980s, it was famously said that the "best way to rob a bank is to own one."[82] In the wake of the role of LCFIs in the 2007–8 financial crisis, Friedrichs suggests the term "bank robbery" should include how the banks themselves steal from "clients and customers, investors, and ordinary taxpayers."[83] According to US Assistant Attorney General Leslie Caldwell, "Simply put, banks and other financial institutions continue to come up on our radar screens because they, and the individuals through which they act, continue to violate the law, maintain ineffective compliance programs or simply turn a blind eye to criminal conduct to preserve profit."[84] Nobel laureate and *New York Times* columnist Paul Krugman laments how "much of the financial industry has become a racket – a game in which a handful of people are lavishly paid to mislead and exploit consumers and investors."[85]

Because this essay is mainly descriptive, it raises more questions than it answers. Given the accumulated evidence, one of the most compelling questions to ask is whether LCFIs – and finance capitalism generally – are inherently criminogenic. Ironically, it may be the legal conditions put in place for common stock corporations that make them prone to unethical and illegal conduct: the limited liabilities borne by modern corporate actors can shield executives and directors from both criminal prosecution and civil suits, which may remove a substantial deterrent to unethical and illegal behaviour. The highly competitive markets in which corporations work is also said to pressure management and employees to break the law. Executive compensation in stock options may be an incentive to cheat in the short run to push up stock prices. Executive authority within a corporation often provides powers and freedom from control that may promote unethical and illegal conduct while "multiple layers of control and ownership insulate individuals from a sense of responsibility for corporate actions."[86]

Within the financial services sector, the ongoing trend of creating and marketing highly speculative financial products, such as mortgage-backed securities or collateralized debt obligations, has helped steer LCFIs into the realm of investment fraud. Indeed, the subprime mortgage market and the securitization of risky overpriced loans that were so aggressively pushed by LCFIs have been called "the largest Ponzi scheme in the history of the capital markets"[87] given they satisfy the three basic legs of the fraud popularized by Charles Ponzi: "debt, speculation or gambling, and the belief in rapid 'investment' growth."[88] The relatively lenient penalties assessed against LCFIs for their offences – deferred prosecution agreements (essentially probation) and monetary penalties (which are a fraction of their profits) – may also undermine any deterrence incentive for future offences. Moreover, the fact that many LCFIs responsible for the financial crisis were bailed out by the US government because they were "too big to fail" sends a clear message to this sector that the state ultimately has their backs regardless of how badly they behave or the extent of their misconduct's impact. In his summary of the "criminogenic conditions complicit in the financial meltdown," Friedrichs includes "financial organizations that are either 'too big to fail' or too interconnected to challenge without harming financial structures." His list of criminogenic risk factors also includes "exorbitant executive compensation and bonuses; excessive leveraging in relation to investments; 'innovative,' complex, and excessively risky financial products or instruments; and pervasive conflicts of interest involving entities that supposedly provide some form of oversight of the activities of financial institutions, including boards of directors, auditing firms, and credit-rating agencies."[89] Much has been written about how few, if any, executives or directors of a LCFI were criminally prosecuted for the role their corporations played in the onset of the 2007–8 financial crisis (let alone any of the other illegal acts catalogued in this essay). The fact that executives and directors escape criminal prosecution may be the result of "crony capitalism," which is "the ability of favored elites to loot with impunity (and be bailed out)."[90]

Questions have also been raised as to whether an organizational pathology exists with LCFIs that drives unethical, unlawful, and even criminal behaviours. Senator Carl Levin, who chaired the Senate subcommittee during its investigation into HSBC, is quoted as saying, "The culture at HSBC was pervasively polluted for a long time."[91] Assistant US Attorney General Leslie Caldwell told a conference on money laundering and financial crimes, "The record of dysfunction that prevailed at HSBC for many years was astonishing."[92] For Ross, the numerous transgressions of HSBC reveal that what is "lacking in these instances is a corporate culture that prizes integrity ... HSBC has been cited in the past and yet committed violations anew. If positive change is to be lasting, so, too, must the culture that fosters it be ingrained throughout the bank."[93] This hypothesis of organizational pathology can be applied beyond the HSBC case study; the National Commission on the Causes of the Financial and Economic Crisis may have intimated a similar argument when it wrote, a "crisis of this magnitude cannot be the work of a few bad actors, and such was not the case here."[94]

It has been argued that corporate executives escape criminal sanctions because corporations are separate and legal entities distinct from management and shareholders; in other words, corporations may be inherently criminogenic beyond the actions of individual executives, directors, and employees. Notwithstanding, the distinct legal status of corporations, the culpability of senior management in corporate wrongdoing, and the nurturing of an organizational pathology are not mutually exclusive but critically interconnected. As Leaf writes, "Of all the factors that lead to corporate crime, none comes close in the importance to the role top management plays in tolerating, even shaping a culture that allows it."[95] Rowan Bosworth-Davies, a former financial crimes specialist with London's Metropolitan Police, blames senior management at HSBC for creating a corporate culture that tolerated and even encouraged its many transgressions. "You don't launder this volume of money by accident, because somewhere along the line, your systems and controls for preventing money laundering just 'broke down'! You do it because you work in a bank which is willing to flout every rule in the book and engage in layer upon layer of criminal conduct if the money is right! You do it because your management structure is defined by a criminogenic determination to amplify the anomic environment within which you operate and in which you expect your staff to co-operate."[96] Regardless of its root causes, the supposed organizational pathology of LCFIs threatens to continue unabated due to the primacy that maximizing (short-term) profits and shareholder returns now assume in the very *raison d'etre* of LCFIs and corporations in general. According to Stephens,

> Profit-maximization, if not the only goal of all business activity, is certainly central to the endeavour. And the pursuit of profit is, by definition, an amoral goal – not necessarily immoral, but rather morally neutral. An individual or business will achieve the highest level of profit by weighing all decisions according to a self-serving economic scale. Large corporations magnify the consequences of the amoral profit motive.[97]

While any hypothesis claiming that LCFIs suffer from an organizational pathology that contributes to the onset of criminal behaviour is tentative, it is incumbent upon researchers, lawmakers, and business leaders to pursue this line of inquiry, given the scope and impact of the lawlessness displayed by LCFIs in both historical and contemporary times.

NOTES

1 US Department of Justice, "HSBC Holdings PLC. and HSBC Bank USA N.A. Admit to Anti-Money Laundering and Sanctions Violations, Forfeit $1.256 Billion in Deferred Prosecution Agreement," *Department of Justice Press Release*, 11 December.
2 United States Senate, Permanent Subcommittee on Investigations, Committee on Homeland Security and Government Affairs, *US Vulnerabilities to Money Laundering, Drugs, and Terrorist Financing: HSBC Case History* (Washington, DC: United States Government Printing Office, 2012).
3 Alastair Jamieson, "Report: HSBC Allowed Money Laundering That Likely Funded Terror, Drugs," NBC News, 17 July 2012.
4 US Department of Justice, "HSBC Holdings PLC. and HSBC Bank USA N.A. Admit to Anti-Money Laundering and Sanctions Violations."
5 Marc Ross, "HSBC's Money Laundering Scandal," Investopedia.com, 29 January 2013.
6 Rob Davies and Tim Shipman, "HSBC Let Drug Gangs Launder Millions: First Barclays, Now Britain's Biggest Bank Is Shamed – and Faces a £640million Fine," *Daily Mail Online*, 17 July 2012.
7 United States Senate, Permanent Subcommittee on Investigations, US Vulnerabilities to Money Laundering, Drugs, and Terrorist Financing: HSBC Case History, 179.
8 United States Senate, Permanent Subcommittee on Investigations, *US Vulnerabilities to Money Laundering, Drugs, and Terrorist Financing: HSBC Case History*; US Department of Justice, "HSBC Holdings PLC and HSBC Bank USA N.A. Admit to Anti-Money Laundering and Sanctions Violations; Dylan Murphy, "Money Laundering and the Drug Trade: The Role of the Banks," *Global Research*, 7 May 2013.
9 Jason Leopold et al., "The FINCEN Files," Buzzfeed News, 20 September 2020; BBC News, "FinCEN Files: HSBC Moved Ponzi Scheme Millions Despite Warning," 20 September 2020a; BBC News, "The FinCEN Files: Your Guide to Eight Years of Finance Leaks," 20 September 2020b; Sasha Chavkin and Patricia Marcano, "How Banks Helped Venezuela's 'Boligarchs' Extract Billions," Organized Crime and Corruption Reporting Project, 20 September 2020; International Consortium of Investigative Journalists, "Global Banks Defy US Crackdowns by Serving Oligarchs, Criminals, and Terrorists," Organized Crime and Corruption Reporting Project, 21 September 2020.
10 Yueqi Yang, Jenny Surane, and Yalman Onaran, "Banks Moved US$2 Trillion amid Laundering Orders, ICIJ Says," *Bloomberg News*, 20 September 2020.
11 International Consortium of Investigative Journalists, "Global Banks Defy US Crackdowns by Serving Oligarchs, Criminals, and Terrorists."
12 Anthony Cormier, "HSBC's Secret Files: The Inside Tale of What Happened after It Apologized for Being Dirt," Buzzfeed News, 21 September 2020.

13 Spencer Woodman, "HSBC Moved Vast Sums of Dirty Money after Paying Record Laundering Fine," *Organized Crime and Corruption Reporting Project*, 21 September 2020.
14 US Securities and Exchange Commission, "SEC Halts Pyramid Scheme Targeting Asian and Latino Communities," US Securities and Exchange Commission Press Release, 28 March 2014.
15 Ivana Kottasova, "The Russian Money Laundering Sandal Exposed: Global Banks Handled Laundered Russian Cash Worth Hundreds of Millions," *Organized Crime and Corruption Reporting Project*, 24 March 2017; Max de Haldevang, "The Top 50 Global Banks Allegedly Involved in a $21 Billion Russian Money-Laundering Scheme," Quartz.com, 21 March 2017; Alun John, "Hong Kong's Currency Issuing Banks Processed Money Laundered by Russian Criminals: Organized Crime and Corruption Reporting Project," *South China Morning Post*, 21 March 2017.
16 Jake Bernstein, *Secrecy World* (New York: Henry Holt and Co., 2017); Tom Burghardt, "HSBC Caught in New Drug Money Laundering Scandal," *Global Research*, 2 November 2015.
17 Bernstein, *Secrecy World*; John Litchfield, "The Assistant Mayor, the Swiss Bank Accounts and the €350,000 of Moroccan Drugs Money," *The Independent*, 9 August 2014.
18 Bernstein, *Secrecy World*, 203; Joshua Franklin and Stephanie Nebehay, "HSBC to Pay $43 Million Geneva Money Laundering Settlement," Reuters, 4 June 2015.
19 Bernstein, *Secrecy World*, 50.
20 Bernstein, *Secrecy World*, 48.
21 Bernstein, *Secrecy World*, 50.
22 Bernstein, *Secrecy World*; David Leigh et al., "HSBC Files Show How Swiss Bank Helped Clients Dodge Taxes and Hide Millions," *The Guardian*, 8 February 2015.
23 Bernstein, *Secrecy World*, 137.
24 Associated Press, "What You Need to Know about the HSBC Scandal: Leaked Documents Show Extent to Which HSBC's Swiss Branch Helped Wealthy Dodge Taxes," MacLeans.ca, 9 February 2015.
25 Burghardt, "HSBC Caught in New Drug Money Laundering Scandal"; Julia Werdigier, "Britain Examines 4,000 HSBC Accounts in a Tax Haven," *New York Times*, 9 November 2012.
26 Burghardt, "HSBC Caught in New Drug Money Laundering Scandal."
27 *Sky News*, "HSBC Faces Fresh Money Laundering Probe," 19 March 2013; RT.com, "Argentina Accuses HSBC of $80mn Money Laundering," 19 March 2013.
28 John Letzing, "Swiss Banks Offer Carrot and Stick in Addressing Hidden Accounts," *Wall Street Journal*, 18 July 2014.
29 US Department of Justice, "Credit Suisse Pleads Guilty to Conspiracy to Aid and Assist US Taxpayers in Filing False Returns," US Department of Justice Press Release, 19 May 2014c.

30 US Department of Justice, "HSBC Holdings PLC. and HSBC Bank USA N.A. Admit to Anti-Money Laundering and Sanctions Violations, Forfeit $1.256 Billion in Deferred Prosecution Agreement."
31 United States Senate, Permanent Subcommittee on Investigations, US Vulnerabilities to Money Laundering, Drugs, and Terrorist Financing: HSBC Case History, 6, 170–6.
32 US Department of Justice, "HSBC Holdings PLC. and HSBC Bank USA N.A. Admit to Anti-Money Laundering and Sanctions Violations, Forfeit $1.256 Billion in Deferred Prosecution Agreement."
33 US Department of Justice, "HSBC Holdings PLC. and HSBC Bank USA N.A. Admit to Anti-Money Laundering and Sanctions Violations, Forfeit $1.256 Billion in Deferred Prosecution Agreement."
34 Glenn Simpson, "ABN Amro to Pay $80 Million Fine Over Iran, Libya," *Wall Street Journal*, 20 December 2005.
35 US Department of Justice, "Barclays Bank PLC Agrees to Forfeit $298 Million in Connection with Violations of the International Emergency Economic Powers Act and the Trading with the Enemy Act," US Department of Justice Press Release, 18 August 2010.
36 Aaron Lucchetti and Jay Solomon, "Credit Suisse to Pay US $536 Million in Iran Probe," *Wall Street Journal*, 16 December 2009; Claudio Gatti and John Eligon, "Iranian Dealings Lead to a Fine for Credit Suisse," *New York Times*, 15 December 2009.
37 Liz Moyer, "Deutsche Bank to Pay 258-Million and Fire 6 in Settlement," *New York Times*, 4 November 2015.
38 US Department of the Treasury and Comptroller of the Currency, Consent Order AA-EC-13-04 in the Matter of JPMorgan Chase Bank, N.A. Columbus, OH; JPMorgan Bank and Trust Company, N.A., San Francisco, CA; Chase Bank USA, N.A., Newark, DE, 1 April 2013.
39 Caldwell, 2015.
40 Matthew Goldstein, "R.B.S. to Pay $100 Million to Settle Inquiries into Violations of Sanctions," *New York Times*, 13 December 2013.
41 US Department of Justice, "BNP Paribas Agrees to Plead Guilty and to Pay $8.9 Billion for Illegally Processing Financial Transactions for Countries Subject to US Economic Sanctions," US Department of Justice Press Release, 30 June 2014b.
42 US Department of Justice, "BNP Paribas Agrees to Plead Guilty and to Pay $8.9 Billion for Illegally Processing Financial Transactions for Countries Subject to US Economic Sanctions."
43 Heidi Moore and Jill Treanor, "BNP Paribas Pleads Guilty to Criminal Charges in Sanctions Case," *The Guardian*, 30 June 2021.
44 New York State Department of Financial Services, *In the Matter of Standard Chartered Bank, New York Branch, New York, New York* (New York: New York State Department of Financial Services, 2012).

45 United States Senate, Permanent Subcommittee on Investigations, US Vulnerabilities to Money Laundering, Drugs, and Terrorist Financing: HSBC Case History, 6–7.
46 United States Senate, Permanent Subcommittee on Investigations, US Vulnerabilities to Money Laundering, Drugs, and Terrorist Financing: HSBC Case History, 239.
47 Jason Leopold et al., "The FinCEN Files."
48 US Department of Justice, "HSBC Holdings Plc Agrees to Pay More than $100 Million to Resolve Fraud Charges," US Department of Justice Press Release, 18 January 2018b.
49 Michael Corkery and Ben Protess, "Rigging of Foreign Exchange Market Makes Felons of Top Banks," *New York Times*, 20 May 2015; Karen Freifeld, David Henry, and Steve Slater, "Global Banks Admit Guilt in Forex Probe, Fined Nearly $6 Billion," Reuters, 20 May 2015.
50 United States District Court District of Connecticut, Plea Agreement, United States of America V. Barclays Plc, Defendant, Violation: 15 USC. § 1 , Filed 20 May 2015.
51 US Department of Justice, "Five Major Banks Agree to Parent-Level Guilty Pleas," US Department of Justice Press Release, 20 May 2015.
52 Amy Tsang, "Europe Fines 5 Banks $1.2 Billion for Their Roles in Foreign Exchange Cartels," *New York Times*, 16 May 2019.
53 Carrick Mollenkamp, "Bankers Cast Doubt on Key Rate amid Crisis," *Wall Street Journal*, 16 April 2008.
54 Carrick Mollenkamp, "Exclusive: US Conducting Criminal Libor Probe," Reuters, 28 February 2014.
55 *The Economist*, "The Rotten Heart of Finance," 7 July 2012.
56 Halah Touryalai, "Big Banks Fined $2.3B Over Illegal Libor Cartels, More Fines on the Way," *Forbes*, 4 December 2013.
57 United Kingdom Financial Services Authority, *The Turner Review: A Regulatory Response to the Global Banking Crisis* (London: Financial Services Authority, 2009); National Commission on the Causes of the Financial and Economic Crisis in the United States, The Financial Crisis Inquiry Report. Final Report of the National Commission on the Causes of the Financial and Economic Crisis in the United States (Washington, DC: US Government Printing Office, 2011); Joseph E. Stiglitz, *Freefall: America, Free Markets, and the Sinking of the World Economy* (New York: W.W. Norton & Co., 2010); John Cassidy, *How Markets Fail: The Logic of Economic Calamities* (New York: Picador, 2010); Susan Will, Stephen Handelman, and David Brotherton, eds.), *How They Got Away with It: White Collar Criminals and the Financial Meltdown* (New York: Columbia University Press, 2013).
58 National Commission on the Causes of the Financial and Economic Crisis in the United States, *The Financial Crisis Inquiry Report*, xvi.
59 National Commission on the Causes of the Financial and Economic Crisis in the United States, The Financial Crisis Inquiry Report, xvii.

60 National Commission on the Causes of the Financial and Economic Crisis in the United States, The Financial Crisis Inquiry Report, xvii.
61 National Commission on the Causes of the Financial and Economic Crisis in the United States, 2011, xviii–xix.
62 National Commission on the Causes of the Financial and Economic Crisis in the United States 2011, xix.
63 Gilbert Geis, *White-Collar and Corporate Crime: A Documentary and Reference Guide* (Santa Barbara, CA: Greenwood Press, 2011), 289.
64 Jessica Silver-Greenberg, "Mortgage Crisis Presents a New Reckoning to Banks," *New York Times*, 9 December 2012.
65 US Securities and Exchange Commission, "SEC Enforcement Actions Addressing Misconduct That Led to or Arose from the Financial Crisis," 7 October 2016.
66 US Department of Justice, "Barclays Agrees to Pay $2 Billion in Civil Penalties to Resolve Claims for Fraud in the Sale of Residential Mortgage-Backed Securities," US Department of Justice Press Release, 29 March 2018a.
67 Jana Kasperkevic, "Goldman Sachs to Pay $5bn for Its Role in the 2008 Financial Crisis," *The Guardian*, 11 April 2016.
68 US Department of Justice, "Credit Suisse Agrees to Pay $5.28 Billion in Connection with Its Sale of Residential Mortgage-Backed Securities," US Department of Justice Press Release, 18 January 2017a.
69 Danielle Douglas-Gabriel, "Citigroup to Pay $7 Billion to Resolve Mortgage Securities Investigation," *Washington Post*, 14 July 2014.
70 US Department of Justice, "Deutsche Bank Agrees to Pay $7.2 Billion for Misleading Investors in Its Sale of Residential Mortgage-Backed Securities," US Department of Justice Press Release, 17 January 2017b.
71 *Wall Street Journal*, "Biggest Bank Settlements," n.d.
72 US Department of Justice, "Bank of America to Pay $16.65 Billion in Historic Justice Department Settlement for Financial Fraud Leading Up to and during the Financial Crisis," US Department of Justice Press Release, 21 August 2014a.
73 This does not include a whole other area of fraud perpetrated in the financial services industry: over-exaggerating the return on an investment of a financial product.
74 Marcy Gordon, "Bank of America Paying $772M in Settlement with US Regulators Over Selling Credit Card Extras," Associated Press, 9 April 2014.
75 Ken Sweet and Stefanie Dazio, "Wells Fargo to Pay $3B to Resolve Probes into Fake Accounts," Associated Press, 21 February 2020; Michael Corkery, "Wells Fargo Fined $185 Million for Fraudulently Opening Accounts," *New York Times*, 8 September 2016; Office of the Attorney General of the Commonwealth of Pennsylvania, "Attorney General Shapiro Announces $575 Million 50-State Settlement with Wells Fargo Bank for Opening Unauthorized Accounts and Charging Consumers for Unnecessary Auto Insurance, Mortgage Fees," 28 December 2018; Matt Levine, "Wells Fargo Opened a Couple Million Fake Accounts," Bloomberg News, 9

September 2016; Jennifer Taub, *Big Dirty Money: The Shocking Injustice and Unseen Cost of White Collar Crime* (New York: Viking, 2020), ix.
76 David Enrich, *Dark Towers: Deutsche Bank, Donald Trump, and an Epic Trail of Destruction* (London: Custom House, 2020); Ed Caesar, "The FinCEN Files Shed New Light on a Scandalous Episode at Deutsche Bank," *New Yorker*, 23 September 2020; Buzzfeed News, "A Small-Scale Con Exposes Deutsche Bank's Lack of Oversight," *Organized Crime and Corruption Reporting Project*, 23 September 2020; Deutsche Welle, "FinCEN Files: Deutsche Bank Tops List of Suspicious Transactions," Dw.com, 20 September 2020; Liz Moyer, "Deutsche Bank to Pay 258-Million and Fire 6 in Settlement."
77 Ben Walsh, "JPMorgan Chase Hit with Multi-Million Dollar Fine for Shady Investment Advice," Huffington Post, 18 December 2015.
78 International Consortium of Investigative Journalists, "Global Banks Defy US Crackdowns by Serving Oligarchs, Criminals, and Terrorists."
79 US Department of the Treasury and Comptroller of the Currency, Consent Order AA-EC-13-04 in the Matter of JPMorgan Chase Bank, N.A. Columbus, OH; JPMorgan Bank and Trust Company, N.A., San Francisco, CA; Chase Bank USA, N.A., Newark, DE.
80 Commodity Futures Trading Commission, "CFTC Orders JPMorgan to Pay Record $920 Million for Spoofing and Manipulation," CFMT Press Release, 29 September 2020.
81 Peter Kuitenbrouwer, "Tom Hayes: First Banker to Walk the Libor Plank," *Financial Post*, 27 May 2015.
82 William Black, The Best Way to Rob a Bank Is to Own One: How Corporate Executives and Politicians Looted the S&L Industry (Austin: University of Texas Press, 2013).
83 Friedrichs, 2013, 11.
84 Leslie Caldwell, "Assistant Attorney General Caldwell Remarks at the ACAMS Anti-Money Laundering & Financial Crime Conference, Hollywood, FL," US Department of Justice, 16 March 2015.
85 Krugman, Paul. "Looters in Loafers," *New York Times*, 19 April 2010.
86 Stephens, 2002, 2.
87 Tavakoli, Janet. "Madoff Deserves Lots of Company," 13 December 2008, www.tavakolistructuredfinance.com.
88 Susan Will, "America's Ponzi Culture," in *How They Got Away with It: White Collar Criminals and the Financial Meltdown*, eds. Susan Will, Stephen Handelman, and David Brotherton (New York: Columbia University Press (Kindle Edition), 2013), 45–67, 48.
89 David, Friedrichs, "Wall Street: Crime Never Sleeps," in *How They Got Away with It: White Collar Criminals and the Financial Meltdown*, edited by Susan Will, Stephen Handelman, and David Brotherton (New York: Columbia University Press, 2012), 15.

90 Black, The Best Way to Rob a Bank Is to Own One: How Corporate Executives and Politicians Looted the S&L Industry, 171.
91 Jamieson, "Report: HSBC Allowed Money Laundering That Likely Funded Terror, Drugs."
92 Caldwell, "Assistant Attorney General Caldwell Remarks at the ACAMS Anti-Money Laundering & Financial Crime Conference, Hollywood, FL."
93 Ross, "HSBC's Money Laundering Scandal."
94 National Commission on the Causes of the Financial and Economic Crisis, *The Financial Crisis Inquiry Report*, xxiii.
95 Leaf, Clifton. "Enough Is Enough," *Fortune* 18 March 2020, 67.
96 Tom Burghardt, "HSBC Caught in New Drug Money Laundering Scandal," Global Research, 2 November 2012, https://www.globalresearch.ca/hsbc-caught-in-new-drug-money-laundering-scandal/5310397.
97 Stephens, Beth. "The Amorality of Profit: Transnational Corporations and Human Rights," *Berkeley Journal of International Law*, 1 (2002): 2.

3 Locating the Centre: State, Capital, and the Political Economy of Money Laundering in Canada

SANAA AHMED

Introduction

In the last ten years, Canada has emerged in the public eye as one of the premier onshore destinations for laundered monies from across the world.[1] In 2015, a government-initiated enquiry into corruption within the construction industry in Quebec showed the intimate linkages between Mafia-type criminal organizations and domestic politicians, big business, and service industry professionals (lawyers, accountants, etc.).[2] Between 2016 and 2017, the Panama and Paradise papers revelations blew the lid off a vibrant, Canadian-made money laundering operation rather poetically referred to as "snow-washing."[3] By the end of 2017, casinos in British Columbia (BC) were running laundering operations sophisticated enough to merit their own name – "the Vancouver model" – while the ongoing fentanyl crisis was also producing a steady stream of illicit monies. In the background, there were also reports of $10 billion having been laundered in Alberta in 2015, reports of how laundered monies had fuelled the meteoric rise of real estate markets in Toronto and Vancouver, and a scandal about a Canadian bank being involved in money laundering.[4]

While each revelation prompted a wave of public opprobrium and calls for greater regulatory oversight, the linkages between them were never mounted into a more meaningful discussion of money laundering in Canada. Collectively, the developments spoke volumes about the "who, why, and how" of laundering. Critically, they also showed just how deeply embedded money laundering practices were in Canada and how significant their scale. However, the attendant policing considerations and implications were either ignored or unrecognized. Why, for example, was the sizeable financial crime policing apparatus in Canada unable to detect, apprehend, or prosecute the launderers? Was the apparatus responsible for these failures, either because of its systemic design flaws or because of its operational inefficiencies? If so, who was to be held accountable and how? Or was continued laundering evidence of a flawed public policy? If so, how was this to be remedied? In the absence of clear answers to any of these questions, the purported laxity of regulation of casinos, the housing and drugs markets became the "face" of laundering in public discourse while policing and other issues receded into the background.

As significant was the widespread neglect of the *politics* of laundering. The nexus between politicians and big business, for example, demonstrated the vulnerability of the polity and its policies to the influence of launderers. However, there was little effort invested in even identifying the extent and the nature of this influence, let alone unpacking the nuances. For example, it remained unknown whether corruption in the Montreal construction industry was state capture (that is, the shaping or the formation of the basic rules of the game via illicit and/or non-transparent private payments to public officials), regulatory capture (that is, the influence that non-state actors – including private individuals, corporations, and business sectors – have on the basic rules *without* making private payments),[5] or just administrative corruption (that is, private payments made to public officials to distort the implementation of official rules and policies)?[6]

The piecemeal analysis of the phenomena generated a slew of seemingly ambitious but essentially unquantifiable policy responses: "rooting out" corruption, increasing regulatory "oversight" at the casinos, "tackling" the opioids crisis, and making housing "affordable" for "ordinary Canadians." The accompanying regulatory initiatives were just as whimsically conceived and often entirely inadequate to their task. For example, there was little explication of how corruption in the Quebec construction industry would be "rooted out" or who would do this when most of the stakeholders and actors (including regulators and politicians) were in on the game. Similarly, when the extent of snow-washing through shell companies was unearthed, finance minister Bill Morneau initially refused to institute a public register containing ownership details of corporations and subsequently instituted one at only the federal level.[7] Given that most corporations are incorporated provincially,[8] the exercise was doomed to failure. In another instance, the BC government commissioned a series of reports into laundering in the province[9] and in 2019 came up with legislation mandating transparency in land ownership[10] and, subsequently, corporate ownership.[11] However, the laws as they stand are unlikely to have the kind of impact on either housing prices or corporate transparency that champions of transparency would have hoped for.[12] Meanwhile, it is significant that Manulife, the laundering bank, did not lose its licence.

The above policy responses and regulatory initiatives corroborate what has long been contended by critics of Canada's money laundering policies: there is little political or corporate will to combat laundering and investigate white-collar crime, particularly once the story disappears from news cycles.[13] This lack of will manifests itself more in action (or inaction)[14] than in words, more in on-the-ground institutional arrangements than in political statements. This chapter unpacks the seeming lack of will in combatting money laundering and argues, instead, that every decision to focus (or not) on a particular set of offences or crimes, to fund (or defund) certain departments and units, is animated by a passionate underlying logic. The flailing governmental/corporate desire to "combat" money laundering is not born of lethargy or apathy: the significant political and economic benefits of laundering necessarily *obviate* every desire to extinguish the phenomenon. More simply: the torpor of Canadian public policy is among the requisite features of vibrant onshore destinations and thus is more likely to be systemic than serendipitous. The laundering industry does not flourish because regulation is *weak*; regulation is weak *because* the industry is strong.

The chapter comprises two parts. The first describes the reasons for the strength of the laundering industry by dilating on what I call the political economy approach to money laundering. This approach necessitates the situation of the *business* of money laundering *within the larger project of the Canadian political economy*. Instead of perceiving the phenomenon of laundering as a law enforcement failure, the political economy approach treats Canadian money laundering "industry" and "businesses" or enablers as economic actors and demonstrates their significance for the economy. While "big crime" focuses on the sordid, *criminal* nature of business and political actions, the political economy approach excavates the mundane and routine aspects of laundering: how "dirty" money creates regular, non-laundering jobs; is taxable; shores up real estate; and finances consumption.

The second part interrogates the role of the state by deploying Michael Mann's insight that "the state" is simultaneously *a place* and *an actor*. As a place, the state is susceptible to prominent power actors who benefit from money laundering – that is, key economic actors – and can leverage their power to exert influence over the policy and enforcement actions of the state. As an autonomous actor, however, the state also operates to protect and propagate its own institutional interests, *which are often entwined with those of big money*. As such, states organize and facilitate certain economic crimes (such as laundering) *in line with their own interests and contrary to the stated objectives of big policing*. More simply: big policing fails to impede or prevent laundering because doing so would be inimical to the interests of both the state as well as the interests of powerful economic actors.

The Political Economy Approach to Money Laundering

In the one hundred years since the term "money laundering" was coined, its praxis *and* theory have undergone several transformations of increasing sophistication. The term "money laundering" originally described the practice of sluicing dirty money through storefront operations (such as laundromats) and cash-intensive businesses (such as car washes).[15] The operation protected the money generated through criminal activities against seizure by law enforcement authorities (LEAs) by creating the impression the money was legitimately earned. However, given how white-collar crime – especially corporate wrongdoing – has evolved in the last three decades, most scholars now refute this crime-laundering causality and take exception to such definitions of laundering. Instead, they insist the offence be expanded to include misdemeanours that embody the spirit of the practice: tax abuse (including tax evasion and avoidance),[16] trade-related malpractices (including transfer pricing and base erosion profit shifting, for example),[17] white-collar crime,[18] capital flight, and the proceeds of informal economies. Ruggiero, for example, contends that it was well known by the 1990s that drug money is a very small component of dirty money and these other categories make up for the rest.[19]

This analysis is borne out by the data regarding the composition of global illicit financial flows (IFFs),[20] currently estimated at between $1.6 trillion and $2 trillion a year.[21] As the analysis shows, *crime accounts for less than one-third of the total volume of the IFFs pie.*[22] That is, trafficking in drugs, sex, humans, and arms corruption and so on comprise between 16 and 33 per cent of IFFs, while the bulk – estimated between a staggering 67 and 84 per cent of total IFFs – comprises trade-related *malpractices* conducted by corporations (for example, over-and under-invoicing, or tax avoidance and evasion).[23] Significantly, since "malpractices" by definition are not criminal acts, the flows they generate are considered beyond the charge of laundering in Canada even though their volume is larger by far.

Even so, the *regulation* of laundering remains inexplicably mired in contexts of crime and criminality. Global and domestic regulators continue to favour the criminalization approach to laundering and trace its origin to profit-generating "criminal acts." They describe the phenomenon as the "processing of these criminal proceeds to disguise their illegal origin ... [so that] the criminal [may] enjoy these profits without jeopardising their source."[24] This fundamental mischaracterization of the nature of the problem inevitably generates flawed policy responses in that it focuses law enforcement attention on the small fry.

The most important omission in such accounts of money laundering is an inability to situate the money laundering industry within the broader political economy.[25] Industries do not operate in hermetically sealed vacuums and are invariably situated within a complex of relationships and horizontal and vertical linkages[26] of varying density and complexity, depending on the scale and scope of the particular industry. The Panama Papers disclosures in 2016 brought Canada's snow-washing industry into the public eye, while the reputation of the country as an onshore destination is of far older provenance, and consequently its roots in the political economy run deep. A political economy approach to money laundering would entail seeing the occurrence of money laundering within Canada as less of a law enforcement failure and more as a systemic response to the peculiarities of the Canadian political economy.

While the Canadian economy is among the ten largest economies of the world,[27] the lingering effects of the 2007–9 global recession have been magnified by certain structural characteristics of the economy. Two of these are particularly relevant for the purposes of this analysis. First and foremost is the question of how the Canadian economy is financed. A look at the numbers through the conventional Keynesian savings-equals-investment lens is particularly instructive. Pre-pandemic figures show revenue as comprising just 17 per cent of GDP.[28] Meanwhile, a 2018 report by the Canada Revenue Agency (CRA) showed that fentanyl peddlers in Vancouver were not the only ones using shell companies and that wealthy Canadians had ferreted away between $76 billion and $241 billion to various onshore and offshore havens.[29] According to the CRA, it was losing some $3 billion in tax annually as a result. The upshot is the economy is not fuelled by "excess" dollars swilling around in the system because Canada does not make enough to support itself.

Predictably, the shortfall is met through government borrowing or by incurring public debt.[30] Canada's gross debt in the third quarter of 2019[31] had ballooned to slightly over 136 per cent of its GDP,[32] which works out to a debt per capita of $71,487.[33] Public debt-to-GDP ratios over 77 per cent are generally believed to have a deleterious impact on long-term economic growth[34] (discussed below) because of the way debt churns through the economy. Obviously, there is the cost of debt servicing, which is almost 7 per cent of federal government revenue funnelled into interest expenses.[35] This takes away from money available for other expense heads. But government borrowing also crowds out private capital investment, both by reducing the pool of monies available to private investors through financial intermediaries as well as by reducing the appetite of lenders for investments in the private sector.[36] (This is because sovereign debt is generally seen as a less risky investment as compared to private investment.) Further, enhanced borrowing by an already heavily indebted government also pushes up interest rates: for example, sovereign bonds issued by a borrowing-prone, indebted government are seen as riskier investments and are priced higher than they would be ordinarily. Since all other debt (including commercial loans, corporate bonds, and residential mortgages) are priced above sovereign bond rates, the higher government bond prices also increase the cost of borrowing money across the board. As financial institutions, businesses, and corporations pay higher rates for raising money, they pass on these costs to their consumers in the form of higher mortgage rates and more expensive goods and services.

Even if one buys into the cheap-debt-is-good argument favoured by some economists and ignores or discounts the impact of government borrowing on other sectors of the economy, rising levels of public debt are rarely, if ever, a worthwhile aim on their own. The more germane issue is always what the debt is being incurred for: is the debt financing projects that will deliver *economic growth*?

This question becomes even more important given the other structural peculiarity of the Canadian economy: its continuing dependence on real estate, rentals, and leasing, as well as construction, for economic growth. The top three contributors to the Canada's economy in terms of the percentage of GDP remain real estate, rentals, and leasing (13 per cent of GDP); manufacturing (10 per cent); and construction (7 per cent). Taken altogether, the real estate and construction sector account for 20 per cent of Canadian GDP.[37] This is significant because, as a general rule, the more advanced economies have successively deindustrialized and moved away from the production of lower-value goods towards the provision of higher-value services as a driver of growth.[38] However, even this figure is a hugely conservative estimate since it does not pick up the elements related to real estate and construction within other sectors of the economy, such as manufacturing;[39] wholesale;[40] retail;[41] financial and insurance services;[42] and professional, scientific, and technical services.[43] As the details in the footnotes show, real estate and construction drive much of the activity within an economy in terms of both output and job creation.

This assertion is borne out by the growth figures for Canada. In 2019, the GDP grew by 2 per cent, a drop from 3.2 per cent in 2017.[44] While Statistics Canada attributed the modest growth to increased exports from most regions and a small rise in household spending, it also acknowledged that growth was pushed downwards by a decline in business investment in non-residential construction, due to the completion of major construction projects in several provinces and territories as well as the downward pressure on housing activity following the implementation of heightened mortgage rules and higher interest rates. Significantly, a breakdown of provincial growth shows that the most growth came from real estate activity as well as construction-related activities.[45]

The interaction of these two characteristics – the paucity of domestic savings and the overreliance on real estate and construction – has significant implications for the Canadian economy. With its savings, investment, debt, and economic growth data being what they are, and with growth inextricably tied to certain sectors of the economy, can Canada afford to be picky about the money it takes? More critically, is it so picky? If history is any indication, the answer is no and is reflected by two examples.

First, business immigration has been a part of Canada's immigration system since the 1952 *Immigration Act*.[46] Since the 1990s particularly, the federal government and Quebec have concurrently been running immigration programs specifically designed to draw foreign capital into Canada. The program logic was to have foreign investors make up for the lack of Canadian capital by financing industries or businesses that would generate income and provide employment.[47] While there appears to be little or no data about the volume of monies Canada has attracted under its business investor program, the 2016 census data shows the number of economic migrants to Canada between 1980 and 2016 was 2,994,135,[48] of which 284,840 (or 9.5 per cent) were applicants under business programs, while 331,800 (or 11 per cent) had applied under provincial and territorial nominee programs.[49] While bringing funds from their home countries to Canada was a precondition for business immigration, even the economic migrants who were workers (2,357,225,[50] or 78.7 per cent) or provincial or territorial nominees must have brought funds for their resettlement costs. Significantly, the economic migration program does not seem to have had any stipulations regarding the source or origin of funds in the home country.[51] This clearly indicates that the cleanliness of the money was not a priority.

The casual assumption that the situation must have changed since then should be treated with extreme scepticism; most indicators – especially findings from the Panama and Paradise papers – suggest Canadian public policy continues on the same path. The Tax Justice Network (TJN) data for 2020 shows that Canada has caused other jurisdictions tax losses worth $8 billion by accepting inbound flows.[52] (It is unclear from the TJN data whether this figure also includes money lost through capital flight from other economies to Canada.) Similarly, the efforts of the federal government to stimulate the moribund pandemic economy include ambitious immigration targets. It will be interesting to see if the government imposes a "cleanliness" requirement on funds being brought in by the new immigrants.

The second example is the financing of public infrastructure projects. Typically, large infrastructure projects create jobs and output while paving the way for sustained future economic growth in line with government priorities.[53] The construction of highways, for example, facilitates interprovincial trade and transport, streamlines supply between farms and cities, allows for the outward expansion of densely populated cities and allows commuters to work within the city while living in the suburbs. This is, of course, in addition to the creation of jobs and goods needed to physically construct highways. Additionally, through toll taxes and other levies, highways generally pay for themselves. Infrastructure projects thus have a significant impact on economic growth. In 2018, more than 585,000 jobs were associated with the production of infrastructure assets – 17,000 more jobs than in 2017. Most provinces and territories had more jobs from infrastructure investment in 2018 than in 2017. Nationally, 54 per cent of the total jobs were the result of direct investment, while 46 per cent were indirectly created from spin-offs in other industries.[54] Typically, since the economic gains associated with large infrastructure projects also deliver significant political gains for incumbent governments, they are seen as an attractive policy tool.

However, the great recession of 2007–9 imposed fiscal constraints on both provincial and federal governments, which turned to public–private partnerships (or P3s) for infrastructure projects, where the private sector supplemented or even replaced public financing.[55] Between 2007 and 2015, some 220 P3s projects worth an estimated $70 billion were completed across Canada.[56] In 2017, the federal government set up the Canada Infrastructure Bank, which was to provide "federal support to attract private sector and institutional investment to new revenue-generating infrastructure projects … in the public interest. By leveraging the capital and expertise of the private sector, the Bank [was to] help public dollars go further and keep … grant dollars for those projects … more appropriate for traditional grant funding mechanisms."[57] At present, Canada is endorsing an ambitious $180 billion infrastructure plan it hopes to implement in line with its Agenda 2030 plans.[58]

Two points merit greater consideration here. First, the state clearly lacks the resources to undertake even productive, employment-generating activities under its own steam. Second, this policy shift came despite the well-documented incidences of and amplified risk of corruption in public infrastructure projects.[59] As Beare contends, corruption is both endemic and "normal" in the construction industry. Instances of corruption are neither one-off events nor episodic; they are just the way the industry operates. She talks about how the *quid pro quo* standard of corruption (that is, the prosecution must show that an amount was provided in exchange for a governmental policy or action) borrowed from US courts is also applied in corruption enquiries in Canada. However, she contends, since one of the hallmarks of corruption in the industry is "rigged bidding," the *quid pro quo* requirement fails to impede corrupt practices.[60] But clearly, the taint of corruption is not significant enough to preclude such partnerships.

The foregoing can be distilled into a few key takeaways. First, ordinary, middle-class Canadians do not save enough to finance investment and increased public borrowing is hurting the longer-term economic interests of Canada. As such, the influx of laundered money (whether through beneficial corporate or land ownership schemes, business immigration programs, or a studied governmental indifference to tax abuse and trade-related malpractices) represents a financial windfall for the economy. Second, Canada derives most of its economic growth from real estate and construction-related activities. As such, even if the bulk of laundered monies were finding their way to the real estate and construction markets across Canada, the economy would be very well served. This will be particularly true in the wake of the 2020 pandemic, as most private-sector investors will shy away from large infrastructure projects. The $2 trillion infrastructure plan of US President Joe Biden is a good example of how strategic investments in infrastructure can stimulate economic growth.[61] The proclivity of the Canadian state towards P3s indicates a similar approach, whereby corruption is deemed an acceptable – if not necessary – price to pay for economic growth.

Role of the State (Actor/Place)

Interrogating the role of the state in the phenomenon of money laundering is inordinately difficult. First, governmental crime gets far less public or scholarly attention than conventional forms of crime.[62] While transnational and other forms of non-conventional crime, such as organized crime, militancy, corporate crime, or even computer crime, are receiving increasing attention, governmental crime remains grossly under-researched.[63] Second, the study of state crime poses multiple definitional issues: what, for example, is "state crime"? Or, what is the difference between "state-organized," "state-initiated," and "state-facilitated" crimes? Third, the ontological issues are multifaceted and complex: who constitutes "the state" and how do various power actors within a polity influence the direction of the state? If only the state can define who a criminal is, how will that state ever be deemed a criminal itself? Fourth, there are also procedural or systemic issues: if the state is organizing crimes itself, how is the integrity of laws and regulations to be preserved or insulated from the influence of *this* state? Further, which agencies of the state are to be held responsible for impeding or preventing such crimes? While a detailed exposition about the first reason is beyond the scope of this chapter, the remaining ones are discussed below.

The primary difficulty with studying state crime is that there is no common understanding of what it entails. Traditionally, the term "state crime" was used to refer to practices including human rights violations, genocide, crimes against humanity, and war crimes.[64] Reaching for a more expansive definition, Kauzlarich, Mullins, and Matthews define state crime as that action or inaction by the state, its agencies, or representatives, which causes harm to individuals, groups, or property. Even so, such in/action must directly relate to an assigned or implied trust or duty and be committed in furtherance of the self-interest of the state itself or the interest of elite groups holding the state.[65] However, even this definition is not broad enough to cover the role of the state in laundering. Part of this has to do with optics: as seen above, while the state and elite groups do benefit immensely from laundering, this fact remains mostly unrecognized and unexamined by even critical scholars.[66] The other part has to do with the demonstration of "harm," which is a much bigger ask as there is little data and even fewer empirically grounded studies conclusively establishing the harm purportedly caused by laundering.[67]

Combined, the definitional issues, the optics, and the lack of evidence establishing harm have implications and consequences beyond the obvious. First, all justice- and accountability-focused efforts to address laundering as a state crime are precluded *if the state is not seen as an actor in the laundering project*. Second, since such justice- and accountability-oriented efforts are instruments originally meant to redress traditional state crimes such as genocide or war crimes, they usually have a "moral and ethical goal,"[68] which helps bolster their legitimacy and popularity. But where, due to the in/action of the state, laundering causes harm to individuals, groups, or property is not conclusively established, conjugating moral and ethical goals becomes extraordinarily difficult. For example, unless clear causality is established between laundering, business investor immigration programs, and housing prices in Vancouver, how is the state to be held responsible for encouraging the inflow of illicit financial flows? Third, even in redressing traditional state crime, justice and accountability instruments are punctured by realpolitik, which Rothe defines as "political decision making based on pragmatic state interests, rather than moral premises." This decision-making takes place in "a fluid world of shifting military, economic and political considerations," which can also be at odds with one another. As such, Rothe concludes, self-interest takes precedence over justice and accountability efforts, which are sacrificed if they conflict with the strategic, political, and economic interests of the state.[69] The natural corollary: if the strategic or economic interests of the state prevail over justice or accountability efforts even where heinous crimes such as genocide are concerned, what hope can there be for redressing state crimes such as the facilitation of laundering?

An associated difficulty is that of determining the *extent* of the state's responsibility based on an analysis of state in/action. Does, for example, a failure to effect meaningful reform of beneficial ownership laws qualify as "state inaction" facilitating laundering? Or is it "criminal" for the state to encourage foreign investment without questioning the source of funds? Here, while the definitions espoused by various criminologists are coloured by the examples they use, the crux remains the same: what states do and don't do *matters*. And, as discussed above, the state's motivations are pegged to its strategic, economic, and political needs.

Criminologist William Chambliss defines state-organized crime as a question of the "relationship between criminality, social structure and the political economy." State-organized crime, he contends, stems from the modern state's ongoing need for capital accumulation to survive and acquire power and wealth. The "duty" of the state, then, becomes to provide a climate and a set of international relations that facilitate this accumulation. State officials are thus judged on *their ability to create these conditions*.[70] As such, insists Chambliss, only those acts count as state-organized crimes which are, first, defined as specifically criminal under the law, and second, committed by state officials in pursuit of their jobs as representatives of the state.[71] Comparatively, Rothe and Friedrichs draw a distinction between "state-facilitated crimes," where the state "fails to take necessary action, thus aiding illegal actions on the part of corporations," and "state-initiated crimes," where the state "sets the stage for, or initiates, illegal corporate activity."[72] While Rothe and Friedrichs are specifically talking about corporate crime here, the argument holds *mutatis mutandis* for individuals and groups too.

While the definitions are useful in delineating the parameters of the debate, they also trigger a series of ontological questions: who constitutes "the state"? Who determines the direction of state policy? And who are the real beneficiaries of these policies? According to Mann's IEMP model, one must look to the *sources* of power that influence social control, such as ideological, economic, military, and political power (the IEMP model), rather than focusing on structures and institutions of power such as the state.[73] This perspective shows how, as a place, the state is open to penetration by different power networks as well as geopolitical concerns.[74] Yet in Mann's reading, as an actor, the state also manifests autonomy, an identity independent of its multiple networks of power. He posits that state autonomy may reside less in elite autonomy than in the autonomous logic of definite political institutions that rose during previous power struggles and were subsequently institutionalized and now constrain present struggles.

Similarly, Kauzlarich, Mullins, and Matthews point to the need to examine the construct of the state within its broader socio-historical context as well as the classes that influence state policy and how they evolve over time.[75] For example, a state's dependence on foreign monies to shore up flagging domestic savings or the influence of the transnational and domestic capitalist class on the state's investment policies says much about *who* the state is or, to be more precise, who is driving state policy. This is why Tombs invokes Gramsci and Poulantzas to contend that the distinction between "public" and "private" spaces is a juridical one sustained by the apparatuses of the state.[76] He sees the state as invariably "capitalist" and maintains that this state values profit above social values. Like others, Tombs challenges the "false assumption" that the state is oppositional and external to corporations[77] or that the state and the power elite are "ontologically distinct."[78] In a similar vein, Pistor also maintains that the role of regulatory agencies is to reproduce the social conditions necessary to sustain the capitalist social order.[79] However, Tombs takes this one step further and provocatively argues that states also create criminogenic markets.[80] Through long-term ideological work, discursive framing (for example, the practice of referring to regulatory protections as red tape), and changes in the day-to-day work of regulators, he says, key law enforcement and regulatory agencies effect the "institutionalization of decriminalization" through "regulatory surrender."[81]

While initially persuasive, Tombs's argument collapses in the absence of the "Other": his state achieves decriminalization by surrendering either to corporations or capitalism in general. More simply, at the behest of its capitalist friends and partners, the state agrees to decriminalize *an activity*, presumably so everyone can profit from it unfettered by law or regulation. But the more interesting question pertaining to laundering is: if only the state can define who is a criminal, who will deem the state a criminal and how will they do so?[82] Following from the above definition of state crime by Kauzlarich, Mullins, and Matthews, does the state have a duty to follow its own laws, or to protect its citizens from illicit financial flows? Is this an implied responsibility or obligation conferred by the broader social contract? While some criminologists believe the social contract confers an implied duty on the state to sanction elite and white-collar deviance and to adhere to the fundamental principles of human rights,[83] even these expectations exist *in rem*. There is a rich literature on how states sanction financial crime, how individuals and corporations are treated differently. However, there is very little available on *whether states practice what they preach and how they are to be held accountable for their transgressions*.

Chambliss's account of state responses to piracy and smuggling as examples of state-organized crime is fascinating because he locates the state within a political economy context. He contends that between the sixteenth and nineteenth centuries, virtually every European state as well as the United States were complicit in piracy. While in theory each state protected only its own pirates, in practice they all protected any pirate willing to share their gains. To resolve the inherent contradiction between the law and the economic interests of the state, he says, states evolved the practice of issuing letters of marque to "regulate" the illegal act by prescribing limitations on the acts that were permissible. While pirates rarely followed these limitations, the illegality was condoned as it fulfilled the state's objective of capital accumulation as a determinant of the nation's ability to industrialize, protect its borders and weaken the enemy.[84] As Chambliss presciently argues, sometimes the interests of the state are served by violating its own laws, especially when those laws contradict other interests of the state (even so, Chambliss does not venture into the justice/accountability terrain).[85] If the Canadian state, for example, sees illicit financial flows as essential to its economic interests, the question of frustrating or even impeding inflows becomes one of normative priorities: is the state to sacrifice economic development in order to uphold the social contract? If not, what would a potential rebalancing of priorities look like? And, most significantly, which option better serves the interests of the average Canadian and how is this to be determined?

This brings us to the fourth and final point: the procedural or systemic issues. If the state is organizing crimes *itself*, how is the integrity of state-sponsored laws and regulations to be preserved or insulated from the influence of *this* state? While the extent of money laundering in Canada would suggest otherwise, the activity is currently governed by fifteen different laws and regulatory instruments.[86] In 2019, the federal government *seemingly* cracked down on beneficial ownership by setting up a public registry at the federal level that was meant to have persons with more than 25 per cent beneficial interest disclose the same. But not only did the initiative ignore the fact that 90 per cent of corporations are registered provincially, not federally, it also ignored the fact that 25 per cent is too high a limit to catch anything worthwhile.[87] Similarly, why would the various organs and institutions of the state,[88] which derive their power, legitimacy, and authority from the state, frustrate the objectives of the same state? Further, where the state determines the funding, the agenda and the scope of state institutions and law enforcement agencies, how are said institutions and agencies expected to remain autonomous? In 2018, for example, the RCMP publicly confessed it had no expertise to conduct sophisticated financial or corporate investigations.[89] And early in 2020, the RCMP disbanded its Financial Crimes Unit in Ontario.[90] Given the overarching influence of the state on such agencies, which agencies are to be held *independently* responsible for impeding or preventing such crimes? And where, precisely, is this justice and accountability initiative meant to attach? For example, if the RCMP disbands a unit, is the RCMP at fault or the government that stopped prioritizing funding for the unit?

Conclusion

Perhaps the most potent argument in favour of the political economy approach is that it accommodates the varying and oftentimes conflicting responsibilities of the modern state to its citizens in a way the criminalization approach to money laundering cannot. A public policy on money laundering predicated on the criminalization approach can only have the state unsuccessfully trying to tamp down on money laundering but cannot satisfy the state's commitment to protect the livelihoods of those lawyers, bankers, accountants, casino workers, and others who are dependent on this business. Since the state is incapable of reconciling and articulating these disparate, conflicting sets of commitments, the actual and the stated public policy objectives and positions assumed by the Canadian state remain riven by a disjuncture.

NOTES

1 Marco Chown Oved, "Corporate Secrecy Makes Canada a Haven for White-Collar Crime, Says Report," *Toronto Star*, 7 December 2016, https://www.thestar.com/news/world/corporate-secrecy-makes-canada-a-haven-for-white-collar-crime-says-report/article_ff790d4b-700e-5a4f-a155-7d3594c820fb.html.

2 Government of Quebec, *Report of the Commission of Inquiry on the Awarding and Management of Public Contracts in the Construction Industry*, Commissioner Justice France Charbonneau, four vols. (Quebec: Government of Quebec, 2015). The Charbonneau Commission was a public inquiry into corruption in the management of public construction contracts in Quebec. The commission was created in October 2011, in response to significant public pressure on the provincial Liberal government and was meant to: (1) investigate and describe acts of collusion and corruption in the provision and management of public contracts

in the construction industry (including private organizations, government enterprises, and municipalities) and to include any links with the financing of political parties; (2) examine the possibility of organized crime infiltration in the construction industry; and (3) suggest solutions and recommendations to identify, reduce, and prevent collusion and corruption in the award and management of public infrastructure projects. For critical reads on the report, see Margaret E. Beare, "Entitled Ease: Social Milieu of Corporate Criminals," *Critical Criminology: An International Journal*, special issue: *Crimes of the Powerful: The Canadian Context* 26, no. 4 (2018), 509–26, DOI:10.1007/s10612-018-9423-x; Margaret E. Beare, "Shadow Boxing against the Crimes of the Powerful," in *Revisiting Crimes of the Powerful*, eds. Steve Bittle, Laureen Snider, Steve Tombs, and David Whyte (New York: Routledge, 2018), 45–59; Denis Saint-Martin, "Systemic Corruption in an Advanced Welfare State: Lessons from the Québec Charbonneau Inquiry" (2015). Osgoode Legal Studies Research Paper Series 115, http://digitalcommons,osgoode.yorku.ca/olsrps/115.

3 The term follows from the original "laundering" phrase with a nod to both the pristine reputations of Canada and its financial regulators as well as the Canadian winter. See Robert Cribb and Marco Chown Oved, "Snow Washing: Canada Is the World's Newest Tax Haven," *Toronto Star*, part 1 of a four-part series, 25 January 2017.

4 The bank was eventually identified as Manulife but was only fined for laundering money.

5 An example of this would be the outsize influence of the finance industry on financial regulation. Since the industry wallahs are assumed to have greater knowledge than public officials in many specialized fields, the preferences of the industry end up coded into government regulation.

6 Joel S. Hellman, Geraint Jones, and Daniel Kaufmann, "Seize the State, Seize the Day: State Capture, Corruption and Influence in Transition," World Bank Policy Research Working Paper 2444 (2000). See p. 2 for a more detailed explication of the three terms. While some authors use the three terms interchangeably, for a nuanced read see, Upendra Baxi, "Market Fundamentalisms: Business Ethics at the Altar of Human Rights," *Human Rights Law Review* 5, no. 1 (2005): 16–17.

7 After the 2019 amendments to the *Canada Business Corporations Act*, companies must disclose true ownership to both shareholders and creditors. However, this information is (1) only provided about individuals who own more than 25 per cent of voting or all shares outstanding, and (2) is not available publicly. See Corporations Canada, "Individuals with Significant Control," https://ised-isde.canada.ca/site/corporations-canada/en/individuals-significant-control.

8 The ratio of federally registered companies to provincially registered ones is 1:9. Marco Chown Oved and Robert Cribb, "Ottawa Vows to Lift Corporate Secrecy in Bid to Stop Tax Evasion and Money Laundering," *Toronto Star*, 18 July 2017, https://www.thestar.com/news/canada/2017/07/18/corporate-secrecy-to-be-lifted-to-help-stop-tax-evasion-and-money-laundering.html.

9 Peter M. German, *Proceeds of Crime and Money Laundering* (Toronto: Thomson Reuters, current service); Peter M. German, *Dirty Money – Part 2* (Vancouver: British Columbia, 2017); Maureen Maloney, Tsur Somerville, and Brigitte Unger, *Combatting Money Laundering in British Columbia Real Estate* (Victoria, BC: Minister of Finance, 2019); Justice Austen F. Cullen, *Commission of Inquiry into Money Laundering in British Columbia : Interim Report* (Victoria, BC: Attorney General and Minister of Finance, 2020).

10 This is the 2019 *Land Ownership Transparency Act* (LOTA) of British Columbia. Meanwhile, in its 2019 budget, Quebec promised to begin consultations regarding the setting up of a public beneficial ownership registry and was followed by BC in early 2020. See Jen St. Denis, "US and Canada Closer to Lifting Veil on Corporate Ownership," *Toronto Star*, 28 June 2019, https://www.thestar.com/vancouver/u-s-and-canada-closer-to-lifting-veil-on-corporate-ownership/article_7a7eded3-cfc7-5daa-93e3-7d4ce1312e11.html.

11 In 2019, the BC Legislature amended the British Columbia Business Corporations Act and Business Corporations Regulation to mandate greater transparency in corporate ownership. The amendments took effect in October 2020. See BC Government, Order of the Lieutenant Governor in Council, Order 169, 6 April 2020, https://www.bclaws.gov.bc.ca/civix/document/id/oic/oic_cur/0169_2020.

12 Space constraints preclude a detailed discussion of the reasons here but the primary problems with the laws are that the additional information about ownership is, first, required only about individuals who own more than 25 per cent of the interest in a property or more than 25 per cent of the voting shares or all shares outstanding, and second, this information is not available publicly. Additionally, the law does not set out specifically what happens in cases where individuals control corporations through legal entities and/or other individuals.

13 Margaret E. Beare, "Entitled Ease: Social Milieu of Corporate Criminals," *Critical Criminology: An International Journal, Special issue: Crimes of the Powerful: The Canadian Context* 26, no. 4 (2018): 509–26, https:// DOI:10.1007/s10612-018-9423-x. Beare contends that street crimes and/or crimes involving visible signs of violence have always been accorded greater political priority than what she scathingly refers to as "*so-called* 'victim-less'" crimes, such as corruption or white-collar crime (emphasis added).

14 The "inaction" piece refers to the fact that governments act *even when they choose not to act*, because inaction is as valid a policy response as action. See generally Frank Pearce, *Crimes of the Powerful: Marxism, Crime and Deviance* (London: Pluto Press, 1976). Pearce develops the idea of an "imaginary social order" to explain why the behaviour of police, state, and corporation diverges from their stated priorities.

15 R.T. Naylor, *Wages of Crime: Black Markets, Illegal Finance and the Underworld Economy* (Montreal: McGill-Queen's University Press, 2004), 134–5. Although Naylor dates the origin of the phenomenon of money laundering to medieval

74   Sanaa Ahmed

Europe and to offshore havens to the early seventeenth century, the term "money laundering" first arose in the 1920s in the United States.
16 See generally Thomas Pogge and Krishen Mehta, eds., *Global Tax Fairness* (Oxford: Oxford University Press, 2016).
17 See generally Nikos Passas for lucid accounts of trade-based money laundering.
18 This would include political, corporate, and criminal corruption. For an neat overview of corruption in Canada generally, see Margaret E. Beare, "Canada: Internal Conspiracies – Corruption and Crime," in *Handbook of Organized Crime and Politics*, edited by Felia Allum and Stan Gilmore (Northampton, MA: Edward Elgar Publishing, 2019), 189–208.
19 Vincenzo Ruggiero, *Dirty Money: On Financial Delinquency* (Oxford: Oxford University Press, 2017), 202.
20 While there is no generally accepted definition of IFFs, the term broadly refers to money illegally earned, transferred, or used that crosses borders. This includes money from illegal acts (e.g., corruption, tax evasion); the proceeds of illegal acts (e.g., smuggling and trafficking in minerals, wildlife, drugs, and people); and funds used for illegal purposes (e.g., financing of organized crime). See the World Bank website, Illicit Financial Flows (IFFs), 7 July 2017, https://www.worldbank.org/en/topic/financialsector/brief/illicit-financial-flowffss-i. Critical scholars insist that commercial activities such as tax avoidance should be considered part of IFFs.
21 United Nations Office on Drugs and Crime, *Estimating Financial Flows Resulting from Drug Trafficking and Other Transnational Organized Crimes* (Vienna: United Nations Office on Drugs and Crime, 2011). https://www.unodc.org/documents/data-and-analysis/Studies/Illicit_financial_flows_2011_web.pdf.
22 United Nations Conference on Trade and Development (UNCTAD), *Urgent Global Action Needed to Tackle Tax Avoidance* (2014), http://unctad.org/en/pages/newsdetails.aspx?OriginalVersionID=838&Sitemap_x0020_Taxonomy=CSO; Global Financial Integrity, "Illicit Financial Flows from Developing Countries: 2004–2013," http://www.gfintegrity.org/wp-content/uploads/2015/12/IFF-Update_2015-Final-1.pdf.
23 Global Financial Integrity 2015; Global Financial Integrity, "Illicit Financial Flows: The Most Damaging Economic Condition Facing the Developing World," September 2015, 38–42, https://www.scribd.com/document/281848024/Illicit-Financial-Flows-The-Most-Damaging-Economic-Condition-Facing-the-Developing-World. The latter also features a lucid description of balance of payments leakages in illicit financial flows as well as a neat discussion of the limitations of using recorded balance of payments figures and trade data for estimating IFFs. The main limitations are that such data do not account for trade in drugs and other contraband, smuggling, hawalas, same-invoice faking, cash transactions, and lack of data on trade in services.
24 Financial Action Task Force, https://www.fatf-gafi.org/content/fatf-gafi/en/pages/frequently-asked-questions.html#tabs-36503a8663-item-6ff811783c-tab. The global

regulator, the Financial Action Task Force on money laundering and terrorism financing (FATF), sees laundering as stemming from, primarily, drugs and arms trafficking, smuggling, and sex work, although it also admits that embezzlement, insider trading, bribery, and "computer fraud schemes" can also generate large profits. While FATF has included terrorism financing, the financing of weapons of mass destruction and corruption within its ambit, the nexus with specific illegality remains intact. The advantages of doing so accrue to the regulators, since money laundering is that rare beast that is simultaneously a crime and evidence of the commission of other crimes. Most strategies to combat laundering are based on "follow the money" methods of crime control. See Naylor, *Wages of Crime*, 248–52, for a useful explication of Levi and Reuter's history of AML-CTF regulation in the United States.

25 "Political economy" is understood here as the interrelationships of individuals, governments, as well as public policy.

26 Horizontal linkages are relationships between firms at the same level in a value chain that cooperate and pool, for example, resources or expertise to achieve outcomes that would elude them individually. Vertical linkages refer to relationships between firms at successive stages in a supply-chain process. See Evan Tarver, "Horizontal Integration vs. Vertical Integration: What's the Difference?" *Investopedia*, 18 January 2021, https://www.investopedia.com/ask/answers/051315/what-difference-between-horizontal-integration-and-vertical-integration.asp.

27 International Monetary Fund, *World Economic Outlook: Managing Divergent Recoveries* (Washington, DC: IMF, 2021), 105, https://www.imf.org/en/Publications/WEO/Issues/2021/03/23/world-economic-outlook-april-2021. In October 2019, Statistics Canada put the size of the GDP at 2012 chained prices at $1.9 trillion, *Historical (Real-Time) Releases of Gross Domestic Product (GDP) at Basic Prices, by Industry, Monthly*, 2019, https://www150.statcan.gc.ca/t1/tbl1/en/tv.action?pid=3610049101&cubeTimeFrame.startMonth=01&cubeTimeFrame.startYear=2019&cubeTimeFrame.endMonth=12&cubeTimeFrame.endYear=2019&referencePeriods=20190101%2C20191201.

28 Revenues include both taxes (individual, corporate, and others) as well as non-tax revenue, such as social contributions; revenue from grants; property income; sales of goods and services; fines, penalties, and forfeits; voluntary transfers other than grants; as well as miscellaneous revenue (e.g., auto premia, drugs plan premia, and other revenue not classified elsewhere). Statistics Canada, Table 10-10-0016-01 Canadian Government Finance Statistics for the Federal Government, https://www150.statcan.gc.ca/t1/tbl1/en/tv.action?pid=1010001601.

29 Marco Chown Oved, "Canadians with Offshore Holdings Evade up to $3 Billion in Tax per Year," *Toronto Star*, 28 June 2018, https://www.thestar.com/news/canada/2018/06/28/canadians-with-offshore-holdings-evade-up-to-3-billion-in-tax-per-year.html.

30 "Public debt" is defined here as the debt incurred by the federal government as distinguished from the debt of provincial governments and/or municipal

76 Sanaa Ahmed

organizations. For a general overview of public debt, see the *Encyclopedia Britannica* website, "Government Budget," https://www.britannica.com/topic/government-budget/Government-borrowing#ref26345.

31 For the purposes of consistency and accuracy of comparison, pre-pandemic figures are used throughout the chapter for the most part. This is because exponential government spending in the wake of the pandemic has worsened the debt situation for both the federal and provincial governments. In the budget announced in April 2021, for example, after announcing a slew of spending measures aimed at resuscitating the pandemic economy, Finance Minister Chrystia Freeland estimated the size of the 2020–1 deficit at $354.2 billion and said she expected the federal debt to peak at 51.2 per cent of GDP in 2021–2 before declining to 49.2 per cent of GDP in 2025–6. See "Takeaways – Canada 2021 Budget in Numbers," Yahoo! Finance, 19 April 2021, https://finance.yahoo.com/news/takeaways-canada-2021-budget-numbers-201120275.html.

32 Canada's gross debt position (domestic debt plus foreign debt) in the third quarter of 2019 was $2,491,758 million (or $2.49 trillion) while the size of its GDP (chained at 2012 dollars) in October 2019 was $1.98 trillion. Statistics Canada, "General Government Gross Debt, Quarterly (x 1,000,000)," Table 36-10-0467-01, December 2021, https://www150.statcan.gc.ca/t1/tbl1/en/tv.action?pid=3610046701. The debt-to-GDP ratio is the former figure expressed as a percentage of the latter. However, the debt-to-GDP ratio varies according to the methodology used by various authors. In a January 2020 op-ed, the Fraser Institute's Jake Fuss and Milagros Palacios put the size of the combined federal-provincial net debt-to-GDP ratio for 2019–20 at 64.3 per cent, while Bank of Canada governor Stephen Poloz put the figure at 90 per cent in his December 2019 address in Toronto. Meanwhile, Philip Cross at the Macdonald Laurier Institute cites the Bank for International Settlements and says Canada's debt-to GDP ratio is 305.7 per cent. See Jake Fuss and Milagros Palacios, "Canadian Governments Ought to Get Serious about Bringing Down Debt," *Globe and Mail,* 15 January 2020, https://www.theglobeandmail.com/business/commentary/article-canadian-governments-ought-to-get-serious-about-bringing-down-debt/; Stephen S. Poloz, "Big Issues ahead – the Bank of Canada's 2020 Vision," Stephen S. Poloz, Remarks to the Empire Club, Canada, Toronto, Ontario, 12 December 2019, https://www.bis.org/review/r191220d.pdf; Philip Cross, "The 2010s Were a Lost Decade of Debt: The Combination of a Decade of Slow Income Growth and Mounting Debt Has Left Canada's Economy Vulnerable to a Shock," *Financial Post,* 8 January 2020, https://business.financialpost.com/opinion/philip-cross-the-2010s-were-a-lost-decade-of-debt#comments-area. However, use of the debt-to-GDP ratio as a measure of a country's ability to service its debt is also fraught with problems and many economists prefer debt per capita figures to explain the extent of the problems of debt. This is because, first, GDP is too complex and too difficult to measure accurately. Second, debt is paid off from revenues a country generates and not the

value of the total amount of goods and services produced by a country. For a neat explainer, see "National Debt," *Investopedia*, https://www.investopedia.com/updates/usa-national-debt/. At $335 billion for the year 2018, Canada's revenues account for just 12 per cent of total debt. See Statistics Canada, "Canadian Government Finance Statistics for the Federal Government x 1,000,000, 22 November 2021, https://www150.statcan.gc.ca/t1/tbl1/en/tv.action?pid=1010001601&pickMembers%5B0%5D=3.2.

33 However, the figure needs to be used with caution as "per capita" by definition applies equally to men, women, children, retirees, etc.

34 Mehmet Caner, Thomas Grennes, and Fritzi Koehler-Geib, "Finding the Tipping Point – When Sovereign Debt Turns Bad," The World Bank Policy Research Working Paper 5391, July 2010, https://documents1.worldbank.org/curated/en/509771468337915456/pdf/WPS5391.pdf.

35 For 2018, this amount was $23 billion. See Statistics Canada, "Canadian Government Finance Statistics for the Federal Government," Table: 10-10-0016-01, https://www150.statcan.gc.ca/t1/tbl1/en/tv.action?pid=1010001601&pickMembers%5B0%5D=3.2, Table: 10-10-0016-01.

36 Critics of neoclassical economics, however, contend that interest rates are too low to have such effects.

37 Statistics Canada, Gross Domestic Product (GDP) at Basic Prices, by Industry, Monthly (x 1,000,000), Table 36-10-0434-01, https://www150.statcan.gc.ca/t1/tbl1/en/tv.action?pid=3610043401.

38 A useful comparison emerges when one looks at the sectoral breakdown of other countries higher than Canada in the GDP rankings. The top two contributors to US growth, for example, are health care and technology. China, meanwhile, has progressively deindustrialized since 2011 and the share of the services sector in the coming decade is pitched at 65 per cent of value added, while industrial activity is expected to fall to 30 per cent of value added See Min Zhu, Longmei Zhan, Daoju Peng, "China's Productivity Convergence and Growth Potential – a Stocktaking and Sectoral Approach," IMF Working Papers, 27 November 2019, 30. https://www.imf.org/en/Publications/WP/Issues/2019/11/27/Chinas-Productivity-Convergence-and-Growth-Potential-A-Stocktaking-and-Sectoral-Approach-48702. While manufacturing in both Japan and Germany account for a large amount of GDP (20 per cent each), the goods produced are high-value engineering-oriented, R&D-led industrial products in Japan's case and high-value capital goods in Germany's. See Trading Indicators, https://tradingeconomics.com/germany/indicators; https://tradingeconomics.com/japan/gdp-from-manufacturing.

39 These would include the manufacture of furniture and related products for kitchens and bathroom cabinets and vanities; veneer, plywood, and engineered wood products; millwork (mouldings, parquet flooring, stairwork); sawmills (lumber, etc.); wood preservatives; structural wood products; particle boards and fibreboard mills; wood windows and doors; pre-fab wood buildings; petroleum

refineries' products (such as asphalt); asphalt paving, roofing, and shingles; adhesives, resins, and synthetic rubbers, chemicals, paints, coatings, plastic plumbing; plastic window and door manufacturing; plumbing fixtures; clay building material and refractory manufacturing (tiles); glass and glass products (including fiberglass installations and windows); cement and concrete products; gypsum products (drywall, ornamental, and architectural plaster work); all other non-metallic mineral products (dimension stone for buildings, dry-mix concrete, stucco and stucco products, tiles); steel products; copper products (copper wires, tubing); architectural and structural metals; hardware (hinges, locks, etc.); spring and wire products; turned product and crew; nuts and bolts; metal valves; construction machinery; sawmill and woodworking machinery; rubber and plastics machinery; ventilation, heating, and air-conditioning equipment; metalworking machinery; electrical equipment, appliances, and components (bulbs, tubes, lighting fixtures); furniture and related products; household and institutional furniture and kitchen cabinets; wood kitchen and cabinets and countertops; upholstered household furniture; other wood household furniture; household furniture (except wood and upholstered); institutional furniture; office furniture; other furniture-related products; mattresses; and blinds and shades. See North American Industry Classification System (NAICS) Canada 2017, Version 3.0, sections 31–3; https://www23.statcan.gc.ca/imdb/p3VD.pl?Function=getVD&TVD=1181553.

40 These would include merchants dealing in linen, drapery, and textile furnishings (for institutional buyers such as hotels, hospitals, offices, etc.); floor coverings; other home furnishings; building material and supplies; electrical, plumbing, heating, and air-conditioning equipment and supplies; lumber, millwork, hardware, and other building material supplies; construction and forestry machinery, equipment, and supplies. See NAICS Canada 2017 Version 3.0, section 41; available at https://www23.statcan.gc.ca/imdb/p3VD.pl?Function=getVD&TVD=1181553.

41 These would include retailers providing furniture, home furnishings, fittings (doors, windows, etc.), building material and supplies (hardware, paints, etc.). NAICS Canada 2017 Version 3.0, sections 44–5; available at https://www23.statcan.gc.ca/imdb/p3VD.pl?Function=getVD&TVD=1181553.

42 These would include financial intermediaries (credit unions, banks, mortgage brokers), insurers, reinsurers (such as property reinsurance carriers), as well as mortgage funds.

43 These would include lawyers, accountants, architectural design services, etc.

44 Statistics Canada. Gross Domestic Product (GDP) at Basic Prices, by Industry, Monthly, Growth Rates (x 1,000,000), Table 36-10-0434-02, 1 March 2022, https://www150.statcan.gc.ca/t1/tbl1/en/tv.action?pid=3610043402&pickMembers%5B0%5D=2.1&pickMembers%5B1%5D=3.1&cubeTimeFrame.startMonth=12&cubeTimeFrame.startYear=2019&referencePeriods=20191201%2C20191201.

45 Statistics Canada, "Provincial and Territorial Economic Accounts, 2018," *The Daily*, 7 November 2019.
46 Statistics Canada, *Evaluation of the Federal Business Immigration Program, 2014*, 2, https://www.canada.ca/content/dam/ircc/migration/ircc/english/pdf/pub/e2-2013_fbip.pdf.
47 Statistics Canada, *Evaluation of the Federal Business Immigration Program, 2014*, 17, https://www.canada.ca/content/dam/ircc/migration/ircc/english/pdf/pub/e2-2013_fbip.pdf.
48 Statistics Canada, 2016 Census of Population, Statistics Canada Catalogue no. 98-400-X2016202, https://www12.statcan.gc.ca/census-recensement/2016/dp-pd/dt-td/Rp-eng.cfm?LANG=E&APATH=3&DETAIL=0&DIM=0&FL=A&FREE=0&GC=0&GID=0&GK=0&GRP=1&PID=110558&PRID=10&PTYPE=109445&S=0&SHOWALL=0&SUB=0&Temporal=2017&THEME=120&VID=0&VNAMEE=&VNAMEF=.
49 Statistics Canada, Immigrant Population by Selected Places of Birth, Admission Category and Period of Immigration, Canada, Provinces and Territories, Census Metropolitan Areas and Areas outside of Census Metropolitan Areas, Census 2016, https://www12.statcan.gc.ca/census-recensement/2016/dp-pd/dv-vd/imm/index-eng.cfm.
50 Statistics Canada, Immigrant Population by Selected Places of Birth, Admission Category and Period of Immigration, Canada, Provinces and Territories, Census Metropolitan Areas and Areas outside of Census Metropolitan Areas, Census 2016, https://www12.statcan.gc.ca/census-recensement/2016/dp-pd/dv-vd/imm/index-eng.cfm.
51 The eligibility and selection criteria include previous business experience, minimum personal net worth, minimum investment in Canada, "post-arrival intentions and ability," education, official language proficiency, age, and adaptability as well as medical, criminality, and security checks. See Statistics Canada, *Evaluation of the Federal Business Immigration Program, 2014*, 3–4, https://www.canada.ca/content/dam/ircc/migration/ircc/english/pdf/pub/e2-2013_fbip.pdf. For example, while the application for business immigration in the start-up business class specifies that the money being brought to Canada must be "available and transferable [as well as] free of debts or other obligations," it specifies nothing about the source of funds or laundering, other than the fact that cash amounts over $10,000 need to be declared when entering Canada, see Immigration, Refugees and Citizenship Canada, Federal Business Program, https://www.canada.ca/en/immigration-refugees-citizenship/services/application/application-forms-guides/guide-5759-application-permanent-residence-business-immigration-program-start-business-class.html. Interestingly, the replication of the Canadian immigration strategy more recently by EU countries such as Cyprus, Portugal, and Malta have drawn vehement criticism by developed countries for selling citizenship in exchange for wads of "dirty money." See Simon Goodley and David Pegg, "Malta

Still Selling Golden Passports to Rich Stay-Away 'Residents,'" *The Guardian*, 23 April 2021, https://www.theguardian.com/world/2021/apr/23/malta-still-selling-golden-passports-to-rich-stay-away-residents.

52 Tax Justice Network, Canada, https://www.taxjustice.net/country-profiles/canada/.
53 For example, US President Joe Biden's infrastructure plan leverages government spending in line with the administration's *political* priorities such as the development of the green technology or the provision of elderly care. See Benjamin Swasey, "By the Numbers: Biden's $2 Trillion Infrastructure Plan," 1 April 2021, https://www.npr.org/2021/04/01/983470782/by-the-numbers-bidens-2-trillion-infrastructure-plan.
54 Statistics Canada, "Infrastructure Economic Account 2018," https://www150.statcan.gc.ca/n1/daily-quotidien/190411/dq190411a-eng.htm.
55 Infrastructure Canada 2018: 8.
56 Infrastructure Canada 2018: 14.
57 Infrastructure Canada 2018: 3. However, everyone is not a P3s fan: for a particularly incisive critique, see Toby Sanger, "A Shareholder Shopping Spree for Public Assets," *CCPA Monitor*, January–February 2018.
58 Infrastructure Canada 2018: 7.
59 See Beare, "Canada: Internal Conspiracies – Corruption and Crime," for an incisive analysis of how corruption dogs infrastructure projects as varied as health care and construction.
60 Beare, Canada: "Internal Conspiracies – Corruption and Crime," 7.
61 Swasey, "By the Numbers: Biden's $2 Trillion Infrastructure Plan."
62 Dawn L. Rothe and David O. Friedrichs, "The State of the Criminology of Crimes of the State," *Social Justice* 33, no. 1 (2006): 155. The authors ascribe this inattention to academic censorship and self-censorship; difficulties in conducting and publishing such research; the consequent inability to demonstrate scholarly prolificacy, which affects academic careers; lack of funding; lack of "official" documents; as well as official and public opposition to the notion of state crime.
63 Rothe and Friedrichs, "The State of the Criminology of Crimes of the State," 147.
64 Dawn L. Rothe, "Exploring Post-resistance to State Criminality: Realpolitik versus Ideology," *Social Justice* 36, no. 3 (2009–10): 111–21.
65 David Kauzlarich, Christopher W. Mullins, and Rick A. Matthews, "A Complicity Continuum of State Crime," *Contemporary Justice Review* 6, no. 3 (2003): 241–54, 244.
66 Tsingou is a notable exception. Eleni Tsingou, "Global Financial Governance and the Developing Anti-money Laundering Regime: What Lessons for International Political Economy?" *International Politics* 47, no. 6 (2010): 617–37.
67 Terence Halliday, Michael Levi, and Peter Reuter, Global Surveillance of Dirty Money: Assessing Assessments of Regimes to Control Money-Laundering and Combat the Financing of Terrorism (Champaign: University of Illinois and American Bar Foundation, Centre on Law and Globalisation, 2014), 7, 47. http://www.undrugcontrol.info/en/issues/money-laundering/item/6740-global

-surveillance-of-dirty-money. While there is a plethora of reports, articles, and studies claiming to provide the same, almost none are supported by data and mostly deal in guesstimates of dubious provenance.
68 Rothe, "Exploring Post-resistance to State Criminality: Realpolitik versus Ideology," 112.
69 Rothe, "Exploring Post-resistance to State Criminality: Realpolitik versus Ideology," 113–15.
70 William J. Chambliss, "State-Organized Crime – the American Society of Criminology, 1988 Presidential Address," *Criminology* 27, no. 2, (1989): 202.
71 Chambliss "State Organized Crime, 183–4.
72 Rothe and Friedrichs, "The State of the Criminology of Crimes of the State," 153.
73 Michael Mann, *The Sources of Social Power*, Vol. 4: *Globalizations 1945 – 2011* (New York: Cambridge University Press, 2012), 1. While he relies on standard understandings of "economic" and "ideological" power, his segregation of military and political power merits further explication. To Mann, military power is focused, furious, lethal violence exercised by armies, terrorists, paramilitaries, and criminals. Political power, on the other hand, is the centralized, territorial regulation of social life, through law and rule-governed political deliberations in centralized courts, councils, assemblies, and ministries. Unlike Weber who thinks any organization (including NGOs, corporations, and social movements) can have political power, Mann sees the state as the only spatial and institutionalized form of centralized, territorial power. However, Mann fails to evaluate judicial power as a source of social power; this is an unfortunate omission.
74 Michael Mann, *The Sources of Social Power*, Vol. 2: *The Rise of Classes and Nation-States 1760 – 1914* (New York: Cambridge University Press, 1993), 56.
75 Kauzlarich, Mullins, and Matthews, "A Complicity Continuum of State Crime," 251–2. Among other factors, the authors point to the need to examine the stage of development of said state as well as how close the state is to achieving its goals.
76 Steve Tombs, "State-Corporate Symbiosis in the Production of Crime and Harm," *State Crime* 1, no. 2, (2012): 170–95. Also see Saskia Sassen, *Territory, Authority, Rights: From Medieval to Global Assemblages* (Princeton, NJ: Princeton University Press, 2006), 381, 403. Sassen discusses how global processes are embedded in what she calls "national strategic spaces": state institutions, territories, and infrastructure.
77 Tombs, "State-Corporate Symbiosis in the Production of Crime and Harm," 171–2, 176.
78 Kauzlarich, Mullins, and Matthews, A Complicity Continuum of State Crime," 242.
79 Tombs, "State-Corporate Symbiosis in the Production of Crime and Harm," 173; Katharina Pistor, *The Code of Capital: How Law Creates Wealth and Inequality* (Princeton, NJ: Princeton University Press, 2019), 3–5.
80 Tombs, "State-Corporate Symbiosis in the Production of Crime and Harm," 176–7.
81 Tombs, "State-Corporate Symbiosis in the Production of Crime and Harm," 177–81.

82 Rothe and Friedrichs, "The State of the Criminology of Crimes of the State," 150.
83 Kauzlarich, Mullins, and Matthews, "A Complicity Continuum of State Crime," 245.
84 Chambliss, "State-Organised Crime," 187–8.
85 Chambliss, "State-Organised Crime," 188. Chambliss uses a particularly telling example of the US National Security Council, the Department of Defense, and the CIA working together to sell arms to Iran in direct violation of the *Illegal Arms Export Control Act* in the late 1980s (pp. 192–6).
86 These include the Criminal Code of Canada, Proceeds of Crime (Money Laundering) and Terrorist Financing Act 2000, Mutual Legal Assistance in Criminal Matters 1985, Income Tax Act 1985, Office of the Superintendent of Financial Institutions Act 1985, Canada Business and Corporations Act 1985, Seized Property Management Act 1993, United Nations Act 1985, Proceeds of Crime (Money Laundering) and Terrorist Financing Suspicious Transaction Reporting Regulations, Proceeds of Crime (Money Laundering) and Terrorist Financing Regulations, Cross-border Currency and Monetary Instruments Reporting Regulations, Proceeds of Crime (Money Laundering) and Terrorist Financing Registration Regulations, Proceeds of Crime (Money Laundering) and Terrorist Financing Administrative Monetary Penalties Regulations, Regulations Implementing the United Nations Resolutions on the Suppression of Terrorism 2001 and United Nations Al-Qaida and Taliban Regulations 1999.
87 Cribb and Oved, "Snow Washing: Canada Is the World's Newest Tax Haven."
88 At the federal level, Canada currently has twelve agencies tasked with anti–money laundering enforcement and prosecution, while there are approximately fourteen at the provincial level. The federal agencies include the Canada Border Services Agency, the Canada Revenue Authority, CSIS, Department of Finance, Department of Justice, Financial Transactions and Reports Analysis Centre of Canada (FinTrac), Public Prosecution Service of Canada, RCMP, Stats Canada, Canada Mortgage and Housing Corporation, Bank of Canada, and the Office of the Superintendent of Financial Institutions. The provincial agencies include the RCMP (except in Ontario and Quebec), municipal police, Crown counsel (e.g., BC Crown Counsel), Civil Forfeiture Office, MoF Revenue Division, Office of the Chief Information Officer (BC), Land Title and Survey Authority (BC), BC Assessment, real estate regulators, financial sector regulators, securities regulators, Financial Institutions Commission (BC), professional regulators (e.g., Law Society of Ontario, Notaries Public, Chartered Professional Accountants, etc.), as well as lottery and gambling regulators.
89 Grant Robertson and Tom Cardoso, "RCMP Aims to Use outside Experts to Crack Down on White-Collar Crime," *Globe & Mail*, 12 April 2018, B1, https://www.theglobeandmail.com/business/article-rcmp-aims-to-use-outside-experts-to-crack-down-on-white-collar-crime/.
90 Oved, "The RCMP Is Shutting Down Its Financial Crimes Unit in Ontario."

4 Policing Financial Crime – Do We Care?

PETER M. GERMAN

Big policing is expensive, the largest budget item for most municipalities, with broad tentacles that also extend deep into provincial and federal budgets. The police and those who superintend their actions are constantly balancing competing demands for service. In recent months and years, this has extended to a broad-based discussion on the very need for police. When faced with difficult choices, governments and, by extension, the police will almost always default to the public's basic need to feel and be safe in their homes and communities. Accordingly, police invariably and understandably give priority to the fight against violent crime.

Where does financial crime fit within this equation? Increasingly, it does not and yet the globalization of financial markets and the unparalleled growth of technology and cyber-based solutions have combined to facilitate an exponential increase in financial crime, much of it linked to transnational organized crime.

This chapter traces the expansion and contraction of federal resources focused on financial crime, the response by provinces, and the increased burden on already overstretched municipal police resources. It argues that proper resourcing of the police is simply part of the cure. In fact, a cacophony of issues has impacted this crime type.

By taking our eye off the spectre of financial crime, Canadians are at considerable risk, and yet there is little clamour for change, leading to even less action by government. A comprehensive national strategy to deal with the existential threats posed by these crimes will serve as a starting point in making Canada a safer place to live and less hospitable to the forces which threaten our economic security.

Financial Crime

It takes little imagination to determine what is meant by violent crime, with the possible caveat that non-physical violence is less easy to identify than physical violence. Most citizens can relate to the imperative of preventing crime that could impact their safety at home, work, and in public settings. Homicides and sexual offences come to mind when considering violent crime. Likewise, public order offences can evoke images of violence, most recently in the inner sanctum of America's citadel of democracy, the Capitol Building. But what image is conjured up when the term "financial crime" is used?

George Gilligan has traced the history of financial crime, which he refers to as a "slippery concept," to the earliest of recorded time, when trade commenced between tribal societies, markets developed, and rudimentary currencies came into use.[1] Michael Levi refers to financial crime as an "administratively functional" category of offences, rather than a legal category. Levi highlights its breadth of definition and notes that a financial crime in one nation may not constitute an offence in another, reflecting different economic and legal structures and policies.[2]

Concern over financial crime is not unique to the Judeo-Christian tradition. General principles in the Qur'an and the Sunnah, including the concepts of trust, fair dealing, and honesty, give rise to prohibitions against forms of financial crime.[3] For example, money laundering offends the equitable distribution of wealth and the principle of not profiting from unlawful activity.[4]

An oft-used fallback position when attempting to discern a definition for financial crime is to borrow from international agencies, which have considered the issue on a global level. Acknowledging the difficulty of definition, the eleventh United Nations Crime Congress in 2005 was persuaded that economic and financial crime refer "broadly to any non-violent crime that results in a financial loss."[5] This is admittedly an all-encompassing definition, designed to garner widespread acceptance among nations. Greater precision inevitably leads to country-specific approaches to many forms of behaviour, such as cartels, insider trading, and counterfeiting. Despite the vagaries of definition, there does, however, appear to be a collective acceptance among nations that money laundering is a subset of this amorphous concept, linked closely to a wide range of predicate offences.

Financial Crime in Canada

Canada is plagued by financial crime, but quantification is difficult. There are few Canadians unaware of mass marketing and internet frauds or the many scams which are the constant staple of consumer news broadcasts. Identity theft has reached new levels as government and corporate websites are attacked and mined for personal information. There has always been and will always be a segment of the population that seeks to increase its worth through fraud and deceit. Their crimes are not solitary in nature, and they have a disproportionate impact on economies and populations. Financial crime distorts the normal economic forces of supply and demand.[6]

A good example is telemarketing fraud, either through phone calls or e-mail messages. Mini-boiler rooms,[7] easily transportable, work out of transient locations in Toronto, Montreal, or as far away as India, using "sucker" lists to call victims in Canada, the United States (US), the United Kingdom (UK), and other English-speaking countries. The truly gullible are duped into meeting their callers in a relatively safe third country, such as the Netherlands, whose citizens have not traditionally been targets of the scammers.

Millions of dollars are lost annually to these frauds, with a disproportionate percentage of victims being seniors. The money obtained by the scammers is laundered by others in the organization, either through bulk smuggling or electronic transfers. Experts within the organized crime ring disguise the money trail, ensuring that an invisible wall exists between the perpetrators of the initial fraud and the money movers.[8]

The upscale version of telemarketing is "phishing" and all its variants, in which criminals mimic or clone financial websites, in the hope of duping persons reading their e-mail into providing passwords and other personal information, which can then be used, traded, or sold for identity theft purposes. These scams are by their nature international in scope. Investigating them requires cooperation among authorities from multiple countries, oftentimes involving different legal systems. Telemarketing and phishing are perfectly quaint, however, by comparison to what is on the horizon, and that horizon is bearing down on us at frightening speed. With the advent of virtual currencies and contactless financial transactions, the opportunities for harm and illegal profits are increasing exponentially.

Despite the simplicity of our definition of financial crime, it would be a mistake to assume that it is the work of lone fraudsters or opportunistic criminals. Virtually all of these schemes are being leveraged by and can be linked to organized crime networks with tentacles in many countries.

The Spectre of Organized Crime

In 1876, the Minister of Justice of Canada stood up in the House of Commons and declared that a "carnival of crime [was] beginning on our border."[9] "Organized crime" and "transnational organized crime" were not part of the lexicon of the day. For Edward Blake it was those perfidious Americans who seemed always to be ignoring the international border by allowing whisky traders in the west and the Fenians in the east to violate Canadian sovereignty.

Little could Blake have imagined that the horse and buggy world of his day would give rise to a global village in which airplanes crisscross the skies and an invisible internet snakes around the world, that international travel would be described in terms of hours and not weeks, and that money would be transmitted between continents in a series of zeros and ones.

Organized criminals have adapted well to the new world. Their traditional structures have given way to modern enterprises, organizations have diversified and adapted, intense rivalry between groups has increasingly been replaced by cooperation and collaboration, domestic borders have been cast aside, and technology has been embraced to instantaneously hide their identity. Organized crime is not unique to one country, one race, one ethnicity, or even one continent. It is a worldwide phenomenon which, due to current technology and transportation systems, can operate internationally with relative ease. Organized crime knows no allegiance to the Rule of Law. It is amorphous and increasingly not commodity specific.

Organized crime is about making money and using money for the benefit of the organization and its members. These groups develop partnerships wherever necessary to further this goal; with politicians, public servants, revolutionary groups, terror networks, other organized crime groups, or even ordinary citizens who wish to make a "quick buck." Organized crime uses people as instruments of crime, whether to procure, transport, or sell illegal substances, or to launder the proceeds of their crime.

When organized crime groups cross international borders they are referred to as transnational organized crime. Whether they are drug trafficking rings, fraud syndicates, protection rackets, human trafficking networks, gaming ventures, or counterfeit rings, the common factors are that their activities are illegal and for profit. It is infinitely more difficult for law enforcement to track criminals outside of a country. Furthermore, criminal law is country specific, such that transnational organized criminals are only prosecuted if they commit an offence against a nation's domestic laws.

Transnational organized crime groups are flexible and will continue to form and reform, while the response by government typically operates with much less flexibility. Some forms of organized crime are quite complex; however, complexity can also lead to managerial difficulties for the syndicates and is not necessarily the preferred option. The ideal criminal enterprise is one which produces high value for low risk.[10]

Money Laundering

Most, if not all crime for profit requires that the proceeds of illegality be disguised in some fashion to allow the perpetrator to "clean" his or her dirty money. Money laundering is the term used to describe this process. Beare and Schneider describe it as a "tactical imperative employed by cash-intensive criminal enterprises."[11] It is a necessary element of the crime cycle and serves as the "back office" of profit-driven crime. The objective is to obfuscate the money trail and, most importantly, its illegal source. This is not easy, however, due to the sheer weight and bulk of cash, the risk of detection which cash poses, and the dangers created by transporting large sums.[12]

The process of money laundering can be quite complex; however, for definitional purposes, it is almost always divided into three stages: placement of the dirty money in the legitimate financial system, layering the money by moving it through other financial vehicles to disguise its origin, and integrating it back into the legitimate economy in a manner that prevents detection of its origins. Each stage can manifest itself in a plethora of ways. The three stages are equated to the three cycles of washing and drying clothes, giving the word "laundering" a meaning quite unintended by its Latin origin. Recent media headlines and studies concerning money laundering in Canada point to the attraction that Canada poses to domestic and international criminal organizations which seek to launder the proceeds of their nefarious activities.[13]

A Global View

Canada is not alone when it comes to the prevalence of financial crime. It is a scourge in many countries and has morphed into a global epidemic of corruption. In recent decades, the world community has recognized that corruption in low- and middle-income countries is a huge impediment to the forward movement of nations. Almost invariably, corruption will take hold in a nation where the rule of law is either weak or non-existent. Although no state is immune from corrupt practices, where institutions are guided by legal process, its impact is minimized. Where the checks and balances do not exist or are not enforced, persons in positions of power are free to benefit personally from their office.[14]

Corrupt practices can spread throughout a government bureaucracy, in which public servants, police, and the military may exact tribute in return for doing tasks that they are already paid to perform. The ripple effect is found in private industry which, in its attempt to satisfy the demands of public officials, will develop its own corrupt practices with respect to contracts and tenders. Eventually, corruption becomes a way of life, accepted by the public as a necessary evil to obtain basic services. Jack Blum notes that corruption is contagious: "If the bosses are stealing, the employees feel that they can steal with impunity," thereby creating a culture of corruption.[15]

Grand corruption, or kleptocracy, is an extension of this criminality – the use of public office for personal gain, sometimes for seemingly no other reason than to accumulate and horde vast quantities of capital. In recent years, grand corruption has captured the attention of governments around the world. The theft of state assets leads to all manner of economic and personal deprivation for the citizens of a country, ransacked of its treasury. Kleptocrats are of every race and religion. Oftentimes, the money paves the way for an exit from their country, a precursor in case their control weakens or is wrestled away in a coup.[16]

Some of the worst offenders in low- and middle-income countries are multinational companies, headquartered in Europe and North America, whose boards of directors would condemn bribery and corruption if it occurred in their own country. Unfortunately, the pursuit of profits and ever-increasing shareholder earnings allows these same directors to view international contracting as somehow different and corruption as acceptable in the context of poorer nations. The extractive industries and defence contractors have traditionally been among the worst offenders.

An incontrovertible fact remains. Money that should remain within a lower income country, which represents the toil and struggle of the peoples of those lands, has found its way into financial institutions that fuel the most powerful economies of the world, including Canada. So, what must Canada do to curb the onslaught of financial crime, both domestic and international in origin?

Constitutional Responsibility

The Canadian policing system is tiered, much like most other activities of government. There are law enforcement agencies operating at the federal, provincial, and municipal levels of government. This obviously reflects Canada's constitutional structure, in which the two senior levels of government are enshrined within the *Constitution*, while the municipal level is a creation of the provinces.[17]

Responsibility for dealing with criminality is bifurcated in the *Constitution*, with the federal government responsible for the making of criminal law under section 91(27) of the *Constitution* and the provincial governments responsible for the more ubiquitous, administration of justice under section 92(14). The latter has been interpreted to include all matters related to the enforcement and prosecution of matters in the *Criminal Code*.[18] This bifurcated approach results from the bartering that led to Canadian Confederation in 1867, whereby both the federal and provincial governments intended to share many tasks which, in a unitary system such as the United Kingdom, would be the remit of one level of government. The development of large municipalities created yet another dynamic as they carved out, in practical terms, a large portion of the provincial mandate. To say that the legal framework for policing in Canada is complicated would be an understatement.

Over the past 150 years, Parliament has passed many statutes containing criminal offences, in addition to those found in the *Criminal Code*. The federal government has a right and responsibility to investigate and prosecute these other criminal offences, leading to the need for a national police force and specialist law enforcement agencies. Provincial authorities may also investigate and prosecute these other criminal offences, if they do not infringe on the federal power. The result is a typically Canadian middle ground, a form of cooperative federalism in policing and prosecution.[19]

A Little Police History

At the time of Canada's Confederation in 1867, British policing was composed of two streams or models of policing – civil and colonial. The civilian police obtained their mission from Sir Robert Peel in his 1829 principles of policing, which continue to be a bedrock of policing in common law countries.[20] The second stream reflected the needs of a far-flung empire, which had been conquered through military force but maintained by a highly developed civil service and, in many colonies, a mounted police force. The latter did not flow from the civilian model of Peel but from a merger of cavalry and police, loosely patterned after the Royal Irish Constabulary.[21]

Canada's first prime minister, Sir John A. Macdonald, was faced with the imperative of settling the North-West Territory, which stretched from the western border of a much smaller Manitoba to the new colony of British Columbia (BC), which had been promised a rail link to the eastern provinces. In the absence of a territorial police, Macdonald devised a force, which came to be the North-West Mounted Police.[22] The existing provinces were policed by an amalgam of provincial, colonial (BC), or municipal police. The federal government had its own Dominion Police force, which served several functions, including security of federal facilities, counter espionage, and subversion. It also investigated offences under federal statutes.[23]

Financial crime in the early years of Confederation was rudimentary by today's standards. Fraud and false pretence were criminal offences, as were bribery and related corruption offences. They were investigated by local authorities for the most part. Little to no action was taken against the cartels and monopolies that existed in the railways and other industries. Corporate directorships and senior political positions were, for the most part, the preserve of an aristocratic cabal of well-heeled men of influence. It was the way business and government operated and few saw any difficulty with this comfortable world of privilege and all its trappings.

Over time, however, the world became much more complex and so did government and law enforcement. In 1920, the Dominion Police was absorbed into what became the Royal Canadian Mounted Police (RCMP), a national police force with a mandate that included federal areas of interest but also responsibility for *Criminal Code* offences in the new provinces of Alberta and Saskatchewan, the newly enlarged province of Manitoba and the far north, from Yukon to Baffin Island. Provincial police forces came and went, until 1932 when all had been absorbed into the RCMP, except for Ontario, Quebec, and British Columbia. The latter entered the fold in 1950, almost contemporaneous to Confederation in Newfoundland and the RCMP also assuming a role there.[24]

The 1960s saw a marked increase in crime of a financial nature, which outraged the nation and required the attention of law enforcement. Various scandals, involving bid-rigging, fraudulent bankruptcies, stock market manipulation, and political corruption called for a federal response, not only because much of this crime fell within its mandate, but because it also crossed provincial borders. In response to these issues, the federal government looked to the national police force.

The RCMP responded by bringing together a small cadre of highly educated and experienced specialist officers who undertook complex investigations of the sort described above. The notion that some crime required specialists was an important recognition in the evolution of policing away from the generalist model which had dominated, with some exceptions, for almost a hundred years. In 1967, commercial fraud sections (later termed commercial crime sections) were rolled out across the country and undertook corporate, federal statute, market manipulation, and bankruptcy investigations. This expanded to include a partnership with the tax authorities, related to organized crime. Until police salaries and budgets increased dramatically in the 1980s, the federal government seemed happy to engage in these investigations, although many were properly the preserve of provincial authorities, whose financial contribution was minimal.[25]

During the 1990s, it became clear that criminals should not be allowed to retain the proceeds of their crimes. Although an obvious proposition today, in previous times there was little done to pursue these proceeds and no legislation that specifically targeted money laundering and proceeds of crime. Canada's ratification of the *Vienna Convention* in 1989 cast a spotlight on this legislative and enforcement gap.[26] Furthermore, US authorities began to take aggressive action against money laundering as a means by which to dismantle organized crime groups. The inclusion of enterprise crime units within the commercial crime sections of the RCMP was the Canadian response.

With the passage of proceeds of crime legislation in 1989, which made laundering a criminal offence, created special search warrants and restraint orders, and allowed for the forfeiture of ill-gotten gains, the RCMP was funded to deal with money laundering.[27] Proceeds of crime sections developed across the country, staffed with police officers who used their expertise to pursue the proceeds of crime. The sections were also integrated by incorporating investigators, accountants, and lawyers from other agencies.[28]

In the past two decades, the exponential increase in both financial crime and cybercrime placed a huge burden on the specialist financial crime sections, as well as on all levels of policing. In Ontario and Quebec, municipal and provincial police continued to investigate many financial crimes, from basic to multi-million-dollar frauds. The Ontario Provincial Police Anti-Rackets Squad and the Sûreté du Quebec developed considerable expertise in this area, while municipal police tended to do what they could within the constraints of municipal finances and competing priorities.

Much of the above changed in 2013, when the RCMP announced a restructuring of its federal investigative resources. The commercial crime and proceeds of crime sections were abolished in all provinces over the next few years, with Ontario and Quebec being holdouts.[29] The staff in these sections was integrated into a new model of organized crime teams under the rubric of Federal and Serious Organized Crime. The new structure resembled that seen in England and elsewhere; however, the net result in the RCMP was for a diminution of financial crime resources. A few specialists in a generalist unit have a habit of becoming generalists themselves. With retirements and transfers, the expertise of the former sections was lost and financial crime took a back seat to other investigations.

The realignment of RCMP resources caused a ripple effect within the contract provinces by downloading huge cases onto municipal detachments and police forces. Suddenly these entities were faced with fraud and other financial files, with greatly increased dollar values than had previously been the case. Likewise, proceeds of crime and money laundering no longer had a dedicated enforcement unit, resulting in those cases taking a back seat in the contract provinces.[30]

Federal regulatory agencies were forced to fill the gap in areas of federal concern that had previously seen RCMP involvement. At the provincial level, securities commissions were increasingly forced to look at their criminal mandate in addition to the bread and butter of regulatory enforcement. Ontario moved to a serious fraud office model, in which the provincial prosecution service partners with the Ontario Provincial Police (OPP) and regional forces to deal with financial crime matters in a model that resembles that of other common law jurisdictions, such as the United Kingdom and New Zealand.[31] The OPP also maintains its Canadian Anti-Fraud Centre (formerly Phone Busters) in North Bay. This, in partnership with the RCMP and the Competition Bureau of Canada, serves as a national clearing house for fraud files, particularly mass marketing schemes engineered by phone and computer.[32]

The work of Justice Charbonneau in Quebec and the subsequent development of an anti-corruption unit in that province,[33] the serious fraud office in Ontario, and the British Columbia government's recent focus on money laundering in casinos and real estate are bright spots set against an otherwise drab landscape.

Who Should Police Financial Crime?

At best, financial crime in Canada is currently an enigma in the broader scope of challenges facing policing. It is not obvious to the naked eye. It has a sinister ability to victimize ordinary citizens in a significant way in their normal daily lives as they use a computer, answer the phone, or make an investment. The sheer volume of financial crime is sufficient to swamp the resources of police forces. The issue begs for a holistic, cross-government approach. What does this look like in reality?

We are already witnessing the devolution of a great deal of responsibility for the prevention of financial crime to the private sector. Banks and credit card grantors, as well as other financial entities, are now heavily invested in security, in both a preventive and a reactive sense. Considerable energy is spent on educating clients on frauds, as well as buttressing internal informatics and other processes to prevent illegal incursions. Similarly, trained investigators pursue those frauds which do occur or, at the very least, monitor what is occurring for trends. They also liaise with police where appropriate.

The self-help witnessed by financial entities is not entirely a voluntary, profit-driven exercise but is also a requirement of Canada's anti–money laundering regime. Under the *Proceeds of Crime (Money Laundering) and Terrorist Financing Act*,[34] reporting entities are required to create a compliance structure which includes a plan, a compliance officer, training in anti–money laundering, knowing one's customer, and reporting large transactions, suspicious transactions, and others.

Regulatory agencies and associations are also helping to fill the gap. A plethora of these bodies are found at both the federal and provincial levels of government, including securities commissions, financial industry regulators, and a host of self-governing professional bodies, such as law and accounting societies. These regulators and quasi-regulators govern admission to a particular industry, undertake investigations of complaints, and impose sanctions.

Other contributors are the entities that provide direct assistance to the public, including consumer protection agencies. These organizations generally provide warnings related to fraud and handle complaints against businesses.

Self-help remedies are also available to the public. These include access to the civil courts for the purpose of suing parties where an individual or collective believes that it has been aggrieved. A wide array of quasi-criminal tools is available from the civil courts, such as *Mareva* injunctions and *Anton Pillar* orders, which can facilitate private investigations.[35] However, other than with respect to small claim matters, access to the civil courts tends to be prohibitively expensive for most citizens.

A remedy which began in Ontario in 2002 and later spread to most provinces, is civil forfeiture.[36] It is a statutory remedy which allows provincial governments to restrain and ultimately forfeit the instruments of crime and proceeds of unlawful activity. They are *in rem* proceedings, against property and not a person, which allow a province to bring action against property which has not been forfeited through the criminal process. The downside of civil forfeiture is the inability to sanction individuals. Essentially, when successful, civil forfeiture removes the proceeds of crime but allows organized crime to continue its business.

As we see from the foregoing discussion, the police cannot, nor can they be expected to deal with all aspects of financial crime. The sheer volume makes it impossible. What then should the role of the police be in these matters, and how should their responsibilities be shared or otherwise allocated among the different levels of government?

If we begin with the constitutional backdrop that exists in Canada, we know that two levels of government have responsibility in terms of criminal law. The federal government creates the *Criminal Code*, and the provinces administer criminal law, through policing, prosecution, and the courts. A parallel structure exists in terms of the investigation and prosecution of criminal offences in other federal statutes. The duality of responsibility in certain areas, such as drug enforcement, requires a coordinated approach. A similar argument could be made with respect to proceeds of crime and money laundering, which can arise from virtually any predicate criminal offence, whether within the *Criminal Code* or in another federal statute. This duality necessitates a commitment by both levels of government as well as an integrated response.

A further issue to be considered is the role of municipal governments. As creatures of the provinces, and not standalone governments within the *Constitution*, municipalities undertake those roles which are delegated to them by the provinces. The practice has been to delegate virtually all frontline policing to municipalities. Inevitably this places them in the position of being the recipient of many complaints of financial crime from the public. The practice has been for departments to triage these complaints, investigating some in the first instance or through specialized units, declining others, or referring them to provincial or federal policing units. This delicate overlap of responsibilities is dependent on each level of government placing commensurate attention and resources on the problem. It requires a high level of coordination, and both bureaucratic and political will at all three levels of government.

A theme which has emerged in recent decades has increased the complexity and the cost of police investigating financial crime. The advent of the *Charter of Rights and Freedoms* in 1982, an integral part of Canada's *Constitution*, spawned a paradigmatic change in how police operate, how prosecutors prosecute, how courts operate, and how offenders are sentenced.[37] These changes include disclosure obligations, the elimination of reverse onus clauses, court-imposed time limits on prosecutions, enhanced search warrant and electronic surveillance requirements, and a host of others.

Despite the importance of the foregoing changes, their unintended consequence has been to increase the cost and duration of criminal investigations. It is probably inevitable that police will seek the best return for their investment and that is seldom seen as a financial crime investigation. A compounding factor has been the increased prevalence of non-custodial sentences for non-violent crimes. This leads to police asking what benefit derives from a successful financial crime prosecution when, in the vernacular, "nobody goes to gaol." All these factors combine to defeat the dominant factor in all sentencing – deterrence. If there is no downside to illegal conduct, one can reasonably expect that it will continue.

A National Strategy

So, what is the answer? By paying lip service to controlling financial crime, Canadians are routinely victimized by cyber and land-based fraudsters. The financial industry has by default become the *de facto* financial crime police. This has led to a certain ambivalence among many who no longer view fraud as a crime but a cost of doing business and for some, a settling of accounts with big business. And yet, it is also the elites, the professionals, the crooked corporate executives, and the foreign dictators, who benefit when we ignore financial crime.

Not surprisingly, international organizations, including the G-7, the Organization for Economic Cooperation and Development, the European Community, and most notably the United Nations, have consistently pointed to the incredible deprivations which people around the world, oftentimes the poor and least protected, suffer when financial crime and corruption are left unchecked. Despite its membership in many of these organizations and its avowed support for strong action to counter these threats, Canada's record in the area is, at best, modest.

Canada must consider a national strategy to deal with organized crime, financial crime, and money laundering. Opening the discussion on these topics would be of immense value to politicians and bureaucracies. Engaging thought leaders in the area would allow for rational decision-making, which considers alternatives and charts a course that will permit forward movement by governments.

If one thing is certain, it is that financial crime, writ large, will become increasingly sophisticated as the world becomes more complex and the risk to economies and individual citizens has the potential to grow exponentially. Although resourcing the police and prosecutors to an acceptable level is needed, ensuring a unified and coherent national strategy will allow for the most efficacious use of these resources and a targeted approach to the problems of today and tomorrow.

NOTES

1 George Gilligan, "Financial Crime: A Historical Perspective," in *Research Handbook on International Financial Crime*, edited by Barry Rider (Cheltenham, UK: Edward Elgar, 2015), 32–3.
2 Michael Levi, "Foreword: Some Reflections on the Evolution of Economic and Financial Crimes," in *Research Handbook on International Financial Crime*, edited by Barry Rider (Cheltenham, UK: Edward Elgar, 2015), xxviii.

3 Siti Faridah Abdul Jabbar and Asma Hakimah Ab Halim, "The Concept of Fraud in Islamic Law," in *Research Handbook on International Financial Crime*, edited by Barry Rider (Cheltenham, UK: Edward Elgar, 2015), 364.
4 *Jabbar*, 365.
5 Cited in Levi, *Foreword,* xxviii.
6 See Maureen Maloney, Tsur Somerville, and Brigitte Unger, *Combatting Money Laundering in British Columbia Real Estate* (Victoria, BC: Minister of Finance, 2019), 44.
7 A "boiler room" is an operation in which salespeople call lists of people to pressure them into buying dubious financial commodities.
8 In 2002, the Government of Canada Anti-Fraud Centre received 70,948 reports of fraud, involving 42,093 victims, amounting to $108.8 million in losses. This accounts for reported crime only by individuals and likely represents a small percentage of the total amount of fraud in the country. In the first quarter of 2021, 17,005 reports of COVID-19 fraud were reported, involving 15,198 victims. Accessed 5 March 2022, https://antifraudcentre-centreantifraude.ca/index-eng.htm.
9 Blake to the Earl of Carnarvon, Colonial Secretary, 7 August 1876, quoted in W.H. Corbett, *Foreword to Law Enforcement in the Global Village* (Ottawa: Supply and Services Canada, 1990).
10 A concise introduction to this topic is Leslie Holmes, *Advanced Introduction to Organised Crime* (Cheltenham, UK: Edward Elgar, 2016).
11 Margaret E. Beare and Stephen Schneider, *Money Laundering in Canada: Chasing Dirty and Dangerous Dollars* (Toronto: University of Toronto Press, 2007).
12 See generally, Peter M. German, *Proceeds of Crime and Money Laundering* (Toronto: Thomson Reuters, current service), chapter 1.
13 Peter M. German, *Dirty Money – Part 2* (Vancouver: British Columbia, 2017).
14 Robert Rubin, Statement to the *Conference on Fighting Corruption and Safeguarding Integrity among Justice and Security Officials* (Washington, DC: US Treasury, 24 February 1999), https://irp.fas.org/news/1999/02/99022403_clt.htm.
15 Jack A. Blum, "Multilateral Assistance to Nigeria and the Recovery of Misappropriated Nigerian Assets," Statement to the US House of Representatives Committee on Banking and Financial Services Subcommittee on Domestic and International Monetary Policy, 25 May 2000.
16 In 2004, Transparency International (TI) released its "Top Ten" list of kleptocrats, including such names as the late president Mohamed Suharto of Indonesia, late president Ferdinand Marcos of Indonesia, late president Mobutu Sese Seko of the Democratic Republic of Congo, late president Sani Abacha of Nigeria, and former president Slobodan Milosevic. See Transparency International, "Where Did the Money Go?" *Global Corruption Report 2004* (London: Pluto Press, 2004), 13, online at https://www.transparency.org/en/publications/global-corruption-report-2004-political-corruption.

17 *The Constitution Act, 1982*, being Schedule B to *The Canada Act 1982* (U.K.), c. 11, https://www.legislation.gov.uk/ukpga/1982/11.
18 *Criminal Code*, R.S.C. 1985, c. C-46.
19 See *Quebec (Attorney General) v. Canada (Attorney General)*, 2015 SCC 14 for a discussion of the limits of cooperative federalism. See also, *Criminal Code*, s. 2 for a definition of "Attorney General."
20 Civitas, "The Nine Principles of Policing," accessed 5 March 2022, https://www.civitas.org.uk/research/crime/facts-comments/principles-of-good-policing/.
21 Emma Bell, "Normalising the Exceptional: British Colonial Police Cultures Come Home," *Cultures coloniales et postcoloniales et decolonization* 10 (2013), translation available Open *Edition Journals*, accessed 5 March 2022, https://journals.openedition.org/mimmoc/1286?lang=en.
22 See generally, Richard Gwynn, *Nation Maker – Sir John A. Macdonald: His Life, Our Times, Volume Two 1867–1891* (Toronto: Random House Canada, 2011). The North-West Mounted Police became the Royal North-West Mounted Police in 1904 and the Royal Canadian Mounted Police in 1920.
23 For an uncritical overview of the history of the RCMP, see Nora and William Kelly, *The Royal Canadian Mounted Police – A Century of History* (Edmonton: Hurtig Publishers, 1973).
24 Peter M. German, "Federal-Provincial Contracting for Royal Canadian Mounted Police Services: A Survey Utilizing the Interplay Model of Public Policy Analysis," MA thesis, 1990, Simon Fraser University.
25 Report of the Royal Canadian Mounted Police – Fiscal Year Ended March 31, 1968 (Ottawa: Queen's Printer, 1969), 23.
26 Convention against Illicit Traffic in Narcotic Drugs and Psychotropic Substances, UNESC Doc. E/Conf. 82/15 (1988).
27 Statutes of Canada, 1988, c. 51.
28 See German, *Proceeds of Crime*, at chapter 20 for a historical overview of financial crime units in the RCMP.
29 The financial crimes unit in Ontario was eliminated in 2020. See Marco Oved, "The RCMP Is Shutting Down Its Financial Crimes Unit in Ontario. Here's Why Former Mounties Say It's a Mistake," *Toronto Star*, 15 January 2020, https://www.thestar.com/news/investigations/2020/01/15/the-rcmp-is-shutting-down-its-financial-crimes-unit-in-ontario-heres-why-former-top-mounties-says-its-a-mistake.html. Quebec appears to have been spared much of the drama seen elsewhere in the RCMP, maintaining its presence in financial crime and proceeds of crime enforcement.
30 See, for example, Paisley Woodward, "Former RCMP Proceeds of Crime Head Warned Bosses of Weakened Dirty Money Investigations," *CBC Investigates*, https://www.cbc.ca/news/canada/british-columbia/former-rcmp-proceeds-of-crime-head-warned-bosses-of-weakened-dirty-money-investigations-1.5099332.
31 Christopher Burkett, "Fraudsters Beware: Ontario Launches Serious Fraud Office," Baker McKenzie, Commentary, News, & Updates, 6 September 2019, Accessed 2

March 2022, https://www.canadianfraudlaw.com/2019/09/fraudsters-beware-ontario-launches-serious-fraud-office/.
32 Canada, "Scams by A-Z Index," Canadian Anti-Fraud Centre, https://www.antifraudcentre-centreantifraude.ca/index-eng.htm.
33 The Commission's appointment is found at https://www.publicationsduquebec.gouv.qc.ca/fileadmin/gazette/pdf_encrypte/lois_reglements/2011F/56587.pdf, and the final report in French can be downloaded at https://www.bibliotheque.assnat.qc.ca/guides/fr/les-commissions-d-enquete-au-quebec-depuis-1867/7732-commission-charbonneau-2015. The Unité permanente anticorruption (*UPAC*) home page is https://www.upac.gouv.qc.ca/.
34 Canada, Proceeds of Crime (Money Laundering) and Terrorist Financing Act, S.C. 2000, c. 17.
35 A Mareva injunction is a civil restraint order, which freezes property on the order of a civil court. An Anton Pillar order is often referred to as a civil search warrant, again issued by a civil court.
36 *Civil Remedies Act 2001*, S.O. 2001, c. 28, in force on 12 April 2002.
37 Part I of The Constitution Act, 1982, supra.

SECTION TWO

Beyond Reach: Crimes of the Entrepreneurial Elites

This section addresses manoeuvres that involve enormous economic gains for those driven by opportunistic, entrepreneurial, or political motives outside of what we envision as formal institutional or corporate settings. By examining tax evasion, art fraud, and banking fraud, the next three chapters present what Margaret Beare has identified as privileged patterns of exchange among elites that have "new and near-limitless opportunities to profit-maximize at public expense."[1] Discrete from what Beare has identified as the "money-grubbing" small-time operators or "in-your-face outlaw biker outfits,"[2] the manoeuvres discussed here involve members of a global capitalist class with unquantifiable private wealth that resides within the orbit of state interest but outside of state prosecution. Through tax havens, thinly regulated art markets, and political muscle-flexing to attain global economic power, those elites can hide money out of reach of national policing and regulatory systems. Regrettably for the bottom 20 per cent, such policing activity that does exist can, when scrutinized for burdens of proof, end up protecting those very people who benefit most from private investment schemes.[3] In each of these chapters, we meet economic elites as individuals, groups, networks, or companies that might be charged for overtly criminal acts as defined in black letter regulations but that, when it comes to legal proof or prosecution, are routinely offered deferred prosecutions due to the off-the-books nature of their activities that occupy the grey periphery of legitimate business.[4]

Transparency is anathema to the success of big crime as these chapters illustrate. For tax evaders and avoiders, secrecy is achieved by hiring wealth managers and accountants who, as we are learning from the Panama Papers revelations, favour offshore companies for opaque investment dealings. The deferential treatment offered to those who do attract criminal prosecution can be seen in the "unnamed" status assigned defendants during judicial hearings.[5] For entrepreneurs who hire tax strategists to deflect their wealth from regulatory authorities, the justifications are wide-ranging. As emerita sociology professor

Laureen Snider notes in her chapter, "Big Money, Small Tax: The Normalization of Tax Evasion," elite corruption is enabled by "the abuse of entrusted power for private gain." She provides several examples of the rationale of the tax evader. Most notable are that tax breaks are the entrepreneur's due under neoliberal policies aimed at freeing up global capital and that the 1980s revolution in shareholder value venerates profit maximization above all else. Snider points to former US President Donald Trump for one of the more sinister excuses. It was his assertion that not paying income taxes makes him "smart," based on his conviction that government would have squandered the money in any event.[6]

Snider criticizes that thinking as hegemonic in its promotion of private-sector projects as cheaper and more efficient than public enterprises, leading to the faulty conclusion that taxation merely encourages wasteful government spending. She observes novel justifications for private profit-maximizing among the 1 per cent. For example, the anti-regulation policies of former President Trump allowed and promoted corporate corruption. One of Trump's first moves in office was to introduce an executive order requiring all agencies to cut at least two regulations for every new one introduced.[7] Snider concludes that neoliberal practices that suffused the money markets in the 1980s and 1990s have created the legitimators and enablers of tax evasion. The factor that speaks most directly to the need for policing in this area, in Snider's view, is that the states *themselves* perpetuate their tax haven status. As her chapter concludes, "What *is* surprising is that governments have done so little to stem the bleeding; indeed they may have facilitated it."[8]

Similar "invisibility advantages"[9] can be found within the art investment world. In "Brushstrokes to Keystrokes: Policing Entrepreneurial Art Crime," law professor Elizabeth Kirley describes a world of privileged access to global art investment where forgery of master artworks, as well as infusion of proceeds of crime, are accepted risks among the moneyed ranks. Forgeries are arranged privately. They are created in secrecy, transferred to favoured agents and middlemen who negotiate with other agents and gallery owners who send out discreet inquiries of prospective buyers and so goes the clandestine transaction wheel for the marketing of illicit art. Invisibility and impunity also follow the investor due primarily to offshore freeport facilities and a policing culture that sees the art world's "entrepreneurial linkages between legitimate and illegitimate exchanges"[10] as less likely to garner a conviction than violent crime.

In addition, the *caveat emptor* principle has coloured art crime trials over the centuries, as brokers, connoisseurs, and historians have traditionally demurred when met with opportunities to comment publicly on the wisdom of the deal. For the art forger, secrecy is double-edged. The artist's deception can be justified as the consequence of derailed ambitions. The artist's talents have been overlooked by the academy, so the forger seeks vindication by using those very talents to defraud the art industry. The forger's identity must remain undisclosed, however, a factor that guarantees fame will remain elusive. Another justification of the forger is that s/he has escaped the circle of cronyism that maintains the salon system. Success in the art world is a feedback loop, and those on the inside do not gain from disrupting the status quo. Outside this salon system, the ultimate winner is the investor, working within networks that perpetuate the misapprehension that art fraud harms no one.[11]

For the third chapter in this section, the theme of secrecy is turned on its head: it is the state actors, not the business elite, who use the criminal law to pull a screen over their political motives. The very public arrest of Meng Wanzhou, a senior executive of the major Chinese telecommunications firm Huawei, in Vancouver in 2018 illustrates the complex strategies employed by heads of state to corral ambitious business elites who become entangled in state struggles for dominance of the global trading system. In his chapter, "Criminal Law as a Proxy for Projecting Global Power: The Case of Huawei," law professor Stephen Wilks uses Meng's arrest to critique the ongoing use of US financial regulations for globalizing American power. While the criminal charges announced against Meng were banking and wire fraud, the alleged felony directly relates to communications with an Iranian-based bank that had been the target of a US-imposed trade embargo. Certain reports characterized Huawei's communications with Iran as violating standard business practices. Those communications took place during "politicized trade tensions between China and the Trump administration." After thirty-two months of house arrest in Canada, Meng was offered a deferred prosecution by the US Department of Justice.[12] This case illustrates the use of criminal prosecution to curb the entrepreneurial activities of a major Chinese enterprise that the United States believed was linked to state security activities of the Chinese government.[13]

Wilks takes a broader view of the manipulations behind the Huawei story. He sees a rising protectionism in the United States combined with a politicized trade war with China that has created a climate in which Huawei embodies two contrasting world views. From the US perspective, the management of Huawei is controlled by the Chinese government through the Chinese Communist Party. Such a firm playing a critical role in building telecommunications infrastructure is problematic given concerns about industrial and military crimes of espionage. In contrast, the Chinese government's historical memories and determination to be a central actor in its country's economic ambitions has created entirely different relationships with private actors, producing structural arrangements that would be unheard of in the United States.

Each activity featured in this section – tax evasion, art fraud, and banking fraud – are big crimes in that they involve big investment gains achieved through the secrecy and anonymity that fixers and middlemen can leverage for the wealthy and influential. Margaret Beare grew impatient with efforts to prosecute grey crime, observing that it "more often looks like normalized on-going exchanges"[14] than inner-circle *quid pro quo* agreements. She advised us not to limit our research to cases that expose the privileges that capital allocates to the wealthiest but, rather, to get at how that access to privilege is legitimized through interactions among clients, enablers, and regulators.

The legal challenges of establishing grey crimes beyond a reasonable doubt can be formidable deterrents to police and victims. Are we to give up chasing these cat-and-mouse manoeuvres of fraudsters and deceivers, then? Snider worries that "corruption is practised in plain sight, and its practitioners are not shamed, but honoured." Recognizing that networks and alliances are constantly in flux, she urges a restoration of the consent of the governed. Even in these times of crisis we must recognize opportunities for transformative social change, "piecemeal and uneven and localized as such change always is." For Wilks, the Meng extradition attempts were performative. One compliance system was used to address contrived grievances originating in another. Such cosmetic stunts in international trade relations need to be recognized as a mere distraction from a much more complex legacy of prioritizing private economic interests above all else. And in the world of art fraud, Kirley looks to vastly improved identification technologies to collect evidence of rogue brushstrokes or the faces of fraudsters on the street. Machine learning has just accomplished the feat of converting computer-generated artworks to collectible assets. Payment has gone digital as well. Those advances favour both the detective and the rogue, so public and private galleries need to continue building advantage by sharing intelligence with on-site IT experts. Where once the "tell" of art fraud was in the chemical composition of the artist's palette (lead, ochre, something blue), now the mark of the forger is "the brushstroke that is too faint, too short, or too inconsistent" as detected by algorithms and directed by human will.

NOTES

1 Margaret E. Beare, "Entitled Ease: Social Milieu of Corporate Criminals," *Critical Criminology* 26, no. 4 (2018): 509–26, at 510.
2 Margaret Beare, "Shadow Boxing against the Crimes of the Powerful," in *Revisiting "Crimes of the Powerful,"* edited by Steven Bittle, Laureen Snider, Steve Tombs, and David Whyte (London: Routledge ,2018), 45–59.
3 Snider's chapter discusses the fact that "after the 2017 tax cuts, the 1% get 20%, the bottom 50% merely 12%," citing E. Saez and E. Zucman, *The Triumph of Injustice* (New York: W.W. Norton, 2019).
4 Sanya Ojo, "The Informal and Illegal Entrepreneurship," in *The Evolution of Black African Entrepreneurship in the UK* (London: IGI Global, 2019), chapter 6.
5 Brenda Medina, "Mass Prosecution Forces Mossack Fonseca Back into the Spotlight in Panama," *ICIJ Investigations*, 31 January 2022, https://www.icij.org

/investigations/panama-papers/mass-prosecution-forces-mossack-fonseca-back-into-the-spotlight-in-panama/.

6 D. Mangan, "Trump Brags about Not Paying Taxes: 'That Makes Me Smart,'" CNBC, 26 September 2016, https://www.cnbc.com/2016/09/26/trump-brags-about-not-paying-taxes-that-makes-me-smart.html, as cited by Snider *infra*.

7 US President, Executive Order 13771, Reducing Regulation and Controlling Regulatory Costs, Federal Register, 30 January 2017, https://www.federalregister.gov/documents/2017/02/03/2017-02451/reducing-regulation-and-controlling-regulatory-costs. As noted in this book's Introduction, corruption is also an element of big crime when "the prospect of financial gain can also lead those in positions of either public or private trust to collude in illegal transactions.

8 Citing B. Harrington, *Capital without Borders: Wealth Managers and the One Percent* (Cambridge, MA: Harvard University Press, 2016); and M. Cuenco, "Oh Canada, Our Home and Native Tax Haven," *The Monitor*, Ottawa: Canadian Centre for Policy Alternatives (2019).

9 Beare, "Shadow Boxing," 51.

10 Beare, "Entitled Ease," 510.

11 Magnus Resch, "Moneyball for the Art World," *ArtNews*, 3 December 2018, https://www.artnews.com/art-news/news/moneyball-art-world-11439/. For a more mathematical calculation of an artist's successful career based on the first five exhibitions, see further, Samuel P. Fraiberger et al., "Quantifying Reputation and Success in Art," *Science*, November 2018, https://science.sciencemag.org/content/362/6416/825/.

12 Department of Justice, Office of Public Affairs, "Huawei CFO Wanzhou Meng Admits to Misleading Global Financial Institution," 24 September 2021, https://www.justice.gov/opa/pr/huawei-cfo-wanzhou-meng-admits-misleading-global-financial-institution.

13 Christopher Balding, "Huawei Technologies' Links to Chinese State Security Services," abstract on Elsevier-SSRN, 5 July 2019, http://dx.doi.org/10.2139/ssrn.3415726.

14 Beare, "Entitled Ease," 513.

5 Opportunistic Prosecution? Huawei and the Role of Banking Regulation in China's Trade War with the United States

STEPHEN WILKS

Overview

This chapter uses historical precursors to the 2018 arrest of Meng Wanzhou, senior executive of a major Chinese telecommunications firm, to examine criminal law's proper place in regulating our global trading system. Meng's arrest occurred amid politicized trade tensions between China and the Trump administration. But these tensions were also the result of equivocal commitments to compliance with World Trade Organization (WTO) rules in the decades since China's 2001 entry into the WTO: Faustian bargains struck in exchange for access to China's cheap labour force and growing consumer markets; and class-based grievances originating from globalization's impact on America's industrial heartland – principally through factory closures, mass layoffs, shrinking tax bases, and other socially disruptive outcomes.

There are legitimate concerns about China exerting geopolitical influence through its international trade practices, which have produced significant US trade deficits. This trend in which imports outpace exports has suppressed wages by replacing high-paying manufacturing jobs with service-sector occupations and by forcing domestic producers to drive down production and labour costs as the only way to compete with the influx of low-cost raw materials and consumer goods. Chinese firms have also leveraged the benefit of state subsidies and forced technology transfer to expand their global market share in key industries. This is especially apparent in sectors with growing demand for telecommunications infrastructure – including 5G networks[1] – considered critical to a technologically dependent economy and where there are persistent claims that this infrastructure may also be vulnerable to commercial and military espionage given its role in supporting large-scale data transmission.

But using criminal law to remedy complex and unresolved trade problems is misplaced logic. The discussion below is organized around two arguments. The first argument contends that using blunt prosecutorial instruments signals a concession that adherence to international trading rules – as originally conceived – continues to wreak havoc with Western political economies. The second argument uses Meng's arrest to insist that relying on criminal law to cure longstanding trade tensions is an ill-conceived, performative exercise that does little more than project strength on the international stage.

Meng's Arrest as the Result of Unresolved Trade Conflict

On 1 December 2018, officials at Vancouver International Airport detained Meng Wanzhou, chief financial officer of Chinese telecommunications giant Huawei Technologies Co., Ltd. (Huawei), during a layover en route to Mexico City.[2] Canadian authorities arrested Meng pursuant to an extradition request issued by the United States (US). American regulators alleged Meng made a series of false statements that downplayed the extent of her involvement in Skycom Tech. Co. Ltd. (Skycom), one of Huawei's Iranian subsidiaries. The focus of these allegations centred on the execution of a $1.5 billion syndicated loan orchestrated by Hong Kong Shanghai Banking Corporation (HSBC); the clearance of dollar transactions by HSBC's US subsidiaries over a ten-year period, contravening the *International Emergency Economic Powers Act* (IEEPA);[3] and statements Meng made to HSBC's compliance officers in 2013, which allegedly understated the extent of Huawei's ongoing relationship with Skycom.[4]

While the US rationale for these proceedings was couched in national security terms, officials also adopted a trade-related posture. Approximately nine weeks after Meng's arrest, the US Department of Justice (DOJ) announced the unsealing of a thirteen-count indictment charging Meng, Huawei, and two of its affiliates.[5] In addition to outlining the allegations against Meng – who was charged with bank fraud, wire fraud, and conspiracies to commit bank and wire fraud[6] – officials characterized Huawei's conduct as evidence of its disregard for "standard global business practices."[7] The "business practices" at issue had evolved over decades, thanks to substantial support from the Chinese government and the Communist Party of China (CPC).

Based in Shenzhen, China, Huawei was founded in 1987 by Ren Zhengfi, an engineer and entrepreneur whose initial business involved the sale, installation, and maintenance of telephone equipment. The company eventually developed expertise in building telecommunications networks and providing consulting expertise to clients worldwide. Huawei was formed at a time when China was already amid a series of reforms initiated by Den Xiaoping in the late 1970s.[8] These reforms included restoring participation in the General Agreement on Tariffs and Trade (GATT), ending a hiatus prompted by the Communist Revolution;[9] pursuing trade agreements with thirty-seven GATT/WTO countries over a fifteen-year period ending in 1999;[10] and gaining entry into the WTO in 2001.[11] In negotiating its entry into the WTO, China undertook to:

(1) open its market; (2) improve protections for intellectual property rights; (3) replace differential treatment enjoyed by developing countries with a most-favoured-nation (MFN) protocol;[12] and (4) agree to other terms under accession protocols.[13]

Enacted in 2000 to complement China's entry into the WTO, Section 421 of the *Trade Act* of 1974 (Trade Act) reflected a US legislative attempt to help liberalize China's economy and to steer it towards integration with Western markets.[14] This provision authorized the president to impose import controls or take other action where the US International Trade Commission (ITC) determined certain imported goods were a "substantial cause of serious injury, or threat" to a domestic industry producing similar or competitive products.[15]

Bilateral commitments to abide by the letter and spirit of WTO rules did not last long. China did lower tariffs and eliminate import quotas. But it also pursued sweeping interventionist programs, including currency manipulation,[16] asserting managerial influence over entities that were either state-owned or heavily subsidized,[17] and resorted to rent-seeking behaviours – such as requiring that foreign firms hand over technical expertise and relinquish intellectual property rights before entering its markets.[18] Between 2006 and 2015, a quarter of all WTO complaints – forty-four in total – involved China.[19]

The United States also failed to fully honour its end of the bilateral bargain by taking an inconsistent approach to enforcing trade rules. George W. Bush was the first American president in office after China became a WTO member. Bush repeatedly rejected ITC recommendations when US businesses brought Section 421 complaints challenging Chinese trade practices – twice in 2003,[20] once in 2004,[21] and again in 2005[22] – out of apparent concern for the entire economy rather than a complaining party's particular industry.[23] Although there were United States Trade Representative (USTR) delegates willing to bring complaints directly to the WTO – it initiated seven between 2004 and 2008[24] – both Bush and the private sector preferred informal dialogue and dispute settlements:[25]

> Bush's advisors ... worried that if one industry got protection under the safeguard, virtually every US manufacturer competing with Chinese imports would be clamoring for similar treatment. That would put the entire US-China trade relationship at risk, and US multinationals – which were reaping big profits in the Chinese market – lobbied heavily to avoid any major disruptions.[26]

Complex co-dependencies gradually emerged to shape China's relationship with the United States. As Americans enjoyed cheap consumer goods, China monetized its vast labour pool, lifting millions of its citizens out of poverty while fuelling rapid middle-class expansion. There were also extensive Chinese reinvestments in capital markets around the world, which included buying US

Treasury Bonds as well as investing in Fannie Mae and Freddie Mac (which helped Americans access affordable mortgages). While their economic relationship had its flaws, neither China nor the United States wanted to risk damaging larger structural arrangements that had become successful by-products of trade liberalization.

But the 2007–9 recession revealed much about the two countries' contrasting responses to what had become a global financial crisis. Whereas the US government prioritized bailing out financial institutions, China faced the prospect of millions of Chinese workers being idled by a drop in orders from Western buyers. The Chinese government issued a $586 billion emergency stimulus package for projects such as low-income housing, education, electrification, education, and transportation.[27] The country's central bank also intervened, cutting interest rates, doubling its lending target, and requiring banks to generously extend credit.[28] While these responses were fundamentally at odds with China's WTO commitments, they revealed how China's interventionism offered a strategic alternative to dependency on a consumptive US economy.

Chinese trade practices have continued to prompt adjudicative and multilateral responses. The United States has initiated nearly two dozen actions as of 2020,[29] and the USTR maintains that China continues to disregard WTO panel or appellate rulings.[30] The USTR also alleges that China abuses WTO remedies, such as anti-dumping and countervailing duty investigations, as a strategy to dissuade WTO countries from exercising rights under existing rules.[31] During his presidency, Barack Obama tried neutering China's regional and global influence through the Trans-Pacific Partnership (TPP). Signed on 5 February 2016, the TPP was a multilateral arrangement that required China to accept new trading terms and submit to additional demands as a condition of congressional ratification.[32] Obama deliberately excluded China from the rulemaking process while making it the TPP's primary target.[33] TPP negotiations gave signatory states better trade privileges than those available to WTO members. The Obama administration also crafted TPP provisions in response to claims that China had used its WTO membership to access foreign markets without honouring rules – particularly through its maintenance of trade barriers, the ongoing subsidy of state-owned enterprises, and the violation of intellectual property rights.[34]

The TPP eventually fell prey to rising disaffection among a swath of US voters. Having experienced some combination of wage degradation, unemployment, and community erosion, these Americans grew hostile to governments presiding over a global trading system that was decimating working classes throughout the industrialized world. As David Frum observed, a mix of politicized nationalism and scepticism about the markets created an outlook that differed from 1980s-era conservative moments:

The rise of these nationalist parties is forcing a rearrangement of the political grammar of the developed world. The conservative parties of the 1980s defended markets and were skeptical of economic redistribution. The nationalist movements of the 2010s are skeptical of markets and defend economic redistribution, provided that the redistribution benefits people of the correct ethnic stock and cultural outlook.[35]

These structural changes altered the consensus historically underpinning liberal democracies. Government, civil society, and the private sector had repositioned themselves in response to globalization. Americans have experienced these trends, most significantly in the declining fortunes of workers across America's industrial heartland and in the corresponding deterioration of their communities due to shrinking tax bases.[36] Widening income inequality and social cleaving along the lines of education – particularly among white, middle-aged men – produced greater receptiveness to politicians openly embracing racism and xenophobia, and it hardened attitudes towards legal and illegal immigration.[37] Once in control of governments, these politicians signalled sympathy for declining faith in trade liberalization – most notably through disengagement from multilateral agreements, protectionist rhetoric, politicized trade disputes, and weakening commitments to existing multilateral trade relationships.

Donald Trump's successful 2016 presidential campaign crafted a populist appeal rooted in this zeitgeist and promised supporters America would get "tough" with China. Trump made good on his promise, albeit in ways that were more performative than constructive. A day after his inauguration, Trump issued a Presidential Memorandum announcing the United States' withdrawal from the TPP on 23 January 2017.[38] In August of the same year, the Trump administration commenced an investigation into China's trade practices under Section 301 of the Trade Act.[39] Sections 301 through 310 are often collectively described as "Section 301" and authorize the imposition of trade sanctions on countries that: (1) violate trade agreements with the United States or (2) resort to conduct deemed an "unjustifiable" or "unreasonable" burden on American commerce. Predating WTO dispute resolution mechanisms, Section 301 was conceived as a means to pressure countries to reduce barriers and open their markets.[40] Looking to this statute as an alternative to initiating further WTO action reflected a new phase in America's relationship with the WTO and fits within a pattern of disengagement from multilateral processes that was a defining feature of Trump's presidency.[41]

The USTR's seven-month investigation culminated in a lengthy report focusing on China's unmet commitments to change its technology transfer strategies.[42] Most relevant to the present discussion, the report alleged: (1) that the Chinese government worked through foreign ownership restrictions to require or pressure the transfer of technology from US companies to Chinese entities;[43] (2) that China used technology regulations to interfere with American firms' freedom to bargain for terms of technology transfer without Chinese government intrusion;[44] (3) that China had heavily invested in Chinese entities as part of a large-scale outbound direct foreign investment strategy to acquire or invest in US firms in an effort to expand its market share and to secure technology assets – especially in Europe and the United States;[45] and (4) that China had resorted to industrial espionage through a program of cyber intrusions into American commercial networks.[46]

As the Section 301 investigations were unfolding over the summer and fall of 2017, the United States and China entered into trade talks, which proved unsuccessful, setting off a series of tariffs and retaliatory tariffs.[47] Starting in January 2018, there were: (1) US tariffs on imported washing machines and solar panels[48] and (2) 25 per cent tariffs on imported steel and 10 per cent on imported aluminium.[49] China retaliated by imposing 25 per cent tariffs on 128 products.[50] Over the next eighteen months, "tit-for-tat" measures between the two countries created supply-chain problems for US firms that were either obtaining raw materials from foreign sources or selling goods to Chinese markets.[51]

The US tariffs between the United States and China, which began in 2018, would continue escalating over the summer of 2019, destroying supply-chain relationships that had been years in the making.[52] Contrary to political campaign promises, surging imports from Canada, Mexico, and other countries diminished any expectation that imposing tariffs on Chinese goods would somehow repatriate American jobs lost during the preceding thirty years.[53]

Huawei as the Corporate Embodiment of US Trade Grievances

By the time of Meng's 2018 arrest, Huawei had become a global behemoth, with hundreds of institutional clients – including thirty-five carriers, over two hundred Fortune Global 500 companies, and more than seven hundred municipalities.[54] Through its workforce of 194,000 employees in more than 170 countries, the company developed and sold a range of products and services that allowed it to secure a dominant share of the global telecommunications market.[55] But Huawei was now caught up in the widening US–China trade dispute where national security concerns were invoked to address long-term consequences of inconsistent adherence to WTO trade rules.

While there is no evidence that Huawei's equipment has supported commercial or military espionage,[56] rhetoric regarding its national security risks have persisted thanks to the company's leadership history, its ties to the Chinese government, and its global reach. Huawei's founder was a member of the People's Liberation Army and remains a member of the Chinese Communist Party (CCP). Huawei's current rotating Chairman of the Board is also a CCP member. Federal Bureau of Investigations (FBI) Director Christopher Wray outlined these concerns during a 2018 Senate Intelligence Committee Hearing, suggesting Huawei might use its infrastructure to harvest data at the Chinese government's behest.[57]

But US efforts to target Huawei transcended national security concerns and reflected perceptions that Huawei was simply an agent of Beijing without overtly saying as much. Wray's comments came six years after a 2012 House Intelligence Committee Report, which expressed broader geopolitical concerns – "that Huawei's global expansion, in and of itself, can serve as vector for Beijing's influence."[58] Yet the national security arguments seemed to serve as the impetus for subsequent legislation banning Huawei from securing contracts with federal government agencies.[59] US officials also discouraged use of the company's handsets and pressured other countries to exclude the company from 5G projects.[60] These efforts produced limited effect, with only Australia, New Zealand, and the United Kingdom acquiescing to American demands.[61]

Remarkably, the narratives surrounding these tactics hardly discuss the degree to which Huawei has benefited from Chinese trade policies, particularly those targeting the telecommunications field. Nor do they acknowledge the extensive role Western firms played in working through joint ventures that served as frameworks for forced technology transfer. In the 1970s, China expressed interest in forming joint ventures with Western telecommunications firms willing to share their technology in exchange for accessing its markets. Only one firm – Bell Telephone Manufacturing Company (BTM), a Belgian subsidiary of US telecom giant ITT – accepted China's proposal.

BTM's joint venture with China's Ministry of Posts and Telecommunications quickly sprang to life after its US parent company and the Belgian government successfully lobbied for an exception to multilateral rules restricting the sale of technologies and strategic assets to Communist countries.[62] Through this arrangement, BTM transferred its US parent's System 12 digital telephone exchange system – then the most advanced of its kind in the world – to its Chinese partner, Shanghai Bell.[63] With support from the Belgian government, the venture not only facilitated the transfer of technologies for chips and components, it provided training to Chinese engineers. The Chinese government leveraged the benefits of the BTM venture in several ways. Domestic firms were required to buy equipment from Shanghai Bell at subsidized rates. Shanghai Bell, in turn, enjoyed reductions in taxes and tariffs on imported goods.[64] This joint venture became the prototypical precondition China imposed on outside firms wanting access to its markets.

Well-known firms, such as Siemens, Fujitsu, Lucent, NEC, Motorola, Ericsson, and Nortel, eventually followed suit, forming joint ventures that did more than simply hand over technology.[65] The Chinese government ensured domestic firms and engineers accessed training opportunities connected to these joint ventures. Western firms established massive research and development hubs where Chinese engineers absorbed much of the technological expertise that would find its way into indigenous production.[66] Similar activities occurred through strategic relationships with universities and research institutes. China's military also contributed to this activity, with the result that more than six hundred thousand engineers were involved in research and development in the telecommunications and high-tech sectors.[67] Huawei benefited from all of these developments. It was not only immersed in the diffusion of technical "know-how" but also secured direct government funding as a "national laboratory" – a designation that unlocked funding historically set aside for universities and research institutions.

Huawei found other ways to benefit from this large-scale, government-driven push to domestically repurpose Western telecommunications expertise. In 1991 the advent of the HJD-04 digital telephone switch – the first system of its kind to be developed in China – spawned the creation of other such systems.[68] Using higher salaries and its desirable Shenzhen location to recruit engineers involved with HJD-04, Huawei eventually created its own system known as C&C08. As China's domestic capabilities took root, the company capitalized on tariffs and government incentives that effectively pressured Chinese telecom providers to buy their equipment from domestic firms[69] – a practice that continues to this day. In April 2020, for example, China Mobile awarded $5.2 billion in contracts to build out 232,143 base stations in connection with the roll out of its 5G network.[70] Even though Ericsson's contract bid appeared to be most competitive in terms of price and quality,[71] it only received 11.5 per cent of the contract – while Huawei received the largest share at 57 per cent.[72]

Tens of billions in state-backed loans, credit lines, tax relief, and tied aid programs also propelled Huawei's global expansion. The company could underbid competitors when competing for contracts and extend more generous financing terms to buyers. Huawei's products and services were also tied to aid to developing countries that were required to use Chinese products and services.

While such trade practices were common throughout many industries, foreign firms that might normally complain were reluctant to challenge China for fear of losing access to its lucrative market. For example, in September 2010, Japan filed a WTO complaint challenging provisions of Ontario's "green energy" statute.[73] The challenge centred on stipulations that local technology producers would provide a minimum percentage of the province's renewable energy. Anxious to avoid any tensions, Japan has never filed such a complaint in connection with China's green energy strategy, which is unfolding on a much larger scale in its backyard.[74] This selective approach to WTO enforcement reveals the nature of China's rent-seeking power in a global trading system where some actors are willing to look past the flouting of trade rules in service of their economic dependency on Chinese markets.

China's trading practices have produced important pricing effects in telecommunications sectors. Complex factors shape the "make or buy" decisions Western firms undertake during supply-chain formation, when the costs of purchasing intermediate goods are weighed against manufacturing them. As beneficiaries of massive state support, firms like Huawei can distort such analyses by flooding the global marketplace with intermediate goods made at a cost Western firms cannot match. China's extensive subsidies also mask the real cost of production, distorting prices to an extent that destroys incentives to pursue research and development in the West where "buying" becomes cheaper than "making," and where new commercial dependencies on foreign production can leave Western firms strategically vulnerable.

The Folly of Jailing Executives to Regulate Trade

In seeking to extradite Meng on the pretext of *International Emergency Economic Powers Act* (IEEPA) violations, the Trump administration purported to rely on one compliance system to address contrived grievances originating from another. But this was largely cosmetic and ineffective. The arrest was part of a larger, ill-conceived strategy of inserting an aggressive tone into the US–China relationship. Despite its populist appeal, this approach was performative at best – resulting in job losses,[75] supply-chain disruptions,[76] and increased costs to manufacturers and consumers.[77] A 2019 study released by the Federal Reserve system concluded Trump's trade dispute with China had produced little economic benefit:

> We find that tariff increases enacted in 2018 are associated with relative reductions in manufacturing employment and relative increases in producer prices. In terms of manufacturing employment, rising input costs and retaliatory tariffs each contribute to the negative relationship, and the contribution from these channels more than offsets a small positive effect from import protection.[78]

While there was some historical validity in Trump's framing of trade-related grievances as giving China the upper hand, the current state of play within the global trading system reflects a set of intentional choices. The mix of diplomatic and commercial calculations that signalled inconsistent commitment to WTO compliance did more than give China the upper hand within the global economy. It revealed the extent to which profit-seeking – often with state support – eclipsed any regard for globalization's social and structural effects on the body politic within Western economies.

In pretending to ignore America's historical role in creating problems it did not intend to fix, the Trump White House also seemed unconcerned with the collateral effects of Meng's arrest on Canada, its largest trading partner.

Trade ties to China and its obligations as signatory to an extradition treaty with the United States put the Canadian government in a difficult position, given China's demands for Meng's release.[79] The three-way impasse has triggered the retaliatory arrest of two Canadians by Chinese police, the blocking of Canadian imports to China, and the denial of entry visas for trade delegates trying to negotiate an end to the impasse.[80] Using criminal law powers to jail a Chinese executive for violating economic sanctions is merely a distraction from a much more complex legacy of prioritizing private economic interests above all else.

NOTES

1 "5G" is shorthand for the telecommunications industry's fifth generation of technical standards for cellular networks. Telecommunications firms around the world began deploying 5G networks in 2019.
2 Daisuke Wakabayashi and Alan Rappeport, "Huawei CFO Is Arrested in Canada for Extradition to the US," *New York Times*, 5 December 2018, https://www.nytimes.com/2018/12/05/business/huawei-cfo-arrest-canada-extradition.html.
3 50 USC. ch. 35 § 1701 *et seq.*
4 Department of Justice, "Chinese Telecommunications Conglomerate Huawei and Huawei CFO Wanzhou Meng Charged with Financial Fraud," *Justice News*, 28 January 2019, https://www.justice.gov/opa/pr/chinese-telecommunications-conglomerate-huawei-and-huawei-cfo-wanzhou-meng-charged-financial.
5 DOJ, "Chinese Telecommunications Conglomerate."
6 DOJ, "Chinese Telecommunications Conglomerate."
7 DOJ, "Chinese Telecommunications Conglomerate."
8 Simon Lester and Huan Zhu, "The US-China Trade War: Is There an End in Sight?" *Cato Journal* 40, no. 1 (2020): 15. Unfortunately, the scope of this discussion does not include examination of China's seventeenth- and eighteenth-century experience with Western powers forcing their way into Chinese markets. For a useful discussion of how this history overshadows China's contemporary trade negotiations with the United States, see Alan Rappeport, "19th Century 'Humiliation' Haunts China-US Trade Talks," *New York Times*, 27 March 2019, https://www.nytimes.com/2019/03/27/us/politics/china-opium-wars-trade-talks.html.
9 Henry Gao, "China's Participation in the WTO: A Lawyer's Perspective," *Singapore Year Book of International Law* (2007): 11, 41.
10 Lester and Zhu, "The US-China Trade War," 16.
11 World Trade Organization, "Member Information: China and the WTO," accessed 11 July 2020, https://www.wto.org/english/thewto_e/countries_e/china_e.htm.
12 Under the WTO rules, a most-favoured-nation (MFN) clause requires signatories to grant concessions, privileges, or immunities granted to one nation in a trade

agreement to all member countries. See World Trade Organization, "Principles of the Trading System," http://tinyurl.com/yfe7z2v.
13 Approval for the entry of a new member into the WTO includes "The Protocol of Accession of the new entrant ... annexed to the Report which states that the country accedes to the WTO Agreement, defines the Schedules and outlines final provisions for timing of acceptance of the Protocol and full membership of the WTO." World Trade Organization, "How to Become a Member of the WTO," accessed 11 July 2020, https://www.wto.org/english/thewto_e/acc_e/acces_e.htm. The Accession Protocols generated in connection with China's WTO entry can be found at: World Trade Organization, Annex 8 (Revised) to the Draft Protocol on the Accession of China of 18 June 2001, WT/ACC/CHN/42 (2001), https://www.wto.org/english/thewto_e/acc_e/a1_chine_e.htm.
14 Trade Act of 1974, § 423(c), 19 USC. § 2451b(c).
15 See generally, United States Senate Committee on Finance, Senate Report on the Trade Reform Act of 1974, Vance Hartke. Report 93–1298, at 210–13, n 406, "Market Disruption," Washington, DC, 1974. The purpose of the report is "to provide an effective remedy against market disruption caused by imports from communist countries."
16 Paul Blustein, "The Untold Story of How George W. Bush Lost China," *Foreign Policy*, 2 October 2019.
17 Blustein, "The Untold Story."
18 Blustein, "The Untold Story."
19 Mark Wu, "The 'China, Inc.' Challenge to Global Trade Governance," *Harvard International Law Journal* 47, no. 2 (2016): 262–3, 57.
20 Pedestal Actuators from China, Inv. No. TA-421-1, USITC Pub. 3557 (November 2002); Memorandum on Pedestal Actuator Imports from the People's Republic of China, *Weekly Comp. Pres. Doc.* 39 (17 January 2003): 82; Certain Steel Wire Garment Hangers from China, Inv. TA421-2, USITC Pub. 3575 (February 2003); Memorandum on Wire Hanger Imports from the People's Republic of China, *Weekly Comp. Pres. Doc.* 39 (25 April 2003): 492.
21 Certain Ductile Iron Waterworks Fittings from China, Inv. TA-421-4, USITC Pub. 3642 (October 2003); Memorandum on Imports of Certain Ductile Iron Waterworks Fittings from the People's Republic of China, 40 *Weekly Comp. Pres. Doc.* 40 (3 March 2004): 331.
22 Circular Welded Non-Alloy Steel Pipe from China, Inv. TA-421-6, USITC Pub. 3807 (October 2005); Presidential Determination on Imports of Circular Welded Non-Alloy Steel Pipe from the People's Republic of China, *Weekly Comp. Pres. Doc.*41 (30 December 2005): 1921.
23 Blustein, "The Untold Story."
24 Request for Consultations by the United States, "China-Value-Added Tax on Integrated Circuits," WTO Doc. WT/DS309/1 (23 March 2004), https://www.wto.org/english/tratop_e/dispu_e/cases_e/ds309_e.htm; Request for Consultations

by the United States, "China–Measures Affecting Imports of Automobile Parts," WTO Doc. WT/DS340/1 (3 April 2006), https://www.wto.org/english/tratop_e/dispu_e/cases_e/ds340_e.htm; Request for Consultations by the United States, "China – Certain Measures Granting Refunds, Reductions or Exemptions from Taxes and Other Payments," WTO Doc. WT/DS358/1 (7 February 2007); Request for Consultations by the United States, "China – Measures Affecting the Protection and Enforcement of Intellectual Property Rights," WTO Doc. WT/DS362/1 (16 April 2007); Request for Consultations by the United States, "China – Measures Affecting Trading Rights and Distribution Services for Certain Publications and Audiovisual Entertainment Products," WTO Doc. WT/DS363/1 (16 April 2007); Request for Consultations by the United States, "China – Measures Affecting Financial Information Services and Foreign Financial Information Suppliers," WTO Doc. WT/DS373/1 (5 March 2008); Request for Consultations by the United States, "China – Grants, Loans and Other Incentives," WTO Doc. WT/DS387/1 (7 January 2009).
25 Lester and Zhu, "The US-China Trade War," 18.
26 Blustein, "The Untold Story."
27 Blustein, "The Untold Story"; Wu, "The 'China, Inc.' Challenge," 277.
28 Blustein, "The Untold Story."
29 US Trade Representative, Exec. Office of the President, 2019 Report to Congress on China's WTO Compliance 7 (2020) [hereinafter USTR 2019 Report] ("The United States ... has brought nearly two dozen cases against China at the WTO covering a wide range of important policies and practices, such as: (1) local content requirements in the automobile sector; (2) discriminatory taxes in the integrated circuit sector; (3) hundreds of prohibited subsidies in a wide range of manufacturing sectors; (4) inadequate intellectual property rights (IPR) enforcement in the copyright area; (5) significant market access barriers in copyright-intensive industries; (6) severe restrictions on foreign suppliers of financial information services; (7) export restraints on numerous raw materials; (8) a denial of market access for foreign suppliers of electronic payment services; (9) repeated abusive use of trade remedies; (10) excessive domestic support for key agricultural commodities; (11) the opaque and protectionist administration of tariff-rate quotas for key agricultural commodities; and (12) discriminatory regulations on technology licensing."); Lester and Zhu, "The US-China Trade War," 19.
30 USTR 2019 Report (2020): 7.
31 USTR 2019 Report (2020): 7.
32 Daniel C.K. Chow, "How the United States Uses the Trans-Pacific Partnership to Contain China in International Trade," *Chicago Journal of International Law* 17, no. 2 (2016): 370.
33 Chow, "Trans-Pacific Partnership," 374.
34 Chow, "Trans-Pacific Partnership," 374.

35 David Frum, "Faith, Reason, and Immigration," *The Atlantic*, 21 March 2019, https://www.theatlantic.com/ideas/archive/2019/03/david-frum-reacts-immigration-responses/585391/.

36 For example, see Robert Ginsburg, "What Plant Closings Cost a Community: The Hard Data," *Labor Research Review* 1 (1994): 22; Wendy Patton and Zach Schiller, "Hard Times at City Halls: Localities Struggle with Damaged Tax Base, State Cuts," *Policy Matters Ohio*, 7 January 2015, https://www.policymattersohio.org/research-policy/quality-ohio/revenue-budget/budget-policy/hard-times-at-city-halls-localities-struggle-with-damaged-tax-base-state-cuts.

37 Stephen C. Wilks, "A Complicated Alchemy: Theorizing Identity Politics and the Politicization of Migrant Remittances under Donald Trump's Presidency," *Cornell International Law Journal* 50, no. 2 (2017): 285.

38 Withdrawal of the United States from the Trans-Pacific Partnership Negotiations and Agreement, 82 Fed. Reg. 8,497 (23 January 2017).

39 Title III of the Trade Act of 1974 (Sections 301 through 310, 19 USC. §§2411–2420).

40 Andres B. Schwarzenberg, *Congressional Research Service*, IF11346, Section 301 of the Trade Act of 1974, 1 (2020),https://crsreports.congress.gov/product/pdf/IF/IF11346.

41 Martin Finucane and Jeremiah Manion, "Trump Has Pulled Out of International Agreements Before. Here's a List," *Boston Globe*, 1 February 2019, https://www.bostonglobe.com/metro/2019/02/01/trump-has-pulled-out-international-agreements-before-here-list/H9zTo2ctVEQ0b8xkUQ2t9J/story.html; Alex Pascal, "Against Washington's 'Great Power' Obsession," *The Atlantic*, 23 September 2019, https://www.theatlantic.com/politics/archive/2019/09/multi-lateralism-nearly-dead-s-terrible-news/598615/.

42 US Trade Representative, Exec. Office of the President, 2020 Report to Findings of the Investigation into China's Acts, Policies, and Practices Related to Technology Transfer, Intellectual Property, and Innovation Under s.301 of the Trade Act of 1974, 6 (22 March 2018) [hereinafter S. 301 Report]. This was not the USTR's first report canvassing pathways to engineer China's compliance with WTO rules. See US Trade Representative, Exec. Office of the President, "US-China Trade Relations: Entering a New Phase of Greater Accountability and Enforcement" (February 2006).

43 S. 301 Report.

44 S. 301 Report.

45 S. 301 Report.

46 S. 301 Report. For a scholarly perspective on these arguments, see Emilio Iasiello, "China's Three Warfares Strategy Mitigates Fallout from Cyber Espionage Activities," *Journal of Strategic Security* 9, no. 2 (2016): 45 ("China is engaged in longstanding cyber espionage against the US, as well as other nations, to collect sensitive public and private information in support of national objectives laid out in its 12th Five Year Plan."); See also Teng Jianqun, "Trump's America First Security Strategy: Impact on China-US Relations," *China International Studies* 70 (2018): 116, 122.

47 "US, China Fail to Agree on Trade, Casting Doubt on Other Issues," CNBC, 19 July 2017, https://www.cnbc.com/2017/07/19/us-china-comprehensive-economic-dialogue-disagreement-over-how-to-reduce-trade-deficit-official-says.html.
48 Richard Gonzales, "Trump Slaps Tariffs on Imported Solar Panels and Washing Machines," NPR, 22 January 2018, https://www.npr.org/sections/thetwo-way/2018/01/22/579848409/trump-slaps-tariffs-on-imported-solar-panels-and-washing-machines.
49 Proclamation No. 9705, 83 Fed. Reg. 11,625 (8 March 2018); Proclamation No. 9704, 83 Fed. Reg. 11,619 (8 March 2018).
50 Heather Timmons, "Timeline: Key Dates in the US-China Trade War," *Reuters*, 15 January 2020, https://www.reuters.com/article/us-usa-trade-china-timeline/timeline-key-dates-in-the-u-s-china-trade-war-idUSKBN1ZE1AA.
51 See David Dollar and Peter A. Petri, "Why It's Time to End the Tit-for-Tat Tariffs in the U.S-China Trade War," *Brookings*, 5 October 2018, https://www.brookings.edu/blog/order-from-chaos/2018/10/05/why-its-time-to-end-the-tit-for-tat-tariffs-in-the-u-s-china-trade-war/.
52 Ronald C. Brown, "Up and Down the Multinational Corporations' Global Labor Supply Chains: Making Remedies That Work in China," *UCLA Pacific Basin Law Journal* 34, no. 2 (2017): 103, 107.
53 Lester and Zhu, "The US-China Trade War," 21.
54 Lester and Zhu, "The US-China Trade War," 3.
55 "IEEE Communications Society, Technology Blog, "Dell'Oro: #1 Huawei Increased Market Share at the Expense of Ericsson, Nokia and ZTE; Mobile CAPEX Flat; 5G Market Forecasts," 10 March 2019, https://techblog.comsoc.org/2019/03/10/delloro-1-huawei-increased-market-share-at-the-expense-of-ericsson-nokia-and-zte-capex-flat-5g-market-forecasts/; Stefan Pongratz, "Huawei and ZTE Increased Their Revenue Shares while Nokia and Cisco's Revenue Shares Declined for the Full Year 2019," The Telecom Equipment Market, Dell'Oro Group: 2019, https://www.delloro.com/the-telecom-equipment-market-2019/.
56 In April 2021 the press revealed a 2010 confidential report concluding that Huawei "could have" been monitoring calls made on a network belonging to KPN, a Dutch mobile phone network. Acknowledging the report's existence, KPN insisted it "never observed that Huawei took client information." The company maintained that none of its suppliers had "unauthorised, uncontrolled or unlimited access to our networks and systems." See John Henley, "Huawei 'May Have Eavesdropped on Dutch Mobile Network's Calls,'" *The Guardian*, 19 April 2021, https://www.theguardian.com/technology/2021/apr/19/huawei-may-have-eavesdropped-on-dutch-mobile-networks-calls?CMP=Share_iOSApp_Other.
57 Open Hearing on Worldwide Threats: Hearing Before the S. Comm. on Intelligence, 115th Cong. 64–65 (2018) (statement of Christopher Wray, Dir., Fed. Bureau of Investigation).

58 Mike Rogers and Dutch Ruppersberger, *Investigative Report on the US National Security Issues Posed by Chinese Telecommunications Companies Huawei and Zte* (2012) 3, 31, 42, 44. Similar comments have come from others. For example, see Elsa Kania, "Much Ado about Huawei," parts 1 and 2, in *Huawei and Australia's 5G Network*, edited by Danielle Cave, Elsa Kania, Tom Uren, et al., Australian Strategic Policy Institute, 10 October 2018, https://ad-aspi.s3.ap-southeast-2.amazonaws.com/2018-10/Huawei%20and%20Australias%205G%20Network.pdf?VersionId=wk2qurC5OGPs1DZmePkkYm_bKw8Rn5Yj. She writes at p. 5: "At a time when Huawei is actively pursuing commercial opportunities and collaborations worldwide, any deliberate introduction of vulnerabilities into its products or networks would clearly contradict its own corporate interests. However, it's clear that Huawei's global expansion, in and of itself, can serve as vector for Beijing's influence."

59 US Congress, John S. McCain National Defense Authorization Act for Fiscal Year 2019 § 889(a), (f(3)(A), 132 Stat. at 1917–18, https://www.congress.gov/bill/115th-congress/house-bill/5515/text.

60 Grace Sullivan, "The Kaspersky, ZTE, and Huawei Sagas: Why the United States Is in Desperate Need of a Standardized Method for Banning Foreign Federal Contractors," *Public Contract Law Journal* 49 (2020): 323, 334.

61 Matthew S. Schwartz, "In Reversal, UK Will Ban Huawei Equipment from Its 5G Network," NPR, 14 July 2020, https://www.npr.org/2020/07/14/890812517/in-reversal-u-k-will-ban-huawei-equipment-from-its-5g-network;"Huawei and ZTE Handed 5G Network Ban in Australia," BBC, 23 August 2018, https://www.bbc.com/news/technology-45281495; Ian Young, "Canada Faces New Pressure to Block Huawei from 5G, after UK Ban Risks Marooning Ottawa from Five Eyes Intelligence Allies," *South China Morning Post*, 14 July 2020, https://www.scmp.com/news/china/diplomacy/article/3093198/canada-faces-new-pressure-block-huawei-5g-after-uk-ban-risks.

62 Xiaobai Shen, The Chinese Road to High Technology: A Study of Telecommunications Switching Technology in the Economic Transition (New York: St. Martin's Press, 1999), 64.

63 Shen, *The Chinese Road to High Technology*, 64. For a useful discussion of telecommunications development in China, see Eric Harwit, "Building China's Telecommunications Network: Industrial Policy and the Role of Chinese State-Owned, Foreign and Private Domestic Enterprises," *The China Quarterly* 190 (June 2007): 311–32.

64 Robert D. Atkinson, "How China's Mercantilist Policies Have Undermined Global Innovation in the Telecom Equipment Industry," *Information Technology & Innovation Foundation*, https://itif.org/publications/2020/06/22/how-chinas-mercantilist-policies-have-undermined-global-innovation-telecom.

65 Atkinson, "China's Mercantilist Policies."
66 Atkinson, "China's Mercantilist Policies."
67 Atkinson, "China's Mercantilist Policies."

68 Atkinson, "China's Mercantilist Policies."
69 There were even governmental evaluations assessing the extent of each firm's support for Chinese firms on the basis of domestically sourced supplies.
70 Mingas, "Huawei, ZTE and Ericsson."
71 Atkinson, "China's Mercantilist Policies."
72 Mingas, "Huawei, ZTE and Ericsson."
73 "*Certain Measures Affecting the Renewable Energy Generation Sector*," Request for Consultations (Japan-Canada), WT/DS412/1, 16 September 2010, http://www.wto.org/english/tratop_e/dispu_e/cases_e/ds412_e.htm; *Green Energy and Green Economy Act, 2009*, S.O. 2009, c. 12 (Can. Ont.).
74 Keith Bradsher, "To Conquer Wind Power, China Writes the Rules," *New York Times*, 14 December 2010, https://www.nytimes.com/2010/12/15/business/global/15chinawind.html.
75 Katia Dmitrieva, "Factory Job Losses Send New Warning Signal to Trump on Trade War," *Bloomberg*, 6 October 2019, https://www.bloomberg.com/news/articles/2019-10-06/factory-job-losses-send-new-warning-signal-to-trump-on-trade-war; Jon Basil Utley, "Trump's Trade War Has Dire Consequences," *The American Conservative*, 6 November 2019, https://www.theamericanconservative.com/articles/trumps-trade-war-has-consequences/.
76 Anthony Rowley, "How Trump's Trade War Has Morphed into an Attack on Global Tech Supply Chain Networks, *South China Morning Post*, 3 June 2019, https://www.scmp.com/comment/opinion/article/3012656/how-trumps-trade-war-has-morphed-attack-global-tech-supply-chain.
77 David Lawder, "Drag from Trump's Trade Wars Continues to Ripple through US Economy," *Reuters*, 14 January 2020, https://www.reuters.com/article/us-usa-trade-china-effects/drag-from-trumps-trade-wars-continues-to-ripple-through-u-s-economy-idUSKBN1ZD2GU; Katheryn Russ, "What Trump's Tariffs Have Cost the US Economy," PBS, 11 October 2019, https://www.pbs.org/newshour/economy/making-sense/what-trumps-tariffs-have-cost-the-u-s-economy; Shawn Tully, "Trump's Tariffs Were Supposed to Ding China, but the US Economy Is Getting Hit 2.5x Harder," *Fortune*, 8 October 2019, https://fortune.com/2019/10/08/trump-china-tariffs-trade-war-us-economy-impact/.
78 Aaron Flaaen and Justin Pierce, "Disentangling the Effects of the 2018–2019 Tariffs on a Globally Connected US Manufacturing Sector," *Finance and Economics Discussion Series* 2019-086. Washington: Board of Governors of the Federal Reserve System (23 December 2019): 3, https://www.federalreserve.gov/econres/feds/files/2019086pap.pdf.
79 David Ljunggren, "Fed up Canada Tells US to Help with China Crisis or Forget about Favors," *Reuters*, 5 May 2019, https://www.reuters.com/article/us-canada-trade-china-huawei/fed-up-canada-tells-u-s-to-help-with-china-crisis-or-forget-about-favors-idUSKCN1SB0IA.
80 Ljunggren, "Fed up Canada."

6 From Brushstrokes to Keystrokes: Policing Entrepreneurial Art Crime

ELIZABETH A. KIRLEY

Introduction

The current art market is both vulnerable and accommodating to forgers and money launderers. Art commodities can gain double or triple asset value over a decade if the market is hot and promotion skilful.[1] For art criminals, there are two advantages to continuing deceptive practices in the current financial markets: prosecution of art crime is expensive and time intensive and so of lesser policing priority than violent offences; and there exists the persistent misapprehension among some businessmen and jurists that art fraud harms no one.[2] Regarding the latter, even today many in the criminal justice sector would tend to agree with English Lord Chief Justice Sir John Holt who admonished legal counsel during the 1703 trial of an accused fraudster, "Shall we indict one man for making a fool of another?"[3]

Policing forgery and money laundering involves penetrating the murky dealings of financial elites working as individuals, groups, networks, or companies. While the occasional arrest serves to invigorate policing efforts,[4] when it comes to legal proof, the offer of deferred prosecutions is often made to offenders due to the off-the-books nature of their crimes that occupy the grey periphery of legitimate business.[5]

Canadian sociologist Margaret Beare recognized the inherent challenge to policing the "entrepreneurial linkages between legitimate and illegitimate exchanges."[6] She studied the many ways in which "the embeddedness of capitalism is exploited and simultaneously denied while serving as a lifestyle of the financially advantaged."[7]

This chapter examines those "entrepreneurial linkages" between forger and investor, as well as sales agent and money launderer. It asks what tools in the hands of art detectives and policing agencies could pierce the opaque layers of brokerage within the privileged milieu of private art collectors. It addresses two enterprises that, if investigated more aggressively, could facilitate art policing efforts: the freeport storage system that perpetuates secrecy for artworld elites, and the increasing recognition of artificial intelligence (AI) as a superior tool for both the investigator and the rogue.[8] The chapter theorizes that the disinclination of domestic and international police to prioritize art crime is shifting with the emergence of independent digital payment systems and the incursion into "grey crime" of algorithmic tools that can spot an outlier brushstroke with record speed and scale.

We use as a case study the 2017 sale of an oil painting catalogued as the *Salvator Mundi*, a slightly larger-than-life portrait on a walnut panel of the Christ figure in a benediction pose, characteristic of late Renaissance Italian master painters.[9] Its emergence as a possible long-lost work of Leonardo da Vinci is the subject of much speculation in art museums as well as art investment and policing circles. If expert attributions are correct, the painting is one of only fifteen to twenty masterworks produced by da Vinci. Oxford University art historian Martin Kemp appraises this painting as "the devotional counterpart to the Mona Lisa"[10] for its idiosyncratic brushstrokes, the decorative origins of its drapery details, and for Christ's gaze that is directed at the viewer located anywhere in the room.[11] Naysayers view the painting as a forgery, or perhaps an example of hyper-restoration that, in the rare air in which such master works become sought-after investments, might amount to the same thing. The cloud of secrecy around the painting's provenance, current location, owner,[12] and funding source, render the *Salvator Mundi* an excellent study in the ease of entry and impunity of networked players in art market big-ticket investments. While the painting is used throughout this chapter as a unifying device, there is no legal proof or formal accusation of either art crime or money laundering involving the work.

This chapter proceeds in three parts: Part 1 introduces the culture of secrecy and cronyism offered by the freeport system to forgers and money launderers; Part 2 details the museum standard tests for authenticating an alleged masterwork that are available to aid police detection; and Part 3 assesses new digital tools that can either facilitate their rogue creation or detect the forgery of master artworks. The chapter concludes with a discussion of the ongoing misapprehension of art fraud as a victimless crime. As emerita professor of Sociology Laureen Snider acknowledges in chapter 7 of this collection, "elites ... have 'new and near-limitless opportunities to profit-maximize at public expense.'"[13]

Part 1 Freeports: Hiding Ill-Gotten Gains in Plain Sight

As the gavel descended on the final bid for the modest-sized *Salvator Mundi* at Christie's Auction House in November of 2017, the jaw-dropping price of $450.3 million in US dollars marked the most expensive artwork ever purchased at private auction.[14] One art consultant has put that increase of market value in graphic terms: if the Christie's auction price were represented by a pile of $100 bills, it would reach higher than the Empire State Building. Using the same metric, the original purchase price would amount to roughly a third of an inch.[15]

According to the global art investment firm Art Basel,[16] despite a dip in art markets during COVID-19, fine art is still the biggest business attracting both legal and illegal money.[17] Gallery and auctions, although not public art museums, are proclaiming art transactions as COVID-proof due to high sales.[18] Those assessments argue for more accountability and improved regulatory scrutiny because certain art transactions remain impregnable to regulators and police. As one academic at the Courtauld Institute of Art observed in 2013, "the more art is useful for investment, tax scams, money-laundering, and entry to the elite," the more it "parades its principled uselessness."[19]

Art, like any present-day commodity, is routinely sold and transported across national borders. In 2020 alone, the Chinese and UK art markets each accounted for one-fifth of the total value sold around the world.[20] The ease with which such works have been circulated among handlers has been fostered over the years by lax disclosure laws and levels of secrecy only the very rich can afford. Such opacity is defended as a means of protecting potential buyers and sellers in highly competitive transactions. The storage location, if offshore, or the corporate entity enabling its removal from public view and from tax requirements are the focus of art detectives and various lawmakers attempting to address those shortfalls, with mixed success.[21]

High bidding auctions can be viewed as conduits for moving large masses of money around the globe. As one CIA investigator stated after the *Salvator Mundi* sale, "The intelligence community is going to want to know where the money is coming from and where it is going."[22] Money laundering within the art investment culture is in need of tighter regulation. While the US Congress initiated such a move in 2021 with proposed revisions of the *Bank Secrecy Act 1970*, a study by the US Treasury Department released in early February of 2022 has concluded that regulation of the art market "needn't be an area of immediate focus given the higher risks posed by other sectors."[23]

And so the veiling of art market activities continues.[24] Even know-your-customer compliance demanded of bricks and mortar banks can be circumvented using blockchain, nonfungible tokens (NFTs), and other technologies offering decentralized financing.[25] Illicit banking arrangements also accommodate the money launderer, such as the "Vancouver Model" that is used to evade detection in transactions within the fertile art markets of South-East Asia.[26] Reporting requirements might be circumvented also if no financial institution appears to be involved and the work is nested in duty-free storage facilities known in the industry as freeports.[27]

Freeports are part of de-territorialized spaces created in the Second World War era by nation states to facilitate transnational commerce.[28] For those in the luxury commodities market featuring fine art, antique cars, and select wines, freeports are an outlet of choice.[29] It is possible that the *Salvator Mundi* painting is being stored in a free trade zone in an oversized warehouse at any of the Geneva International Airport, Luxembourg Findel Airport, Le Freeport in Singapore, or New Castle County, Delaware. The advantages for art investors are many: permanent secure storage until their asset matures in value; framing and restoration services; earthquake, hurricane, and climate control protection; on-site exhibition space and sale rooms; dealers who can represent both vendor and purchaser without the need for conflict-of-interest disclosure; anonymity and protection from taxation and regulatory scrutiny; and, above all, less intrusion by detectives with warrants.[30] The latter benefits both the forger and money launderer for extended periods of time and, if an in-storage sale should take place, the provenance trail can be obscured completely.

Freeport owners promote a variety of tax advantages because they argue the goods they store are technically in transit.[31] In addition to regulatory evasion, freeport storage creates socio-cultural disadvantages: major artworks are being removed from circulation and so are no longer available as a public good to art institutions, art museum goers, researchers, or educators. For the duration of their storage, master paintings like *Salvator Mundi* have their cultural capital traded for tax-free investment. In this sense, it really is all about the money. Unless collectors decide to lend or donate their works of art to public museums, their investments are in a vault, out of circulation, and preserved for the privileged few.[32]

Artist John Zarobell sees a conflict in the development of freeports: they exist "at the convergence of national sovereignty and transnational economic developments in the luxury commodities market."[33] He observes that the market processes that countries have introduced in the pursuit of "secrecy jurisdictions" are being transformed into a system where our most valuable possessions are converted into capital market structures, "harnessed for their potential to generate more value through new instruments of financialization."[34] Columbia University sociologist Saskia Sassen would agree: she views the freeport system as a threat to state economic autonomy in that it represents "states legislating to the benefit of multi-national corporations and foreign investors at the expense of their own territorial authority."[35]

Policing freeports can be a bit of a mug's game. Akin to the numbered Swiss bank account, the freeport fortress with its opaque economic activity can discourage scrutiny by enforcement authorities. Policing authorities have penetrated freeport security in certain high-profile cases, but mainly related to cultural property, which does not usually include fine art purchased by private auction.[36] The transcontinental nature of global trading means that artworks can be crossing borders with great frequency, an activity that can incur considerable customs duties and attract domestic laws and regulatory authorities. That activity can produce a paper trail of immense assistance to policing efforts. Freeports have mostly eliminated those footprints in the art trade.

Release of the Panama Papers in 2016, however, has incentivized policing of freeports in some jurisdictions.[37] Yves Bouvier, for example, as owner of the company Natural Le Coultre that controls freeports in Luxembourg, Monaco, and Singapore, was criminally indicted in 2017 by Monaco authorities for victimizing "high net worth individuals" and for tax evasion. He is also the subject of an ongoing civil suit by Russian oligarch Dmitry Rybolovlev for double invoicing for the sale of Picasso works.[38] Rybolovlev was a previous owner of the Leonardo *Salvator Mundi* before it was placed for auction in 2017.

Such high-level indictments, however, have not established that laws were broken inside the freeport facility, nor revealed in any detail how offshore mechanisms have altered the art market. Freeports are similarly opaque to the collection of legal evidence: detectives have difficulty building a case file that connects current owners with ultimate beneficial owners, and artworks with money from the predicate offence.[39] The secrecy of freeports, in combination with a lack of government authority to regulate, tax, or investigate property stored inside a secrecy jurisdiction, comprises an almost insurmountable investigative hurdle for police agents. Such commodities belong to an "informal economy" identified by US economist Edgar Feige as a blend of black and grey markets with the legitimate, if less regulated, market.[40] Using Margaret Beare's typology, freeports encase the unreachable cache of "entitled ease."[41]

This is particularly the case when artworks are bought and sold without ever having left the freeport facility. As the editors of *Artsy* magazine point out, "Invisible to tax authorities, foreign governments, and even insurers of the artworks themselves, art could be stored there with complete anonymity and sold without any taxes being paid."[42]

Part 2 Policework to Detect Forgeries

The *Salvator Mundi* that was the subject of the Christie's auction was attributed to Leonardo by several art professionals long before the gavel fell in 2017. An attribution is a professional opinion that an artwork is by a particular artist. For the painting to become accepted as a genuine work of art, however, and a trusted commodity in the art market, a higher level of proof is required: its authenticity.[43] There exist many tools to assist police professionals in reaching what the Smithsonian Institute calls "the real thing."[44]

a) Authenticity

Discussions about authenticity usually begin with the semantics of art identification. Terms that art historians use – "painted by," "by the hand of," "from the studio of," "circle of," "style of," or "copy of" – each mark a progressive step away from active involvement of the attributed artist in the physical, creative act of painting.[45] Within the studio system in which Renaissance artists traditionally worked, students were encouraged to copy masterworks and, once that master had completed the central figure or landscape in a commissioned work, less experienced hands might add the finer strokes. The challenge to authenticity in such a system is quickly apparent.

Another aid in authenticating a painting necessarily involves tracing its ownership across time. This establishes the artwork's provenance, to "capture[s] the ownership history of a piece all the way back to the artist's studio."[46] A document containing that ownership history is also referred to as a provenance. Among forgers, it is often falsified as part of the deception.[47]

In the case of *Salvator Mundi*, the written provenance has provoked as much interest as the painting itself. Each missing time period can fuel suspicions of forgery and other criminality. As can be seen from the reference to two kings and other notables, the provenance of *Salvator Mundi* is impressive but with gaps, as indicated by the bold text in Table 6.1 below.[48]

The management of provenance risk is a professional field that addresses certain threats to transactional integrity such as insider trading, conflicts-of-interest, money laundering, art forgery, and other systemic issues revealed by the infamous Panama Papers.[49] New York art insurance specialist Lawrence Shindell points out that any *perceived* risk of artwork provenance can create as much havoc and suspicion as proven or legal ownership because they are "highly portable, high value art objects which physically move and actively trade throughout a globalized marketplace."[50]

In Figure 6.1 we are faced with another more nuanced challenge to the authenticity of *Salvator Mundi*: the extensive restorative work provided by the reputable conservator Diane Modestini several years before its most recent sale. A team of respected art experts determined in 2008 that the work was by Leonardo's hand. The lengthy conservation by Modestini raises the critical question of whether the painting had been so over-worked that it was too far removed from the master's hand. As Thomas Campbell, former director of New York's Metropolitan Museum, posted on social media after the Christie's sale, "450 million dollars?! Hope the buyer understands conservation issues."[51] The implication was that Modestini's restoration might have gone beyond usual limits of art conservation. The result could be viewed by some as the conservator inserting herself into the creative act.[52] Some art historians insist that only work by restorers and conservators that is visually apparent to the observer is permitted to keep the work authentic. As Italian conservation theorist Cesare Brandi commented in support of that view, "For restoration to be a legitimate operation, it cannot presume that time is reversible or that history can be abolished."[53]

Comparing the images from left to right in Figure 6.1 below, you might note a colour and sfumato difference in the face, garment, and background; a

Table 6.1. Chronology of *Salvator Mundi* attributed to Leonardo da Vinci Compiled from Various Sources in this Chapter

Date	Event	Price at sale
1500–15	Likely created by Leonardo for King Louis XII of France	
1625	Transported to England in 1625 to the court of King Charles I	
1660	Catalogued in the collection of King Charles II; his widow commissioned an etching of the work	
?	**Passed to Duke of Buckingham**	
1763	Sold by son of Duke of Buckingham	
	Missing from the Royal collection (137 years)	
1900	Purchased in Virginia, US by Sir Frederick Cook	
1958	Purchased at Sotheby's UK sale by Warren Kunst	£45
2005	Purchased by Robert B. Simon and Alexander Parish from St Charles Gallery, New Orleans	US $1,175
2005–17?	**Placed with Diane Modestini as commissioned restorer**	
2017	Purchased by Swiss dealer Yves Bouvier	US $80 million
2017	Purchased by Dmitry Rybolovlev	US $127.5 million
2017	Purchased, possibly by Crown Prince Mohammed bin Salman Al Saud of Saudi Arabia	US $450.3 million

Source: Author

reshaping of the face through shadowing: a deepening of skin tones; and some alteration to Christ's beard. At a certain undefinable point, the viewer is presented with a new work, not a reworked Leonardo construction. The question for conservators, valuators, investors, and lawyers becomes, where is that point for the *Salvator Mundi*?

The controversy continues. For example, since hearing of the Christie's sale in 2017, Modestini herself has commented that the work was in such a deteriorated state that she was called upon to make some subjective decisions about restoration methods. The legal question of forgery is just as controversial. A more granular definition of "restoration" would clearly help to settle the question.[54]

Figure 6.1. *Salvator Mundi* before treatment, 2005 (left); after cleaning by Modestini, 2006 (middle); after Modesti restoration, 2011 (right).
Source: Salvator Mundi LLC

b) Forensics to Determine Materials and Techniques

The second step in assessing "the real thing" is scientific analysis. Technical assessment focuses on analysing the surface of the painting, the underpainting, and the canvas or wooden material using chemicals or light.

Laboratory tests can contribute significantly to the authentication conversation. The *Salvator Mundi* painting would have undergone a range of physical chemical tests before restoration, such as stereomicroscopy, visible and fluorescent light microscopy, Raman microspectroscopy, scanning electron microscopy with energy dispersive spectroscopy, and stratigraphy. Such chemical analyses would determine the composition of paint, environmental factors causing corrosion or fading, and paint layering that could indicate previous restorations.

Further analysis using X-rays could offer another valuable clue to attribution: a *pentimento* showing that the thumb of Christ's right hand had originally been painted in a different position.[55] Such change of heart would not be something a forger would do.[56] In addition, infrared imaging would reveal that the painter had pressed his palm against the wet paint above Christ's left eye while working *sfumato* or a blurring technique into that area. That imprint was distinctively Leonardo, according to both art historian Martin Kemp and biographer Walter Isaacson. Those clues can assist the study of the creative process as revealed in the underlayers of a painting and can be compared to other works by Leonardo showing a similar appearance and style. Even a combination of all those techniques, however, can render results that are not dispositive.[57]

A team headed by art analyst Nica Gutman Rieppi conducted forensic tests on the *Salvator Mundi* and made two observations: the original work was executed using a relatively limited palette; and the painting's sophisticated visual effects were achieved through a complex sequence of layers. The Rieppi team concluded that the underlying layers provide insights of "an artistic mind actively at work during the various stages of painting."[58] The combination of technique and the addition of pulverized glass to the paint helped achieve the "luminosity, translucency and depth that characterize the *Salvator Mundi*."[59] That analysis supports the Leonardo attribution.

c) The Connoisseur's Eye

He was seeking to understand not just what Leonardo did but why he did what he did the way he did it.[60]

Those words reflect the passion and precision with which British art historian Kenneth Clark approached the idiosyncratic paintings of Leonardo da Vinci. Similar scrutiny is recommended for potential buyers to distinguish forgeries from originals.[61] When owners of an unknown work represent it as painted by a certain artist, the art historian attempts to fit it into the artist's known body of work. The subject matter, the brushwork, the choice of colours, and the type of composition are all consistent idiosyncrasies in an artist's *oeuvre*. Any variation could immediately arouse suspicion. Morellian analysis was developed to verify an artist's work by looking for the artist's unique quirks of style, such as the minute details of facial features or the precise fingerprint of a brushstroke.[62] Those can be identified, mapped out, and predicted for future output by that artist.

In that way, an art forgery can be detected in much the same way as a handwriting forgery. With masterworks, the scholar or detective examines the iconography of a piece. As most policing specialists in art crimes know, forgers rarely have the scholarly background to combine iconographic elements correctly, and their errors often betray them.[63]

Martin Kemp has studied Leonardo and his works for fifty years and has performed a closer examination of the painting's iconography and design. He has focused on two features: the "mundus" or clear orb held in Christ's left hand as "Saviour of the World" and Christ's hair. In examining the rock crystal of which the orb would be composed he has noted that air bubble inclusions are correctly represented which "extends the reach of the iconography from the earth to the wider cosmos."[64] He expresses confusion, however, over the abrasion shown on the surface of the orb, giving its surface an uneven quality.[65]

Kemp next focuses on the portrayal of Christ's hair. "It's very characteristic, this vortex hairstyle. Now the followers and boys could do curly hair pretty nicely. But Leonardo had a theory about the curling of hair."[66] That theory held that hair must portray the movement of water. Kemp saw that there is a "logic to the vortex formation. It has a kind of anatomy." Those clues reinforced Kemp's opinion that this is authentic, what historians call an autograph work.

The educated eye has long been a necessary feature of authentication. For dedicated "art cops" such as Rene Allonge in Europe's art crime epicentre, Berlin, an eye for forgeries has "enthralled the public with one dramatic investigation, arrest, or recovery after another."[67] Stylistic analysis is a subjective task: experts would argue you cannot simulate this gift or teach it to a computer. The experts we examine next would challenge that assertion.

Part 3 New Digital Tools for Policing Art Crime

In this section we look at how new tools using AI (artificial intelligence) to detect forgery and money laundering are progressively taking a more dominant role in art sales and police investigations. Art museums, galleries, and other art institutions have traditionally been more conservative in changing their rule-based systems. There are newer, more flexible firms, however, that are proving that machine learning and neural networks can quite ably signal criminality, with their calculations that work on probabilities, not definitive conclusions or subjective assessments.[68]

Both Sotheby's and Christie's art auction firms, for example, have hired in-house digital experts that use AI to vet forgeries before sales. Sotheby's has put digital technology to other uses as well due to plummeting sales in the early months of the pandemic. It has launched its own Gallery Network, promoted as a "digital marketplace for blue-chip galleries" as well as hosting an online auction on behalf of private galleries and dealers in masterworks from various locations worldwide.[69] Those progressive strategies show promise for more transparent transactions and hence more accessibility to police.

a) Forgery

When testing for authenticity using algorithmic tools, the larger the body of work, or *oeuvre*, the easier it is to find idiosyncratic marks of the artist's style. With Leonardo's attributable *oeuvre* calculated at less than twenty major works over his entire career, AI tools must be trained on a vastly larger data reservoir and respond faster than humans can. That is why human–machine interaction works well for authentication tasks. Humans balance the equation with their ability to read human motivation that drives the rogue mind.

b) Reading the Forger

For the art forger, the deception of the con is often justified as the consequence of derailed ambitions: the artist's talents have been overlooked by the academy and so the forger feels vindicated in using those very talents to anonymously defraud the art industry. There is a cruel irony in the fact that the forger's identity must remain undisclosed, a factor that guarantees fame will remain elusive. Another justification offered by the forger is that s/he has escaped the circle of cronyism that maintains the salon system. Success in the art world is a feedback loop, and those on the inside do not gain from disrupting the status quo. The loop is self-sustaining due to its networks within networks: the same collectors who buy an artist's work most likely sit on a museum board to whom they will ultimately donate the work, which then further promotes the artist and the institution by attracting visitors, media, exhibition sponsors, and donors. Outside this salon system, the ultimate winner is the investor, working within networks that perpetuate the misapprehension that art fraud harms no one.[70]

c) Reading Brushstrokes

Where once the physical proof of forgery was in the chemical composition of the artist's palette (lead, ochre, azul) now the digital mark of the fraudster can be found in brushstrokes that are too faint, too numerous, or too inconsistently applied to convince the expert. The concept of "fingerprinting" artists using their brush strokes can be dated to the 1950s when a Dutch art historian, Maurits Michel van Dantzig, developed pictology, a manually coded version of brushstroke identification.[71]

In 2017 a team of art researchers from Rutgers University, working with a restoration team in The Hague, Netherlands, refined that process with a form of AI known as recurrent neural networks (RNN).[72] The researchers examined 297 works mostly by four major artists: Pablo Picasso, Henry Matisse, Amedeo Modigliani, and Egon Schiele, focusing on about 80,000 individual strokes.[73] By running those strokes through RNN and machine learning, they were able to identify the original artist about 70–80 per cent of the time. They could identify forgeries 100 per cent of the time, an impressive result for AI when working from a single stroke. "A human cannot do that," the principal investigator observed at the time.[74]

In Switzerland, two innovative researchers use a single photograph and AI to correctly detect several known forgeries – all without setting eyes on the original.[75] Their methodology includes supplying their art recognition algorithm with "characteristic features of the artist from a set of photographs of the artist's original paintings."[76] The algorithm "looks" at brushstrokes and produces a heat map that pinpoints the areas of the painting that are most suspect.[77]

Similar technology that works with the principles of entropy, or the amount of disorder contained within a given volume, has been developed by computer scientist Stephen Frank and art historian Andrea Frank. That team has examined various parts of an image and assigned importance to each part, including biases, to differentiate among those parts. Working with convolutional neural networks (CNNs), these art detectives have overcome the formidable problem of distinguishing an artist's *oeuvre* using an AI training sample that is quite small: the very problem presented by Leonardo da Vinci's lifetime oeuvre of fewer than twenty paintings.[78] Their self-reported success rate at deciphering original works from forgeries was 90.4 per cent in 2019.[79]

The Frank research team has now applied its algorithmic method to the "Leonardo" *Salvator Mundi*. The latest challenge to attribution has arisen around the possibility that Christ's hands were not included contemporaneously with the head but were added later, with the implication that the addition was not done by Leonardo. The painting's restorer, Diane Modestini, is adamant that the arms are a later addition but by the original artist. Some experts accept the painting as partially by Leonardo,[80] while others reject the attribution entirely.[81]

By far the most controversial AI tools to enter the crime detection field are large language models (LLMs) released by OpenAI in 2021 and 2022: the *image*-generating model DALL-E and its *text*-generating companion, Chat-GPT.[82] They can create and edit images when given a natural language prompt. Those prompts are part of massive data troves freely supplied by us through our online activities.

One news source characterizes this extraordinary jump in scale and speed as akin to taking "our whole world knowledge and building on it cumulatively to get smarter and smarter" ... but in seconds.[83]

Chatbots are not people, however, despite industry statements to the contrary, such as the Google AI engineer who professed: "I know a person when I talk to it."[84] Many results are inaccurate, even fictional, as the latest iteration of ChatGPT has shown. As well there are limits, for now: the technology can satisfy requests for summary business reports but not in-depth market analyses, descriptive essays for undergraduates but not prescriptive papers for upper-level students, and the occasional verifiable footnote,[85] although one journalism source has described most citation results as "hallucinogenic!"[86] More broadly, academics are reacting to submissions to peer-reviewed or other scholarly journals that contain "major errors and biases," a tendency to veer from the truth, and possible weaponizing of search results to spread disinformation.[87] More than one such submission has listed a chatbot as author.[88]

Policing agencies have further concerns: no data we have released onto the internet are safe from exploitation to train these bots,[89] from our uploaded photos to artworks, "liked" content, searches, social media postings, and personal profiles.[90] Europol clarifies the advantage: "With the help of LLMs, various types of phishing and online fraud can be created faster, much more authentically, and at significantly increased scale."[91] Cautionary concerns expressed by policing agencies include the notable acceleration in synthetic media production, such as deepfakes, and AI's ability to mimic human-like sensory abilities, such as seeing, hearing,[92] and emoting.[93] Other rogue behaviours include the emergence of LLMs from the dark web that can be disseminated without any safeguards against data that could be "harmful" to humans.[94]

Small wonder that tech entrepreneurs Elon Musk (X, formerly Twitter), Steve Wozniak (Apple), and others have released a public letter urging AI labs to pause development of LLMs until such "profound risks to society and humanity"[95] can be addressed. Developers' liability might also be on that agenda.

As LLMs gain their footing in the open market, can police agencies intensify their use of AI to track down forgers and other art criminals? That conversation has already begun within Interpol[96] and Europol,[97] and among open-source researchers,[98] as well as artist communities.[99] Interpol's introduction of their free ID-Art app expands the policing playbook for art detectives to upload images or input keywords to search for suspicious artwork or transactions.[100] The public, including collectors and investors, can access this resource as well merely by swiping a smartphone screen and reporting art scams and forgeries to police. More colloquial police training advice is also available on YouTube channels to advise officers on dos and don'ts of ChatGPT use.[101]

One research team has proposed a quick identifier for bogus bot-created artwork: inserting digital watermarks into original digital images that can easily verify the work's provenance.[102] While several researchers have proposed inserting digital watermarks as a quick identifier of bot-created artwork, another source reports that those watermarks can be digitally overridden with relative ease. Another team proposes injecting poison samples into text-to-image training data that would look visually identical to benign images with matching text prompts but would skew the data, disabling its ability to generate meaningful images.[103] That tool could act as a last defence for content creators against random, malicious web scrapers. An additional corrective is for police agencies to intensify their training to spot the shortcomings of LLM technologies, such as bias in visual imaging and learning gaps in police AI training.

Another algorithmic development uses facial recognition tools, such as Clearview, to give police access to graphic details of people's faces as they go about their daily lives. Genealogy software is another innovation that has facilitated the identification of perpetrators in cold murder cases. Those inventions might have crossover applications in the art detection field, notably for comparing faces on the canvas with other artworks by the same artist for stylistic similarities. While such technologies promise major advancement in the policing of art crime, they are meeting formidable resistance from civil libertarian organizations and privacy advocates.[104] The technologies are welcomed, however, by government agencies tasked with national and individual security protections. For example, in 2020 it was determined that surveillance technologies such as Amazon's Rekognition software that promotes the computational ability to monitor "people of interest," is under consideration (and possibly is already in use) by some governments.

One of the more egregious mistakes made by automated programs has been revealed by the US National Institute of Standards and Technology: the majority of facial recognition technologies in use by government agencies have performed worse on non-white faces.[105] The data used by such AI programs have been scraped from over 18 million online images (2019 figures), primarily mug shots of US residents as well as photographs collected for specific governmental uses, such as visa applications and identification shown to customs agents by those entering the United States.[106] Commercial access to such personal information is prompting litigation by privacy advocates and educating us all on the extent of non-consensual data retention prevalent in online transactions.

If the challenges listed above can be legally addressed, the impact of AI on art crime detection could be transformative. One key question to sooth human apprehension about collaborative human–computer interactions is whether there are capabilities of the human mind that will forever escape computer performance. Current indications are that creativity, understanding, natural language, and consciousness are examples of human exceptionalism that artificial intelligence has not yet commercially replicated.[107] As British mathematician and codebreaker Alan Turing observed, computers are only capable of executing algorithms – step-by-step recipes for performing a task. The novel LLM capabilities under discussion in this chapter could post a stark challenge to that truism. We might find some consolation in the fact that, so far, computers lack sentience and do not appear to be cognizant of the operations they perform.[108]

d) Money Laundering

The challenge of policing money laundering that has art forgery as the predicate (underlying) offence is even more daunting. Forensics and other authentication tools discussed above might be just as accessible to forgers and felons as they are to police. While formalized money laundering laws and reporting procedures have been initiated in most countries, several factors from staff resistance to a global pandemic can deter the best transnational policing intentions.

The message from the World Economic Forum (WEF) is that, if price tag alone is determinative, our current methods of combating money laundering are just not working. The WEF calculates that, in the United States alone, the cost of anti–money laundering compliance is $23.5 billion a year, closely followed by costs for European banks of $20 billion annually.[109] Art fair organizer Art Basel has reported that the art market generated US$67.4 billion in 2018.[110] The total loss in that time to money laundering has been calculated by the United Nations Office on Drugs and Crime to be between 2 and 5 per cent of global GDP – between $800 billion and $2 trillion by current figures.[111] Those numbers signal an unimpressive return on investment. Most money laundering goes undetected due to the clandestine nature of the crime. Further, current estimates suggest that only around 2 per cent of profits earned by criminals is forfeited upon conviction.

With lockdowns during the COVID-19 pandemic forcing the closure of many legitimate businesses, money launderers are compelled to get more creative to move money around. It is reported that, with government bailouts propping up some small- to middle-income businesses, "vast sums of money have started flowing into small businesses once again."[112] The Financial Transactions and Reports Analysis Centre of Canada (FINTRAC) has attributed to the COVID-19 pandemic an overall decrease in large cash transaction reporting as a result of the physical distancing and public health measures implemented.[113] The independent, intergovernmental body, Financial Action Task Force (FATF) sees money laundering activity during the pandemic differently.[114] It reports "mounting cases of the counterfeiting of medical goods, investment fraud, adapted cyber-crime scams, and exploitation of economic stimulus measures put in place by governments."[115] Also observed are increases in online child exploitation due to an increase in the time spent online, increases in property crime due to properties being left uninhabited, and corruption in relation to contracts for medical supplies.[116] The British Institute of Art and Law reports that in early 2020 the sale of a John Constable painting to a Dutch museum by a London dealer was infiltrated by hackers with a resultant $3.1 million loss and court action between the parties.[117] The organization cautions that, with a large number of art sales to raise money for coronavirus causes occurring online, there is increased risk of scams of this sort.

This imposes greater pressure on extant anti–money laundering programs. Some firms that use machine learning to detect suspicious financial activity have expanded into hybrid investigative approaches that integrate computer and human efforts, thereby cutting down on false positives and errant alerts. The pivoting to other tactics required of money launderers during the pandemic is challenging police flexibility with their AI solutions. Police need to keep pace, however. Rogue opportunism must be caught as it happens. "Otherwise," warns a crime expert at the adaptive behavioural analytics firm Featurespace, "by the time you've detected something and alerted the people who need to know, the money is gone."[118]

At this time, improvements in AI technology favour both the detective and the rogue.[119] While future AI software will sharpen fraud detection, and emerging technologies are refining privacy enhancing technology to support data sharing to reduce individual internet user exposure,[120] it will also offer the fraudster the ability to produce more sophisticated and timely forgeries and to sell them in a totally digital market, beyond regulatory oversight. Another layer of secrecy has been created with cryptocurrency payment systems using non-fungible tokens (NFTs) that use a blockchain accounting system.[121] NFT crime is gaining ground, using ransomware attacks and scams. In 2021, crypto crime hit an all-time high of US$14 billion while comprising a lower percentage of all cryptocurrency activity, according to one report from the private sector.[122]

The pace of competition for pixels and mega-data between rogue and policing sectors has been compared to an "arms race."[123] As fraudsters improve their techniques, the authentication tools of experts, auction houses, art museums, and galleries will need to improve two-fold in accuracy and alacrity to outsmart the forger's software. For example, machine learning has just accomplished the feat of converting user-generated artworks to collectible online assets. The first such work has garnered US$69 million at a public auction.[124] The digital work exists only online; its promise for art markets can be seen in the fact that thirty-three active bidders had contested the winning bid, and the final price marked the third highest ever achieved for a living artist, after artists Jeff Koons and David Hockney.[125]

Conclusion: The Harm Done

The fraudster has long been despised by those who live by the rules. In his allegorical poem *The Divine Comedy*, the Italian author Dante Alighieri relegated fraud and deception to the eighth circle of hell. That decision located "the opportunists who were for neither good nor evil, merely concerned with themselves" closer to the eternal fires and deeper in the mire of ignominy as imposed by Catholic dogma of Fourteenth-century Italy.[126]

In our times, forgery of artistic artefacts is dealt with not as immoral opportunism but as a serious crime with real victims. The delict is creating a work that is intentionally meant to deceive.[127] Forgers have skills and tools to create an artistic illusion by copying an artist's style and, often, these include the provenance documents that falsely authenticate the resulting artwork. Money launderers can also move with ease within the art market. Digital tools as reviewed in this chapter can enable those deceptions of the rogue opportunist, but they can also offer quantum improvements to police investigations, leading to prosecutions for the financial harm they inflict.[128]

Art criminals are no different in their risk analyses from other malefactors or felons, according to Vernon Rapley, former Scotland Yard detective and the Director of Cultural Heritage Protection and Security at the Victoria and Albert Museum. "It all boils down to the core criminal considerations: supply, demand, opportunity and risk."[129] He cautions that those apprehended for major crimes understand only too well that prosecutors must prove dishonesty beyond all reasonable doubt. With experienced co-conspirators or legal counsel, they will use this to their litigatory advantage.

This chapter has argued that the conspiracy of silence and obfuscation around high-yielding art crimes can cause calculable harm that expands far beyond the perpetrators. Current initiatives at law reform focus on "know who benefits" and disclosure of key actors at each transfer point in ownership. This involves replacing backroom deals and a wink and a nod between owners and sales agents with compliance rules that grant police the details of provenance and ownership they require. Law reform and enforcement, however, rely on able detection, the kind that a combination of connoisseur skills and new AI tools are now poised to deliver.

Dr. Peter German, a former RCMP deputy commissioner, quite ably speaks to the particular harm done by money laundering: "It is both an embarrassment and a threat to a society that adheres to the rule of law, for organized crime to take advantage of all that is good in our society and subvert it for pecuniary advantage."[130] German cautions that laundering deprives governments of tax revenue and enables corruption, as it disguises the proceeds of bribery, embezzlement, illicit drug sales, and other financial crimes. He is also alerted to the "steep human cost" of dirty money.[131]

The other major activity in art fraud – forgery – is best addressed by visual artists themselves. Artist Jason Bailey, who writes about the benefits of technology to the art world, cautions: "We need to stop celebrating forgers as lovable rascals getting one over on rich collectors … The reality is that art forgers undercut our shared humanity by compromising the historical record of our most important cultural objects: our art."[132]

Meanwhile, there is no record of any public sighting of the Salvator Mundi painting since its record-breaking auction purchase in 2017. Its ownership remains contested in certain circles, as does its authenticity. As its principal conservator and a staunch believer in its authenticity over a 15-year period, Diane Modestini might possibly have spent more intimate time with the painting than anyone else in today's world. She describes her moment of absolute conviction:

> One evening, I was trying, once again, to retouch a loss in the upper lip. I could not master the imperceptible transition to my satisfaction and had removed my retouch numerous times. I had a copy of a book the Louvre had recently published about the Mona Lisa, which was lavishly illustrated (Mona Lisa: Inside the Painting). I removed the page with the detail of the mouth and pinned it to my easel. At that moment I realized that the Salvator Mundi could not have been painted by anyone except Leonardo[133]

Modestini points out the 'untouchable' or unsalable status of Salvator Mundi among select museums and private collectors over the decade before its Christie's record sale. Ironically, it continues to lure commercial interest from "the underworld of Freeports, shell companies, and money laundering. This is the great tragedy in the saga of this painting."[134]

NOTES

1 James Tarmy, "Here's How to Make Millions as an Art Forger," *Bloomberg*, 21 May 2015, https://www.bloomberg.com/news/articles/2015-05-21/here-s-how-to-make-millions-as-an-art-forger.
2 The term "art crime" is used expansively to capture deceptive practices such as forgery of art and authentication papers, copying of artworks that are falsely attributed to masters (also referred to herein as "art fraud"), and excessive restoration or conservation of an original masterpiece that, it is argued, produces a new artwork. It includes money laundering activities that involve such predicate crimes as terrorism or human trafficking.
3 Vernon Rapley, "The Police Investigation of Art Fraud," in *Art Crime: Terrorists, Tomb Raiders, Forgers and Thieves*, edited by Noah Charney (London: Palgrave MacMillan, 2016), 33–40.
4 United States Attorney's Office, "Seller of Forged Basquiats and Harings Arrested on Fraud Charges," Southern District of New York, 9 July 2021, https://www.justice.gov/usao-sdny/pr/seller-forged-basquiats-and-harings-arrested-fraud-charges.
5 Sanya Ojo, "The Informal and Illegal Entrepreneurship," in *The Evolution of Black African Entrepreneurship in the UK*, edited by Sanya Ojo (London: IGI Global, 2019).

6 Margaret Beare, "Entitled Ease: Social Milieu of Corporate Criminals," *Critical Criminology* 56, no. 4 (2018): 526.
7 Beare, "Entitled Ease," 510.
8 Art fraud can be defined as "the deliberately false representation of the artist, age, origins, or ownership of a work of art in order to reap financial gain." See further, Marguerite Keane, *Britannica*, https://www.britannica.com/topic/art-fraud. For present purposes it includes art forgery and money laundering but excludes the art "fake" that is a copy, a replica, or misattributed work.
9 Measuring 65.5 cm. in height and 45.6 cm in width along the top edge and 45.1 cm along the bottom edge.
10 Martin Kemp, Robert B. Simon, and Margaret Dalivalle, *Leonardo's* Salvator Mundi *& the Collecting of Leonardo in the Stuart Courts* (Oxford: Oxford University Press, 2019).
11 Stephanie Pappas, "Mystery of Orb in a Record-Breaking Leonardo da Vinci Painting Deepens," *Live Science*, 13 January 2020, https://www.livescience.com/da-vinci-light-orb-mystery.html. Pappas comments, "that orb defies the laws of optics, creating a controversy over just what da Vinci was using as his inspiration. Now, a new study argues that the orb may be a realistic depiction of a hollow glass ball."
12 Rumoured to be the Saudi Crown Prince Mohammed bin Salman.
13 Laureen Snider, "Big Money, Small Tax: The Normalization of Tax Evasion," infra., chapter 13.
14 Andreas Koefoed, *The Lost Leonardo*, Sony Pictures Classics, https://www.sonyclassics.com/film/thelostleonardo.
15 Scott Reyburn, "How This Leonardo's Mind-Blowing Price Will Change the Art Market," *New York Times*, 24 November 2017, https://www.nytimes.com/2017/11/24/arts/design/salvator-mundi-leonardo.html.
16 Self-described as "the leading global platform connecting collectors, galleries, and artists," Art Basel is a for-profit, international art fair promoting art investment annually in Basel, Switzerland; Miami Beach, Florida; and Hong Kong. The organization's website offers statements of Principles and Best Practices to increase the transparency and accountability of the art market. See further, "About/Overview," *Art/Basel*, https://www.artbasel.com/about.
17 Art Basel and USB, *The Art Market 2021*, reports that 2020 global sales of art were valued at an estimated $50 billion, down from approximately $67 billion worldwide just a few years earlier, "likely primarily due to the ongoing COVID-19 pandemic." See also, Clare McAndrew, "The Art Market 2021," *Art Basel and USB*, https://www.artbasel.com/about/initiatives/the-art-market.
18 James Tarmy, "Art Galleries Discover That Their Business Model Is Covid-Proof," *Bloomberg*, 23 February 2021, https://www.bloomberg.com/news/articles/2021-02-23/art-galleries-have-been-thriving-while-museums-suffer-during-covid.
19 Julian Stallabrass, "Manifest Opulence," *London Review of Books*, 18 October 2013, https://www.lrb.co.uk/blog/2013/october/manifest-opulence.

140   Elizabeth A. Kirley

20 Clare McAndrew, "The Art Market 2021," *Art Basel and UBS*, 2021, https://d2u3kfwd92fzu7.cloudfront.net/The-Art-Market_2021.pdf.
21 For example, the newly revised *Bank Secrecy Act* in the United States includes disclosure requirements for antiquities and digital currencies but not, as of this writing, for fine artworks. The US Anti-Money Laundering/Combating Financing of Terrorism legal framework, as amended by the Anti-Money Laundering Act of 2020, is codified at 12 U.S.C. 1829b, 12 U.S.C. 1951–1959, and 31 U.S.C. 5311–5314 and 5316–5336. This set of laws is commonly referred to as the Bank Secrecy Act, or BSA. Implementing regulations are codified at 31 CFR Chapter X.
22 Koefoed, "The Lost Leonardo."
23 US Department of the Treasury, "Study of the Facilitation of Money Laundering and Terrorist Finance through the Trade in Works of Art," February 2002. The study noted, "Most art market participants, including some entities that provide financial services within the high-value art market, are not subject to anti-money laundering/countering the financing of terrorism (AML/CFT) obligations" (Executive Summary). See further, Dylan Tokar, "Art Market Poses Money Laundering Risks, but Treasury Weighs against Regulation for Now," *Wall Street Journal*, 4 February 2022.
24 One notable exception is the European Union's *Fifth Money-Laundering Directive* that dictates that all European art dealers and intermediaries must now obtain documentation to identify clients for all art transactions totalling ten thousand euros or more. Directive (EU) 2018/843 of the European Parliament and of the Council of 30 May 2018 amending Directive (EU) 2015/849 on the prevention of the use of the financial system for the purposes of money laundering or terrorist financing and amending Directives 2009/138/EC and 2013/36/EU. The legislation is more sweeping, capturing paintings under "works of art" that also includes drawings or collages executed by hand, photographs, and limited-edition engravings, lithographs, and prints.
25 Mieke Marple, "Why I Believe NFT Will Benefit Artists," *Artsy*, 29 April 2021, https://www.artsy.net/article/artsy-editorial-nfts-will-benefit-artists. Non-fungible tokens are digital assets encoded on a blockchain that represent a set of rights.
26 Peter German, "Dirty Money: Turning the Tide – An Independent Review of Money Laundering in B.C. Real Estate, Luxury Vehicle Sales & Horse Racing," *The Cullen Commission, Part 2*, 2019, https://cullencommission.ca/files/Dirty_Money_Report_Part_2.pdf.
27 *The Financial Recordkeeping and Reporting of Currency and Foreign Transactions Act of 1970* (the *Bank Secrecy Act* or BSA), 31 USC §5311 et seq., as amended. The purpose of the BSA is to require US financial institutions to maintain appropriate records and file certain reports involving currency transactions and a financial institution's customer relationships. The BSA is significantly altered by the 1 January 2021 amendment of the *National Defense Authorization Act* that introduces Section F "The Anti-Money Laundering Act, 2020." While "dealers in antiquities" and

virtual currencies" are now included in the "financial institutions" that are subjected to reporting requirements, art dealers and corporate investors are not specified. Canada prosecutes money laundering under the *Criminal Code of Canada*, s.462.31; reporting is administered through the *Proceeds of Crime (Money Laundering) and Terrorist Financing Act*, S.C. 2000, c. 17. "Art as property" is not defined in the Act.

28 John Zarobell, "Freeports and the Hidden Value of Art," *Arts* 9, no. 4 (18 November 2020): 117ff., https://www.mdpi.com/2076-0752/9/4/117/htm.

29 Samuel Weeks, "A Freeport Comes to Luxembourg, or, Why Those Wishing to Hide Assets Purchase Fine Art," *Arts* 9, no. 3 (2020): 87.

30 "The Black Box of the Art Business," *Best Documentary*, 1 February 2019, YouTube video, [47:12], https://www.youtube.com/watch?v=5TSE2TcMduc.

31 Talia Bernicker, "Behind Closed Doors: A Look at Freeports," *Center for Art Law*, 3 November 2020, https://itsartlaw.org/2020/11/03/behind-closed-doors-a-look-at-freeports/.

32 Michael Kosmides, "The Art of Disguise," *Money Laundering Bulletin*, 29 May 2019.

33 Zarobell, "Freeports."

34 Zarobell, "Freeports."

35 Saskia Sassen, "Locating Cities on Global Circuits," *Environment and Urbanization* 14, no. 1 (2002): 13–30 passim.

36 UNESCO, Convention on the Means of Prohibiting and Preventing the Illicit Import, Export and Transfer of Ownership of Cultural Property, No. 11806, 823 U.N.T.S. 231, 14 November 1970. Beyond the scope of this chapter is the complex area of international law pertaining to the policing or recovery of cultural property that is stolen or misappropriated in any way. Of historical interest is the 1995 UNIDROIT Convention on Stolen or Illegally Exported Cultural Objects as an example of international intergovernmental efforts to harmonize private, and particularly commercial law between states and groups of states for the recovery of cultural property which, under the Convention, includes "pictures, paintings and drawings produced entirely by hand."

37 "Panama Papers Case Revives Concerns about Fine Art as Money Laundering Conduit," *Thomson Reuters*, 18 February 2020, https://blogs.thomsonreuters.com/answerson/panama-papers-fine-art-money-laundering/.

38 Eileen Kinsella, "Swiss Authorities Investigate Charges That Freeport King Yves Bouvier Owes More Than 100 Million in Back Taxes," *Art Net*, 6 September 2017, https://news.artnet.com/art-world/yves-bouvier-swiss-tax-charges-1072205.

39 To prosecute money laundering, a predicate or original offence such as theft, embezzlement, forgery, or extortion must be proven beyond a reasonable doubt.

40 Editorial staff, "What Actually Happened in the Art Market's Informal Economy," *Artsy*, 2 August 2017, https://www.artsy.net/article/artsy-editorial-art-markets-informal-economy.

41 Beare, "Entitled Ease."

42 Editorial Staff, "The Role of Freeports in the Global Art Market," *Artsy*, 14 July 2017, https://www.artsy.net/article/artsy-editorial-freeports-operate-margins-global-art-market.
43 Alan Bamberger, "Authenticating and Attributing Art: What You Need to Know," *ArtBusiness.com*, n.d., https://www.artbusiness.com/artauth.html.
44 Menachem Welker, "The Imitation Game," *Washington Post Magazine*, 27 February 2019.
45 "AI Can Detect Art Forgery – and That's Not All," *Mind Matters*, 19 June 2019, https://mindmatters.ai/2019/06/.
46 "Provenance: What Is It and Why Should It Matter to You?" *Artwork Archive*, http://www.artworkarchive.com/blog/provenance-what-it-it-and-why-should-it-matter-to-you.
47 As was the case in *Hearn v. McLeod Estate* 2019 ONCA 682, where a false provenance for a forgery of Indigenous artist Norval Morrisseau's work was issued to the buyer by a gallery. For reasons relating to Canadian federalism, sales of art with a private gallery come under provincial sale of goods legislation and, in this case, a breach of contract was found based on finding that provenance documentation is an essential part of the contract. See generally, Alexander Herman, "The Art Law Review: Canada," *The Law Review*, 11 January 2022, https://thelawreviews.co.uk/title/the-art-law-review/canada/.
48 "Timeline: How 'Salvator Mundi' Went from £45 to $450 Million in 59 Years," *Artnet*, 15 November 2017, https://news.artnet.com/market/timeline-salvator-mundi-went-45-to-450-million-59-years-1150661. For a more detailed, art historical description of this process, see also Martin Kemp, "Rediscovering Leonardo's Salvator Mundi," Oxford University Press, YouTube, 14 October 2019, https://www.youtube.com/watch?v=VDozBKAFTH0; and Martin Kemp, "Leonardo's Salvator Mundi: Scholarship, Science and Skulduggery," YouTube, 13 May 2019, https://www.youtube.com/watch?v=KIUP8l7HUWI.
49 Lawrence M. Shindell, "Provenance and Title Risks in the Art Industry: Mitigating These Risks in Museum Management and Curatorship," *Museum Management and Curatorship* 31, no. 5, (2016): 407.
50 "Provenance: What Is It."
51 Thomas Campbell, Instagram, https://www.instagram.com/p/BbidIPrHIv_/?taken-by=thomaspcampbell/.
52 David A. Scott, *Art: Authenticity, Restoration* (Los Angeles: Cotsen Institute of Archaeology Press at UCLA, 2016), 25.
53 Cesare Brandi, *Theory of Restoration*, edited by Giuseppe Basile and translated by Cynthia Rockwell (Florence: Istituto Centrale Per Il Restauro, 1977), 75.
54 For example, the Criminal Code of Canada (RSC, 1985, c. C-46) defines the crime of forgery thus: "366(1) Every one commits forgery who makes a false document, knowing it to be false, with intent (a) that it should in any way be used or acted on as genuine, to the prejudice of any one whether within Canada or not; or (b)

that a person should be induced, by the belief that it is genuine, to do or to refrain from doing anything, whether within Canada or not." In the United States criminal prosecutions of art forgers are possible under federal (RICO), state, and/or local laws. Civil actions can also be brought; in the United Kingdom, for example, the *Sale of Goods Act 1979* or the *Consumer Rights Act 2015* are preferred vehicles.

55 "A pentimento (pl. pentimenti) is a visible trace of earlier painting beneath a layer or layers of paint on a canvas or wooden panel," *Oxford Languages*, Oxford online, https://languages.oup.com/google-dictionary-en/.

56 Isaacson, "Leonardo."

57 Güngör Polatkan, Sina Jafarpour, Andrei Brasoveanu, et al., "Detection of Forgery in Paintings Using Supervised Learning," *16th IEEE International Conference on Image Processes*, 2006, https://ieeexplore.ieee.org/document/5413338.

58 Nica Gutman Rieppi, Beth A. Price, Ken Sutherland, et al. "*Salvator Mundi*: An Investigation of the Painting's Materials and Techniques," *Heritage Science* 8, no. 39 (2020): passim, https://doi.org/10.1186/s40494-020-00382-3A.

59 Rieppi, Price, Sutherland, et al., "*Salvator Mundi*."

60 Francesca Fiorani, "Kenneth Clark and Leonardo: From Connoisseurship to Broadcasting to Digital Technologies," in *Leonardo in Britain: Collections and Historical Perception*, Proceedings of the International Conference, edited by Juliana Barone and Susanna Avery Quash (Florence: Olschki, 2019), 363.

61 See further, Leila Amineddoleh, "Purchasing Art in a Market Full of Forgeries: Risks and Legal Remedies for Buyers," *International Journal of Cultural Property* 22, nos. 2–3 (2015): 419–35.

62 Megan McHugh, Grace DiFrancesco, Joe Gencarelli, and Cai Debenham, "Art Forgeries and Their Detection." *Nature*, n.d., https://nature.berkeley.edu/garbelottoat/wp-content/uploads/art4.pdf.

63 Britannica. "Forgery in the Visual Arts," n.d., https://www.britannica.com/art/forgery-art/Considerations-of-aesthetics-and-risk.

64 "Martin Kemp, Behind the Scenes of Leonardo da Vinci's Salvator Mundi," YouTube, 10 December 2017, https://www.youtube.com/watch?v=hMsg7kWge6A&t=1407s.

65 This account is based on "Rediscovering Leonardo's Salvator Mundi," YouTube, 14 October 2019, https://www.youtube.com/watch?v=VDozBKAFTH0, and Leonardo's Salvator Mundi: "Skulduggery," YouTube, 13 May 2019, https://www.youtube.com/watch?v=KIUP8l7HUWI&ab_channel=GreshamCollege.

66 Kemp, "Skullduggery."

67 Joshua Hammer, "Confessions of an Art World Detective," *Town and Country*, 28 January 2022, https://www.townandcountrymag.com/leisure/arts-and-culture/a38678240/rene-allonge-art-theft-detective/.

68 In its 2019–20 Departmental Report, FINTRAC acknowledged that AI advancements serve both detective and money launderer: "With the advent of artificial intelligence, machine learning, big data, predictive analytics, and

distributed systems, the financial services industry is seeing an unprecedented level of digital disruption, such as the growing use of fintech, blockchain and cryptocurrencies. These same technologies create additional avenues for money launderers and terrorist financiers. FINTRAC also recognizes, though, that artificial intelligence and other evolving technologies can also provide the tools with which to combat this activity."

69 Eileen Kinsella, "'Business as Usual Went Right out the Window': How Lockdown Forced Auction Houses into the Future – For Good," *ArtNet*, 24 September 2020, https://news.artnet.com/market/covid-19-auction-houses-intel-report-2020-1909853.

70 Magnus Resch, "Moneyball for the Art World," *ArtNews*, 3 December 2018, https://www.artnews.com/art-news/news/moneyball-art-world-11439/. For a more mathematical calculation of an artist's successful career based on the first five exhibitions, see further, Samuel P. Fraiberger, Roberta Sinatra, Magnus Resch, et al., "Quantifying Reputation and Success in Art," *Science*, November 2018, https://science.sciencemag.org/content/362/6416/825/tab-figures-data.

71 Andrew Dickson, "The New Tool in the Art of Spotting Forgeries: Artificial Intelligence," *The Guardian*, 6 August 2018, https://www.theguardian.com/us-news/2018/aug/06/the-new-tool-in-the-art-of-spotting-forgeries-artificial-intelligence.

72 Sarah Cascone, "Artificial Intelligence Can Now Spot Art Forgeries by Comparing Brush Strokes," *ArtNet*, 21 November 2017, https://news.artnet.com/art-world/artificial-intelligence-art-authentication-1156037.

73 Ahmed Elgammal, Yan Kang, and Mildo Den Leeuw, "Picasso, Matisse, or a Fake? Automated Analysis of Drawings at the Stroke Level for Authentication and Attribution," *arXiv*. 1711.03536, no. 1 (13 November 2017): 1–24, https://authenticationinart.org/pdf/literature/ai-brushstroke-recognition.pdf.

74 Jackie Snow, "This AI Can Spot Art Forgeries by Looking at One Brushstroke," *MIT Technology Review*, 1 November 2017, https://www.technologyreview.com/s/609524/this-ai-can-spot-art-forgeries-by-looking-at-one-brushstroke/.

75 "Instant Evaluation of Art Authenticity," *Art Recognition*, https://query.prod.cms.rt.microsoft.com/cms/api/am/binary/RWB9bl.

76 Jason Bailey, "Can AI Art Authentication Put an End to Art Forgery?" *Artnome*, 12 September 2019, https://www.artnome.com/news/2019/9/12/can-ai-art-authentication-put-an-end-to-art-forgery.

77 Bailey, "Can AI."

78 Stephen J. Frank and Andrea M. Frank, "A Neural Network Looks at Leonardo's (?) Salvator Mundi," *Leonardo* 54, no. 6 (20 December 2021): 619–24. doi: https://doi.org/10.1162/leon_a_02004. See also Mark Anderson, "Amateurs' AI Tells Real Rembrandts from Fakes," *IEEE Spectrum*, 25 April 2019, https://spectrum.ieee.org/tech-talk/computing/software/the-rembrandt-school-of-ai-an-algorithm-that-detects-art-forgery.

79 Sumbo Bello, "Researchers Train AI to Spot Art Forgery," *Edgy*, 29 April 2019, https://edgy.app/ai-to-spot-art-forgeries.
80 Carmen Bambach, "Seeking the Universal Painter: Carmen C. Bambach Appraises the National Gallery's Once-in-a-Lifetime Exhibition Dedicated to Leonardo da Vinci," *Apollo Magazine*, 1 February 2012, https://www.thefreelibrary.com/Seeking+the+universal+painter%3A+Carmen+C.+Bambach+appraises+the...-a0281460849.
81 Charles Hope, "A Peece of Christ," *London Review of Books* 42, no. 2 (2 January 2020), https://www.lrb.co.uk/the-paper/v42/n01/charles-hope/a-peece-of-christ.
82 "Models: Overview," OpenAI, https://platform.openai.com/docs/models/gpt-3-5. OpenAI's models are based on Generative Pre-trained Transformer (GPT) technology. Competitive LLMs in 2023 include Bing 16 (Microsoft) and BARD (Google).
83 "Artificial Intelligence Is Rapidly Developing, but How Does It Work? Experts Explain," NBC News, YouTube, 22 March 2023, https://www.nscan youtube.com/watch?v=APliuwGYDNc&ab_channel=NBCNews.
84 Ian Bogost, "Google's 'Sentient' Chatbot Is Our Self-Deceiving Future," *The Atlantic*, 14 June 2022, https://www.theatlantic.com/technology/archive/2022/06/google-engineer-sentient-ai-chatbot/661273/.
85 Aaron Welborn, "ChatGPT and Fake Citations," Duke University Libraries, 9 March 2023, https://blogs.library.duke.edu/blog/2023/03/09/chatgpt-and-fake-citations/.
86 "Beyond ChatGPT: What Chatbots Mean for the Future," *The Economist*, YouTube, 23 March 2023, https://www.youtube.com/watch?v=dctcfxw13AQ&ab_channel=TheEconomist.
87 James A. Lubowitz, "ChatGPT, an Artificial Intelligence Chatbot, Is Impacting Medical Literature," *Journal of Arthroscopy and Related Surgery* 39, no. 5 (2023): 1121–2, DOI: 10.1016/j.arthro.2023.01.015.
88 Ju Yoen Lee, "Can an Artificial Intelligence Chatbot be the Author of a Scholarly Article?" *Journal of Educational Evaluation for Health Professions*, 20 June 2023, doi: 10.3352/jeehp.2023.20.6.
89 Nick Vincent and Hanlin Li, "ChatGPT Stole Your Work. So What Are You Going to Do?" *Wired*, 28 January 2023. Authors discuss four "data leverage" activities that users can choose to regain power over their data: *direct action* (such as redirecting data); *regulatory action* (through data protection policy); *legal action* (pursuing a lawsuit); and *market action* (demanding consent for use of data).
90 "How DALL-E 2 Is Changing the Art World with Words and Images," Today/CNN, YouTube, 30 August 2022 [3:36], https://www.youtube.com/watch?v=hiSgpZUAy2c&ab_channel=TODAY.
91 Europol, "ChatGPT: The Impact of Large Language Models on Law Enforcement," *Tech Watch Flash*, 27 March 2023, https://www.europol.europa.eu/publications-events/publications/chatgpt-impact-of-large-language-models-law-enforcement.
92 Karen Hao, "AI Armed with Multiple Senses Could Gain More Flexible Intelligence," *MIT Technology Review*, 24 February 2021, https://www.technologyreview.com/2021/02/24/1018085/multimodal-ai-vision-language/.

93 Christine Caron, "The A.I, Chatbots Have Arrived, Time to Talk to Your Kids," *New York Times*, 22 March 2023, https://www.nytimes.com/2023/03/22/well/family/ai-chatgpt-parents-children.html referencing Sherry Turkle.
94 Hao, "AI Armed."
95 Cade Metz and Gregory Schmidt, "Elon Musk and Others Call for Pause on A.I., Citing 'Profound Risks to Society,'" *New York Times*, 29 March 2023, https://www.nytimes.com/2023/03/29/technology/ai-artificial-intelligence-musk-risks.html.
96 "INTERPOL Introduces Art App to Better Protect Cultural Heritage," *Interpol.int*, 6 May 2021, https://www.interpol.int/en/News-and-Events/News/2021/INTERPOL-launches-app-to-better-protect-cultural-heritage.
97 Europol, "ChatGPT."
98 Nicholas Vincent, "Why You're an Expert 'Language Model Trainer'!" *PSA Research Group*, 31 March 2021. The author points out that "GPT-3 is one of the largest and most powerful language processing AI models to date, with 175 billion parameters."
99 Vanessa Thorpe, "'ChatGPT Said I Did Not Exist': How Artists and Writers Are Fighting Back against AI," *Guardian*, 18 March 2023, https://www.theguardian.com/technology/2023/mar/18/chatgpt-said-i-did-not-exist-how-artists-and-writers-are-fighting-back-against-ai.
100 Nora McGreevy, "Interpol's New App Combats Art Crime and Protects Cultural Heritage," *Smithsonian Magazine*, 12 May 2021.
101 "ChatGPT for Law Enforcement: Unlocking the Potential for Beat Cops, Detectives and Admin," DopeCop, YouTube, 13 January 2023 [11:01], https://www.youtube.com/watch?v=hByXi92ir1Q&ab_channel=DopeCop.
102 Kate Knibbs, "Researchers Tested AI Watermarks — and Broke All of Them," *Wired*, 3 October 2023, https://www.wired.com/story/artificial-intelligence-watermarking-issues/
103 Shawn Shan, Wenxin Ding, Josephine Passananti, et al., "Prompt-Specific Poisoning Attacks on Text-to-Image Generative Models," *arXiv*, 20 October 2023, https://doi.org/10.48550/arXiv.2310.13828.
104 Karen Hao, "The Two-Year Fight to Stop Amazon from Selling Face Recognition to the Police," *MIT Technology Review* (12 June 2020), https://www.technologyreview.com/2020/06/12/1003482/amazon-stopped-selling-police-face-recognition-fight/.
105 "NIST Study Evaluates Effects of Race, Age, Sex on Face Recognition Software," *National Institute of Standards and Technology*, 19 December 2019, https://www.nist.gov/news-events/news/2019/12/nist-study-evaluates-effects-race-age-sex-face-recognition-software.
106 Kayla Kibbe, "Government Study Confirms Face Recognition Technology Is Racist," *Inside Hook*, 23 December 2019, https://www.insidehook.com/daily_brief/news-opinion/government-study-confirms-face-recognition-technology-is-racist.
107 Walter Bradley Center for Natural & Artificial Intelligence, "What's at Stake in the Debate over AI?" 4 July 2018, https://centerforintelligence.org/2018/07/04/whats-at-stake/.

108 Bogost, "Google 'Chatbot.'"
109 Ellen Zimiles and Tim Mueller, "How AI Is Transforming the Fight against Money Laundering," *World Economic Forum*, 17 January 2019, https://www.weforum.org/agenda/2019/01/how-ai-can-knock-the-starch-out-of-money-laundering/.
110 Dropped to 50 US billion in 2020 due to pandemic economic forces, according to Angelica Villa, "2021 Art Basel Global Market Report Reveals 22 Percent Drop in 2020 Sales to $50 Billion," *Artnews*, 16 March 2021, https://www.artnews.com/art-news/market/2021-art-basel-report-says-50-billion-1234586822/.
111 United Nations Office on Drugs and Crime, "Money Laundering," UNDOC, https://www.unodc.org/unodc/en/money-laundering/overview.html.
112 William Douglas Heaven, "The Pandemic Has Changed How Criminals Hide Their Case," *MIT Technology Review* (6 August 2020), https://www.technologyreview.com/2020/08/06/1006104/covid-pandemic-criminals-cash-money-laundering-financial-crime-ai-machine-learning/.
113 Financial Transactions and Reports Analysis Centre of Canada, "Special Bulletin on COVID-19: Trends in Money Laundering and Fraud," July 2020. In the United States, see Richard Summerfield, "Heightened Vigilance: COVID-19 Creates Fraud and Money Laundering Vulnerabilities," *Financier Worldwide*, reporting that "the Financial Crimes Enforcement Network (FinCEN), the Financial Industry Regulatory Authority (FINRA), the Securities and Exchange Commission (SEC) and the Commodity Futures Trading Commission (CFTC) have all advised financial institutions to be on high alert for a potential increase in 'illicit financial activity.'"
114 Financial Action Task Force, "Update: COVID-19 Related Money Laundering and Terrorist Financing," December 2020.
115 "Financial Action Task Force," 6.
116 "Financial Action Task Force," 6.
117 Charlotte Dunn, "Art Crimes in Current Times," *Institute of Art & Law*, 1 May 2020, https://ial.uk.com/art-crime-in-current-times/. For a more legal oriented analysis, see Katie Dixon and Zachary Shufro, "Risky Business: Fraud, Authenticity, and Limited Legal Protections in the High Art Market," *New York University Journal of Intellectual Property & Entertainment Law* 10, no. 2 (2021): 246.
118 Heaven, "The Pandemic."
119 Parag S. Chandakkar, and Baoxin Li, "Investigating Human Factors in Image Forgery Detection," *Computer Science*, 5 April 2017, https://arxiv.org/abs/1704.01262.
120 World Economic Forum, "The Next Generation of Data-Sharing in Financial Services: Using Privacy Enhancing Techniques to Unlock New Value," White Paper, 12 September 2019, https://www.weforum.org/whitepapers/the-next-generation-of-data-sharing-in-financial-services-using-privacy-enhancing-techniques-to-unlock-new-value.
121 Clive Thompson, "The Untold Story of the NFT Boom," *New York Times Magazine*, 12 May 2021, https://www.nytimes.com/2021/05/12/magazine/nft-art-crypto.html.

122 "Crypto Crime Trends for 2022: Illicit Transaction Activity Reaches All-Time High in Value, All-Time Low in Share of All Cryptocurrency Activity," *Chainalysis*, 6 January 2022, https://blog.chainalysis.com/reports/2022-crypto-crime-report-introduction/.
123 Dickson, "The New Tool."
124 Scott Reyburn, "JPG File Sells for $69 Million, as 'NFT Mania' Gathers Pace," *New York Times*, 11 March 2021, https://www.nytimes.com/2021/03/11/arts/design/nft-auction-christies-beeple.html. The NFT artwork was titled *Everydays: The First 5000 Days*, 2021, and completed by "Beeple."
125 Reyburn, "JPG File."
126 Dante Alighieri, *The Divine Comedy* (Indiana: Indiana University Press, 2004).
127 Artwork Archive, "Biggest Art Fakes and Forgeries Revealed in 2018," *Artwork Archive*, 2018, https://www.artworkarchive.com/blog/biggest-art-fakes-and-forgeries-revealed-in-2018.
128 All FINTRAC guidance, https://fintrac-canafe.canada.ca/guidance-directives/guidance-directives-eng.
129 Rapley, "Police Investigation."
130 German, "Dirty Money."
131 Adrienne Tanner, "Peter German Is on a Mission." *CPA Canada*, 24 April 2020, https://www.cpacanada.ca/en/news/pivot-magazine/2020-04-24-peter-german-dirty-money.
132 Jason Bailey, "Can AI Art Authentication Put an End to Art Forgery?" *Artnome*, 12 September 2019, https://www.artnome.com/news/2019/9/12/can-ai-art-authentication-put-an-end-to-art-forgery.
133 Diane Dwyer Modestini, Salvator Mundi Revisited, at https://salvatormundirevisited.com/History-of-the-Salvator-Mundi.
134 Modestini, Salvator Mundi Revisited.

7 Big Money, Small Tax: The Normalization of Tax Evasion

LAUREEN SNIDER

Introduction

Margaret Beare famously argued that "ongoing patterns of exchange" and the "normalization of corruption" are the hallmarks of corporate corruption in Canada.[1] She examined circumstances that allow elite cultures to believe that if an act has not (*yet*) been declared illegal, it is justifiable. No "ethical or fairness considerations" are relevant.[2] This article explores factors behind this licence to evade/avoid rules among the most adept practitioners of big money/big crime, those who practise tax avoidance. It makes two claims: first, that neoliberalism carries a social, moral, and cultural agenda that infuses all societal practices, institutions, and values. Second, while non-elites have adjusted their moral imperatives to survive the neoliberal economy, elite corruption has become endemic because elites have the most opportunities to exploit their advantages without fear of negative repercussions, legal or otherwise. The impact and implications of these factors are explored in the third section of the chapter, an empirical examination of the legitimizers, enablers, and participants who practise tax evasion.

1. Neoliberalism as a Moral Imperative

Whyte and Wiegratz define neoliberalism as "an analytic category used to identify, describe and make sense of a system of sometimes interconnected and sometimes disparate, but always contradictory truth claims."[3] No one package of dogma defines all neoliberal agendas. Nor has it been defined, understood, and implemented in the same way in different societies. Major societal change is *always* chaotic, partial, and resisted, varying with historical and cultural specificities, with timing, and with the presence or absence of champions. Nevertheless, it is worth outlining the basic claims of neoliberalism: a set of policy prescriptions that sees *free* markets as the only efficient way to distribute resources and manage a capitalist economy. Markets are free when there is no government "interference." Governments, and public services in general, restrict individual liberty and impede efficiency. Neoliberalism is also an ideology that posits competitiveness as a universal and desirable human trait. It promotes specific economic and social policies that facilitate "the commodification of all forms of social provision, consumption and distribution."[4] It is hard to imagine a better facilitating recipe for big crime and big money.

The ideal human being under neoliberalism is an independent individual who is always seeking ways to maximize his (*sic* – it is a uniquely, albeit not exclusively, male-gendered vision) economic opportunities. If this self-maximizing individual finds a socio-political environment that values and rewards these traits and has the opportunity to control the behaviour of others as, for example, the CEO of a major corporation, he will prosper. Moral and ethical issues are second-order considerations. This is why Whyte and Wiegratz, among others, claim that fraud, "the use of deception to make an economic gain," is now endemic.[5] As the authors state, "the apparent rapid rise in a range of business and consumer frauds [is] a direct consequence of the liberalization of market, the re-regulation of particular economic sectors and the restructuring of the state."[6] This is partly because neoliberal states have privatized and downsized those agencies responsible for monitoring and sanctioning corporate crime, but the deepest damage is rooted in the social practices and values, rationalizations, and moral justifications that are part and parcel of the neoliberal agenda. Its moral narratives encourage corruption because the logic of neoliberal capitalism is not public service or social responsibility, but self-interest, self-maximizing, and individualism. As Makovicky points out, "the moral economy of modern quango-culture regularly conflates the pursuit of private gain with the production of public good," making greed and corruption "a routine side-effect of neoliberal policymaking" rather than the practice of a few rogue individuals.[7]

Nor does corporate/business corruption arise in a vacuum. Like the corruption of individuals, corporate wrongdoers have a set of market values derived from neoliberalism that explain and justify their behaviour to themselves and to broader institutions and publics. Though these rationales serve their own interests, they are presented as benefitting everyone – they create prosperity, jobs, and fuel competitiveness. These values and policies are normalized in dominant discourse and institutions. And they are ubiquitous – entwined with and engrained in our day-to-day practices. "The morality of neo-liberalism is able to confront other moralities and give impetus to a process of substantial and lasting moral change," change that "shapes the structures and practices of accumulation and making a living."[8]

There is little empirical work tracing how new ways of thinking and acting become "standard practice" (hegemonic), but one lens is the phenomenon of "moral regulation,"[9] defined as "a project of normalizing, rendering natural, taken for granted, obvious, what are in fact ontological and epistemological premises of a particular and historical form of social order."[10] Feminist works have documented regulatory efforts to shame, tame, and discipline women through constructing the unwed mother, the slut, and the hysterical woman.[11] Others have documented the creation of the child abuser, the alcoholic, and the psychopath.[12] These are all attempts to shape the morality of particular subjects and change attitudes and behaviour. They are typically initiated by more powerful groups (patriarchal elites, for example) and aimed at the less powerful (poor women and men).

The transition from feudalism to capitalism made it imperative to change the beliefs, practices, and culture of land-based peasants and shape them into an industrial proletariat. The original autonomous self-actualizing individuals – owners of cotton mills and aristocrats who realized that sheep were more productive than people – proclaimed their emancipation from age-old social ties to their land and tenants/serfs. Peasants pushed off the land had few means of resistance other than riots, since many if not most were illiterate and universal suffrage was two centuries away. At the moral level, as Carrier argues, the rioters were protesting the loss of a way of thinking that linked social and economic relations.[13] Landowners were abandoning historic responsibilities that were part and parcel of the feudal order[14] Carrier argues that we see a similar disavowal of public responsibility – to states, communities, employees, and the environment – in the practices and rationales of global capitalism today.

While it is difficult to link neoliberalism to specific moral shifts, we *can* document the values that are most useful to living the ideal neoliberal life. Swader showed the "dark side ... of individualization" in Eastern European countries after the fall of communism in 1989.[15] The successful post-communist "homo-economous" has to develop "flexible morality."[16] The most rewarding traits at the individual (micro), institutional (meso), and societal (macro) levels of analysis are promoting one's own interests, independence, and self-maximizing. The prototypical individual must be more egoistic than altruistic, quick to spot and seize opportunities, more interested in his own well-being than that of a collective or amorphous public. The ability to see others' points of view is a disadvantage – empathy gets in the way of success. Individuals must be constantly alert to different ways of commodifying their talents and possessions. Unused bedrooms can become sources of income; the family car can become a taxi; one's clothing, genes, food, music, or children can all be turned into moneymaking "brands."[17] And cornering the market on masks and ventilators during a COVID pandemic is a clever move.

Like the neoliberal individual, businesses must be nimble, efficient, and constantly on the lookout for ways to cut costs and expand and develop profitable new ventures. Maximum profit at minimum risk to the bottom line is sought.

Establishing and avoiding risk is the basic criterion of neoliberal decision-making. Whether a particular decision is ethical, moral, or harmful to employees and/or communities has no place in the equation. A policy decision may be reversed to avoid state sanctions or publicity, but this is an expedient, instrumental consideration not an ethical one.

A central characteristic of neoliberal governance is its faith in free markets. Money should be *put to work* by lending it out in as many ways as possible and profiting from each transaction. Financialization is the practice of applying a monetary value to everything that can be touched or imagined. Tangible goods, services, or natural resources and intangible, imagined concepts and futures are turned into commodities, valued solely for their exchange value. The goal is to turn *it*, whatever *it* is, into a financial instrument, or a derivative of a financial instrument, something that can be traded on some kind of exchange. Key factors in the mortgage credit collapse of 2007–8 where millions lost their homes were new mathematically based ways of hiding risk by conceptualizing, bundling, and selling assets through over-the-counter derivatives such as credit default swaps. By slicing high-risk mortgages into "tranches" and selling them in huge bundles, the riskiness of any one mortgage disappeared – and the bank profited not once, as in traditional house mortgages, but many, many times. Regulators lacked the resources and, in many cases, the will to stop these practices because they also believed that "the market would sort it out." Neither individual bankers nor their institutions questioned the morality of their transactions – leaked e-mails show them revelling in the power they wielded over the "suckers" who bought "garbage mortgages."[18]

Perhaps the clearest example of neoliberal dogma is found in New Public Management (NPM), a program that has radically modified the philosophy and practice of public service in modern states, first in the United Kingdom under Margaret Thatcher, then New Zealand, Sweden, North America, and beyond.[19] Traditional public service goals, particularly democratic accountability and service, were derided as obsolete, and public servants who resisted were made redundant, transferred, and (wherever unions were weak) fired.[20] Efficient governments cut the size of the public sector and the power of public service unions and implemented professional management techniques that divided departments into small units forced to compete against each other for budgets and staff. Performance measures determined the winners.[21]

To sum up: individual, institutional, and macro factors inhibiting corruption have been eroded or replaced, material and moral incentives promoting self-serving practices have increased. At the individual level, self-maximizing is the new norm; cost-cutting, efficiency, and profits are seen as more worthwhile than social responsibility or public service; and states have downsized, defunded, privatized, or abolished many of the agencies and personnel responsible for policing business. Neoliberal fraud is "the outcome of a broader process that has restructured the ... assemblage of power relations, accumulation imperatives, subjectivities, common sense and modes of thinking."[22] Thus it is reasonable to assume that elite crimes have increased. And there is ample evidence this is the case.

2. Elite Corruption

In the early 1980s, the eras of Thatcher and Reagan, neoliberalism fuelled unchecked globalization and corporations accelerated their search for new resources to exploit, new markets to develop. In 1989, the Soviet Union collapsed and another vast swathe of the globe opened to capitalist expansion. International institutions such as the World Bank (WB) and International Monetary Fund (IMF) provided capital to promote resource development and the transition to capitalist economic systems (under the guise of promoting "democracy"). Millions of development aid dollars went into the pockets (and Swiss bank accounts) of national and local elites in developing countries. In return, dissent was suppressed and docile labour forces were delivered to corporate factories and mines. The world was suddenly awash in big money.

As the environmental damage and cultural costs became visible to all, globalized capital went on the defensive. The problems, they claimed, were due to corrupt governments and greedy officials in the host countries. Thus, corruption was defined as "the abuse of public office for private gain"[23] and the prescribed remedies were wholesale privatization of formerly public goods and services. This "woefully deficient" concept of corruption ignores and minimizes corporate responsibility for the types of corruption practised and promoted by the private sector.[24] This is not to deny the existence of public-sector corruption, but this is a very partial, neoliberal, and Western perspective of globalized capitalism.[25]

While bemoaning the role of those who accept illicit funds, international bodies and governments have been slow to act against those who offer the bribes. But with the World Bank estimating dollar losses through corruption in the trillions,[26] the Organization for Economic Cooperation and Development (OECD) asked its thirty-four members to pass a series of anti-corruption laws by the end of 1998.[27] Canada yielded to this pressure by adopting the Corruption of Foreign Public Officials Act (CFPOA), which prohibits "offering, promising or giving [payments or gifts] ... to a foreign public official directly or indirectly ... in exchange for using his/her position or influence to obtain a business advantage."[28] But the legislation was full of loopholes and lacked enforcement mechanisms. In 2014, Canada finally established an International Anti-Corruption Unit in the RCMP's Commercial Crime Branch, but the Crown still had to prove both *actus reus* (the actual act) and *mens rea* (guilty mind) to get a criminal conviction.

Few scholars have examined private-sector corruption in high-income countries, the home base of the primary offenders. Exceptions include Beare, Friedrichs, and Wedel.[29] Beare's intensive investigation of the corruption revealed by the Charbonneau Report, a bid-rigging scandal involving the governing Liberal party, organized crime and the construction industry in Quebec, identified a wide array of political officials, bureaucrats, political parties, organized crime, unions, and entrepreneurs who worked together to skim off public money for private ends.[30] The Charbonneau Commission revealed "a culture of impunity," a long-standing network of exchanges and interactions that were not defined as corruption by the participants.[31] Key actors avoided criminal charges because these networks do not operate the way law defines and criminalizes corruption.

Beare addresses the decline of institutional and individual factors that inhibit corruption through cases of tax evasion.[32] She argues that elites in Canada have special legal privileges because their harmful acts, if illegal at all, are covered by corporate law, which grants corporations special privileges (incorporation, limited liability, the assumption of corporate personhood and ambiguity). Canada has no transparency laws allowing corporate ownership (particularly of shell companies) to be traced.[33] Legal judgments that conflate the legal with the ethical/acceptable nourish a "corruption-permissive" elite culture that allows elites to see their advantages as legitimate. Beare states, "There is an acceleration of impact driven by the development of niche professional areas of expertise that specialize in exploiting every advantage that the laws allow" and "sharing values that see the 'legality' of the actions as adequate justification."[34] She comments further, "A system that operates on capitalistic principles that value profit and personal gain [as neoliberal capitalism does] must have ... countermechanisms that can prevent corruption."[35] And (despite ever more promises of new legislation)[36] ours does not.

Hypothesized increases in elite corruption are most dramatically validated in the United States where the neoliberal, anti-regulation policies of former President Trump have allowed and promoted corporate corruption.[37] While most Western governments have downsized and starved regulatory agencies, the speed and depth of Trump's measures is both unprecedented and extreme.[38] One of Trump's first moves was Executive Order 13771 requiring all agencies to cut "at least" two regulations for every new one.[39] As of December 2019, twenty-four financial regulations have been amended, delayed, deregulated, or rescinded; nineteen in telecommunications (including the Net Neutrality repeal in June 2018); twenty-five in health (including no mandatory coverage of birth control, October 2017); seventeen in labour; ten in education; twenty in transportation; five in housing; fourteen unclassified "other"; and a mammoth fifty-four in the Environmental Protection Agency.[40]

The Trump presidency provides a dramatic illustration of Tombs and Whyte's argument that all corporate corruption and crime under neoliberalism is state enabled.[41] The loss of continuity and experienced staff will make it impossible for President Biden to reverse most of these changes or undo the damage done.[42]

Predictably, then, prosecutions for white-collar crime in the United States have declined to their lowest point since tracking began in 1998. Criminal penalties fell from $3.6 billion in 2015 (the last year of the Obama presidency) to $110 million in 2019. Illicit profits seized by the Securities and Exchange Commission have dropped by half.[43] And Trump continually used his powers to pardon corporate criminals. On Tuesday, 18 February 2020, for example, seven new pardons and four sentence commutations went to the former police commissioner of New York, convicted of tax fraud, to "Junk Bond King" Michael Milken, convicted of violating securities laws, and to Edward de Bartolo Jr., convicted of gambling fraud.[44]

3. Tax Avoidance and "Wealth Managers"

This section looks at the exponential growth of tax evasion under neoliberal policy changes to "free" capital in the 1980s and 1990s. Limits on the convertibility of national currencies and the amounts that could be taken outside a country were removed, technological changes in the 1990s allowed 24/7 stock trading, and the 1980s "shareholder value revolution" made profit maximization the primary, indeed the only, goal of business.[45] It is estimated that governments regularly lose at least US$20 billion annually due to tax avoidance (legal) and tax evasion (illegal).[46] We look first at the enablers of tax avoidance, the "wealth managers" who devise the tools that allow top income holders and corporations to evade taxes; second at the 1 per cent and their morality; and third at the consequences, the damage done.

Until the nineteenth century the main source of wealth was land ownership, and family wealth was defended through intermarriage and primogeniture. The earliest form of *trusts* was an informal arrangement which involved the temporary transfer of land ownership to a third party, usually a relative or friend, "in trust" for the benefit of the owner's wife and children. This prevented seizure by "the church, the state, or rival noblemen."[47] As capitalism expanded ownership of the means of production – factories, railroads, and banks – and trade became the dominant sources of great wealth. Wealth was largely confined to a small number of white, upper-class families in North America and Europe. With the introduction of income tax in the United States in 1913 as a temporary provision to fund the First World War, corporate wealth began moving off-shore and profit-sheltering, tax-exempt vehicles such as foundations and think-tanks became more common. While ostensibly dedicated to social welfare, these institutions are allowed to use their riches to influence policies and engage in electoral politics in an unregulated, non-transparent way, thanks to a loophole in the US tax system known as 501(C)(4).[48] In their roles as politicians, donors, and lobbyists, this class has prevented states from taxing newly mobile global wealth, forcing them to engage in an endless war to the bottom to attract capital investment by cutting corporate taxes, abolishing unions, creating special trading zones, and granting tax holidays.

Wealth management was professionalized in 1991 with the founding of the Society of Trust and Estate Practitioners (STEP) to train accountants, bankers, and lawyers as "wealth managers" who engage in "the business of deploying legal and financial expertise to defend the fortunes of high net-worth individuals and families."[49] STEP now has over 20,000 members in over ninety-five countries. Wealth managers put the assets of high-value individuals into a "trust" in tax havens such as the Cayman Islands, Switzerland, Luxembourg, Jersey, Bermuda, Hong Kong, Lichtenstein, and the Seychelles (to name only a few). Clients must have at least US$30 million in investable assets, and the contemporary client base for STEP professionals includes the world's 167,669 "ultra-high worth individuals," 0.7 per cent of the global population who own 41 per cent of global assets.[50] Each trust will hold shares in multiple corporations in different countries, allowing assets to be swiftly transferred if national governments raise taxes or legislate transparency. Corporations make billions in profits in one country but register and pay taxes wherever tax rates are lowest. In 2017 Google, for example, shifted US$23 billion through a Dutch shell company to Google Ireland Holdings, an affiliate based in Bermuda where companies pay no income tax. This legal manoeuvre allowed Google to avoid paying US income tax or European withholding taxes on its overseas profits.[51]

Getting information on the culture, practices, and rationale of wealth management professionals is difficult because their success depends on arranging complex secret deals. However, two recent studies have penetrated the veil of secrecy. In 2014–15 John Christensen did interviews with twenty tax professionals from the Big Four transnational accounting firms, Pricewaterhouse Coopers, Deloitte, KPMG, and Ernst and Young,[52] and from 2008 to 2015 Brooke Harrington interviewed sixty-five wealth managers in eighteen countries.[53] To gain access and establish trust, Harrington completed STEP's two-year trust and estate planning (TEP) certification program.[54] Both authors laid bare the enormous influence global accounting firms have on politics and the economy. They market tax avoidance schemes to favoured clients and shape tax policies by intensive lobbying of politicians by funding academic research, making large political donations, hiring former tax officials and politicians as advisers, and publishing commentaries on what they saw as sensible tax policy in national and international media. Christensen points out that professional accountants once saw themselves as having a duty to balance their commercial interests with their public service duty, but his subjects admitted that their professional codes of conduct were "weak or non-existent on the ethics of tax avoidance."[55] This is no surprise since the Big Four firms "play an influential role in shaping the ethical norms and wider culture of the tax advisory industry" and write new accounting rules.[56] Accountants also enjoy a state-guaranteed monopoly over bankruptcy proceedings and external audit markets, and the privilege of self-regulation. They justify their roles as "helping business grow," making "efficiency gains," and "reducing client costs," but "profit maximization" is their over-riding duty.[57]

Harrington's study reveals a wealth management culture hostile to outsiders and resentful of "misguided" and "naïve" press coverage.[58] Many of her interviewees see themselves as providing a vital public service – preventing feckless children of the very rich from squandering family wealth or preventing "unethical" "onerous" tax grabs which fund "generous government spending" on the unworthy and undeserving.[59] They believe taxes act as a "chill on the entrepreneur as a creator of wealth" and encourage the poor to rely on welfare instead of taking jobs and resent being forced to pay for services they do not use, such as public education or Medicare.[60]

The clients of wealth managers also have numerous justifications for avoiding/evading taxation. Former President Trump epitomized this when he asserted that not paying income taxes makes him "smart" because the money would be "squandered."[61] Bankers complicit in crimes such as interest rate fixing, bribery, issuing sub-prime mortgages, and fraud offered similar rationales. As individuals they said their crimes were necessary to meet company targets, keep their job, defend or advance their career, and sometimes "to make a killing and then retire."[62] At the societal level they believed that "what is good for business is good for all," that free markets, flexible workers, open societies, and economic freedom make for competitiveness, growth, and "a good society."[63] As Wiegratz observed, "their moral compass is firmly anchored in the magnetic field of late capitalism."[64]

One of the few quantitative studies of elite attitudes to tax evasion and bribery used World Values Survey data from 2005 to 2009 from forty-seven developed and less developed countries.[65] The goal was to discover whether capitalism itself is criminogenic[66] or whether fraudulent behaviour is correlated with the personal characteristics, values, and culture of national elites. Swader found that the capitalist class in all countries shows more "moral flexibility" and sees fewer ethical problems with, for example, paying workers "less than they [are] worth" than middle- or lower-class groups.[67] "Fraud support rises steeply with income," but this drops off slightly at the top level in developed countries, somewhat more in the less developed world. Swader argues that "the structural demands on a capitalist enterprise … to *achieve profit through the most efficient techniques available*" are universal, but there is "cultural variability in the *individual profit motive*."[68] That is, capitalism *is* criminogenic, but primarily because it promotes materialistic values, and the most materialistic populations, whatever their class or gender, are more in favour of fraud.

Studies elsewhere have shown that tax evasion varies directly with wealth – the top 0.01 per cent richest households in Scandinavia evade "about 25 per cent of the taxes they owe" by concealing "assets and investment income abroad."[69] A series of studies[70] have shown that the rich are more likely than the less rich to act unethically: drivers of high-status cars are four times more likely to cut off those driving lower-status cars and more likely to fail to yield right of way to pedestrians at crosswalks (these findings were controlled for traffic density, age, and gender – since young men in all classes drive faster and more aggressively than women or older people). In laboratory experiments students primed to feel rich took twice as much candy from a jar supposedly meant for underprivileged children as those who were not primed. High-status job seekers are more likely to lie when applying for jobs, cheat at computer games, and support tax evasion and bribery to secure contracts. And rich people are more likely to blame others rather than themselves for failures. In every sense, they feel *entitled*.

Generalizations are always dangerous. There are many empathetic, non-materialistic people in top income groups, and numerous differences between new money and old money. While possibly more cohesive,[71] the very rich are more ethnically diverse that they used to be, albeit not in gender (they are still predominantly male). Billionaires from the Middle East (oil sheiks, for example) and Asia (particularly China) have different attitudes to wealth and privilege than Anglo-Saxon elites from Northern Europe and the United States. Wealth managers report that Arabs, for example, are less happy with surrendering ownership; they prefer to own assets outright, while Chinese billionaires want tax-evading structures consonant with traditional patriarchal authority that extend beyond the grave – for instance, grandson x only receives y if he behaves in a certain way.[72] Despite these differences Urry argues that the growth of offshoring has created homogeneity among the global rich. They have become a "class for itself" not a "class in itself."[73] In tastes, travel destinations, schools attended, and attitudes to wealth, the Swedish billionaire has more in common with the Turkish or Chinese billionaire than with his/her fellow citizens.

Why does this matter? What damage does it do? In the eyes of the super-rich their actions prevent governments from wasting money and facilitate entrepreneurship. While 59 per cent of Americans (71 per cent of Democrats, 60 per cent of Independents, and even 45 per cent of Republicans) support tax increases on those earning over US$10 million a year, elites argue that this will cause capital flight and destroy corporate and national competitiveness. They lobby instead (usually successfully) for tax cuts.[74] But when nations cut taxes on the very rich, corporations use their windfalls on stock buybacks that reward the richest Americans who own 80 per cent of all shares.[75] For example, Trump's *Tax Cuts and Jobs Act* (2017) generated a record $1.1 *trillion* buybacks; wage rates grew 1.9 per cent and job creation was a meagre 2.9 per cent in 2018. The very rich evade the lower tax rates as assiduously as they did the higher rates. Estimates of global offshore wealth range from $8.2 trillion to $32 trillion *despite* historically low tax rates, special concessions, and subsidies.[76] Taxes in many developed countries are now regressive rather than progressive: the poor subsidize the rich. Only four countries, Costa Rica, Mexico, Turkey, and Chile, have a lower tax rate for top income earners than the United States.[77] Income tax rates for the richest four hundred families have fallen from 70 per cent in 1950, 47 per cent in 1980, to 21 per cent after Trump's tax cut. As recently as 2001, the rich were assessed inheritance taxes on estates worth $650,000 or more; now the cut-off point is $11 million. In 1950 the top 1 per cent of Americans received 10 per cent of all income, the share of the bottom 50 per cent was 20 per cent. After the 2017 tax cuts, the 1 per cent gets 20 per cent, the bottom 50 per cent merely 12 per cent.[78] Over 90 per cent of major corporations and high–net worth individuals have offshore accounts; one-quarter to one-third of all global wealth is offshore.[79]

With nation-states losing trillions in tax revenues annually, the escalation in inequality is not surprising. What *is* surprising is that governments have done so little to stem the bleeding; indeed, many have facilitated it.[80] As Urry demonstrates, major states "engender and facilitate" their own havens, with "geographic, historic, symbolic ties to the homeland."[81] The tax-free status of the City of London goes back centuries – the City is 1.2 square miles in the heart of the financial district where the usual laws and taxes of Britain do not apply. The City is a legally registered *corporation* with municipal authority that functions as a giant, rich international offshore lobbying group, one that incessantly argues for international financial deregulation, tax-cutting and more tax havens. Its assets are beyond state authority; the king himself has to ask permission to enter.[82] Tax havens such as Jersey, Guernsey, and the Isle of Man are referred to as extensions of the City of London – they have governors appointed by the British monarch and multiple ties to the British government but retain sufficient autonomy that Britain is powerless to end their tax haven status. One step removed from the City of London are British overseas territories, such as the Cayman Islands and Bermuda.[83] Beyond these are havens such as Mauritius in the Indian Ocean, Hong Kong, and the Bahamas, which Britain does not control but which still "feed billions in business to the City from around the world."[84] The City of London acts as "the hub of a global network of tax havens sucking up offshore trillions from around the world and sending it, or the business of handling it, to London."[85,86]

Other countries have passed special laws to accommodate the cultural preferences of the very rich. The British Virgin Islands, for example, crafted VISTA (Virgin Islands Special Trusts Act) to attract Asian billionaires who want complete anonymity – even the wealth managers who created their trusts are ignorant of the daily operations of those billionaires' businesses. VISTA has been "a resounding success."[87] A similar arrangement, Special Trusts Alternative Regime (STAR) was created in the Cayman Islands in 1997.[88]

As noted earlier, since the 2007–8 financial crisis the OECD has pressured its members to pass anti-corruption laws to force tax havens to reveal the source, ownership, and amount of hidden money. In 2010, the United States passed the *Foreign Accounts Tax Compliance Act*, a law that requires foreign financial institutions to submit the financial information of US citizens in their countries to the Internal Revenue Service (IRS) or face a 30 per cent withholding tax. This is an attempt to regain national fiscal self-determination, something lost when capital was "set free."[89] However, FATCA exempts the United States! Financial institutions in the United States are *not* required to share foreign account holders' information with their respective countries, so the United States is "rapidly becoming the new Switzerland."[90] Delaware, South Dakota, Wyoming, and Nevada have functioned as tax havens for decades – over 65 per cent of Fortune 500 companies and more than half of all US publicly traded companies are incorporated in Delaware, and eighty-one of the 206 trusts revealed in the Panama Papers are in South Dakota.[91] Similar problems have plagued the efforts of other countries to reclaim misappropriated tax dollars. The European Union still loses over $27 billion in corporate tax a year due to US firms shifting profits from where they were earned to tax havens where corporate income tax rates range from 10 per cent to 0.08 per cent. It is estimated that Luxembourg alone costs EU nations $12 billion per year in lost corporate taxes, the Netherlands $10 billion, Switzerland $3 billion, and the United Kingdom $1.5 billion.[92] These four countries "are responsible for half of the world's corporate tax avoidance risks"; they have been labelled the "axis of tax avoidance."

In April 2016, leaked documents from the law firm Mossack Fonseca in Panama, as revealed in the Panama Papers, published details about tax avoidance/evasion by 894 Canadian individuals, corporations, and trusts.[93] Three years later only twelve had been ordered to pay anything back,[94] but the Canada Revenue Agency reported that it was investigating fifty-two international and offshore tax evasion cases, five of which were named in the Panama Papers.[95] For the five-year period ending 31 March 2022, there were 140 convictions of tax evasion and more than $72 million in federal tax collected.[96] However the government's primary focus has been on money laundering by organized crime, not on policing the very rich.[97] Since the capitalist state has created and nourished these tax havens, and neoliberal morality celebrates tax avoidance/evasion, it would be foolish to expect significant penalties.

Conclusion

This chapter has argued that neoliberalism has dramatically shifted practices and values in countries dominated by global capitalism. Behaviours once considered immoral and illegal have been normalized. Corruption is practised in plain sight, and its practitioners are not shamed but honoured. States not only turn a blind eye to big money corporate crime, they enable and facilitate it.

The exercise of power always generates resistance, and there is plenty of "push-back" from activist groups of all persuasions. But the very rich present a united front, and they have unparalleled cultural, political, and economic resources. The opposition is weakened by divisions across class, race, and identity, and by the need to fight many battles, offensive and defensive, at once. Public education, health care, the environment, and broader democratic freedoms are all threatened by the ability of those with the most resources to shape policy and avoid paying their fair share of taxes.

Balancing the contradictions between capital's incessant drive to accumulate and the need to legitimate an exploitative capitalist social system is a constant challenge, and networks and alliances are constantly in flux. Unexpected events such as earthquakes, invasions, and most recently the COVID-19 pandemic have to be managed and manipulated to prevent crises and restore the consent of the governed. These times of crisis offer opportunities for transformative social change – piecemeal and uneven and localized as such change always is.

NOTES

1 Margaret Beare, "Canada: Internal Conspiracies, Corruption and Crime," in *Handbook of Organizational Crime and Politics*, edited by F. Alum and S. Gilmour (Cheltenham, UK: Edward Elgar Publishing, 2019), 189–208; Margaret Beare, "Entitled Ease: Social Milieu of Corporate Criminals," *Critical Criminology* 26, no. 4 (2018): 509–26, https://doi.org/10.1007/s10612-018-9413-z.
2 Beare, "Entitled Ease," 9.
3 D. Whyte and J. Wiegratz, eds., *Neoliberalism and the Moral Economy of Fraud* (London: Taylor & Francis, 2016).
4 Whyte and Wiegratz, eds., *Neoliberalism*, 182.
5 Whyte and Wiegratz, eds., *Neoliberalism*, 2.
6 Whyte and Wiegratz, eds., *Neoliberalism*, 5.
7 N. Makovicky, "Public Good for Private Gain: Public Sector Reform, Bureaucrats and Discourses of Moral Accountability in Post-Socialist Central Europe," in *Neoliberalism and the Moral Economy of Fraud*, edited by D. Whyte and J. Wiegratz (London: Taylor & Francis, 2016), 159–69, at 162.
8 Whyte and Wiegratz, eds., *Neoliberalism*, 12.
9 P. Corrigan and D. Sayer, *The Great Arch: English State Formation as Cultural Revolution* (New York: Basil Blackwell, 1985); M. Valverde, "Moral Capital," *Canadian Journal of Law & Society* 9, no. 1 (1994): 213–32. DOI: 10.1017/S0829320100003574; C. Smart, "The Woman of Legal Discourse," *Social & Legal Studies* 1 (1992): 29–44.
10 Corrigan and Sayer, "The Great Arch," 4.
11 Smart, "The Woman."

12 Carol Smart, *Feminism and the Power of Law* (London: Routledge, 1989); Michel Foucault, *Discipline and Punish: The Birth of the Prison* (New York: Pantheon, 1979).
13 James Carrier, "Economic Wrong and Economic Debate in the Neoliberal Era," in *Neoliberalism and the Moral Economy of Fraud*, edited by D. Whyte and J. Wiegratz (London: Taylor and Francis, 2016), 17–28.
14 E. Thompson, *The Making of the English Working Class* (Harmondsworth, UK: Penguin, 1963); E. Thompson, *Whigs and Hunters: The Origin of the Black Act* (New York: Pantheon, 1975); D. Hay, P. Linebaugh, J. Rule, et al., *Albion's Fatal Tree: Crime and Society in Eighteenth-Century England* (New York: Pantheon, 1975); A. Sayer, "Moral Economy, Unearned Income and Legalized Corruption," in *Neoliberalism and the Moral Economy of Fraud*, edited by D. Whyte and J. Wiegratz (London: Taylor and Francis, 2016), 43–53; Carrier, "Economic Wrong."
15 C. Swader, The Capitalist Personality: Face-to-Face Sociality and Economic Change in the Post-Communist World (London: Routledge, 2013): 6.
16 Swader, The Capitalist Personality, 12.
17 Laureen Snider, "How Do I Discipline Thee: Let Me Count the Ways: Tightening the Screws on the 99%," in *The Class Politics of Law: Essays Inspired by Harry Glasbeek*, edited by J. Fudge and E. Tucker (Winnipeg: Fernwood, 2019), 135–51.
18 Laureen Snider, "Interrogating the Algorithm: Debt, Derivatives and the Social Reconstruction of Stock Market Trading," *Critical Sociology* 40, no. 5 (2014), https://doi.org/10.1177/0896920513504603.
19 E. Ferlie, "The New Public Management and Public Management Studies," *Oxford Research Encyclopedia of Business*, 2017, https://doi.org/10.1093/acrefore/9780190224851.013.129.
20 Ferlie, "Public Management."
21 The impact of NPM in Ontario Works, the ridiculously named agency responsible for delivering welfare to those in need (such as single mothers) in Ontario has actively tried to subvert the "ethic of care" social workers are trained in and to replace it with instrumental neoliberal attitudes and practices. See further, K. Maki, "Neoliberal Deviants and Surveillance: Welfare Recipients under the Watchful Eye of Ontario Works," *Journal of Surveillance and Society* 9, no. 1 (2011): 47–63; and K. Maki, "Automating Social Inequality," in *Infrastructures of Citizenship: Digital Life in the Global City*, edited by D. Cowen, A. Mitchell, B. Story, and E. Paradis (Vancouver: University of British Columbia Press, 2020).
22 Whyte and Wiegratz, eds., *Neoliberalism*, 11–12.
23 J. Wedel, "Rethinking Corruption in an Age of Ambiguity," *Annual Review of Law and Social Science* 8 (2012): 453–98, at 478.
24 Wedel, "Rethinking," 480.
25 Wedel, "Rethinking."
26 In 2018 the estimated cost of corruption was US$2.6 trillion, approximately 5 per cent of World GDP, UN Security Council, 2018, https://www.un.org/press/en/2018/sc13493.doc.htm.

27 M. Barutciski and S. Bandali, "Corruption at the Intersection of Business and Government: The OECD Convention, Supply-Side Corruption and Canada's Anti-Corruption Efforts to Date," *Digital Commons* 12, no. 3 (2016), https//digitalcommons.osgoode.yorku.ca.
28 Corruption of Foreign Public Officials Act, *Justice Laws Website,* https://laws-lois.justice.gc.ca/eng/acts/c-45.2/.
29 Beare, "Conspiracies"; Beare, "Entitled Ease"; D. Friedrichs, "Crimes of Globalization and Asian Dam Projects: Powerful Institutions and Slow Violence," in *Revisiting "Crimes of the Powerful,"* edited by S. Bittle, L. Snider, S. Tombs, and D. Whyte (London: Routledge, 2018), 231–42; and Wedel, "Rethinking."
30 Charbonneau Commission Report, "Review and Relevance of Recommendations for Toronto's Purchasing and Materials Management Division," 6 September 2017, https://www.toronto.ca/legdocs/mmis/2017/gm/bgrd/backgroundfile-106799.pdf.
31 Beare, "Conspiracies," 194.
32 Beare, "Entitled Ease," passim.
33 Harry Glasbeek, *Class Privilege. How Law Shelters Shareholders and Coddles Capitalism* (Toronto: Between the Lines, 2017); Harry Glasbeek, *Capitalism: A Crime Story* (Toronto: Between the Lines, 2018).
34 Beare, "Entitled Ease," 9.
35 Beare, "Conspiracies," 203.
36 Government of Canada, Department of Revenue, "How We Combat Tax Evasion and Avoidance," https://www.canada.ca/en/revenue-agency/programs/about-canada-revenue-agency-cra/compliance/how-combat-tax-evasion-avoidance.html.
37 Whyte and Wiegratz, eds., *Neoliberalism,* passim; Beare, "Entitled Ease," passim.
38 Laureen Snider, "Beyond Trump: Neoliberal Capitalism and the Abolition of Corporate Crime," *Journal of White Collar and Corporate Crime* 1, no. 2 (June 2020): 86–94.
39 Federal Register, Presidential Documents, 9339 Executive Order 13771, *Reducing Regulation and Controlling Regulatory Costs,* 30 January 2016, vol. 82, no. 22, 3 February 2017, https://www.govinfo.gov/content/pkg/FR-2017-02-03/pdf/2017-02451.pdf; Nolan D. McCaskill and Matthew Nussbaum, "Trump Signs Executive Order Requiring That for Every One New Regulation, Two Must Be Revoked," 30 January 2017, https://www.politico.com/story/2017/01/trump-signs-executive-order-requiring-that-for-every-one-new-regulation-two-must-be-revoked-234365.
40 "Tracking Regulatory Changes in the Biden Era," Brookings Institute, https://www.brookings.edu/interactives/tracking-deregulation-in-the-trump-era/.
41 S. Tombs and D. Whyte, "The Shifting Imaginaries of Corporate Crime," *Journal of White Collar and Corporate Crime* 1, no. 1 (2020), https://doi.org/10.1177/2631309X19882641.
42 Laureen Snider, "Beyond Trump," 86–94.
43 M. Hobbes, "The Golden Age of White-Collar Crime," *Highline Huffington Post,* 10 February 2020.

44 Derrick Bryson Taylor, Heather Murphy, and Mariel Padilla, "A List of Trump's Pardons and Commutations," *New York Times*, 18 February 2020, https://www.nytimes.com/2020/02/18/us/politics/trump-pardons.html.
45 J. Christensen, "Do They Do Evil? The Moral Economy of Tax Professionals," in *Neoliberalism and the Moral Economy of Fraud*, edited by D. Whyte and J. Wiegratz (London: Taylor & Francis: 2016), 64–73.
46 B. Harrington, *Capital without Borders: Wealth Managers and the One Percent* (Cambridge, MA: Harvard University Press, 2016), 11.
47 Harrington, Capital without Borders, 4.
48 J. Mayer, Dark Money: The Hidden History of the Billionaires: Behind the Radical Right (New York: Doubleday, 2016).
49 Harrington, Capital without Borders, 2.
50 Harrington, Capital without Borders, 11.
51 D. Sirota, "Microsoft Admits Keeping $92 Billion Offshore to Avoid Paying $29 Billion in US Taxes," *International Business Times*, 22 August 2014. In 2018 the estimated cost of corruption was US$2.6 trillion, approximately 5 per cent of World GDP, according to the UN Security Council, https://www.un.org/press/en/2018/sc13493.doc.htm.
52 Christensen, "Do They Do Evil?"
53 Harrington, Capital without Borders.
54 Harrington, Capital without Borders, 20.
55 Christensen, "Do They Do Evil?" 66.
56 Christensen, "Do They Do Evil?" 67.
57 Christensen, "Do They Do Evil?" 65.
58 Harrington, Capital without Borders, 68
59 Harrington, Capital without Borders, 68.
60 Harrington, *Capital without Borders*, 65–85.
61 D. Mangan, "Trump Brags about Not Paying Taxes: 'That Makes Me Smart,'" CNBC, 26 September 2016, https://www.cnbc.com/2016/09/26/trump-brags-about-not-paying-taxes-that-makes-me-smart.html.
62 Mangan, "Trump Brags."
63 Whyte and Wiegratz, eds., *Neoliberalism*.
64 J. Wiegratz, "Bankers Have a Moral Compass, It Just May Not Look Like Yours," *The Conversation*, 3 March 2015.
65 C. Swader, "Fraudulent Values, Materialistic Bosses and the Support for Bribery and Tax Evasion," in *Neoliberalism and the Moral Economy of Fraud*, edited by D. Whyte and J. Wiegratz (London: Taylor & Francis, 2016), 170–81.
66 Glasbeek, *Class Privilege*; Glasbeek, *Capitalism: A Crime Story*; S. Tombs and D. Whyte, *The Corporate Criminal: Why Corporations Must Be Abolished* (New York: Routledge, 2015): Whyte and Wiegratz, eds., *Neoliberalism*; J. Wiegratz and D. Whyte, "How Neoliberalism's Moral Order Feeds Fraud and Corruption," *The Conversation*, 16 June 2016, https://theconversation.com/global/search?q=How+Ne

oliberalism%E2%80%99s+moral+order+feeds+Fraud+and+Corruption%2C%E2%80%9D+The+Conversation%2C;Steven Bittle, *Still Dying for a Living* (Vancouver: University of British Columbia Press, 2012).
67 Swader, "Fraudulent Values," 171.
68 Swader, "Fraudulent Values," 170–1 (italics in original).
69 Niels Johannesen, Gabriel Zucman, and Annette Alstadsæter, "Tax Evasion and Inequality," *VoxEU CEPR Policy Portal*, 9 May 2018, https://cepr.org/voxeu/columns/tax-evasion-and-inequality.
70 M. Szalavitz, "Why the Rich Are Less Ethical: They See Greed as Good," *Time*, 28 February 2012; U. Shashikant, "Why Poor People Tend to Be More Generous than the Rich," *The Economic Times Wealth*, 20 July 2018.
71 J. Urry, *Offshoring* (Cambridge, UK: Polity Press, 2014).
72 Harrington, Capital without Borders, 113.
73 Urry, *Offshoring*, 10.
74 M. Cuenco, "Tax Sovereignty in the Age of Global Capital," *American Affairs*, 20 November 2019.
75 Cuenco, "Tax Sovereignty."
76 A. Zakrzewski, B. Beardsley, D. Kessler, et al., *Global Wealth 2018: Seizing the Analytics Advantage*, Boston Consulting Group, June 2018.
77 E. Saez and E. Zucman, *The Triumph of Injustice* (New York: W.W. Norton, 2019).
78 Saez and Zucman, *The Triumph*.
79 Urry, *Offshoring*.
80 Harrington, *Capital without Borders*; Cuenco, "Tax Sovereignty."
81 Urry, *Offshoring*, 54.
82 N. Shaxson, "The Tax Haven in the Heart of Britain," *New Statesman*, 4 February 2011, https://www.newstatesman.com/economy/2011/02/london-corporation-city.
83 Shaxson, "The Tax Haven."
84 Shaxson, "The Tax Haven."
85 Shaxson, "The Tax Haven."
86 It is unclear how or whether Britain's departure from the European Union has jeopardized their status.
87 Harrington, Capital without Borders, 115.
88 Harrington, Capital without Borders, 170.
89 Cuenco, "Tax Sovereignty."
90 Cuenco, "Tax Sovereignty."
91 Rachel Curry, "What US States Are Tax Havens? You May Be Surprised," *Market Realist*, 8 October 2021, https://marketrealist.com/p/what-us-states-are-tax-havens/.
92 "Taking Back Control of Our Tax Systems," *Tax Justice Network*, https://taxjustice.net/take-back-control/#taken_over.
93 T. Wright, "Nearly 900 Canadians Found in Panama Papers, but No Charges Have Yet Been Laid," CTV News, 2 April 2019, https://www.ctvnews.ca/business/nearly-900-canadians-found-in-panama-papers-but-no-charges-have-yet-been-laid-1.4362518.

94 C. Nardi, "Panama Papers: 12 sur 900 identifiés doivent rembourser," *Le Journal de Quebec*, 18 February 2019, https://www.tvanouvelles.ca/2019/02/18/panama-papers-12-canadiens-sur-900-identifies-doivent-rembourser.
95 Government of Canada, Department of Revenue, "Panama Papers: CRA Executing Search Warrants in $77 Million Tax Evasion Case," 28 March 2019, https://www.canada.ca/en/revenue-agency/news/newsroom/criminal-investigations-actions-charges-convictions/20190328-panama-papers-search-warrants-tax-evasion-case.html.
96 Government of Canada, Department of Revenue, *How We Combat Tax Evasion and Avoidance*, https://www.canada.ca/en/revenue-agency/programs/about-canada-revenue-agency-cra/compliance/how-combat-tax-evasion-avoidance.html.
97 Financial Action Task Force (FATF), *Anti-money Laundering and Counter-terrorist Financing Measures – Canada. Fourth Round Mutual Evaluation Report*, 2016, www.fatf-gafi.org/publications/mutualevaluations/documents/mer-canada-2016.html.

SECTION 3

Big Police: If We Can't Live with Them, Can We Live Without Them?

This section contains two starkly different views of the police. One presents evidence of police dysfunction and resistance to change; political, racial, and gender bias; repression; and even illegal behaviour. With equally compelling evidence the other depicts the police as useful social agents fulfilling an essential role of maintaining and restoring equilibrium and safety when events destabilize established order or harm humans. Neither version is wrong, although both can at times be overstated. Although there are shadings in between, they describe two coexisting contradictory states in policing that ultimately frustrate reform. With each acting as a countervailing force on the other, the result is stalemate. Only in exceptional cases such as policing in apartheid South Africa or factional Northern Ireland does the dysfunctional prevail to the point where there is complete restructuring and reform of the police; but good policing is similarly unable to dominate sufficiently to banish the dysfunctional.

In the opening chapter, Peter Manning reviews the history of police reform efforts in Anglo-American policing in the eighty years or so from the end of the Second World War until the present and concludes that they have all failed to bring real change. The result is a pattern of policing that is much the same as it was in 1829. Manning identifies and discusses some of the factors contributing to the failure, such as the superficial nature of the research informing change or the persistent view of police as solely crime fighters. Consequently, reforms tend to be fads with no staying power or focused too narrowly on crime control. Moreover, some of the much-touted reforms, such as the Compstat model or predictive policing, have made policing at least potentially more repressive in its treatment of poor, racialized, and marginalized groups.

Margaret Beare traces a similar experience with policing in Canada. She points out that even the recommendations of numerous public inquiries have had little success in bringing about the reforms needed to remedy demonstrated flaws in policing. This situation resonates with Manning's "scandal-based reform," a phenomenon that is not solely the experience of the United States or Canada, but also shared by any number of other countries, not the least being the United Kingdom, Australia, or Belgium.[1] Too often dysfunctional police organizations or policing situations are neglected, ignored, or knowingly allowed to continue until scandal erupts. Then reforms have to be introduced, ostensibly to prevent such situations arising again but also to stem public outrage and criticism. Yet, as both Manning and Beare observe, all big reform ideas tend to slide back to the crime control mode, so the change does not move much beyond words.

Above all, Beare is interested in the concept of policing the police. She therefore delves into the nature of governance and accountability of the police. She explores problems with police use of discretion and the political influences that affect police behaviour, including the political manoeuvring of the police themselves to protect their own interests. While showing scepticism for the notion of police governance, her account is nevertheless nuanced in showing how police legitimacy frequently depends on negotiation with different constituencies so compromise is often the result. Ultimately, she believes that police can be externally directed to move beyond self-interest to achieve better outcomes for people.

On the other hand, Anna Willats's passionate but coherent and well-argued chapter is unequivocal in stating that vulnerable women and racialized communities are over-policed and under-served so police should be defunded and the resources diverted to community agencies that can provide expert services. Whether one agrees with her conclusions or not, we can follow her on her trajectory of disillusion with the police. As a community worker, she has personal experience and intimate knowledge of the "streets" and the interactions between its largely powerless inhabitants and the police who can use their authority for good or ill. She therefore brings verisimilitude and immediacy to the academic accounts of low policing in this section of the book. Her chapter also complements the discussions of the concurrent activities in the "suites" described in the other two sections. The crime is predatory in both cases; in one causing harm mainly to personal well-being and in the other mainly to economic well-being, but cumulatively causing great harm to social well-being. In a less than perfect world, we rely on the remediating actions of the police who are present in both street and suite and have the authority to intervene. When they fail, for whatever reason, trust and confidence are shaken and collective disillusion and cynicism can set in.

Laura Huey and Lorna Ferguson restore some balance in their presentation of the results of a study of police response to missing persons in one Canadian municipality. Many of those reported missing were persons with mental illness. They point out that police interventions with mentally ill persons are complex and cannot be described as simply the "criminalization" of the mentally ill. In fact, many police interventions are of a welfare nature and are resolved informally and successfully. The researchers' findings further show that far from police diverting resources from social agencies, the social agencies in fact "download" both the operational and financial responsibility for dealing with mental health crises to the police. Such findings challenge proposals to defund the police and divert the resources to social agencies.

Kevin Haggerty, Sandra Bucerius, and Daniel Jones examine a less well-known reaction to the recent high-profile police shootings of African Americans and African Canadians. Protests against systemic racism in policing and militaristic tactics against the mentally ill in crisis have included some academics and university departments that have cancelled or paused cooperation on research or student placements with police. The authors' perceptive exploration of the dynamics of demonization or "evilization" of the police that in some instances replaces rational criticism, and of the ultimate effect on both policing and scholarship, leads them to the conclusion that police are not alone in practising systemic racism and that if police did not exist there would be a need to invent them to control predatory and violent behaviour and to maintain order.

All of the contributors to this section examine police activities from the point of view of interactions with members of the public rather than with their crime-fighting activities. This could be coincidence or reflect Manning's contention that to view police as primarily crime fighters is to misunderstand their role. Tonita Murray takes up the same theme in arguing that the primary police role is keeping the peace. She takes as her evidence the ever-rising calls for police service in Canada and contends that given the complexities of modern society and the number of vulnerable people, the cost of the police response is cheap at the price of roughly $15 billion a year. The drawback is that the structure and training of police as "specialized generalists" for providing services to people or investigating tangible crime, impairs their effectiveness in controlling the other modern social phenomenon of ever-expanding financial and corporate crime that is a potential threat to Western economies.

The financial, corporate, and other organized and international crimes analysed in the first two sections of this book are a strong indication that public police are not addressing the problem of financial and corporate crime adequately. Some of the gap is filled by investigators in other regulatory and law enforcement agencies, as well as the internal "policing" of banks and other financial institutions, which is a regulatory requirement. This is an aspect of policing that is often overlooked but which collectively may well rival the power and cost of the policing that takes place in the public eye. The moot question is whether public police and regulatory agencies under current arrangements are best organized between them to deal effectively with the problem of financial, corporate, organized, and international crime.

Taken together the chapters in this section reflect the notion inherent in the general introduction to the book, that big crime and big policing involving big money represent a "wicked problem" for Canadian governments. A wicked problem is insoluble because seeming solutions only succeed in making the problem more complex. Policing is only one of a number of wicked problems that elude social or economic policy resolution in modern societies.

But the discussion which follows in this section introduces a further dimension into the discussion by identifying another inextricably entwined strand in the wicked problem. This is the question of whether current policing arrangements in their broadest sense can truly change for the better to meet the needs of vulnerable people adequately and acceptably, while at the same time effectively protecting the financial integrity of the Canadian economy.

Police are a pivot between the rights and security needs of people and a stable, confidence-inspiring crime-free business sector; they are stretched between ameliorating social turmoil and economic threat. They fall short in protecting both because of their own weaknesses. This should be a matter of concern for governments at all levels in Canada. Yet governments have also been falling short in their own responsibility to provide clear and decisive governance and policy direction to the police to address the structural and systemic problems that cause the police to fall short. Instead they have concentrated on containing the size and costs of public policing, which, despite the importance of good public management, may be the least of the policing problems facing governments. The apparent failure of political will is perhaps the first and final strand in the wicked problem. Without political will there can be no start to addressing the wicked problem of efficient, effective, and just policing, and without it the wicked problem remains insoluble.

NOTE

1 See, for example, Tim Newburn, *Literature Review – Police Integrity and Corruption* (London: Her Majesty's Inspectorate of Constabulary, 2015), www.justiceinspectorates.gov.uk/hmi; New York, Knapp Commission, *Report on Police Corruption* (New York: G. Braziller, 1975); Louise Porter and Tim Prenzler, *Police Integrity Management in Australia: Global Lessons for Combating Police Misconduct* (Boca Raton, FL: CRC Press, 2021); Jeroen Maesschalck, "When Do Scandals Have an Impact on Policy Making? A Case Study of the Police Reform Following the Dutroux Scandal in Belgium," *International Public Management Journal* 5, no. 2 (January 2002): 169–93.

8 Reform of the Police

PETER K. MANNING

Introduction

Reform of the police in Anglo-American societies is as old as the creation of the Dublin Metropolitan Police in 1785 and extends to the situation in the Anglo-American world in late 2021. The connection of police to danger, insecurity, crime, and risk, and therefore their necessity, is a recent theme. The idea of a police emerged from several strands: the failures of colonial policing,[1] the protection of the gentry and their property,[2] and control of internal threats – the poor and indigent, Indigenous peoples and immigrants. In the United States the constabulary model is seen in slave patrols (more or less bounty hunters) and local policing in the South, and in Canada the emergence of the Royal Canadian Mounted Police from the Northwest Mounted Police who dealt with strikes and Indian resistance. The Peel model,[3] traced falsely to Peel's efforts to control the Irish, was much admired and featured in every criminal justice textbook and was held up as a paradigm of policing. It was always a contrast conception, a contrast to colonial policing of "the others." This illusion served well until the late 1920s in the United States when violence and corruption drew the attention of the media and politicians, and the pattern of scandal-based attempts at political reform unfolded. Some reforms arise from corruption and others from major violent events. In Canada, the major reorganization, an agency dealing exclusively with national security came after a scandal. In Ireland the recent vision report[4] urged the same: creating a separate agency apart from the An Garda for dealing with national security. In 2021 the killing of a Black man, George Floyd, and a series of violent killings and beatings of Black men led to a reform movement.

In the past, attempts to reform the police in Anglo-American societies[5] have been modest failures because each new effort was cosmetic: the structure and practice did not change much. This is due in part because the audiences of the police are in conflict about the why, what, and how of policing and in part because of their political role of security (under various names in the Anglo-American world). While the claim is repeated that the police are apolitical and neutral, they are, in fact, a political entity with political interests of their own as an organization and occupation.

Some further background on efforts to reform police in democratic societies is necessary,[6] but the problem remains: the police are a secretive organization; they gather and analyse data by which they are judged; they maintain the illusion that their mission (as they define it) is crime control and their efforts to reform are more of the same, now rationalized by technology.[7] They maintain their mandate via dramas of various sorts: police deaths and funerals, fancy dress parades, announcements of major drug seizures, arrests, and miscellaneous charity activities. These are versions of self-celebration. These are control dramas, representing and amplifying the importance of the police. They are completed by dramas of control when police intervention is heralded in an event or series of events. In effect, the police are viewed as idealized "mock-ups" of their actual practices, except in known "rare" instances. In this brief overview I focus on direct attempts to reform the police rather than agencies that work indirectly, such as citizen advice boards, external complaint-processing, ombudsmen [sic], and attempts to reshape internal modes of police handling of violations of law or procedure, such as internal affairs units and in-house investigations.[8] As Stoughton, Noble, and Alpert[9] have written, the absence of valid data on any crucial aspect of police organization and practice is shocking but also true in the Anglo-American world. I suggest that known efforts at police reform have in the past been unsuccessful for known reasons. I later make some comment on current reform efforts.

Early Efforts

The post–Second World War efforts to reform the police, after Vollmer's claims[10] that policing was a profession based on science, were tactical: police needed more rational means to produce something and show something. It became officially recognized and recorded crime. Like firemen who were cast as "firefighters," they were posed as "crime-fighters." How can you fight a category? In the United States, after the burst of research created after the 1967 *President's Crime Commission*,[11] change was in the air. There was little current research to hand at that time.[12] Although the commission dominated by lawyers produced a number of important studies, little change in internal organization or practice occurred. Because they focused on legalistic versions of equality and justice, there was little concern for race, class, and gender as policed, and no concern for the virtually white male nature of police forces. The commission, the research, and publications made no impact on policing-as-a-practice. It did, however, draw attention to an otherwise ignored subject.[13]

In the 1980s one theme emerged: "community policing" (CP), and efforts to move police towards more engagement with neighbourhoods were popular in North America.[14] In short, the effort was popular but a failure. The implicit aim of this tactic was simple but unstated: alter policing in centre cities to reduce violent policing of the poor. It was based on a nostalgic myth about policing in the good old days.[15] The data, indices, and official statistics could not be used to address the issue of equality and fairness because the police gathered, analysed, and stored the data and the typical police answer to the question, "What is good policing?" was, "I know when I see it." The quality of the work and how it might be achieved was unexamined, and when it was raised in training by academic "talking heads" it fell on deaf ears – by that I mean the answer was embedded in the oral culture. The officer has original authority. The research on community policing was inconsistent and ambiguous as to the causes of failure, but the conclusions drawn were simple: there was no program, no implementation, and no consistent type of analysis. Assessment was difficult because some organizations created a community policing unit, some named an officer in each precinct, others claimed that the department as a whole was doing community policing. The aims of such programs were not specified and so could not be measured directly,[16] and the continuing claim: crime control is the job of the police.

A related theme emerged in the early 1980s. A shabby set of ideas first published in a popular magazine[17] was soon truncated and elided into a journalistic catchphrase, "broken windows."[18] Somehow this was transmuted into a theory. This data-free sketch caught the attention of grant funders, the media, and some academics. It was a simple, conservative middle-class notion: neighbourhoods should be tidy and feature no disorder, such as a broken window, trash outside, untrimmed hedges or lawns, abandoned vehicles in sight, or people in T-shirts on the front porch (my summary). Note! The claim was that if even a few of these are present, the neighbourhood (undefined) will deteriorate, dangerous villains either inside or outside the neighbourhood will be predators of your property, and crime will increase. Police by implication are the thin blue line but also are "partners" with "communities." While the broad aim of studying and supporting neighbourhood coherence or sense of mutual obligation or "efficacy" was attempted in Chicago,[19] the data of actual mobilization and the nature, quality, and direction of this "efficacy" were ambiguous and unrelated to participation in community policing activities.[20]

Reduced crime was a surrogate measure for success. The conservative criminologist James Q. Wilson claimed that policing for arrests or reducing crime was a fallback option. In his book of essays[21] Wilson claimed that high crime areas could be ignored, middle-class areas were not at issue, but that areas in transition could be policed to control crime. Kelling advised William Bratton, the then head of the New York City Transit Police, and the police attacked the homeless in the subways, moving them out, calling the art on the subway trains "graffiti" and erasing it. Mayor Giuliani, in his wisdom, supported the idea.[22] This was in aide of civility, as the police defined it. Over time, the police in the New York Police Department (NYPD) and elsewhere took this as an invitation to employ the usual tactics, stop and frisk in "dangerous areas," round up the usual suspects, do sweeps for all at risk, concentrate on the usual areas, and "crack down on crime." This of course is "working backward," as the inference is that areas cause crime and if areas are unchanged the same pattern of arrests and recorded crime would little alter the quality of life in the heavily policed areas.

This was policing the poor on behalf of the status quo. This was not Kelling's original intention,[23] as he sought a civil and open street environment. A police version of broken windows soon became a mantra. This included crackdowns on "J-Walking" (not crossing the road at marked crosswalks); increased stop-and-frisk interventions; and expanded hiring of officers,[24] concentrated patrol in areas with officially reported crime, and increased arrests. The media featured this and made Mayor Giuliani and Commissioner Bratton magazine cover material (as a result Giuliani, in a fit of pique, fired Bratton).

Again, no research demonstrated any positive consequences, unnamed but implied, if measured from lowered crime rates resulting from intense policing of inner-city areas.[25] These were quantitative studies absent any data from the ground, social organization, mini-cultures, and local effort. These did not include better public services, educational opportunities, or well-being as measures. Reduced officially registered crime was enough. The narrow focus on what could be measured and some minor changes within statistically defined areas (*not* social units) obviate actual social organization.[26] The focus on police actions absent any close study of social organization on the ground was the result of mannered ignorance of ongoing interaction orders. In this context, there was neither reorganization of police units nor changes in practices or deployment. The police seized on arrests, raids, and sweeps as solutions to the problem of "disorganization." These little statistical essays altered the narrative in criminal justice's theology, even as these essays denied the past and current ethnographic work and reified criminology's pungent anti-theoretical pose. Ironically, the police actions and claims had their moment. As crime continued to fall for more than twenty years, and they abandoned the public rhetoric, earlier police claims were shown to be fatuous. In many ways, the research was not the driving force: the fad lost its traction.

Later Efforts

A third theme emerged. As officially reported crime in North America dropped through the 1990s, a social fact that experts could not explain,[27] police searched for new rationales for their standard tactics: response to 911 calls, random patrol, and crime investigation. These were surrogate measures at best for the quality of community service. The NYPD, following the initiative of Bratton and Jack Maples in the New York Transit Police,[28] in parallel with broken windows ideas, began to plot crimes using computer-based data: the "Compstat" model. This was not new; the Nazis plotted the homes of Jews and their businesses in Amsterdam and used data to confiscate their art and other possessions in Paris after the occupation.[29]

Bratton, now Commissioner of the NYPD, claimed that the Compstat system of computer-based data and meetings associated with these data caused the crime drop.[30] In due course, it was revealed that the data were patterned in advance by how incidents were defined by supervisors who actually approved the definitions of an incident;[31] the data were disorganized and often absent in discussions;[32] and fundamental questions about procedure, egregious violent events, and the internal politics of the police organization were prohibited.[33] Claims made in funded research to further evaluate Compstat showed negligible results in regard to crime reduction.[34] It was impossible to separate police effects from the effects of various socio-economic factors in the crime drop and tendencies for data to regress to the norm.[35] This did and continues to confound claims made later for evidence-based policing. Again it was tautological, as the information used in their deployment and tactics was police-based. Furthermore, no explanation has been offered for how, where, when, and why Compstat reduced officially recorded crime.[36] And, even if it dips at the time of an "experiment," does this indicate continuous reduced crime? The answer is no. This crime-arrest focus creates further disorganization.[37]

Although the fad was not embraced fully as a package in Canada or the United Kingdom, these attempts at rationalizing police work were a turning point. Whereas crime is a small part of police work, rare in fact in the course of patrol, it has been highlighted, dramatized, and danced in the media: crime control is *the* police job.[38] This reification of the job enhanced the mandate and made later aspects of reform problematic. This strategic rhetoric has enormous staying power and is often centred on merely the need for even more police and a protection of the perks of office – overtime, contractual agreements in favour of officers, retirement benefits, and a wide range of salaries for parallel positions.

The debate about crime control and policing continued through the late 1990s. As crime fell, the Canadian government did not adopt police increase or decrease as an approach to social ordering. In the United Kingdom the Conservative government cut police budgets by approximately 12 per cent.[39] While the racial patterning of police data was well known, police and their academic acolytes dependent on external funding were creating new forms of policing which I would call "rationalized statistically-generated racism perpetuating inequality" (all one term). Funded research continues to use police-based data to chart "crime," not quality of life. "Evidence-based" is simply another buzzword, a version of applying police data to more sophisticated targeting of the same people, areas, and traffic patterns. The nature and character of the evidence have not been well-studied. The latest fads are named and re-named: predictive policing (using police data to reify the sources of crime by area); intelligence-led policing (the claim that feedback alters practices but without data);[40] and big data policing,[41] which is full of hypotheticals and possible consequences of loose integration, big data sets based on different platforms, databases, and validity.

The claims for these vague programs have of late been enhanced by the illusion of "experimental methods." These approaches seldom work except as a reification of data absent a critique of the methods used; controlled data absent interviews, observation of known practices, the extent to which the actual research met idealized standards; and the ever-changing shifts, officers, and organizational deployment of resources.

Desperate claims for the value of police use of "personal electronic devices" is the latest "silver bullet," the ultimate tool to slay the elusive demon: crime. With respect to the latest fad of body cameras and videos, a number of observations suggest the limits of these ideas both ethically and operationally.[42] Research is still in the works, but there is no agreement on what is to be explained or reduced. Is it less violence or fewer complaints, reduced crime in an area, citizen satisfaction, or renewed neighbourhood solidarity? If so, are these a result of police action? What other indicators could be used? The journalists and people active in social media focus on the most outrageous examples of police conduct, such as beatings, shootings, or murder, thus maintaining the focus on extreme examples, as egregious as they are, and ignoring the everyday incivility that is differentially present, given the economics of areas of cities. The hope is perhaps that visual evidence will reduce violence. The events of the last two years in North America do not support this claim. Data on reduced complaints turned into lower costs are economistic re-formulations which have no bearing on the cost of police operations. The police work on an open-ended budget because disasters, riots, demonstrations, and celebrations are unpredictable and require police action. They stand ready: they are not therefore efficient and cannot be. As one mythical quote from an economist notes, "If someone could have made money on this function (police), it would have been privatized long ago." Private prisons are a case in point.

The Present

No serious attempt at reform of the structure and function of policing has succeeded: the pattern has little changed since 1829. Systematic evaluation of these technologically driven initiatives under various names reveal the same pattern:

- The data used are some combination of police-generated data with little material from interviews and observations.

- Claims are made on an ad hoc basis of "success." An example is ShotSpotter, which is sound detection by sensors in high crime areas. The ability to detect the sounds of gunshots is notoriously questionable because it can be confused with noise from firecrackers, loud exhausts, flawed microphones, and cameras. Multiple calls to police about the same sounds result in redundant facts. And to what advantage: faster response to a sound? Basically, such systems are surveillance techniques used in high crime neighbourhoods, which provide symbolic reassurance to others. The value and utility of "personal recording devices" of various sorts has not been proven, and it might be asked why they are even used.
- Police data when fed into algorithms *reify* the previous police-created patterns of stops, disorder, arrests, and calls for service.
- Monitoring and surveillance are narrowly focused in what are deemed high crime/disorder places in cities, whether in Toronto, New York, Boston, or Los Angeles.
- There are no independent data to validate or invalidate police data that are the dependent variables, for example, burglaries, robberies, and drug arrests.
- There are no systematic audits of police data.

These patterns have not changed the funding of police research: it is more of the same superficial studies absent ethnographic research, crime-focused and fundamentally racist in focus. To repeat, even small changes in arrests or disorder based on measurable police interventions show little if any long-term consequences, that is, more than six months. Studies in recent years of the day-to-day negative impact of policing have not changed funding.[43]

Change

Any discussion of change in the Anglo-American police world requires reflection: what are the bases of the stability of the police mandate over these last three hundred or so years since the Dublin Metropolitan Police? The basic structure in North America and the United Kingdom with officers on random patrol (which is not random) and responding to 911/999 calls remains the same. Slight structural differentiation, such as detective work, marine, air, and specialized units, or tactical units, simply reinforce the basic strategy and tactics of the organization. Training varies little and focuses on the here and now and discipline rather than abstract principles such as fairness, equality, and civility. "Human rights" training that patterns training and practice in Canada, the United Kingdom, and the Republic of Ireland is not acknowledged in the United States and has no purchase on training or practice. In North America, occasional "talking head" experts of various kinds are seen by officers as side shows.[44] Outside of elite organizations such as national forces in Canada, the United Kingdom, New Zealand, and Australia, promotion is based on seniority, and movement to command is shaped by local criteria.

Forces in the United States are essentially local enclaves, as there is no set of national criteria or bases for promotion; no system of local or national police academies; and no national system of "fast tracking," lateral entry or advanced training of any kind. In the United States, there is little transfer or movement across organizations except at the top, and there is a weak national system of evaluation, which is based on police-reported data of police organizations. Federal consent decrees after violations of civil rights are agreements to negotiate. The status of police is based on civil service, union contracts, and local hiring practices.

While the percentage of non-sworn employees varies widely in the Anglo-American world (from about 10 to 27 per cent of the total), these jobs are clerical and secretarial. Typically there is a handful of people in management and skilled jobs such as computer maintenance and lawyers, and then others such as cooks, janitors, and part-time employees. The benefits of each are managed on separate tracks: police officers and others. In addition, as Holdaway, O'Neil, and Loftus have shown in the United Kingdom,[45] racism and bias based on gender remains a powerful force impeding promotion and innovation because of tacit racism on the job. There is little or no evidence that increased numbers of people of colour or different genders, including the LGBTQ community, have altered police cultures or practices.

Prospects

Democratic policing in the twentieth century adopted a standard theme from the beginning and continues to play variations on it in the twenty-first century. The theme is flexible and the idea takes on new and varied targets such as immigrants, the homeless, people of colour, those with past records of varying significance, or areas known as sources of trouble. Deployment is based on this self-created myth of where crime lies. The law in this regard is, as Bittner wrote, a flexible resource.[46] The research most honoured and cited in the past twenty years is work that celebrates "crime control" using police data and features studies of high crime areas that are Black.[47] This produces another affirmation of policing inequities based on algorithms. The repetitive focus on "crime" and its nominal statistical control reinforces the notion that Black people cause crime rather than noting that crime is where police find it through the practices of patrol, surveillance, warrant-serving, search, arrest and the local knowledge they use to account for these practices.[48] It is very clear that there are several mini-systems of justice in Anglo-American societies: that of assistance to the wealthy and middle classes, that of surveillance and confrontation of people of colour, and recently, that of deep suspicion towards "immigrants" with various socio-legal statuses. The pattern of practice is acceptable unless or until a major visible incident occurs. This generalization omits situations of policing insurrection as in Northern Ireland and the insurrection and attack on the US Capitol in January 2021. These anomalies are outliers that reflect a form of civil war.

The history of police reform efforts shows that they often arise after a major, visible, and often violent event, or a sequence seen as cumulative, as in the United States in the last ten years, amplified and dramatized by media attention. These indicate and stir associations of other past and future events and are associated with one or more egregious examples.[49] The pattern in the United States is striking, and escalating with known incidents in South Carolina; Baltimore; Cleveland and Columbus, Ohio; Lexington, Kentucky; and Minneapolis (convicted officer Derek Chauvin) and a nearby Minneapolis suburb. The correlation of these policing incidents, demonstrations, and mass shootings at public places, schools, churches, and synagogues seem related, yet this remains difficult to explain. Although mass shootings have increased in the United States, no one has offered an analysis. The explanations are rooted in individualistic motives: revenge, mental illness, domestic conflicts, or are unknown. Response to these events by police has increased agitation because in addition to their immediate response with automatic weapons, gas, rubber bullets, and aggressive no-knock or warrantless entries, command staff have vacillated between defence and claiming investigations are ongoing, to vague apologies for failing to follow procedure (as if that would have avoided the incident or that it is in itself appropriate or just). The responses have been variable and unrelated to the nature of the violence of the event: suspension for a time; a desk job (the "rubber gun" squad); firing; or no announced penalty. Even the April 2021 conviction of Chauvin for murder is seen as a one off, a "rotten apple" instance.

Some Efforts at Reform

Observers such as Bayley and Stenning[50] note that reform and seeking accountability confronts a number of obstacles. First, trust in the police by the vast majority of the population (with some variation given a shocking event) is high and reinforced by tacit beliefs in the necessity to control the poor and unknown others. Second, patterns of experience with the police are bilateral: on the one hand, most people have limited experience with the police, while on the other a few have extensive and constant surveillance.[51] Third, tradition places original authority in the officer on the ground and protects this person by degrees of immunity to prosecution. Fourth, the police are in effect monitors of the ordinary and processors of anomalies or what is unusual: noises, smells, costumes, odd behaviour in an area, and movements of people or vehicles,[52] and as such they proceed by exception and make up the drama of investigation as they go along. Actions on the ground are simply what is written up. Fifth, there is a tendency of politicians to deal with crises by ignoring them, allowing the police to do internal investigations, or creating weak monitoring organizations. Ombudsmen, complaints agencies, or citizens groups constitute the modal approach. Sixth, the history of politicians' "interventions" in "non-political policing" in Anglo-American societies shows the uneven territory of reform and accountability.[53] In addition, the *focus of reform* is inconsistent in the sense that some observers focus on the violations of civil rights arising from surveillance and algorithms that reproduce inequality,[54] others seek police reform via external budgetary means such as "defunding the police," which is associated with the social movement Black Lives Matter, and yet others implicitly defend police tactics and emphasize the value of crime control. One variation is that the state of California banned named tactics in 2021. Other cities have sought reorganization and deployment.

These features of police accountability and organizational structure often ignore the police patrol officer's perspective: from an officer's point of view. *Actions on the ground are situated, and behaviour therefore is driven by the officers' definition of that particular situation.* Thus, the officer's assessment of the situation is "common-sense" actions driven by perceptions such as "I thought it was a gun," "I thought she would stab someone," or "I had to act" (viewed as true at law). The status of the victim is irrelevant, whether she or he is developmentally challenged, disabled, drunk, aged, mentally ill, or a child in a dangerous situation. This creates a constant tension between supervisors, top command, and officers at the "cutting edge"[55] and makes the locus of reform uncertain and politically debatable.

These changes are embedded in a turgid, unchanging, almost flat organizational structure with ranks, positions, and duties ossified, and at the same time recreated by entrepreneurial officers (a niche for special talent), while personalistic evaluations and promotion patterns sustain it. Anglo-American police organizations are changed modestly for three major reasons. The first is significant shifts in *resources* from outside, either local or national as seen by the results of the Patten Report.[56] The second and more benign is structural differentiation, the creation of *specialized units* as seen in the growth of military-simulation in weapons, tactics, and costumes (camouflage, heavy padded bulletproof vests, combat boots). These merely echo the police wish to engage in violence and action rather than talk and negotiation. The degree of restraint and supervision varies within the Anglo-American police world.[57] Other units dedicated to domestic violence and, to a lesser degree, cybercrime units could be paralleled by creating a unit of non-uniformed, unarmed officers. The problem here is deployment or allocation of personnel. While large departments have domestic violence units they are totally reactive to the request of an officer. Other modes of deployment via 911 or 311 (non-emergency calls) are not valid enough to be the basis for allocation.[58] The third source is the hoped-for changes in levels of education required and increased lateral entry (at lieutenant or equivalent rank rather than at the lowest rank). Other recruiting aims to create more diversity. This recruiting takes many forms, including seeking minorities and those with non-binary gender orientation. Training, focused on discipline, running, shooting, driving, and "how to stay out of trouble" has not changed in content since after the Second World War.

Comment

Given the constraints emphasized here, change at best would be graduated. I emphasize the misleading crime focus that continues, contractual obligations negotiated by police unions and associations, research focused on crime control, and the idea that crime is like witchcraft – an unpredictable dangerous force. The research on controlling crime assumes present organizational structure and character of policing, and training that focuses on the "crime" and ignores other types of police work. As a result, efforts at reallocating resources to police and manipulating budgets will produce more of the same. Police rarely share "good cases" or other information with other police agencies or social agencies. The "same" here means a new specialized unit created as a response to reform.

NOTES

1 S.H. Palmer, *Police and Protest in England and Ireland 1780–1850* (Cambridge: Cambridge University Press, 1988).
2 A. Silver, "The Demand for Order in Civil Society," in *The Police*, edited by D. Bordua (New York: Wiley, 1967), 1–24.
3 One irony to be considered is that the Dublin Metropolitan force, created in 1785, was unarmed, peace-keeping in focus and not a constabulary concerned with national security.
4 Republic of Ireland, Minister of Justice, The Future of Policing in Ireland, Commission on the Future of Policing in Ireland (Dublin: Minister of Justice, 2018).
5 I consider Anglo-American modern democratic public police to be represented by forces in the United Kingdom, Canada, the United States, New Zealand, and Australia. The police of the Republic of Ireland, An Garda Siochana, could be included.
6 Peter Manning, *The Technology of Policing* (New York: New York University Press, 2008); Peter Manning, *Democratic Policing in a Changing World* (Boulder, CO: Paradigm Publishers, 2010); Peter Manning, *Policing the Other: The Drama of Policing in Ireland*, forthcoming.

7 S. Brayne, Predict and Surveil: Data, Discretion and the Future of Policing (New York: Oxford University Press, 2020).
8 I mean here that such efforts have neither been fully investigated nor reformed properly, as the boundaries on investigation of the police procedures are even stronger than those around corporations. They begin with known scandals and inevitably focus on individuals rather than procedures. This sustains the notion that police are good; there will always be "rotten apples."
9 Seth W. Stoughton, Jeffrey J. Noble, and Geoffrey P. Alpert, "How to Actually Fix America's Police," *The Atlantic Magazine*, 2 June 2020, 3–13.
10 Sam Walker, *A Critical History of Police Reform* (Lexington, MA: Lexington Books, 1977).
11 President's Commission on Law Enforcement and Administration of Justice, The Challenge of Crime in a Free Society (Washington, DC: 1967).
12 M. Banton, *The Policeman in the Community* (London: Tavistock Publications, 1964); John Rex and Sally Tomlinson, *Colonial Immigrants in a Brutish City: A Class Analysis* (London: Routledge, Kegan, Paul 1963); J.H. Skolnick, *Trial: Law Enforcement in Democratic Society* (New York: Wiley, 1966); W.A. Westley, "Violence and the Police," *American Journal of Sociology* 59, no. 1 (1953); W.A. Westley, *Violence and the Police – A Sociological Study of Law, Custom and Morality* (Cambridge, MA: MIT Press, 1970); J. Wilson, *Varieties of Police Behavior* (Cambridge, MA: Harvard University Press, 1968).
13 Criminology was an important subject throughout the Anglo world. It was focused generally on theory, prisons, and crime more than police. Ironically, the key words invented by an engineer-cum-criminal justice student, Alfred Blumstein, that drove future research, media reports, and the creation of colleges and departments of criminal justice in the United States, "the criminal justice system," were omitted. The title was attached in *The Challenge of Crime in a Free Society* (1967) to an imagined set of subsystems: police, prosecutors, courts, and correction and an imagined flow from arrest to various kinds of exits. The fundamental issues of deciding, power, race, and class.
14 See summary in Manning, *The Technology of Policing*; Manning, *Democratic Policing in a Changing World*; Christopher Murphy, "Policing Postmodern Canada," *Canadian Journal of Law and Society* 13, no. 1 (1998); D. Weisburd and A. Braga, eds., *Police Innovation: Contrasting Perspectives* (New York: Cambridge University Press, 2006).
15 Peter K. Manning, "Community Policing," *American Journal of Policing* 3 (1983): 205–27.
16 Weisburd and Braga, eds., Police Innovation: Contrasting Perspectives.
17 J.Q. Wilson and G. Kelling, "The Police and Neighborhood Safety: Broken Windows," *Atlantic Monthly* 249 (1982): 29–38.
18 Manning, Democratic Policing in a Changing World.
19 W.G. Skogan, Disorder and Decline: Crime and the Spiral of Decay in American Neighborhoods (New York: Free Press, 1990); "Community Policing: Can It

Work?" in The Challenge of Community Policing: Testing the Promises, edited by Dennis P. Rosenbaum (Thousand Oaks, CA: Sage Publications, 1994); W.G. Skogan and S.M. Hartnett, Community Policing, Chicago Style (New York: Oxford University Press, 1997); R. Sampson, The Great American City (Chicago: University of Chicago Press, 2012).

20 W.G. Skogan, *Police and Community in Chicago: A Tale of Three Cities* (New York: Oxford University Press, 2006).
21 J. Wilson, *Thinking About Crime*, rev. ed. (New York: Vintage, 1985).
22 Peter K. Manning, "Theorizing Policing: The Drama and Myth of Crime Control in the NYPD," *Theoretical Criminology* 5, no. 3 (August 2001): 315–44.
23 W. Sousa and G. Kelling, "'Of Broken Windows,' Criminology and Criminal Justice," in *Police Innovations*, edited by D. Weisburd and A. Braga (New York: Cambridge University Press, 2006).
24 Manning, "Theorizing Policing."
25 J. Eck, J. Maguire, and E. Maguire, "Have Changes in Policing Reduced Violent Crime? An Assessment," in *The Crime Drop in America*, edited by A. Blumstein and J. Wallman (New York: Cambridge University Press, 2010); Weisburd and Braga, eds., *Police Innovations*.
26 B.D. Warner, "Community Characteristics and the Recording of Crime: Police Recording of Citizens' Complaints of Burglary and Assault," *Justice Quarterly* 4, no. 4 (1997): 631–50; "The Role of Attenuated Culture in Social Disorganization Theory," *Criminology* 4, no. 1 (2006): 73–98; B.D. Warner, "Directly Intervene or Call the Authorities? A Study of Forms of Neighborhood Social Control within a Social Disorganization Framework," *Criminology* 45, no. 1 (2007:, 99–129; P.J. Carr, L. Napolitano, and J. Keating, "We Never Call the Cops and Here Is Why: A Qualitative Examination of Legal Cynicism in Three Philadelphia Neighborhoods," *Criminology* 45, no. 2 (2007): 445–80. Research for some fifty years has shown no correlation of police numbers and the level and kinds of recorded crime. This is a theme echoed in Weisburd and Braga (2006). Unfortunately, advocates of crime reduction by police tactics, journalists, and the public believe the myth that police control crime.
27 Blumstein and Wallman, *The Crime Drop in America*.
28 Manning, "Theorizing Policing"; Manning, *The Technology of Policing*.
29 W. Scott, *Seeing Like a State* (New Haven, CT: Yale University Press, 1998).
30 Manning, The Technology of Policing.
31 J.A. Eterno and E.B. Silverman, "The New York City Police Department's Compstat: Dream or Nightmare?" *International Journal of Police Science and Management* 8, no. 3 (1 September 2006): 218–31.
32 W.F. Walsh, "Compstat: An Analysis of an Emerging Police Managerial Paradigm," *Policing: An International Journal of Police Strategies and Management* 24, no. 3 (2001): 347–62.
33 Manning, Technology of Policing.

34 Weisburd and Braga, eds., Police Innovation: Contrasting Perspectives.
35 B.E. Harcourt, *Illusion of Order: The False Promise of Broken Windows* (Cambridge, MA: Harvard University Press, 2001).
36 Manning, "Theorizing Policing."
37 D.R. Rose and T.R. Clear, "Incarceration, Social Capital and Crime: Implications for Social Disorganization Theory," *Criminology* 36, no. 3 (1998): 441–80.
38 This is not the time to repeat critiques of lack of validity (accurate measures) and reliability (repeated findings using the same measures with new data) of police statistics that began more than one hundred years ago. Recent influences of clichéd business speak on policing have produced a harvest of nonsense: police chiefs as "CEOs" or using efficiency and "smart policing" as standards, a new version of "crime management": vision statements, strategic planning documents, and management by objectives. These have little or no relationship to policing on the ground. In fact, "ticking the boxes" and "working against the numbers" often obscure the work on the ground. They don't measure it.
39 J. Brown, ed., *The Future of Policing* (London: Routledge, 2013).
40 J.H. Radcliffe, *Intelligence-Led Policing* (Portland, OR: Willan Publishing, 2008).
41 A. Ferguson, *The Rise of Big Data Policing* (New York: New York University Press, 2017).
42 Ibid., 89–90; S. Brayne, *Predict and Surveil: Data, Discretion and the Future of Policing* (New York: Oxford University Press, 2020).
43 Alice Goffman, *On the Run: Fugitive Life in an American City* (Chicago: University of Chicago Press, 2014).
44 A Canadian student of mine was studying training in the Royal Canadian Mounted Police. He spoke to several instructors who were frustrated by trying to encourage "thinking outside the box." They averred that the young recruits did not even yet know the box.
45 S. Holdaway, *The Racialization of British Police* (London: Macmillan, 1996); S. Holdaway and M. O'Neill, "Institutionalized Racism after McPherson: An Analysis of Police Views," *Policing and Society* 16, no. 4 (2006): 349–69; Megan O'Neill, *Police Community Support Officers: Cultures and Identities within Pluralised Policing* (Oxford: Oxford University Press, 2019); B. Loftus, *Police Culture in a Changing World* (Oxford: Oxford University Press, 2012).
46 E. Bittner, The Functions of the Police in Modern Society: A Review of Background Factors, Current Practices, and Possible Role Models (Washington, DC: National Institutes of Mental Health, 1972).
47 Ferguson, *The Rise of Big Data Policing*, especially chapters 3 and 4.
48 Manning, Democratic Policing in a Changing World, chapter 9.
49 M.E. Beare and T. Murray, eds., *Police and Government Relations: Who's Calling the Shots?* (Toronto: University of Toronto Press, 2007); D.H. Bayley and P.C. Stenning, *Governing the Police: Experience in Six Democracies* (New Brunswick, NJ: Transaction Publishers, 2018).

50 D.H. Bayley and P.C. Stenning, *Governing the Police*.
51 Ferguson, The Rise of Big Data Policing.
52 J. Rubinstein, *City Police* (New York: Farrar, Strauss and Giroux, 1973).
53 Bayley and Stenning, *Governing the Police*.
54 Ferguson, The Rise of Big Data Policing, 121–4.
55 This phrase is popular in England, where "cutting edge" and "at the coal face" employ the synecdoche taken from coal mining to characterize the work of constables.
56 Independent Commission on Policing for Northern Ireland, *A New Beginning: Policing in Northern Ireland* (Belfast: 1999).
57 P.A. Waddington, *The Strong Arm of the Law: Armed and Public Order Policing* (New York: Oxford University Press, 1991).
58 Research on police processing of calls for service, the operative euphemism, shows many repeat calls for the same incident; too precise or too broad modes of categorizing the call (about one-half are not "sent down" to an officer at all); screening that relies on "trust" in the caller – many calls are questions, lies, or pranks – only the trusted are sent down; and another one-quarter sent are not attended. The basic rule is, if trusted, categorize it generally and let the officer who answers the call decide the nature, content, and importance of the now incident (Manning 1989). Given these procedures, it is impossible to decide on the basis of calls alone what the incident portends. Special units, social services, and support of other kinds still rely on the ad hoc judgment of officers. For example, I went on a drug raid in a large city and found several families with children sitting around. Some drugs were found. The officers debated whether they should call social services to collect the children. The parents were docile and the children well behaved, so the officers decided they would not call social services.

9 Inquiring into Public Policing

MARGARET E. BEARE

This chapter was motivated in part by promises from various governmental levels of substantive "transformation" to Canadian policing.[1] There have been previous promises of holistic change but little success in determining whether the promises have been adequately fulfilled. The chapter therefore examines the factors that led to calls for change, the resistance encountered, and the impact of the change processes. The examination suggests that there has been more talk than action.

We can see how this is the case by tracing from a Canadian perspective the "route from idea to change" of four of the items on David Bayley's list of "big reform ideas": community policing; problem-oriented policing; signs of crime policing ("broken windows"), and hot-spots policing.[2] Whatever the intended objective, all the big reform ideas tend to slide towards a common end of crime control so that change does not move much beyond words. Community policing can lead to more surveillance and investigation and even to a former chief of the Toronto Police Service referring to "carding"[3] as a form of community policing. Problem-oriented policing and hot-spot policing approaches targeted Toronto neighbourhoods containing gangs and guns with TAVIS-style[4] policing, while broken windows policing is recognized to have a potential for harsh, zero-tolerance control measures.

The tendency of policing to return to its original state can be explained by Bourdieu's differentiation between *field*, *habitus*, and *capital*.[5] Police *habitus* does not readily change even in the face of significant changes to the *field*.[6] The policing *field* as a "site of struggle" is changed when different social actors competing for dominance shift the balance among such factors as social class, types of crime, technology, demographic developments, and so on. The police *habitus*, "durable dispositions," or ingrained and often unconscious practices, perceptions, and attitudes that build up over time do not change or do not change in the same way as the field. Tension is created when the new field and the old habitus do not interact smoothly and the expected change is not realized.

According to Manning and Ericson, among others, the police come to know their "fields" from limited information that results in a socially constructed, redefined, or rationalized version of their environment; but, because it is only selected knowledge, it is an "enacted environment" or, in other words, an environment perceived by means of organizational processes such as resource allocation, human interactions, human memory, and traditional police case-by-case building processes. Weick observes that, "the human creates the environment to which the system then adapts. The human does not react to any environment, he enacts to it."[7] The enacted environment therefore is a part but not the whole of the policing environment, but it is what helps determine police action.

There is also a literature that analyses how the durable aspects of the habitus come to be. Manning refers to the management of appearance and the oral culture of the police[8] and elsewhere refers to "rules of thumb" and "recipe knowledge" to describe how police culture directs police actions. Building on Lyotard's[9] notion of narration as the quintessential form of customary knowledge, Shearing and Ericson[10] argue that the stories police relate to each other or share more widely are "the key to understanding the practical knowledge police officers use to produce action."[11] They believe police culture is not driven by rules, even "cookbook rules," but by the stories that "capture the insights of countless officers" and make police participants in the construction of police actions. How compelling the stories are may determine the change potential within policing. In Bourdieu's *hysteresis effect*, the durable dispositions of the *habitus* "outlive the economic and social conditions in which they were produced." The *field* changes, the economic, cultural, social, and symbolic *capital* may also change,[12] but the built-up thinking and actions based on previous histories, practices, and expectations fail to adapt.[13]

Another insight into the lack of change in policing is provided by Erving Goffman's dramaturgical sociological approach, which Manning applied to policing. Police action can be seen as symbolic and structural in nature. Observing police behaviour is analogous to seeing a drama in which some aspects of policing are hidden and others are visible, or, to use Goffman's terminology, some aspects are "frontstage" and others "backstage." Examining individual events as smaller parts of a larger production allows us to differentiate between the messages and the realities – what is advertised (or the propaganda), how it is symbolically conveyed, and how it is interpreted. What can also be exposed is the relative balance between performances the "actor" believes in versus those that are cynically motivated.

Uniforms, rituals, traditions, ceremonies, and settings, together with established rhetoric and beliefs, are the embedded symbols that serve to "define, construct and manage situations."[14] The process also binds members together within an organization. Manning uses the example of the police funeral to demonstrate the weight of the symbolic meanings that surround policing and even penetrate the rhetoric of politicians, media accounts, and the public consciousness.[15] All the symbolic themes that dominate policing are on display: drama, ritual, costumes, as well as the backstage and frontstage management, teamwork, the presentational strategies, and the control tactics.

As in other policing performances, even funeral ceremonies may have a different backstage from their frontstage performance. In 1998, a young detective constable was killed as he sat in an unmarked van in a shopping-centre parking lot in Toronto. While respecting the Canadian police officer who died, we can examine the circumstances of his case to see how his police organization used dramaturgical techniques to manage his funeral while using other techniques to cover up the facts of his death. The funeral was estimated as the largest in Canadian history and included the first ever global internet coverage. All the provincial and city political and policing elite were in attendance. The themes of the speakers were about the brotherhood of police, the danger of the job, and the sacrifice police make to serve the public. There were calls to be "tough on thugs" and rhetoric on the Toronto police needing to work more closely with immigration officials to activate deportation orders against immigrant criminals. Insufficient resources were seen to be restricting these efforts.

In fact, the police officer had not been killed by dangerous Jamaican criminals, as the police first suggested, but by two homeless drug-addicted women wanting to steal his van. Undercover and in an unmarked van, the women had no idea they had killed a police officer. The linking of the police death to immigration and resource issues was therefore misplaced and opportunistic. Moreover, it was eventually revealed that the two officers who were supposed to be working with the officer's surveillance team had been drinking at bars too far away for them to reach him in time, even though he was able to radio to them that he had been stabbed. After the subsequent investigation, an official police statement said that the death and the absentee drinking colleagues were not related,[16] although five officers later faced *Police Services Act* charges and were disciplined for deceit and for neglect of and drinking on duty.

Official inquiries are useful for gaining the knowledge of police conduct necessary to know where change needs to be made. When things are running smoothly policing operations tend to be invisible, so few notice until something goes wrong and a crisis or scandal erupts. A serious matter can then result in some form of fact-finding that forces transparency on what is a generally secretive occupation. To paraphrase Leonard Cohen, the fact-finding is the crack where "the light gets in" to reveal the hidden or unnoticed anomaly. The unusual event of an officer being stabbed to death while sitting in a vehicle in a shopping mall plaza is an example. If the incident had not occurred, we would not have known that his fellow undercover officers had abandoned work to drink at a hockey rink. Nor would the question about the frequency of officers neglecting their duties have arisen.

A variety of legal processes can be engaged to scrutinize police misconduct. Whether royal commissions, public inquiries, criminal or civil court cases, coroner's inquiries or inquests, and task forces, they are all intended in some manner to seek the truth, and the reports and recommendations they make can become tools for police reform. While any of these fact-finding processes can be affected by politics and power, we can learn from them as long as the critical gaze is maintained. All fact-finding mechanisms have two important elements: an exploratory function where contested facts concerning what happened are negotiated and resolved, and a conclusion and/or resolution of the presenting issue. While the degree of compliance with the results of fact-finding mechanisms may fall short of perfect, the findings remain a signpost to where to take police reform and a yardstick for measuring the degree of police change thereafter.[17]

Within Canada, the police have been the subject of significant legal scrutiny, from criminal trials and lawsuits to public inquiries, all of which have repeatedly identified the same problems. The Royal Canadian Mounted Police (RCMP) and other municipal and provincial police services have all generated incidents that later became targets for legal review, which identified persistent problems and made similar recommendations as previous studies.

Adversarial legal processes, including civil proceedings, can produce factual conclusions, rulings, or recommendations that directly or indirectly influence police practice and behaviour, even though they may in fact conflict with or contradict each other. Such decisions can become rules or tools for police to adapt their operations:[18] however, the effect of a ruling or judgment is limited by the level of court and the rules of precedent, or how the challenged conduct is described in testimony in subsequent cases.[19] Ultimately, therefore, it may result in only slight changes to police practice. When a ruling does not result in change, there is no further opportunity to reiterate it, unless a similar case arises in the future. Changes driven by case rulings can therefore take many years and may never happen.

The second category of legal process includes non-adversarial inquiries that examine collective as opposed to individual police behaviour. In some senses these are political exercises given that governments authorize them and allocate resources for them to function. Calling for an inquiry has been part of political platforms in several Canadian elections, as in the case of the 2006 Ipperwash Inquiry in Ontario, which was created by a new government to examine the actions of the premier of a previous government. To avoid being adversely affected, some governments might refuse to contemplate an inquiry even when there is a clear indication that one should be held. Macdonald believes: "This is related to the fact that the independence of a public inquiry implies that government loses control over what happens during the inquiry, including what may be said in the report.[20] This is only partially true, however, since terms of reference are usually politically determined, as are the appointment of commissioners, and reports on findings and recommendations are largely made with little if any public debate.[21] Nor is there an obligation for governments to accept inquiry recommendations, while the inquiries themselves may vary in utility. Some have proven to be excellent fact-finding processes, while others became mired in legal disputes or deviated from their mandate, and in some cases it was the mandate itself that was the problem.

Inquiries are also expensive. They can also take years to report; their mandates are often narrow or biased so produce limited or slanted findings; they can assign blame but not guilt, and they can destroy reputations without the benefit of a trial.[22] The advantages, however, often compensate for the flaws. They can be as broad as their terms of reference permit, so they can inquire into patterns and practices and systemic and structural questions. An inquiry witness is compelled to testify in exchange for protection against self-incrimination.[23] Inquiries are not judicial proceedings, however, so information provided by witnesses cannot be used as evidence in criminal proceedings, although witnesses can be charged with giving false evidence.[24] The ability to compel testimony is advantageous in examining such matters as political or police corruption or organized crime, where intimidation, violence, or the threat of loss of job, wealth, or status, would otherwise deter witnesses from testifying. Moreover, unlike trials, which focus on a specific incident, inquiries permit examination of policies and underlying issues, and because they are public, they tend to receive media coverage that diffuses information to a wider public.

Inquiry reports into matters touching on the police are useful guides for assessing the various attempts that have been made over the years to improve, change, or hold the police to account. But given their non-coercive character, ultimately their utility may lie more in serving as a marker for such attempts and in providing the cracks into which we can peer to view the workings of the police. The Ipperwash Inquiry report into the 1995 Ontario Provincial Police (OPP) shooting of Dudley George[25] noted that it was the fifth major Canadian public inquiry in twenty-five years to consider relations between police and government and the issues of police independence and accountability in detail.[26] Why are these questions regarding the relationship between the state and the police important? During the proceedings of a 2001 House of Commons committee, one member succinctly described the inherent weakness in the accepted arrangement between police and government: "if we're going to give the RCMP the right to restrict, in their best judgment, the behaviour of Canadian people, then we should make sure it's the RCMP making the decision and not the government using the RCMP for their particular political purposes."[27] Silver observed that as early as 1829 the introduction of the new police in London represented the "penetration and continual presence of central political authority"[28] and thereby established a quite different relationship between the citizenry and the state. Then, as now, the objective was to create a balance that allows for state oversight without becoming a police state.

Of course, police in many countries are directly controlled by government and their mandates are specifically to protect state rather than public interests, and the closer we look at our own system, the muddier the principle of independence appears. There are dangers in believing we are guided by an essential principle when the evidence suggests otherwise.[29] Pue makes the point that the powerful image of the "police as helpers" has remarkable strength and can obscure their immense discretion in deciding when, how, and against whom to apply the law.[30] Few situations allow us to scrutinize this degree of police power; however, incidents that result in public inquiries, saturation media coverage, reports, and studies can provide some insight into the power available to the police, how it is mobilized, and whether in mobilizing their power the police do it as independent and accountable agents of government or as functionaries acting on behalf of political rather than public interests. As Glasbeek commented after the Toronto G8 and G20 summit demonstrations in 2010:

> The righteous anger aimed at the police behaviour during the G8/G20 is aroused because it was made clear to the demonstrators that their liberal democratic rights could be subjugated to force ... But, concentration on The Force ... tends to obscure a question that should be confronted directly: Who has an interest in having The Force frontally attack and diminish our democratic institutions and potential?[31]

Lesley Wood also argues that beyond seeing the police as the demon during extreme actions they can be seen as "a tool of economic elites and political powerholders" and "as a force with relative autonomy which struggles to maintain its own position."[32]

Police Independence

Many discussions of police independence start from the 1968 *obiter dicta* of Lord Denning, which emphasized that police were above all answerable to the law, not governments.[33] This has led to the generally accepted principle that police must be operationally independent but follow the policy direction of ministers. While this seems clear, what happens when police meet politicians and confront political issues may be quite different. Part of the purpose of the Ipperwash Inquiry was to settle the question of whether the Premier directly or indirectly ordered the OPP to take a specific operational action at Ipperwash Provincial Park that resulted in a violent confrontation and the death of Dudley George. The Premier did not give a direct order, but he gave a sufficiently clear message to those who served him that specific policing action was desired "to get the natives out of the park." The inquiry concluded that while communication between government officials and the OPP was important, no government official should have been present at the police command post and that a liaison officer should have passed information between the police and government without distracting the incident commander from police operations.[34]

An opposite finding to political interference is the conclusion reached in the Morden Independent Review of matters relating to the 2010 G20 Summit in Toronto. Morden found that the Toronto Police Service Board, to which the police are accountable, took virtually no part in providing policy direction or operational policies for the planning and execution of policing strategies such as "kettling,"[35] mass arrests, or use of the *Public Works Protection Act*. The incident illustrated the direction police actions can take when legitimate governance is absent. During one weekend, over 1,100 people were arrested, over $1 billion were spent, more than 20,000 police and military were deployed, and the police chief fell short of his promise that the police would protect protestors.[36] Critics were hoping to learn what went wrong through a formal national inquiry. No such inquiry able to compel testimony was ever held, but there were eleven separate reports[37] treating some of the "backstage" decision-making. While the Toronto police chief took some responsibility for the way the G20 unfolded, even after the ten reports were published the public never discovered whether there were other actors, such as the US Secret Service presidential security team influencing some of the more extreme policing tactics. Also left largely unexplained was the role of the Canadian government and its agencies in the incident.

Both police and their political masters can gain advantage from the confusion or overlap between policy and operational decisions. Roach refers to "political shirking" when responsible ministers fail to accept responsibility and to be held accountable for policing decisions they could have influenced. He quotes Edwards, who argued that "undue restraint on the part of the responsible Minister in seeking information as to police methods and procedures can be as much of a fault as undue interference in the work."[38] That was arguably the situation outlined in the Morden Report. Similar cases include the circumstances in the 1984 McDonald *Commission of Inquiry into Certain Activities of the RCMP Security Service*, where the director of the Security Branch had expressed verbally and in writing that certain actions of his officers were "close to the line" with respect to the "commission of crime in the national interest."[39] With respect to one operation, the view appears to have been that sharing the information would have put ministers in an "untenable position" and "given a political flavour to the operation." Government appears to have preferred to remain ignorant of lawlessness so as to deny knowledge if the occasion arose.

It is not clear whether ministers are in fact kept in the dark about police decisions. In the Airbus Affair, the RCMP requested through the Department of Justice assistance from the Swiss authorities for an investigation into potentially criminal dealings involving a former prime minister.[40] When the request became a major media story, the Solicitor General stated that "the minister or the solicitor general does not get involved in operational matters" and that he had merely been informed by the RCMP that the request had been made. Similarly, the Minister of Justice stated that he was not personally aware of the request letter.[41] Yet it is hard to imagine that a Department of Justice lawyer would sign off on a request under a mutual legal assistance treaty (MLAT) concerning a former prime minister without seeking ministerial approval and possibly engaging the Prime Minister's Office. Even at a basic level, the relationship between policy decisions and operational decisions and between police and elected officials is blurred. If elected representatives influence police action, they should do so in an open and accountable manner.[42] Stenning notes that transparency, the written and published directives that outline the relationship between the police and the government, is missing.[43] Morden outlines three principles to aid transparency:

1. Reciprocal information exchange between police and governing body
2. A governing body actively seeking operational information from a chief of police when a critical point arises.
3. Collaboration in defining with the police the "what" but not the "how" of an operation.

As Manning observes, "In practice ... police organizations function in a political context; they operate in a public political arena and their mandate is defined politically ... Patterns of police and politics within the community are tightly interlocked."[44]

Police Dependence on Politics

The police are dependent on government at various levels of jurisdiction for their existence, authority, and resources. They are a resource-dependent agency for funding. Increasingly, the employment contracts of police chiefs specify policies such as community policing to be achieved, and those policies may indirectly or directly bear on operational matters. While this does not necessarily mean a loss of operational independence it may encourage a police chief to maintain favourable relations with the government. At the local level, the political complexion of government officials on social issues may also be an issue. The police must maintain the status quo until it is changed by legitimate political processes. The police therefore enforce particular political positions as enacted into laws but must change with every switch in political policy, while supposedly remaining politically neutral.

On occasion, the police may be required to take action to meet public or government requirements to address specific situations such as social unrest or violence, and urgent action may be required. On examination, some of these matters may reveal a manipulation of the demand for action either by the media, the politicians, government spokespersons, or members of the public with a self-interested agenda, and all the various voices will have had an effect on the policing decision, as will the fear of adverse publicity should the police fail to respond as expected. We have already discussed the political master sidestepping responsibility when blame is being assigned, but C.D. Robinson suggests that the political role of the police may be "to accept the punishment that might otherwise be received by others … police serve as the convenient scapegoat for a variety of error, ineptitude, malfeasance, misfeasance, nonfeasance, committed or permitted."[45]

Concerning the impact of resources on police decisions, Alan Grant does not ask, "Where, as a matter of discretion have the police decided to concentrate their efforts?" but, "Where, as a matter of political discretion have the police been given the capability to engage in enforcement efforts?"[46] With respect to the RCMP, a continual list of government policy decisions are directly linked to earmarked resources for specific activities. For example, during the 1990s, some major government policing-related initiatives that received earmarked resources included child sexual abuse; missing children; family violence and justice for victims of crime; the Canada drug strategy; and Aboriginal justice.

The Justice for Victims of Crime initiative is one example of many complex interactions between government and police for new police policy direction to have effect. Rock analyses how this unfolded.[47] The initiative arose from the desire of the incumbent Government to avoid a free vote in the House of Commons that might have restored the death penalty. The plan was to win support with a package of initiatives to address the public fear of crime, restore confidence, and focus on crime prevention. The answer was the peace and security initiatives, which involved consultation with victims and the use of data from various surveys and research projects to inform the policy actions. Rock details the importance attached to finding resonant terminology and the prolonged negotiations with the police community that led to police buy-in. A diffuse notion of "victims" became concretized in the term "victims of crime," and victimization studies were categorized under the heading of "preventive policing," thus associating victims and the federal initiatives with police work. Police then became willing agents in the complicated transformation from the ambiguities of order maintenance in domestic crises to preventive policing.

Apart from terminology, there had to be those who believed in the initiatives, significant funding, and a structure compatible with those of both the government policy apparatus and policing, to encourage the confluence of interests and efforts. Rock concludes that, "At the very core of any piece of action will usually be found those officials who have staked something of their identity and reputations."[48] That applies equally to the police, who during this analysis were shown to be as committed and as invested as were the government police officials. Not all initiatives were as complicated or had so much to lose if they failed as the Justice for Victims of Crime initiative, but it illustrates the complexity of implementing government policy that has significant change implications for police operations.

Police Discretion and Political Priorities

Once it became obvious to academics that the police make hundreds of conceivably significant discretionary decisions per day, it became important to examine how those decisions were made. The policing literature from the 1960s to 2017 is instructive in showing how thinking about police discretion has evolved and affected policing practice. First, the literature examines interaction between discretion and the law and questions what degree of restraint the legal system can exert on the police; second, it examines the discretion police exercise regarding who to target, that is, who gets "policed" as opposed to who receives policing services.

Goldstein,[49] Lafave,[50] and Davis[51] are credited with recognizing the existence of police discretion. Until then, the police were viewed as mere functionaries of the law.[52] The fault appeared to be a lack of clarity in the law or ambiguous police policies. This freedom to make decisions in police work was seen as an unavoidable aspect of policing due to the "inadvertent ambiguities and omissions in the way statutes and regulations were drafted, exacerbated by the absence of explicitly formulated law enforcement policies."[53]

The next wave of theorists included Skolnick,[54] Bordua and Reiss,[55] Niederhoffer,[56] Wilson,[57] Bittner,[58] and Rubinstein,[59] who saw the police role as more ambiguous and involving competing expectations within policing, although they still regarded the law as the source of accountability and as a restraint upon police behaviour. Skolnick spoke confidently of a concern for "due process of law," and Wilson referred to law as a "constraint that tells the police officer what he must not do." However, a different idea emerged: that there are many different elements of the law which can be used by the police to persuade the courts to uphold their desired actions. During this period there was an emphasis on the conflict and contradictions in policing which created a tension between the adherence to the law and the realities of policing. Academics also attempted to identify a police "personality" but generally concluded that the promotional system, the element of danger, and the authority of police created rather than attracted a particular type of "working personality."[60]

Rumbaut and Bittner claim that Wilson's work was "among the first attempts to demystify the relationship of police work to law."[61] This may be true to the extent that Wilson acknowledges that law is only "one resource among many" that the police can use, and he begins the process of enlightening researchers on the ways in which the police may use the law to their advantage, that is, to manipulate, circumvent, or re-interpret the laws.[62]

This view of the law links us to a third phase in which Richard Ericson and Doreen McBarnet perhaps best represent the idea that "law provides 'cover.'" It does this in two ways: first as blanket cover over a range of offences available for an officer to apply to any troublesome situation, and second, in the legal procedures that are so enabling for the police that there are few occasions when the decision of an officer cannot be legitimated or justified.[63]

In the case of corporate or financial crime, however, legislatively supported discretion may be less helpful to the police. Apart from police being impeded by lack of training or organizational priority-setting, there is bias in the laws that can protect corporate and financial criminals. As Tombs and Whyte argue, such protection shows "a form of criminal law that can barely mask its inherently structural class bias." This bias is inherent in the fabric of both laws and courts. It undermines the ability of states to hold corporations and/or their directors and top management criminally liable for the harms they inflict, and few courts have demonstrated a willingness to pierce the "corporate veil" to prosecute the human agents behind the offending actions of the corporation.[64] Given the circumstances, it is more difficult for the police to exercise discretion effectively in corporate and financial crime cases.

There are also discretionary linkages between police and politics. Alan Grant argues that, in reality, resource allocation influences much police discretion and in that sense is an exercise of political discretion. The allocation of resources determines where police focus attention, for example, on "predatory arrests" or on fraud and corruption enforcement.[65] Grant's point links the arguments raised by those who discuss discretion as a general issue, such as Cain[66] and Chambliss,[67] who study the sources of legal discretion. Grant's emphasis on political discretion suggests that laws can be passed and enforced according to larger political demands.

An example is politically induced concentration on "predatory" arrests. This was the focus of my longitudinal study of policing in Toronto where I found that when racial conflict was rising in the 1970s, the provincial attorney general and solicitor general required community programs seeking funding to focus on what they termed the "symptoms" not the "disease"; in other words, not on root causes but on an aggressive police presence to curb what was portrayed as a "Less stable and less disciplined society."[68] Hickling-Johnston recommended in its Report 5 that the Toronto Police adopt a high-profile policing strategy including intensive community involvement and visibility, high levels of moving vehicle violation stops and street stops, together with quick response capability.[69] Critics, including former Toronto mayor, John Sewell, responded with some of the earliest criticism of "stop and search" strategies, while the community organization Citizen Independent Review of Police Actions (CIRPA), referencing Ericson's findings that officer-initiated proactive encounters with the public had little impact and were often directed at "street cleaning" marginal people, argued against that approach.[70] Martin also observed that governments choose to focus on "street crime" or public order and morality at the expense of "crime in the suites," or crimes involving worker or consumer safety, the environment, or the economy, and that law enforcement not only follows that direction but intensifies it.[71]

The Toronto Board of Commissioners of Police and the police chief responded to the public reaction against high-profile policing by arguing that it was determined by local community discretion and needs, and was "tangible evidence to the community that the police are in touch with and responding to the community."[72] What experience shows is that the intentions of a police chief, board of commissioners, or expert reports notwithstanding, if police are not sensitized to the communities in which they work, the communities may regard increased police presence as discriminatory or harassing rather than increasing safety.

The notion of identifying a dangerous class for increased policing only works if there is a marginalized minority segment of the population that is powerless to protest. Once such individuals or groups obtain a voice it becomes increasingly risky for the police to target them with saturation policing or derogatory media rhetoric. While the hippies and the prostitutes in Toronto of the 1970s might have been considered sufficiently illegitimate and vulnerable to become targets for both police and politicians, there were concerns in the 1980s about how far and how blatantly Black people and homosexual people could be described as "dangerous." These two groups participated in the call for equal rights, and both were diverse enough to include affluent and professional participants as well as political activists in resisting discriminatory policing strategies.

The order maintenance role is problematic because it forces police into certain activities to meet certain societal expectations which evidence confirms cannot be adequately accomplished.[73] In addition to the impossibility of the role is the question Chambliss asks: "whose order?" The authority of the police is most challenged when it is instilled in numerous petty situations rather than against serious criminals.

From the opening of the Canadian West, maintaining legitimacy has therefore involved the police in continual negotiation. Two studies, one by Muir in North America,[74] the other by Punch in Amsterdam,[75] reveal the accommodations that are made in order to meet the expectations of different community constituencies. There is often a three-way process, with the public holding a variety of views of the police, the police holding different views about different segments of society, and individual police officers holding individual views about different constituencies of the public. Potentially, it is an individual officer's view that is most significant because individual officers have the power of discretion at their disposal.

Punch states that individual police officers are aware of the need to adjust policing to meet the expectations of individual members of society: "he subtly but largely unconsciously changes his performance to fit situated encounters ... He does this both on common sense factors – sex, age, race, clothes, etc., and also on their place in the moral hierarchy of people who conform to, or threaten, his ideological jig-saw of what is right and proper."[76]

Punch emphasizes that police have several publics, including legitimate street users, "disreputable" groups, and illegitimate street users. Individual circumstances and demeanour results in these three categories being differentiated still further, which can introduce the potential for discriminatory "adjustments." If someone is defined as low in the moral hierarchy, an officer's behaviour towards that individual may not be designed to win their favour but to meet some notion of how that individual member of a certain class in society ought to be treated. The Canadian example is Ericson's observation that members of the Peel Regional Police regarded the "pukers" and "scum of the earth" as the source of all their policing problems.[77] Van Maanen also noted the police designation of less desirable elements of society as "the assholes."[78]

Conclusion

Ultimately, the power of discretion, whether legal, administrative, or political usually gives police an advantage over circumstances, even when they have to negotiate or accommodate to maintain legitimacy. As Kelly argues, police–community interaction is based upon police power,[79] and even governments who grant the power are reluctant to challenge it. Discretion provides flexibility to deal with circumstances outside the established framework, but as the numerous inquiries into the police have shown, it can be easily misused, whether deliberately or not, and it can be used politically by the police to protect their own interests. When it is misused it is usually those who lack power, influence, or status who feel the adverse effects. The recommendations of public inquiries have prescribed ways for remedying the misuse of power, including the power of discretion, but police discretion has then been used to ignore or only half-heartedly accept outside direction. Despite all the plans and rhetoric about change and transformation, policing then has tended to stay the same or eventually to revert to the norm when changes have been instituted.

NOTES

1 Civilian Review and Complaints Commission, *Report into Workplace Harassment in the RCMP*, April 2017, https://www.crcc-ccetp.gc.ca/pdf/harassmentFinR-eng.pdf; Sheila Fraser, *Review of Four Cases of Civil Litigation against the RCMP on Workplace Harassment*, Report to the Minister of Public Safety and Emergency

Preparedness, March 2017, https://www.publicsafety.gc.ca/cnt/rsrcs/pblctns/rcmp-wrkplc-hrssmnt-css/rcmp-wrkplc-hrssmnt-css-en.pdf;*Auditor General Report on Mental Health Support for Members of the Royal Canadian Mounted Police*, http://www.oag-bvg.gc.ca/internet/English/parl_oag_201705_04_e_42226.html;Toronto Police Service, *Action Plan: The Way Forward: Modernizing Community Safety in Toronto*, January 2017, https://www.torontopolice.on.ca/TheWayForward/files/action-plan.pdf;Ontario Provincial Government, *Strategy for a Safer Ontario*, 12 February 2016, https://www.ontario.ca/page/strategy-safer-ontario-public-discussion-paper; *Action Plan: The Way Forward: Modernizing Community Safety in Toronto*, 26 January 2017, https://www.torontopolice.on.ca/TheWayForward/files/action-plan-printer-friendly.pdf; See also Tonda McCharles, "Two New Reports Urge Radical Reform of How the RCMP Is Managed," *Toronto Star*, 15 May 2017, https://www.thestar.com/news/canada/2017/05/15/mounties-are-incapable-of-policing-themselves-rcmp-watchdog-report-says.html.
2 David H. Bayley, "Police Reform: Who Done It?" *Policing and Society*, 18, no. 1 (2008): 7–17, DOI: 10.1080/10439460701718518.
3 Carding is the practice of police collecting and recording information on individuals obtained from street contacts or stops. It is defended by some as a way of police knowing their community and criticized by others as a discriminatory practice since it disproportionately targets young Black men and can be used for profiling.
4 Toronto Anti-Violence Intervention Strategy (TAVIS).
5 Pierre Bourdieu, *Language and Symbolic Power*, edited by John B Thompson and translated by Gino Raymond and Matthew Adamson (Cambridge, MA: Harvard University Press, 1991).
6 Fergus McNeill, Nicola Burns, Simon Halliday, et al., "Risk, Responsibility and Reconfiguration," *Punishment & Society* 11, no. 4 (October 2009): 419–42.
7 Karl E. Weick, *The Social Psychology of Organizing*, (Reading, MA: Addison-Wesley, 1969), 63–4, quoted in Peter Manning, *The Narcs' Game: Organizational Limits on Drug Enforcement* (Cambridge, MA: MIT Press, 1980), 43. See also Peter K. Manning, *Organizational Communication* (New York: Aldine De Gruyter, 1992).
8 Peter K. Manning, *Democratic Policing in a Changing World* (New York: Routledge, 2010), 202.
9 Jean-François Lyotard, *The Postmodern Condition: A Report on Knowledge*, translated by Geoff Bennington and Brian Mossumi (Manchester: Manchester University Press, 1984).
10 Jean-François Lyotard, *The Postmodern Condition: A Report on Knowledge*, Conclusion (Minneapolis: University of Minnesota Press, 1984).
11 Clifford Shearing and Richard Ericson, "Culture as Figurative Action," *British Journal of Sociology* 42, no. 4 (1991): 481–506.
12 Pierre Bourdieu, *The Logic of Practice*, translated by Richard Nice (Cambridge, UK: Polity Press, 1990).

13 Megan O'Neill, "Revisiting the Classics: Janet Chan and the Legacy of 'Changing Police Culture.'" *Policing and Society* 26, no. 4 (2016).
14 Peter K. Manning, *Police Work* (Long Grove, IL: Waveland Press, 1977), 8.
15 Peter K. Manning, *Police Work*, 20–5.
16 Gay Abbate, "Officers Charged with Drinking on Job," *The Globe and Mail*, 28 April 2000, https://www.theglobeandmail.com/news/national/officers-charged-with-drinking-on-job/article1039106/.
17 Myron W. Orfield Jr. and Myron W. Orfield, "Deterrence, Perjury, and the Heater Factor: An Exclusionary Rule in the Chicago Criminal Courts," *University of Colorado Law Review* 63 (1992); Cyril D. Robinson, "Police and Prosecutor Practices and Attitudes Relating to Interrogation as Revealed by Pre- and Post-Miranda Questionnaires: A Construct of Police Capacity to Comply," *Duke Law Journal* 1968, no. 3 (June 1968): 425–524; R.S.M. Woods, *Police Interrogation* (Toronto: Carswell, 1990).
18 Woods, *Police Interrogation*; Doreen McBarnet, "Book Review: Jury Trials," review of *Jury Trials* by J. Baldwin and M. McConville. *Sociology* 13, no. 3 (1979): 511–13.
19 Woods, Police Interrogation.
20 Roderick Macdonald, "The Rule of Law and Economic Development in Russia: An Analysis of the Forms and Functions of Independent Commissions of Inquiry (Royal Commission) in Canada, Executive Summary and Bibliography," McGill University, https://www.mcgill.ca/roled/files/roled/roled_commissioninquiries_en_-roderick_macdonald.pdf.
21 Phil Scraton, "From Deceit to Disclosure: the Politics of Official Inquiries in the United Kingdom," in *Crime, Truth and Justice: Official Inquiry, Discourse, Knowledge*, edited by George Gilligan and John Pratt (Cornwall: Willan, 2004).
22 There is a requirement under the Canadian *Inquiries Act* that when an inquiry is contemplating making a finding of wrongdoing for the person to be notified in advance of the commission's intention and for the person to be able to make representations in relation to that potential finding. See Macdonald above.
23 Although there have been Canadian royal commissions that, depending on how they were appointed, did not have the power to compel witnesses to attend or provide testimony.
24 For example, an RCMP officer who lied in the *Braidwood Inquiry* into the tasering death of Mr. Dziekanski was convicted of perjury. There are in Canada "Royal Commissions" that, depending on how they are appointed, may not have power to compel witnesses to attend or coercive powers to force testimony.
25 Sidney B. Linden, *Report of the Ipperwash Inquiry*, 4 vols. (Toronto: Attorney General, May 2007), https://www.attorneygeneral.jus.gov.on.ca/inquiries/ipperwash/report/index.html. In 1995 a group of approximately thirty members of the Stony Point First Nation band, including a number of children, began to peacefully occupy Ipperwash Provincial Park in Ontario to assert their claim to the land. The Conservative Ontario government wanted them removed as quickly as possible. On 6 September the Ontario Provincial Police (OPP) staged a nighttime raid on the camp.

26 Other inquiries included the Royal Commission of Inquiry into Certain Activities of the RCMP (McDonald Commission 1981); Rapport de la Commission d'enquête sur des opérations policières en territoire québécoise (Keable Commission Report 1981); the Nova Scotia Royal Commission on the Donald Marshall, Jr., Prosecution, (Hickman 1989; and the Commission for Public Complaints Against the RCMP, RCMP Act – Part VII Subsection 45, 15 (14), (Hughes Inquiry 2001).

27 House of Commons Standing Committee on Foreign Affairs and International Trade. Relevant remarks recorded in the transcript on Thursday, 8 November, 2001, at 10.20 a.m., http://www.ourcommons.ca/Content/Committee/371/FAIT/Evidence/EV1041146/faitev41-e.htm.

28 Allan Silver, "On the Demand for Order in Civil Society: A Review of Some Themes in the History of Urban Crime, Police and Riot in England," Paper 11, Working Papers of the Center for Research on Social Organization Department of Sociology, Michigan State University, 1965.

29 Jean-Paul Brodeur reminds us that there was a different model in France in 1667 under Louis X1V which advocated for, rather than warned against, the blatant use of police powers to advance state interests. Likewise, Louise Shelley in her analysis of Soviet policing describes the police involvement in the intimidation of political opponents for the benefit of political bosses as being an explicitly stated function of the police.

30 Wesley Pue, "The Prime Minister's Police? Commissioner Hughes' APEC Report," *Osgoode Hall Law Journal* 39, no. 1 (2001): 165–85, http://digitalcommons.osgoode.yorku.ca/ohlj/vol39/iss1/5.

31 Harry Glasbeek. "G8/G20, 25 – 27 June, 2010, Toronto: Observations, Questions, Opinions." Unpublished, 2010.

32 Lesley Wood, *Crisis and Control: The Militarization of Protest Policing* (Toronto: Between the Lines, 2014), 162.

33 *R v. Metropolitan Police Commissioner, ex parte Blackburn* [1968] 2 QB 118. In this case, the chief justice and master of the rolls remarked" "By common law police officers owe to the general public a duty to enforce the criminal law. However, police are servants of no one but the law itself, and a chief officer of police has a wide discretion as to the manner in which the duty is discharged. It is for him to decide how available resources should be deployed, whether particular lines of inquiry should or should not be followed and even whether or not certain crimes should be prosecuted. It is only if his decision upon such matters is such as no reasonable chief officer of police would arrive at that someone with an interest to do so may be in a position to have recourse to judicial review. The police do not act under the direction of the Home Office or any other part of the Executive."

34 Ipperwash Inquiry, Executive Summary, Vol. 4, p. 24.

35 "Kettling" is controlling demonstrators by confining them into a small geographical area.

36 Mid-May 2010, one month before the G20 at Bistro 990, Toronto.
37 See Margaret Beare, Nathalie Des Rosiers, and Abigail Deshman, *Putting the State on Trial: The Policing of Protest during the G20 Summit* (Vancouver: University of British Columbia Press, 2015). Some of the eleven separate studies are archived in the Ontario Legislative Assembly Library at http://lois.ontla.on.ca/vwebv/searchAdvanced?sk=exte and with Government of Canada Publications at https://publications.gc.ca/site/eng/home.htm and can be accessed through their catalogues. The separate studies are: *Toronto Police G20 Report* (2011), http://www.torontopolice.on.ca/publications/files/reports/g20_after_action_review.pdf; Parliament of Canada, Standing Committee on Public Safety and National Security (2011), http://www.parl.gc.ca/HousePublications/Publication.aspx?DocId=5054650&Language=&Mode=1&Parl=40&Ses=3&File=9; Ontario Ombudsman Report, *Caught in the Act* (2010), http://www.ombudsman.on.ca/Files/sitemedia/Documents/Investigations/SORT%20Investigations/G20final-EN-web.pdf; John Morden, *Independent Civilian Review into Matters Relating to the G20 Summit* (2012), http://www.tpsb.ca/g20/ICRG20Mordenreport.pdf; Honourable Roy McMurtry, *Report of the Review of the Public Works Protection Act* (2011), https://collections.ola.org/mon/25004/309314.pdf; Gerry McNeilly, *G20 Systemic Review Report: Policing the Right to Protest*, Office of the Independent Police Review Director, Report (2012), https://www.oiprd.on.ca/CMS/getattachment/Publications/Reports/G20_Report_Eng.pdf.aspx; Civilian Review and Complaints Commission for the RCMP, *Public Interest Investigation into RCMP Member Conduct Related to the 2010 G8 and G20 Summits* (2012), https://www.crcc-ccetp.gc.ca/en/public-interest-investigation-rcmp-member-conduct-related-2010-g8-and-g20-summits-0; National Union of Public and General Employees and Canadian Civil Liberties Association, *Breach of the Peace: G20 Summit: Accountability in Policing and Governance* (2011), https://collections.ola.org/monoth/15000/307839.pdf; Royal Canadian Mounted Police, *RCMP 2010 G8 and G20 Summits RCMP-led Horizontal Evaluation Report*, Final Report (2014), https://www.rcmp-grc.gc.ca/en/2010-g8-and-g20-summits-rcmp-led-horizontal-evaluation-report#Findings; Office of the Auditor General, *Report of the Auditor General of Canada to the House of Commons. Chapter 2: G8 Legacy Infrastructure Fund* (2011), http://www.oag-bvg.gc.ca/internet/English/parl_oag_201104_e_35230.html; and OPP, *Consolidated after Action Report: 2010 Muskoka G8 Summit. 2010 Toronto G20 Summit* (2011), https://www.publicsafety.gc.ca/lbrr/archives/cnmcs-plcng/cn31069-eng.pdf.
38 John Edwards, Ministerial Responsibility for National Security, Special Study for the McDonald Commission of Inquiry Concerning Certain Activities of the Royal Canadian Mounted Police (Ottawa: 1984), 97.
39 McDonald Commission of Inquiry Concerning Certain Activities of the Royal Canadian Mounted Police, Second Report, Vol. 2, p. 668, and Third Report, p. 74 (paras. 173–202).
40 International assistance is obtained through a legal process involving signed "mutual legal assistance treaties" (MLATS).

41 Philip Stenning, "Someone to Watch over Me: Government Supervision of the RCMP," in *Pepper in Our Eyes: The APEC Affair*, edited by Wes Pue (Vancouver: University of British Columbia Press, 2000), 111.
42 Stenning, "Someone to Watch over Me," 76.
43 Philip Stenning, "Political 'Independence' of the Police," in *Police & Government Relations: Who's Calling the Shots?*, edited by Margaret E. Beare and Tonita Murray (Toronto: University of Toronto Press, 2007), 183–256.
44 Peter K. Manning, "Police: Mandate, Strategies and Appearances," in *Criminal Justice in America*, edited by R. Quinney (Boston: Little, Brown and Co. 1974), 181–3.
45 C.D. Robinson, "The Mayor and the Police: The Political Role of the Police in Society," in *Police Forces in History*, edited by G.L. Mosse (London: Sage, 1975), 278.
46 Alan Grant, "The Criminal Justice System – Where Are We Going?" *Can. Police Chief* 39 (1980); Alan Grant, *The Police: A Policy Paper* (Ottawa: Law Reform Commission of Canada, Ministry of Supply and Services, 1980).
47 Paul Rock, A View from the Shadows: The Ministry of the Solicitor General of Canada and the Making of the Justice for Victims of Crime Initiative (Oxford: Clarendon Press, 1986).
48 Paul Rock, *A View from the Shadows*, 149–63 and 386.
49 Joseph Goldstein, "Police Discretion Not to Invoke the Criminal Process: Low-Visibility Decisions in the Administration of Justice," *Yale Law Journal* 69, no. 4 (1960): 543.
50 W.R. LaFave, Arrest – The Decision to Take a Suspect into Custody (Boston: Little, Brown, 1965).
51 Kenneth Culp Davis, *Discretionary Justice: A Preliminary Inquiry* (Baton Rouge: Louisiana State University Press, 1969).
52 Ruben Rumbaut and Egon Bittner, "Changing Conceptions of the Police Role: A Sociological Review," in *Crime and Justice: An Annual Review*, edited by N. Morris and M. Tonry (Chicago: University of Chicago, 1979).
53 Rumbaut and Bittner, "Changing Conceptions of the Police Role," 243.
54 Jerome Skolnick, Justice without Trial: Law Enforcement in Democratic Society (New York: Wiley, 1966).
55 David J. Bordua and Albert J. Reiss Jr., "Command, Control, and Charisma: Reflections on Police Bureaucracy," *American Journal of Sociology* 72, no. 1 (July 1966): 68–76.
56 Arthur Niederhoffer, *Police in Urban Society* (Garden City, NY: Doubleday, 1967).
57 James Q. Wilson, Varieties of Police Behavior: The Management of Law and Order in Eight Communities (Cambridge, MA: Harvard University Press, 1968).
58 Egon Bittner, "Police Discretion in Emergency Apprehension of Mentally Ill Persons," *Social Problems* 14, no. 3 (Winter 1967): 278–92.
59 Jonathan Rubinstein, *City Police* (New York: Farrar, Straus and Giroux, 1973).
60 Wilson, Varieties of Police Behavior, 31.
61 Rumbaut and Bittner, "Changing Conceptions of the Police Role," 257.
62 Wilson, Varieties of Police Behavior, 145.

63 Richard Ericson, *Reproducing Order: A Study of Police Patrol Work* (Toronto: University of Toronto Press, 1982), 13; see also Doreen McBarnet, "Book Review: Jury Trials," in *Review of Jury Trials*, edited by J. Baldwin and M. McConville, *Sociology* 13, no. 3 (1979): 511–13; Doreen McBarnet, "The Royal Commission and the Judges' Rules," *British Journal of Law and Society* 8, no. 1 (1981): 109–17; Bittner, "Police Discretion"; Egon Bittner, "The Police on Skid Row: A Study of Peace Keeping," *American Sociological Review* 32, no. 5 (1967): 699–715; Egon Bittner, *The Functions of the Police in Modern Society* (Rockville, MD: National Institute of Mental Health, Center for Studies of Crime and Delinquency, 1970); and M.R. Chatterton, "Police Arrest Powers as Resources in Peace-Keeping," *Social Work* 7 (1976): 234–7.
64 Steve Tombs and David Whyte, *The Corporate Criminal: Why Corporations Must Be Abolished* (New York: Routledge, 2015), 85.
65 Alan Grant, "The Criminal Justice System – Where Are We Going?"; Grant, *The Police: A Policy Paper*.
66 M. Cain, *Society and the Policeman's Role* (London: Routledge & Kegan Paul, 1973).
67 W. Chambliss, and M. Mankoff, *Whose Law? What Order? A Conflict Approach to Criminology* (New York: John Wiley & Sons, 1976).
68 Hickling-Johnston Study, Productivity Improvements – Delivery of Cost Efficient Police Services to Metropolitan Toronto, Report no. 2 (Toronto: Toronto Police Service, 1981).
69 Hickling-Johnston Study, *Productivity Improvements – Delivery/Cost Efficient Police Services to Metropolitan Toronto Citizens,* Report no. 5, Recommendation no. 29 (Toronto: Toronto Police Service, 1981).
70 Citizens' Independent Review of Police Actions (CIRPA), Final Response, p. 37; see also Richard Ericson*, Reproducing Order*, 206.
71 Dianne Martin, "Police Lies, Tricks and Omissions: The Construction of Criminality," Draft presentation to the meeting of the Canadian Association for Legal Ethics (CALE) held in Quebec City, 29 May 2001.
72 Toronto Board of Commissioners of Police, Response to the Public Submission on the Hickling-Johnston Reports, 27 January 1983, p. 4.
73 Manning, *Police Work*, 29.
74 W. Ken Muir, *Police: Street Corner Politician* (Chicago: University of Chicago Press, 1977).
75 M. Punch, *Policing the Inner City* (London: Macmillan, 1979).
76 Punch, Policing the Inner City, 123, 128.
77 Ericson, Reproducing Order, 66.
78 John Van Maanen, "Epilogue on Watching the Watchers," in *Policing: A View from the Street*, edited by Peter Manning and John Van Maanen (Pacific Palisades, CA: Goodyear Publishing, 1978), 319.
79 R.M. Kelly, "On Improving Police-Community Relations: Generalization from an OEO Experiment in Washington, D.C.," *Journal of Social Issues* 31, no. 1 (1975): 57–87.

10 Nowhere to Turn for Survivors of Gender-Based Violence: Misogyny in Policing

ANNA WILLATS

It's long past time to de-task, defund, and ultimately abolish policing as it is practised now – even when it comes to addressing gender-based crimes, including sexual assault and rape. I didn't always recognize this. No one has done more to convince me of this than the police themselves. My experience as a rape crisis worker working with survivors of sexual violence in the 1980s and 1990s, and as a social justice advocate in Toronto after, has taught me to thoroughly question the role of the police and the legal system in addressing sexual assault, criminal harassment, intimate partner violence, and other forms of gender-based violence. I echo the calls of those who say we need to find better ways to prevent and address this violence.[1]

Following are my personal reflections on some of those experiences and how they have added up to an undeniable (to me at least) body of evidence that policing (and the legal system it is part of), no matter how it is reformed, will never be the vehicle for preventing or addressing gender-based violence, largely because it sucks financial and human resources away from the remedies that would be meaningful and effective. And beyond that, I've become convinced that policing and other legal responses will not and cannot bring anyone justice.

As a working-class white kid growing up in the 1960s and 1970s in Milton, Ontario, I did not have much knowledge of police and policing other than what I saw on television and Elmer the Safety Elephant's visits to my public school. Police officers were either silly and hapless (*Car 54 Where Are You?* and *The Andy Griffith Show*), unthreatening white guys (*Adam-12* and *Columbo*), or adventurous and cool (*Hawaii Five-O*). My first memory of interacting with police was when our neighbour, who was a Milton police officer, came to my high school to take my sister and me home after our father died when I was fifteen. The only other time I remember talking with an officer was when my overwhelmed mother asked the local police if they could send someone to speak to me about underage drinking. I clearly remember this very young fellow awkwardly speaking to my seventeen-year-old self through our front door, not sure what he was supposed to say. It was a five-minute interaction where I felt embarrassed and a little ashamed, but never threatened, and able to end it quickly. My mother did not have to worry that I would end up arrested or killed, and I had a funny story to tell my friends. As far as I knew, police were a benign and low-key presence, with seemingly little to do in our quiet, majority-white small town except to deal with public drunkenness and young men getting into trouble. Nowhere did I find or learn accurate information about the origins of policing in North America – in the enslavement and ongoing criminalization of African descended people, and in the enforcement of white-settler land theft and the ongoing genocide of Indigenous peoples.[2]

In 1981, I came out as both a feminist and a lesbian and moved to Toronto. In February 1981 the Toronto police had raided gay bathhouses and arrested over three hundred men, giving rise to an inspiring resistance movement.[3] One of the first demonstrations I ever attended was on the first anniversary of these raids, and it marked the beginning of my realization that the police were not our friends and that their actions could lead to serious consequences for marginalized people, including death by suicide.[4] This early lesson was reinforced almost twenty years later, with the "Pussy Palace" raid in September 2000. Toronto police intimidated and objectified women and trans/non-binary people at the bathhouse event, one of many times the police used *Liquor Licence Act* regulations to disrupt and harass bars, events, and other spaces where what are now known as 2SLGBTQI+ people gathered.[5] I was engaged to conduct a consultation and write a report in 2005 for the Toronto Women's Bathhouse Committee, which was the organizer of the Pussy Palace. This report was mandated by the Ontario Human Rights Commission as a result of a complaint brought by the Committee against the Toronto Police Service (TPS), who were ordered to pay an award of $350,000 to the event organizers. I organized and conducted focus groups, interviews, and a community meeting with members of the 2SLGBTQI+ community, bar owners, and licensees, where I heard about the ways that TPS was collaborating with liquor licence control officers to target 2SLGBTQI+ bars and events, particularly during annual Pride festivities. The findings led to several recommendations and the report contributed to raising the curtain on this issue, as well as the development of equitable policy and practices in regard to strip searches of transgendered people who are detained by police.

I also became a volunteer and then staff counsellor/advocate, media spokesperson, and later a board member at the Toronto Rape Crisis Centre (now TRCC/MWAR) from 1982 to 2000, during a time when survivor-led movements ensured that the undeniable reality of sexual violence and other forms of gender-based violence were made clear to all levels of government, most institutions, and to the public at large. Throughout my time on our twenty-four-hour crisis line, I spoke to survivors from all walks of life. It became clear to me from our callers' experiences with police and other parts of the legal system that misogyny, colonialism, racism, homophobia, transphobia, classism, and ableism in society is embedded in policing and other institutions that are male-dominated, top down, and paramilitary in nature.[6] It became impossible to deny that anti-female attitudes within policing were systemic and not merely a case of a few bad apples or outliers.[7] My conversations with survivors, church groups, union members, community members, other services, and my own 2SLGBTQI+ community confirmed over and over again that when women and trans/non-binary people experienced gender-based violence they often faced double victimization when they came in contact with the police, due to chauvinistic, racist, colonialist, anti-immigrant, homophobic, transphobic, and ableist behaviour and responses, ranging from belittlement, shaming, patronization, abandonment, detention, assault, and more.

The first time I interacted with police in Toronto in a professional capacity was in 1982, when Jack Ackroyd was the chief of the then Metropolitan Toronto Police Force. Beginning in the late 1970s, the Toronto Rape Crisis Centre where I worked had sent members to do training with police constables on sexual assault. It was a frustrating task, as members were met over and over with disbelief about the levels of violence women faced, and a lack of interest in addressing it in any effective way. I facilitated one of these "trainings" with another colleague, where we were met by officers who clearly didn't want to be there, who questioned us about our personal lives, including why we weren't married, and stubbornly refused to take anything we said seriously. This was just as Canadian laws were beginning to change and, in 1983, to recognize that rape within marriage is illegal. These guys did not want to hear it. This was just a taste of what was to come.

Women who chose to report to police in the hopes of having their rapist charged and convicted were disbelieved and dismissed routinely, just as my colleague and I had been. They had to wait for hours in emergency rooms to be seen by doctors and counsellors.[8] Police routinely dismissed and failed to thoroughly investigate the complaints of Indigenous and racialized women, sex workers, women who were raped by someone they knew, trans and queer women, and women with disabilities. The unfounded rate for sexual assaults was higher than for other reported crimes, and of those that did get to court, the likelihood of conviction was incredibly low.[9] Officers assigned to the Sexual Assault Squad (established in 1989) talked openly and often about high levels of false allegations by women.[10] A 2017 *Globe and Mail* series of articles found that although more serious criminal offences should have a lower rate of "unfounded" (particularly with rape because victims are less likely to report), one of every five sexual assault allegations in Canada was dismissed as baseless and unfounded.[11] The report cites misclassification, inadequate training, dated interview techniques; and the persistence of rape myths among law enforcement officials. These realities were also reflected in our work with survivors at the TRCC from the time it was established in 1974.

My experience as a phone counsellor during the 1980s and 1990s also disabused me of my early learning about police officers as benign, friendly, and neutral. Over the years I received many calls from women who were stalked, beaten up, raped, threatened, and mentally tortured by police officers, either in their relationships or as a result of being in conflict with the law or doing criminalized work. Of all of the callers I spoke with in my seventeen years as a counsellor, these were the women who were the most isolated, the most terrified, and who felt most trapped and hopeless in their situations. Sex workers, including erotic dancers, massage parlour workers, and escorts, were very vulnerable to corrupt and violent police officers. They were afraid to report what was happening. Police access to guns and powers of arrest, as well as control over the investigation process, together with sex workers' fear of arrest combined to make reporting crimes against them highly unlikely.[12]

Police were and are abusers in relationships more often than the average.[13] Women who were trying to leave a relationship told us about police sitting in cars outside their home at times throughout the day, about mysterious visits from unknown people, about the presence and display of weapons by their police officer partners at home, and about their fear of what might happen next, while they had no options for reporting the violence and threats. We talked with colleagues working in towns and small communities across the province who reported the same phenomena.

And in small towns the ability to report crimes of gender-based violence was doubly difficult because of the fact that police officers often knew the men against whom women were bringing complaints. These women faced pressure from investigators to make up with their abusers, talk it out, and avoid breaking up the family. This dynamic also affected my colleagues working in rape crisis centres in smaller towns and cities. We talked at our Ontario Coalition of Rape Crisis Centres meetings about the pressures to work with police these advocates dealt with, along with the consequences they faced if they dared to criticize or question how police were doing, or not doing, their jobs.

My education about the danger that policing as it was practised in Toronto posed to women was really brought home by the cases of three women in the 1980s, all of whom were known as Jane Doe.

The first was in February 1984, when nineteen-year-old Robin Gardner Voce was driving home late one night and was stopped by two constables, Rodney Pugh and Gordon Trumbley. Robin had been drinking and was vulnerable. Instead of taking her home, the two cops drove her to the underground parking lot of Gerrard Square in East York and took turns "having sex" with her in their cruiser. Robin forced the police authorities to charge them after bravely confronting the two the next day while carrying a hidden tape recorder that captured them boasting about the incident. After six years of delay they were eventually found guilty of discreditable conduct, and were fired from the service.[14]

Tragically, Robin died (the coroner said by suicide, although her family disputed that finding) just two months before they were found guilty. The case had dragged on and on and caused her a great deal of suffering. I participated in a campaign launched by Robin's parents that successfully exerted pressure on Ontario's Chief Coroner to conduct an official inquest into Robin's death. The coroner found that she likely took her own life in response to the ongoing pressure of the case and the violation she had experienced by the Toronto police. In 1995, a new Scarborough housing project was named after Robin. It devotes 35 per cent of its units to women who have been assaulted or abused.

The director of Robin Gardner Voce Non-Profit Homes was a housing rights advocate who was also known as Jane Doe when she experienced sexual extortion by then Sergeant Brian Whitehead in November 1989. He was eventually charged under the *Police Services Act* and found guilty of "corrupt practice and deceit," leading to a loss of rank to constable.[15] This Jane Doe struggled for years to seek justice from the Metropolitan Toronto Police Force. During this process, she faced a constant uphill battle: her request for criminal charges were ignored; she was not notified of the disciplinary hearing around her case; her request for anonymity was ignored as then Chief William McCormack threatened to reveal her identity to the media, causing her to have to seek an emergency court injunction;[16] and no victim support services were offered to her by the police. "Jane" was a victim of a conspiracy of silence in the police force. Even though the hearing officer described Whitehead's conduct as "a totally despicable abuse of police power and authority,"[17] Whitehead was deemed fit to continue to "serve and protect" the people of Toronto. But "Jane" was indomitable. She also appeared at an inquiry into the sex assault against a sex worker in 1989 by Constable Gordon Junger, who was running an escort agency while working as a police officer.[18] He had been caught but was allowed to resign complete with a letter of reference from Chief McCormack.[19] Media got hold of the story, leading to a scandal that became known as the Junger/Whitehead affair.

This Jane Doe's case led to an inquiry into the administration of internal investigations by the Toronto police (known as the Junger/Whitehead Inquiry).[20] The inquiry was conducted by the Ontario Civilian Commission on Police Services and lasted for one and a half years. The inquiry made twenty-four recommendations. In 1991, it became clear that the Toronto police internal affairs unit was withholding files that were complaints of criminal misconduct by officers – 192 of them.

Jane Doe paid dearly for her efforts. She faced death threats, was beaten up, and had to enter a witness protection program. She regretted ever getting involved in the inquiry and lost any faith she might have had in the justice system by the end of it.[21] She died on October 19, 1996, still traumatized by all that had happened to her, and still without justice. What happened to her confirmed everything I was hearing from women on our crisis line: that some police officers regularly used their powers to detain, arrest, and extort sex from sex workers.

Between these two cases, there was another involving the most well-known of the women known as Jane Doe. In 1986, a serial rapist was targeting single women in the Church-Wellesley neighbourhood of Toronto. He was entering apartments through second-floor balcony doors. The police opted not to issue a warning about "the balcony rapist," as he became known, for fear that women in the area "might get hysterical" – that was what Jane Doe was told when she asked why no warning was issued. "They were using me and all of the other women in my neighbourhood as bait in the hope of catching him in the act," she later told the press, explaining why, using the pseudonym "Jane Doe," she decided to sue the police force.[22]

Jane Doe carried on her efforts to sue the Toronto police force for gender discrimination and failure to protect her and other women for a further eleven years before finally winning her case and a $220,000 award. Her efforts led to the Toronto City Auditor's Review of the Investigation of Sexual Assaults by Toronto Police, an award-winning social audit published in 1999 that resulted in fifty-seven recommendations for change.[23] Jane Doe won many rights for sexual assault survivors and others, including the right to separate legal representation in court for the survivors of sexual assault and the right to sue the police. In 1998, with the support of community advocates and services, she argued that the police under then Chief David Boothby be advised by an advisory committee made up of members of the women's anti-violence community to oversee the audit, the implementation of its recommendations, and the training of police regarding sexual assault investigations, particularly their policies regarding warnings.

While some of these recommendations were carried out, under Chief Julian Fantino we stalled in many areas as he resisted the recommendations and work of the steering committee from day one (he was also prone to gesturing with air quotes every time he said the words sexual assault – I'll never forget that). Jane, supported by advocates, battled long and hard for a meaningful commitment to an end to misogynistic, anti–sex work, and racist practices by the police. We were met with resistance and obstruction every step of the way.[24] A follow-up review by the city auditor found that while a number of the recommendations had been adopted since the original audit, many had not, and others were not being followed by rank-and-file police officers. The sexual assault squad had expanded to encompass child sexual abuse and pornography (not requested by anti-violence advocates in the original audit) and had taken on a broader mandate in regard to what adult sexual assaults it investigated, but had not been provided with additional resources. The auditor also found that even the no-cost recommendations had not been implemented, such as adding to the squad's website (now called the Sex Crimes Unit) information about sexual assault investigative processes so that women could be informed about what to expect, and that the police had not worked collaboratively with women's groups to achieve the changes that were required.[25]

In the late 1980s, Susan Eng joined the Metro Toronto Police Services Board (now the TPSB) and became chair in 1991. A former colleague of mine at the Toronto Rape Crisis Centre, Laura Rowe, was also appointed to the board that year. Rowe immediately faced allegations against her family members, which were leaked to the *Toronto Sun*. She was also accused of being in a car with the sex worker who had been victimized by Gordon Junger (of the Junger/Whitehead affair). Laura was treated like a criminal from the moment she joined the board, for no reason other than she was seen to be a voice for progressive values (being the first out lesbian in her position was also likely a factor). In a 3 July 1997 article in *XTRA!*, a 2SLGBTQI+ community newspaper, she talked about the institution of policing and police oversight: how resistant to change it was, how vulnerable marginalized police officers were, and the negative impacts of partisan politics on policing reform.[26] She persisted and became an effective advocate for progressive policies, such as requiring police to record their reasons for drawing their guns. Her experience, along with those of Susan Eng, Olivia Chow, Arnold Minors, and other board members who advocated for accountability over the years, demonstrated the absolute refusal of police officers and management to respect civilian oversight, or change their practices to protect human rights.

The shooting of Sophia Cook in October 1989 and the shocking public strip search of Audrey Smith in 1993 demonstrated that Black women face particularly egregious violence and degradation from police. These two women were assumed to be involved in criminal behaviour by the police and then violated based on those assumptions. Sophia Cook was a passenger in a car that the police alleged was stolen. She had taken a ride in the car after missing her bus, and for this "crime" was shot (while wearing a seatbelt) and temporarily paralysed.[27] Following this shooting and police killings within a four-month period of Lester Donaldson and Michael Wade Lawson, two Black Toronto-area residents, police representatives tried to shut down any criticism of their actions or suggestions that anti-Black racism was a problem in policing. This was met with a powerful statement of refusal to be silent by a coalition of thirty-five Toronto-based organizations called the Women's Coalition Against Racism and Police Violence in December 1989.[28] This was a period of powerful public resistance and mobilization against anti-Black racism and police brutality led by groups such as the Black Action Defence Committee and the Black Women's Collective.

Audrey Smith, a visitor from Jamaica, was accused by police of carrying drugs, detained, and then stripped and humiliated in public on a Parkdale neighbourhood street in August 1993.[29] As in the Sophia Cook case the police who harmed Audrey Smith were acquitted of any wrong-doing, while both women's characters and reputations were shredded in the media, which is another common police tactic to deflect and deny blame and accountability. In its 2001 *Golden* decision, the Supreme Court found that strip searches are experienced as humiliating and degrading, and many people, particularly women, regard them as sexual assault. There was no video evidence of Audrey Smith's sexual assault, but the 2008 strip search and cruel treatment of Stacy Bonds was captured on police station video.[30] She was another Black woman subjected to violence at the hands of Ottawa police, after being detained for demanding to know why she was being stopped and questioned one night after she leaned into a car to talk to some friends.[31]

These incidents, combined with the numerous killings of Black, Indigenous, and other racialized men by Toronto police over the years undeniably demonstrated that women from these communities could not rely on the police for protection or for access to justice when they experienced gender-based violence. How could Black, Indigenous, and other racialized women, particularly immigrants and refugees, call on the police when they had been hurt by men that they knew? The women who I and other service-providers spoke to did not want their abusers killed, injured, and deported. They wanted the violence to stop. They wanted access to unbiased support for themselves and their children. They wanted safe, affordable housing and good jobs so they could take care of their families. They talked often about the ways that police were ever-present in their communities, randomly stopping their sons and daughters or partners, cruising around and around their children's schools, asking people for identification or justification for being in their own neighbourhoods. And at the same time, they talked about being afraid to call police when they experienced partner violence or needed help for other reasons, for fear of being charged or detained themselves, or of being disbelieved after police talked to their abuser to get "his side of the story" or of being acknowledged but not offered any support. And often, the police just wouldn't respond at all.

In *If Low Income Women of Colour Counted in Toronto*, the 2003 final report of the action-research project Breaking Isolation, Getting Involved, researcher and author Punam Khosla described how police targeting of low-income communities and under-funding of services and supports such as transit, childcare, and recreation programs for marginalized women and communities, together with increased funding of a police service ($634.5 million, or 22 per cent of the total City of Toronto program expenditures) that was in denial of and resistant to acknowledging the pervasiveness of racism and racial profiling, combined to put low-income women into a "lethal catch 22" when it came to protecting themselves and their children.[32] These communities experienced both over- and under-policing at the same time – and were exposed to worse violence as a result. This was in addition to the heartbreak of so many mothers, sisters, aunts, and grandmothers in over-policed and under-served communities when their children, partners, and family members were killed or injured by police.

Over the years I have sat on many task forces, advocated for justice in dozens of presentations to the Toronto Police Services Board and Toronto City Council, developed training on gender-based violence for the Ontario Provincial Police, and worked with community groups on police accountability strategies. It took me far too long to recognize that there is no chance that the police can be significantly changed through engaging with them. And even if they could be compelled to change through sustained political will and enlightened management, the fact is that they enforce laws that are arbitrary and discriminatory, and most often applied to people who are just trying to survive. The power of police officers and other public employees to detain, threaten, control, and interact with marginalized people and communities is destined to result in personal and systemic violence. In my many engagements with police decision-makers and representatives, their need for control and their resistance to change, while protecting their budget and police jobs, was and I believe always will be their priority in coalitions and partnerships.

I also mistakenly believed that it was possible to significantly change how policing is done through greater hiring of under-represented groups, better training by people most affected by violence, advisory committees made up of advocates and community members, neighbourhood-focused policing where cops become better known to residents, and other popular reforms. I believed there was promise in a 1995 report released by Chief David Boothby known as Beyond 2000.[33] I wrongly believed that the police could somehow be shifted to a more empathetic, community-controlled, and service-oriented response to survivors of crime, and that this was a desirable outcome. But over time it became apparent that the language of progress was just a cover for maintaining the status quo while calling it something different. To placate critics and justify their existence and ever-expanding budget[34] in a changing context, the only pivot the police (and other legal and medical institutions) consistently made was to co-opt progressive ideas and language in exercises in image-management and public relations.[35]

Faced since the 1990s with dropping levels of crime and growing calls for accountability, police in Canada have looked for ways to take on more activities and functions to maintain and expand their ever-growing budgets.[36] In Ontario and Toronto, they have had willing partners in local and provincial governments, the better to ensure less criticism and resistance to neoliberal agendas. The Mike Harris government (1995–2002) was a prime example of this dynamic. Its brutal cuts to social assistance, cancellation of social housing builds, closure of psychiatric treatment beds and services, downloading of services and responsibilities to municipalities with no accompanying financial resources, deregulation, and deep cuts to funding for violence against women services were accompanied by a transfer of wealth to cronies, consultants, and corporate interests.[37] The resulting homelessness, violence, and social unrest spilled into neighbourhoods and parks. In response, under the rhetoric of community policing, Boothby introduced Community Action Policing (CAP) in the summer of 1999, which paid officers overtime to patrol what were called "hotspots" in the city. These were in the same communities that had always been over-policed, as well as parks where homeless people and racialized immigrant people gathered.[38] Extra funding for CAP was expanded by Mayor Mel Lastman not long after, and the province pitched in under Premier Dalton McGuinty. This targeted policing program was the forerunner of the expensive, racist, and discredited Toronto Anti-Violence Intervention Strategy under Chief Bill Blair.[39] The money taken out of the already inadequate resources and services that supported communities to prevent violence and go beyond surviving to thriving happened at the same time as funding for police services increased, enabling them to repress and endanger those communities instead.[40]

The 1990s and early 2000s were also a time of frustrating and ultimately unsuccessful engagement with the police around sexual assault and intimate partner violence. In addition to the struggles in implementing the recommendations of the Jane Doe audit, workers representing emergency shelters for women escaping abuse met with Toronto police to establish protocols for engagement, only to have the proposal arbitrarily put on a shelf.[41] While there was significant and effective push back from cross-sectoral coalitions of anti-violence activists and service providers demanding all provincial parties to support and fund feminist, anti-racist responses to gender-based violence that did not depend on the criminal justice system, it was an uphill battle. The provincial and federal governments defunded advocacy and cut funding to independent anti-violence services, while pouring money into duplicate, apolitical victims' services programs that worked closely with courts and the police.[42] The folly of working with the police to address gender-based violence, or any issue with roots in systems of heteropatriarchy, colonialism, and white supremacy, became more and more apparent to me. The energy that we were spending in engagement and efforts to reform police practices needed to be directed to building up community power and skills to address the root causes of the violence they faced.

As the years went on there was more undeniable evidence of the folly of seeking answers for gender-based violence that relied on policing and carceral responses. In 1994, the Canadian Panel on Violence against Women issued its final report, which among other recommendations called for the creation and application of "zero tolerance" policies in many sectors of society, including educational settings.[43] In Ontario these policies were supported by many mainstream feminist agencies and were further entrenched in public schools by the Harris government in 2001 in the Ontario Safe Schools Act.[44] While the original intention may have been to protect girls from sexual harassment and violence, the lack of an anti-racism and disability lens on the experiences of marginalized students in schools, coupled with the law-and-order approach of the Conservative government resulted in disproportionate numbers of suspensions and involvement with police and carceral systems for marginalized students, while Black girls continued to experience gender bias and anti-Black racism ("misogynoir").[45]

There are other examples of policies promoted by anti-violence agencies and advocates that have ended up harming marginalized women because of the gender-neutral, racist, ableist, and homophobic approaches of the legal system. Mandatory charging policies were established to address police hesitancy to lay assault charges against male perpetrators but have instead resulted in increasing numbers of women partners being charged with assault, as police interpreted the policy to mean that if both partners claim that they have been assaulted (even if the impacts and histories of violence are clearly different) then both will be charged. This is particularly true for Indigenous and Black women, who are perceived as angry and aggressive, and for lesbians and gender non-binary people, as police can't rely on their assumptions about gender presentation to determine who the victim is.[46] Survivors who have less skill in English than their partners are also charged more often, as police allow the perpetrator's version of events to frame the situation.[47]

Policies that initially required people who work with children and vulnerable adults (seniors and dependent disabled adults) to pass a vulnerable sector police record check have been expanded to include everyone who wishes to volunteer or work in social and community services, even though most perpetrators of child abuse, sexual assault, and other kinds of violence are known to their victim and not ever charged, let alone convicted. I have seen in my many years of work as a field placement coordinator and supervisor in a community college how this has blocked those who are most likely to have had interactions with police, such as Black, brown, and Indigenous people living in low-income communities, people with mental health disabilities, and people who do criminalized work, from gaining employment, completing practicum placements, and volunteering.

There are too many more examples to count of how the police have demonstrated the danger they pose to women who are vulnerable to gender-based violence. In November 2004, Wyann Ruso was almost murdered by her husband after taking his gun to her local police station and reporting his threats against her. Even when Chief Julian Fantino acknowledged the fact that the police had made errors in this case, it took concerted effort on the part of Wyann, her union, and other legal and community advocates to achieve some accountability to her for police endangerment and neglect in her case.[48]

In 2007, activists with the advocacy group No One Is Illegal (NOII) exposed the fact that police were cooperating with agents of the Canada Border Services Agency to search for women without legal status in Canada who were fleeing abuse and staying in emergency shelters for women. In 2010, I worked with NOII and other migrant rights and anti-violence advocates to stop CBSA officers from attending anti-violence shelters (overturned by the national office CBSA not long after) and to emphasize the need for anti-violence services to take up the cause of migrant survivors of violence and their need for status.[49] This campaign was part of a larger campaign to convince the TPS to implement a "don't ask, don't tell" policy, which called for police officers to stop asking people for their immigration status and, in situations where they became aware of it (for example, when investigating domestic violence complaints), to refuse to disclose the information to immigration enforcement authorities. While we were able to convince them to adopt a "don't ask" policy, they insisted they were obliged to share immigration status with the CBSA. Even so, a 2015 report by NOII found that TPS officers routinely ignored the part of the policy that had been agreed to.[50] I and many other advocates warned that this refusal to protect the immigration status of gender-based violence survivors with immigration enforcement has prevented many abused women from accessing any services at all, effectively trapping them with their abusers.[51] The harassment of migrant women who don't have legal status by police and by by-law enforcement officers still continues, particularly under the guise of police responses to human trafficking and sex trafficking.[52]

Every year brings more evidence of the need to take police out of the role of responding to people in crisis, public complaints, conflicts and disputes, and yes, to gender-based violence. The phenomena I observed up close in my seventeen years as a front-line support worker continue to occur regularly, with widespread tragic consequences. On a regular basis there is another report or inquiry that exposes police negligence at the local, provincial, and national levels – their violations of human rights[53] and their continued inability to collaborate across departments and jurisdictions and to warn the public properly about murderous misogynists. As Justice Archie Campbell noted in his 1996 review of the investigations into the crimes of serial rapist and killer Paul Bernardo, "Because of the systemic weaknesses and the inability of the different law enforcement agencies to pool their information and co-operate effectively, Bernardo fell through the cracks."[54] Despite the history of court decisions calling for effective and timely public warnings, as well as the ongoing calls for thorough investigations of sexual assault, municipal and provincial police failed to do either in the case of ex-colonel Russell Williams, a serial rapist and murderer who terrorized women in small communities near Belleville, Ontario, in 2009/10. A police review of their investigation continued a pattern of denial that police had anything to learn from their mistakes, although they were forced to pay an undisclosed settlement to one of his victims.[55]

These types of failures were echoed across the country at all levels of policing. In 2012, the Missing Women Commission of Inquiry described how Vancouver police and the Royal Canadian Mounted Police (RCMP) in British Columbia ignored community and family members who tried to have them investigate the disappearances of women living in the downtown east side of the city, and refused to act on tips about violence against sex workers and other mainly Indigenous women at serial killer Robert Pickton's farm.[56] Again and again, the themes of lack of cooperation and collaboration across jurisdictions, systemic failures to investigate and take complaints seriously, dismissal of marginalized women, and failure to warn are exposed by investigators. In 2019, the final report of the National Inquiry into Missing and Murdered Indigenous Women and Girls outlined the systemic failures of police and legal systems and their roles in the high levels of gender-based violence, incarceration and denial of justice experienced by First Nations, Metis, and Inuit women, girls, trans, and 2 Spirit people across this country.[57]

There are many more examples of police negligence and harm that have had serious impacts on women and 2SLGBTQI+ people in all walks of life. Constable Michael Sanguinetti's declaration to a York University student audience in 2011 that women need to stop dressing like sluts if they want to prevent rape launched an international Slut Walk movement.[58] Leadership in the RCMP makes the case for its own disbandment as they are unable to identify the obvious systemic racism and sexism rampant in their ranks.[59] Toronto police chief Mark Saunders tells the 2SLGBTQI+ community that there is no evidence of a serial killer, as Bruce McArthur kills repeatedly.[60] A grieving mother is left to find the body of her missing daughter in a stairwell, and 2SLGBTQI+ community members are left to find the remains of their transgender friends in the city morgue.[61] Police protection bodies, such as the Special Investigation Unit (SIU), cannot hide the fact that police are a danger to marginalized and vulnerable people in crises, such as those of Regis Korchinski-Paquet and Chantel Moore.[62,63] And survivors of all forms of gender-based violence continue to be left on their own as their reports are discounted, their restraining orders unenforced, and warnings of danger come too late or not at all.

The police are clearly unable to adjust to and keep up with the progress society has made in our understanding of gender-based violence and the need for bias-free public services and workplaces, the prevalence of anti-Indigenous and anti-Black bias in all Canadian institutions, and the demands for compassionate and non-violent responses to people in crisis. Despite the tremendous investment of time, energy, resources, and money by anti-violence advocates, task forces, citizen juries, commissions, trainers, and survivors, policing continues to fail those who are targeted by gender-based violence. Police services betray their ignorance and determination to continue with the status quo despite their "spin," endless public relations exercises, quarterly reports, and promises to change. Their actions consistently show us why policing must be defunded and dismantled. When will we believe them?

It's undeniable. Misogyny, ableism, and racism are tolerated at the highest levels of policing. Victims of violence are blamed and persecuted, while perpetrators are protected. Public relations and reputation management are prioritized over real change, while mistakes are minimized and ignored. Inquiries show that policing systems are not working, but no effective solutions are implemented. Those who should enact sanctions fail to do so but also face no consequences. Despite these failures, police officers increasingly fill more social work roles. New specialty squads to address online child sex abuse, human and sex trafficking, and sexual assault continue to be created and resourced at considerable cost, and at the expense of services and programs that could make a real difference to survivors who need secure housing, childcare, social supports, and more to protect themselves and their children.

In the many years since I became a crisis counsellor and advocate in 1982, whether the Toronto police leadership was progressive, regressive, or neither, the results for women and other gender marginalized survivors of male violence have been the same. We cannot and must not continue this charade if we hope to prevent and end gender-based violence. In a *Toronto Star* opinion column in October 2020, Professor Mariana Valverde argued for dismantling the RCMP,[64] and I agree with her. Former Toronto Mayor John Sewell and my colleagues with the Toronto Police Accountability Coalition (TPAC) have been calling for over twenty years for significant changes to how policing is done.[65] There is a growing movement for defunding and abolishing the police systems that continue to devour billions of dollars of public funds countrywide – funds that would be better used to address the problems that plague the very communities that police target for surveillance and enforcement. We must address the ways that people are criminalized as they try to survive poverty, white supremacy and white nationalism, colonization, misogyny, ableism, and homo/transphobia. We must listen to the voices of survivors of gender-based violence who are arguing for transformative justice approaches to harm to replace criminalization, policing, and prisons.[66] We must envision something radically different and propose systems of accountability and responses to socially unacceptable behaviour that are not enforced by armed individuals who know nothing about the social determinants of health, oppression, and marginalization. As the chant goes – the system is working exactly the way it was designed to, and efforts to reform it while maintaining its foundations will not lead to the change we need. The case for transformative change is undeniable, and a vision for a better future is being articulated and created neighbourhood by neighbourhood, in large and small communities across the country and around the world.

NOTES

1 See the work of Robin Maynard, *Policing Black Lives: State Violence in Canada from Slavery to the Present* (Halifax, NS: Fernwood Publishing, 2017); Andrea Ritchie, Invisible No More: Police Violence against Black Women and Women of Color

(Boston: Beacon Press, 2017); Jane Doe, The Story of Jane Doe: A Book about Rape (Toronto: Random House Canada, 2003); and the work of Audrey Huntley and the advocacy group No More Silence for critiques and ideas about alternative legal, medical, and other state-sponsored responses to gender-based violence.

2 Many authors and reports have explored and exposed the roles of the Northwest Mounted Police (now the Royal Canadian Mounted Police, RCMP) and successive Canadian governments in colonialist and racist projects. For example, see Maynard, *Policing Black Lives*; Arthur Manuel and Grand Chief Ronald M. Derrickson, *Unsettling Canada: A National Wake-up Call* (Toronto: Between the Lines, 2015); Arthur Manuel and Grand Chief Ronald M. Derrickson, *The Reconciliation Manifesto: Recovering the Land, Rebuilding the Economy* (Toronto: Lorimer, 2017); Government of Canada, *Reclaiming Power and Place: The Final Report of the National Inquiry into Missing and Murdered Indigenous Women and Girls*, 2 vols. (Ottawa: Privy Council Office, 2019); Steve Hewitt, *The RCMP: A History* (Toronto: University of Toronto Press, 2013); Government of Canada, *Final Report of the Truth and Reconciliation Commission of Canada: Honouring the Truth, Reconciling for the Future* and *Calls to Action* (Ottawa: Government of Canada, 2015).

3 Historian, educator, and activist Tim McCaskell writes about these raids and others conducted by the Toronto Police Service since that time in his 2016 book *Queer Progress: From Homophobia to Homonationalism* (Toronto: Between the Lines, 2015).

4 James Dubro, "Toronto's Stonewall," *Now Magazine*, 3 February 2016, https://nowtoronto.com/news/torontos-stonewall/.

5 Jessica Taylor and Amy Powell, "The Pussy Palace Raid: A Brief Herstory," *The ArQuives*, 26 September 2019, https://arquives.ca/latest-news/the-pussy-palace-raid-a-brief-herstory.

6 Steve Hewitt, *Riding to the Rescue: The Transformation of the RCMP in Alberta and Saskatchewan, 1914–1939* (Toronto: University of Toronto Press, 2006). Also see Kevin Walby and Brendan Roziere, "Rise of the SWAT Team: Routine Police Work in Canada Is Now Militarized," *Maclean's*, 25 January 2018; Shiri Pasternak, Kevin Walby, and Abby Stadnyk, *Disarm, Defund, Dismantle: Police Abolition in Canada* (Toronto: Between the Lines, April 2022); Akwasi Owusu-Bempah, "Race and Policing in Historical Context: Dehumanization and the Policing of Black People in the 21st Century," *Theoretical Criminology* 21, no. 1 (2017): 23–34, https://doi.org/10.1177/1362480616677493https://doi.org/10.1177/1362480616677493; Fiona G. Kouyoumdjian, Ri Wang, Cilia Mejia-Lancheros, et al., "Interactions between Police and Persons Who Experience Homelessness and Mental Illness in Toronto, Canada: Findings from a Prospective Study," *Canadian Journal of Psychiatry* 64, no. 10 (2019): 718–25, http://doi.org/10.1177/0706743719861386. In addition, the House of Commons Standing Committee on Public Safety and National Security, *Report on Systemic Racism in Policing in Canada* (43rd Parliament, 2nd Session, 2021) calls for the overhaul of the RCMP's paramilitary structure.

7 One clear example of systemic and bureaucratic discrimination is the July 1998 decision by Justice Jean McFarland in the precedent-setting civil suit brought by Jane Doe against the Toronto Police Service. McFarland found that the TPS had violated Jane's equality rights and had used her and other women as bait while a serial rapist was on the loose, as a result of widespread sexism, adherence to rape myths, and gross negligence. A summary of the decision can be found at Women's Legal Education and Action Fund (LEAF), *Jane Doe v. Metropolitan Toronto Commissioners of Police (1998)*, https://www.leaf.ca/case_summary/jane-doe-v-metropolitan-toronto-commissioners-of-police-1998/. An award of $220,000 was made to Jane Doe, along with court costs to her lawyers and LEAF. Jane points out that police lawyers are also paid out of public funds – adding up to millions of dollars for this case alone. Jane Doe, *The Story of Jane Doe: A Book about Rape* (Toronto: Random House Canada, 2003).
8 Ontario Network of Sexual Assault/Domestic Violence Treatment Centres, *Our History*, https://www.sadvtreatmentcentres.ca/our-history.html.
9 Lorenne Clark and Debra Lewis, *Rape: The Price of Coercive Sexuality* (Toronto: Women's Press, 1977).
10 Christie Blatchford, "Crying Wolf," *National Post*, 8 September 2001, http://fact.on.ca/news/news0109/np010908.htm.
11 Robin Doolittle, "Unfounded: Why Police Dismiss 1 in 5 Sexual Assault Claims as Baseless," *The Globe and Mail*, 23 February 2017, https://www.theglobeandmail.com/news/investigations/unfounded-sexual-assault-canada-main/article33891309/.
12 Jane Doe writes about this in her book, *The Story of Jane Doe*, noting that sex workers organized to protect themselves in the face of police violence against them, and because they could not get complaints of sexual and domestic assault against them taken seriously. Sex worker advocacy groups were founded, including Maggie's (https://www.maggiesto.org/about), the Canadian Organization for the Rights of Prostitutes (CORP), and the Sex Workers Alliance of Toronto (https://walnet.org/csis/groups/swat/index.html). A short film, *Prowling by Night*, was created in 1989 as part of the National Film Board's "Five Feminist Minutes" (Studio D), which documents police harassment of sex workers.
13 Alex Roslin, *Police Wife: The Secret Epidemic of Police Domestic Violence* (Lac Brome, Québec: Sugar Hill Books, 2016).
14 Jim Rankin, "Sex Case Woman Mourned as Project Opens," *Toronto Star*, 1 October 1995, A4. See also Doe, *The Story of Jane Doe*.
15 Ontario Civilian Police Commission, *Report on an Inquiry into Administration of Internal Investigations by the Metropolitan Toronto Police Force*, 1992, 16. See also Andrew Duffy, "Police Board May Discipline Chief McCormack," *Toronto Star*, 24 February 1993, A8.
16 Ontario Civilian Police Commission on Police Services Report, 16, 18. See also Editorial, "The Case of Jane Doe," *Toronto Star*, 8 September 1992, A20.

17 Ontario Civilian Commission on Police Services Report, 18, 44. See also Michele Landsberg, "Police Owe Explanation on Jane Doe," *Toronto Star*, 12 July 1998, A2.
18 Ontario Civilian Commission on Police Services, Report, 13.
19 Duffy, "Police Board May Discipline Chief McCormack."
20 Ontario Civilian Commission on Police Services, Report. See also Doe, *The Story of Jane Doe*.
21 Doe, The Story of Jane Doe; See also Punam Khosla, If Low Income Women of Colour Counted in Toronto: Final Report of the Action-Research Project Breaking Isolation, Getting Involved (Toronto: Community Social Planning Council, 2003).
22 Phinjo Gombu, "Rape Victim Sues Police," *Toronto Star*, 9 September 1997, A3. See also Doe, *The Story of Jane Doe*.
23 Doe, *The Story of Jane Doe*. See also Jeffrey Griffiths, *Review of the Investigation of Sexual Assaults Toronto Police Services* (Toronto: City of Toronto Audit Services, October 1999), http://www.toronto.ca/audit/1999/102599.pdf.
24 Doe, *The Story of Jane Doe*. See also Mitch Potter, "Fantino's Way," *Toronto Star*, 24 February 2001, A21; and Michele Landsberg, "Police Failing to Heed Voice of Women," *Toronto Star*, 22 April 2000, J1.
25 Toronto Police Services Board, Extract of minutes of the public meeting: Follow-Up Review on the October 1999 Report Entitled "Review of the Investigation of Sexual Assaults – Toronto Police Service," Board Minute No. P34/05, 2005, Toronto, ON, https://www.toronto.ca/legdocs/2005/agendas/committees/au/au050405/it001.pdf.
26 Katherine Payne, "Conspiracy Flowers in Police Force: Laura Rowe Ruefully Discovers It's Hard to Change 'Terrified' Cops," *XTRA!* 3 July 1997, No. 331.
27 Maynard, *Policing Black Lives*; see also Ajamu Nangwaya, "Factsheet on Police Containment of and Violence in the African Community," *Toronto Media Co-op*, 7 February 2021, Accessed 28 November 2021, http://toronto.mediacoop.ca/blog/ajamu-nangwaya/6183.
28 Women's Coalition Against Racism and Police Violence, *Statement on the Police Shooting of Sophia Cook*, 16 December 1989, Accessed at https://riseupfeministarchive.ca/activism/organizations/black-womens-collective/blackwomenscollective-dec1989-womcoalstatementagainstracismpoliceviolencestatement-toronto/.
29 Maynard, *Policing Black Lives*; Roger Metivier*, Audrey: The Fight for Justice*, video directed by Roger Metivier, Toronto, 1999. Accessed 25 February 2022, https://www.youtube.com/results?search_query=Audrey+Smith%3A+The+Fight+For+Justice.
30 David M. Tanovich, "Bonds: Gendered and Racialized Violence, Strip Searches, Sexual Assault and Abuse of Prosecutorial Power," *Criminal Reports* 79, no. 6 (2011): 132–50.
31 Maynard, Policing Black Lives.
32 Khosla, If Low Income Women of Colour Counted in Toronto.
33 Metropolitan Toronto Police, Restructuring Task Force, *Beyond 2000: Final Report*, 1994.

34 The Toronto Police Accountability Coalition (TPAC) has kept track of and called for limits on the Toronto Police Service budget for many years. A list of TPAC bulletins containing commentary on the growth of the police budget for most years between 2001 and 2014 can be found at https://tpac.ca/issue.php?id=94.
35 Mandy Bonisteel and Linda Green, "Implications of the Shrinking Space for Feminist Anti-Violence Advocacy," paper presented at the *Canadian Social Welfare Policy Conference*, Fredericton, NB, 2005, https://www.oaith.ca/assets/files/Publications/ShrinkingFeministSpace.pdf; Eileen Morrow, *Advocating for Advocacy: The "Harris Disorder" and How Women Tried to Cure It*, n.d. Accessed 10 March 2022, https://www.oaith.ca/assets/files/Publications/HarrisYears_Jan11.pdf.
36 Anthony Doob, *Thinking about Police Resources* (Toronto: University of Toronto Press, Centre of Criminology, 1993). Doob notes that it is estimated that policing costs rose approximately 15 per cent from 1986 to 1990, although the size of the police establishment changed very little. See also Statistics Canada, "Canada's Crime Rate: Two Decades of Decline," *Canadian Megatrends*, Last modified 17 May 2018, https://www150.statcan.gc.ca/n1/pub/11-630-x/11-630-x2015001-eng.htm; Statistics Canada, "Current and Constant (2002) Dollar Operating Expenditures on Policing, Canada, 1986/1987 to 2017/2018," *Police Resources in Canada, 2018*, Last modified 3 October 2019, https://www150.statcan.gc.ca/n1/pub/85-002-x/2019001/article/00015/tbl/tbl01-eng.htm.
37 Bonisteel and Green, Implications of the Shrinking Space for Feminist Anti-Violence Advocacy; Morrow, Advocating for Advocacy: The "Harris Disorder."
38 Committee to Stop Targeted Policing, *Who's the Target? An Evaluation of Community Action Policing* (Toronto: CSTP, 2000), https://view.officeapps.live.com/op/view.aspx?src=http%3A%2F%2Ftdrc.net%2Fresources%2Fpublic%2FReport-00-08.doc&wdOrigin=BROWSELINK; Khosla, *If Low Income Women of Colour Counted in Toronto*, https://www.academia.edu/7934967/If_Low_Income_Women_of_Colour_Counted_in_Toronto_full_report.
39 John Sewell and Christopher Williams, *Crisis in Canada's Policing* (Toronto: Lorimer, 2021). See also Jim Rankin et al., "Known to Police," *Toronto Star*, Series, 9 March 2012–21 August 2013.
40 Morrow, Advocating for Advocacy: The "Harris Disorder" and how women tried to cure it; Khosla, If Low Income Women of Colour Counted in Toronto.
41 Khosla, If Low Income Women of Colour Counted in Toronto.
42 Doe, *The Story of Jane Doe*; Morrow, *Advocating for Advocacy*; The Cross-Sectoral Violence Against Women Strategy Group (CVAWSG), *Emergency Measures and Beyond: Immediate and Long Term Recommendations For Change*, March 2004, https//:www.learningtoendabuse.ca/resources-events/pdfs/pub_emergencymeasures1.pdf.

43 Sandra Harder, *Violence Against Women: The Canadian Panel's Final Report*, Parliamentary Research Branch, Political and Social Affairs Division, 1994, https://publications.gc.ca/Collection-R/LoPBdP/MR/mr122-e.htm.
44 Ken Bhattacharjee, "The Ontario Safe Schools Act: School Discipline and Discrimination," report to the Ontario Human Rights Commission, 2003, http://www3.ohrc.on.ca/sites/default/files/attachments/The_Ontario_Safe_Schools_Act%3A_School_discipline_and_discrimination.pdf.
45 Maynard, Policing Black Lives.
46 Metrac, *Mandatory and Dual Charging*, pamphlet, December 2008, https://metrac.org/content/user_files/2022/04/dual.charging.criminalized.pdf .
47 Shoshana Pollack, Melanie Battaglia, and Anke Allspach, *Women Charged with Domestic Violence in Toronto: The Unintended Consequences of Mandatory Charge Policies* (Toronto: Woman Abuse Council of Toronto, 2005, https://www.oaith.ca/assets/files/Publications/womenchargedfinal.pdf.
48 Dale Anne Freed, "Police 'Lapse' in Axe Attack," *Toronto Star*, 6 November 2004, A1. See also S. Fraser, "The Agitator," *Toronto Life*, 1 January 2008, https://torontolife.com/city/peter-rosenthal-the-agitator/; Peter Rosenthal was able to negotiate a settlement for Wyann of an undisclosed amount. Nineteen years later, in a similar case, current Toronto police chief Myron Demkiw expressed condolences to the family of twenty-three-year-old Daniella Malia, who was killed by her ex-partner in late March 2023, seventy-two hours after complaining to Toronto police that he was threatening to do exactly that. Two officers are facing misconduct charges for failing to conduct a proper investigation or follow up, Chris Fox, "Toronto Police Officer Accused of Failing to Properly Investigate Woman's 'Repeated Pleas' for Help before Her Murder," CTV News Toronto, 29 March 2023, https://toronto.ctvnews.ca/toronto-police-officer-accused-of-failing-to-properly-investigate-woman-s-repeated-pleas-for-help-before-her-murder-1.6334024.
49 Farrah Miranda and Cathryn Atkinson, "Resisting Deportation of Women Fleeing Violence," *Rabble.ca*, 6 December 2010. Retrieved from https://rabble.ca/anti-racism/resisting-deportation-women-fleeing-violence/.
50 David Moffette, Karl Gardner, and No One is Illegal, *Often Asking, Always Telling: The Toronto Police Service and the Sanctuary City Policy* (Toronto: No One is Illegal, 2015), Accessed 25 February 2022, https://www.flipsnack.com/9FE9E7FD75E/often-asking-always-telling.html.
51 Moffette, Gardner, and No One is Illegal, *Often Asking, Always Telling*.
52 Elene Lam, *Behind the Rescue: How Anti-Trafficking Investigations and Policies Harm Migrant Sex Workers*, revised (Toronto: Butterfly Asian and Migrant Sex Workers Support Network, June 2018), https://d8dev.nswp.org/resource/member-publications/behind-the-rescue-how-anti-trafficking-investigations-and-policies-harm.
53 The Ontario Human Rights Commission has produced many reports on racism in policing over the last thirty years, including *A Collective Impact* (2018) and *A*

Disparate Impact (2020). These reports and others can be found at http://www.ohrc.on.ca/en/framework-change-address-systemic-racism-policing.
54 Justice A. Campbell, *Bernardo Investigation Review Summary Report* (Toronto, Solicitor General and Minister of Correctional Services, Ontario, 1996).
55 Michael Friscolanti "What Did Police Learn from the Russell Williams Investigation?" *Maclean's*, 8 May 2014, https://www.macleans.ca/news/canada/what-did-police-learn-from-the-russell-williams-investigation/.
56 Hon. Wally T. Oppal, *Forsaken: The Report of the Missing Women Commission of Inquiry*, Missing Women Commission of Inquiry (Victoria, BC: Government of British Columbia, 2012).
57 Government of Canada, *Reclaiming Power and Place: The Final Report of the National Inquiry into Missing and Murdered Indigenous Women and Girls*, 2 vols. (Ottawa: Privy Council Office, 2019), https://publications.gc.ca/site/eng/9.867037/publication.html.
58 Joetta L. Carr, "The SlutWalk Movement: A Study in Transnational Feminist Activism," *Journal of Feminist Scholarship* 4 (Spring 2018): 24–38.
59 Hon. Michel Bastarache, *Broken Lives, Broken Dreams: The Devastating Effects of Sexual Harrassment on Women in the RCMP*, report prepared for the Royal Canadian Mounted Police (Ottawa, ON: Royal Canadian Mounted Police, 2020), https://www.rcmp-grc.gc.ca/en/final-report-implementation-merlo-davidson-settlement-agreement.
60 Jessica Patton, "Toronto Police Chief Defends Handling of Bruce McArthur Investigation after Sentencing," *Global News*, 18 February 2019, https://globalnews.ca/news/4940125/toronto-police-chief-saunders-bruce-mcarthur-investigation/.
61 Justice Gloria Stein, *Missing and Missed: The Report of the Independent Civilian Review into Missing Person Investigations*, 2021. The report examines the systemic failure of the Toronto police to work with the 2SLGBTQQIA community to adequately investigate the disappearances of men who were victims of serial killer Bruce McArthur, of Tess Richey, who was raped and murdered and left for dead in a downtown stairwell, and of Aloura Wells, a trans woman of colour whose remains were unidentified for months.
62 Alex Cooke, "Recent Deaths Prompt Questions about Police Wellness Checks," *CBC News*, 23 June 2020. Retrieved from https://www.cbc.ca/news/canada/nova-scotia/police-wellness-checks-deaths-indigenous-black-1.5622320.
63 Regis Korchinski-Paquet was a twenty-nine-year-old Afro-Indigenous woman who fell to her death from a twenty-fourth-floor apartment balcony in an incident involving TPS officers, who were called for help by her family. Chantel Moore was an Indigenous woman and mother of a six-year-old, who was shot by a police officer responding to a request to check on her well-being.
64 Mariana Valverde, "Why the RCMP Should Be Given an Expiry Date," *Toronto Star*, 28 October 2020, https://www.thestar.com/opinion/contributors/2020/10/28/why-the-rcmp-should-be-given-an-expiry-date.html.

65 See https://tpac.ca/ for the issues Toronto Police Accountability Coalition (TPAC) has worked on an index of the monthly bulletins produced by the group since May 2003. See also Sewell and Williams, *Crisis in Canada's Policing*, chapter 6 for many ideas about significant police reform.
66 There are many people in Canada and the United States doing this work, among them are Ejeris Dixon and Leah Lakshmi Piepzna-Samarasinha, editors of *Beyond Survival: Strategies and Stories from the Transformative Justice Movement* (Scotland: AK Press, 2020).

11 Offloading, Upstreaming, Defunding, and Costing: Re-thinking Calls to Police for Absconding Social Work and Mental Health Clients

LAURA HUEY AND LORNA FERGUSON

Introduction

In Canada, much of the public discourse on "defunding the police" has centred on demands for police to be removed from calls for service involving persons with mental illness (PMI). As we have argued before,[1] what remains unacknowledged is an underexplored aspect of police reform: missing persons and the extent to which mental health is an underlying issue in many single and repeat cases of missing persons. Calls for "defunding the police" and creating police non-attendance or diversion policies for mental health calls, as has happened in cities such as San Francisco and New York, occur in a policy space that is completely lacking robust evidence of the current situation and how best to proceed. Missing person cases illustrate how complex the situation is: many missing persons are eloping from hospitals, mental health facilities, and group homes. In other words, they are already plugged into "upstream" institutional resources and networks. When these people go "missing," those same social and health care providers "offload" responsibility onto the police to locate and/or return them.

In this chapter, we draw on police data on missing person calls for service from 2019 from a municipal police service to identify the extent to which missing person reports are generated by social and health care services, looking at how many of these reports involve individuals with mental illness. We then introduce a cost analysis to assess how much this one aspect of "offloading" onto police services is being subsumed within police budgets as a "hidden cost." Our focus then shifts into considering what "upstream" solutions currently exist for preventing and thus reducing these calls for service.

1. Offloading

Much has been written on the effects of deinstitutionalization on individuals with mental illness and on urban communities that were largely under-funded and thus unprepared to provide the community-based resources required to assist vulnerable individuals, often lacking strong social supports.[2] Many of those individuals, lacking employment opportunities and facing stigma and other structural barriers, were largely warehoused in low-income housing stock – often single-resident occupancy hotels – in inner-city neighbourhoods with significant drug problems.[3] Not surprisingly, many PMI struggle with substance abuse and homelessness.[4] These factors combine, it has been argued, to create situations that inevitably lead to police interventions and thus to an increased likelihood of arrest and incarceration for PMI.[5] Despite decades of research that have painted a more complex,[6] if not sometimes contrary,[7] picture of police decision-making with respect to PMI, the "criminalization hypothesis," as this line of thinking has been termed,[8] remains a dominant theme in much public discourse.[9]

In relation to calls to defund the police, there is another problem with invoking the criminalization hypothesis: police arrests only account for a portion of the overall interactions police have with PMI. As one of us has documented elsewhere,[10] other types of interactions can include wellness checks, suicide calls, mental health apprehensions, and situations in which an individual has been the victim of a crime or is a complainant on a disorder call, among others. We are not alone in making this point. Short[11] similarly notes that "it has been argued that policing services have had to pick up the slack, acting as a sort of triage service for psychiatric facilities, apprehending unwell individuals, transporting patients to the hospital, and conducting welfare checks in homes and on the streets." Much of the work generated by such interactions is handled through informal measures typically referred to as "peacekeeping" or "social work" depending on the context.[12] None of these are new observations, either. Egon Bittner's seminal field-based studies of policing in the 1960s documented the challenges police then faced in trying to come up with actions that would resolve situations involving those experiencing mental illness. Where possible, Bittner noted, officers tended to rely on informal actions and sanctions to "keep the peace," reserving law enforcement for more serious offences or those situations in which jail was a safer option for a vulnerable person than leaving them alone on the street.[13] More recent studies on police decision-making in the grey zone – that is, in those situations in which police have limited choices for responding to situations involving PMI – have drawn similar conclusions. Police interact with PMI in a variety of different situations, and how they will resolve a call is guided mainly by situational constraints; legal, policy, and regulatory guidelines; as well as by individual preference and occupational norms.[14]

2. Upstreaming/Defunding

There is now a growing body of public health and related research focused on what is termed the "social determinants" of health – those non-medical factors that can influence health outcomes, such as poverty, racism, and family dysfunction. More recently, this literature has grown to include not only health and mental health but also such behavioural phenomena as "violence," "crime," and "disorder."[15] Those working within this model advocate for interventions aimed at addressing the "root causes" of a social ill, rather than relying on the police and the criminal justice system to effect "downstream" or "Band-Aid" fixes that can worsen health and other outcomes.

With increased recognition of the social determinants of both health and crime, over the past decade, there have been significant efforts made by Canadian policymakers, public health officials, police organizations, and community groups, among others, to promote the adoption of "upstream" solutions to a wide variety of downstream issues. It might surprise some to know that police organizations – in particular, both the Canadian and Ontario Associations of Chiefs of Police – have been actively promoting a "community safety and well-being" model aimed at cross-sector collaboration on addressing root causes of crime, that was also vigorously adopted by the previous Ontario provincial government. To date, such efforts have primarily centred on the creation of "Situation Tables," wherein representatives from the police, social services, health care, and other public-sector groups identify "high-risk" individuals and attempt to secure them housing, rehabilitative, mental health, and other resources to help stabilize their situation.[16] Beyond the promotion of this program, which was also the cornerstone of much police reform work by the Saskatchewan Ministry of Corrections, Policing and Public Safety, most other efforts have been local, frequently underfunded, *ad hoc*, and un-evaluated. This state of affairs has also been true in relation to upstream initiatives in other public sectors, including social work and health care.[17]

Arguably, a significant stumbling block to taking a broader social determinants approach to crime, health, or any other major social issue is the emphasis advocates have placed on the need to address overarching structural issues – such as economic inequality – as *the* primary solution to mental health, homelessness, and so on.[18] To date, we have yet to see a strong majority of Canadians demanding income redistribution or housing on demand schemes, likely because of fears of increased public costs and therefore rising taxation. Perhaps in partial recognition of this fact, activist groups began advancing calls for a different form of redistribution: transferring public funds from police budgets to fund increased social and health care services.[19] Presumably, expanding these services would address needs gaps experienced by PMI, thus reducing the number of vulnerable individuals who experience mental health crises and come into contact with police. What we argue is that there are some simple steps that could be immediately taken to reduce the demand for police services in relation to mental health–related occurrences: health care and social work services could take preventative actions to reduce their reliance on police with respect to PMI who abscond from services – that is, we could start by "responsibilizing" those groups who have, to some extent, benefited from the offloading of certain responsibilities to police.[20]

3. Costing

Hundreds of thousands of Canadians are reported missing to the police each year.[21] This is hardly a homogenous group, and previous research has well documented the variety of factors that contribute to this phenomenon.[22] In this section, we focus solely on individuals with serious psychiatric illnesses who have absconded from forensic and/or other health care facilities. When such individuals leave or otherwise fail to return to a health care setting (such as failing to return after a cigarette break outside the facility), it is a common practice in most, if not all, Canadian jurisdictions for a police report to be filed. In Canadian provinces such as British Columbia (BC), legislation dictates that such a report will be treated as a high priority call ("person at risk" or "high-risk"), necessitating urgent police response.

Information on the prevalence of absconding cases among missing persons reports is not readily available. Fortunately, we can refer to some recent Canadian research, which used closed police files to look at various aspects of missing persons cases. For example, in one recent study, approximately 11.5 per cent of those reported missing to a municipal police service were found to have absconded from a hospital or mental health facility.[23] In this study, the strongest predictors of absconding were cognitive impairment, substance dependency, and mental health issues. A follow-up study examined the demographic, health, and other risk profiles of those who abscond from hospitals and mental health facilities, finding that individuals with schizophrenia and/or dementia were more likely to abscond from mental health facilities, whereas those diagnosed with depression or bipolar disorders were more frequently reported missing from hospitals.[24] In terms of demographic factors, White males were the most frequent absconders from both settings; however, Indigenous patients were over-represented at 9.7 per cent of the total sample. Conversely, Black patients and individuals from other racial or ethnic groups were significantly less likely to abscond from these locations.

In a previous study using the same dataset, researchers identified adults and youth with histories of repeatedly being reported missing.[25] Armed with this information, they looked at the locations from which "repeat missing people" are most likely to abscond. They found that for adults, the top five locations included three health facilities and two homeless shelters/mission centres, thus indicating that individuals under MHAs not only abscond, but some do so repeatedly.[26] Regarding the rate at which such individuals are reported missing, we have little to go on. An earlier study found that within a one-year span, 230 individuals under MHAs were reported missing to police from two Vancouver-area hospitals.[27]

PMI abscond from hospitals and psychiatric and social service facilities for various reasons. Previous research shows that such reasons include seeking freedom, accessing drugs or alcohol, negative treatment experiences, negative experiences with other service users, and/or feelings of boredom, insecurity, or a lack of safety, among others.[28] When this happens, protocol at most, if not all, facilities is to report the individual missing to police as soon as their absence is noticed.[29] In one case we previously documented, an individual was reported missing despite the fact it was known she was on a bus with two security guards from the hospital from which she had absconded.[30] It wasn't that she was actually missing; it was that the security guards were unable to convince her to return. In this and similar other instances in which someone has absconded, a report is taken, a call is dispatched, responding officers typically file a "risk assessment" form to determine the level of response and then, depending on the assessed risk, one, several, or all units on patrol may be requested to look for this person. If the individual has absconded from a psychiatric facility, police have to have the appropriate committal forms to take the person into custody and transport them back.

Where that is not the case, a wellness check occurs, the complainant is notified the person will or will not return voluntarily, and the case documented and closed. In a small proportion of cases, fortunately very few, a formal search must be conducted, drawing on not only uniformed patrol but also a search manager and members of the service's search and rescue team. Each of the steps described is a use of police resources that produces hidden costs typically "absorbed by police services."[31] To date, published Canadian studies that have looked at costs for mental health–related police calls have focused nearly exclusively on mental health apprehensions and police wait times in hospitals.[32] Significantly less is known about other types of MH-related activities – including missing persons inquiries involving absconders – with the exception of two UK-based studies[33] and one Canadian study that estimated costs of PMI involvement in different types of offences as a portion of a police budget.[34]

Scholars are frequently known to cite a "gap in the literature" as a rationale for conducting a study. In the instant case, we are attempting to begin the process of addressing a critical gap in knowledge on an important public policy issue. How we intend to do this is by demonstrating the existence of service issues that are both easily identified through analysis and remedied through practical strategies aimed at reducing service demands. Rather than taking a "whole apple" approach to shrinking the size of the policing footprint, we are showing how "small bites" can work to achieve this objective while realizing service efficiencies and cost benefits. To do this, we have chosen to analyse missing person calls for service as a starting point in a much larger project.

4. Data and Methods

Materials

As previously stated, to explore this matter, we used data obtained from a crime analyst at a Canadian municipal police service who extracted all police calls for service over 2019 from their services record management system (RMS). These data contain particulars on each police report, such as the dispatcher comments, event synopses, occurrence details, type of report initially determined by the dispatcher, the final type of report concluded after a police investigation, final Uniform Crime Report (UCR) categorization, times and locations, and other additional information acquired by police (for example, event address, time cleared, and so on). Data were then anonymized by this crime analyst, who then extracted all calls for service and generated an Excel spreadsheet documenting these occurrences split by crime-related calls and social-related calls. This provided a total of 42,996 files (12,910 crime-related call records and 30,086 social-related) over this one year. From this, any files related to missing persons in both crime- and social-related records were extracted into a separate dataset. These are the data from which we draw for this study. Therefore, our final sample includes 2,033 missing person calls for service over 2019 from one Canadian police agency.

Coding and Variables

The covariate "Location Type" was a pre-existing category within the missing person calls for service Excel dataset. These were generated by the police service RMS (were not research-determined) and resulted from the dispatcher taking information on the location from which the call originated. However, as police data quality is a known issue, we also read each missing person file in full to extract addresses and locations, verify the coding, or adjust the coding if necessary. At this time, we intended to exclude any files in which we could not confirm the location type or if this information was missing completely – a process known as listwise deletion. However, we were able to verify all files and, as such, no missing person records were removed from our final sample.

The RMS-generated categories under the "Location Type" covariate included the following: "group home," "hospital," "mental health facility," "private dwelling," "school," "retirement home," "mission centre and homeless shelter," "mall," "park," "streets/roads/highways," "parking garage," "other non-commercial/corporate places," and "other public, commercial dwelling unit." The classifications of "group home," "hospital," "mental health facility," "private dwelling," "retirement home," and "mission centre and homeless shelter" were coded just as they were assigned in the police RMS and, as previously stated, were verified through our coding process. The categories of "public park," "mall," and "other public, commercial dwelling unit" were collapsed into one. This category was labelled "public." At this time, the remaining uncoded categories of "streets/roads/highways," "parking garage," and "other non-commercial/corporate places" were collapsed into an added group named "other." The "other" category was created as these location types and/or addresses could not be determined as either public or private, and so were thought appropriately placed within an "other" grouping.

For coding whether mental health–related issues were implicated in the police missing person call for service, we generated a binary dummy variable created to represent whether each report had mental health considerations documented throughout or not (0 = mental health not implicated, 1 = mental health implicated). To create this covariate, we coded all of the files manually within the Excel spreadsheet. This was performed through the following steps. First, we conducted an initial manual review of any available qualitative or free text information in the police report (for example, event synopses, dispatcher comments, and event occurrence detail). This occurred to reveal any words within the records representing mental health components. Through this, we were able to collate a broad list of keywords to search through all the reports and extract whether mental health was implicated or not. These keywords included, for example, "ADHD," "OCD," "Bipolar," "Depressed/Depression," "Suicidal/Suicidal Ideation," "Anxiety/Anxious," and others. Then, we manually searched for these keywords throughout all of the missing person records (i.e., "CTRL + F" within the Excel dataset).

After locating files through a keyword search, we finally read each file individually in full before coding to ensure mental health was implicated within the record, instead of only relying upon the keyword search to code. This process occurred as some files had one or several keywords in the qualitative information but did not explicitly state or show that mental health was implicated in the call for service. Put another way, it was necessary to manually read each file before coding to ensure coding accuracy and that codes were not formed based on assumptions about the meaning of the comments. Once it could be verified that the file did include mental health considerations, the record was subsequently coded as "1" to indicate this implication.

Analytical Approaches

For the analytical approaches undertaken, descriptive and statistical analyses were employed first to identify the extent to which missing person calls for service were generated by social and health services. Frequency and cross-tabulation analysis were used to examine the location types and show how often mental health is and is not implicated across all police calls for service categories based on the "Mental Health" variable. Then, logistic regression was used to predict the extent to which mental health is implicated in police missing person calls for service and the different call types. This model was selected as, given that the dependent variable in the analysis is binary (mental health implicated; 0 = no and 1 = yes) and involves bounded categories, the application of a linear probability model violates the standard Ordinary Least Squares (OLS) assumptions. For predicting location types generating police missing person service calls, we employed multinomial logistic regression. This occurred as "Location Type" is a categorical variable that has unordered groupings of location types.

After this, a cost analysis was introduced across the cases identified as from social and health services and those involving mental health implications to assess the hidden cost of this offloading of responsibilities by other services for the police. For conducting this analysis, we utilized the first logged time in which the dispatcher received the call for service and calculated the number of minutes passed until the service call was marked as "cleared." This information was extracted from the data columns titled "Date Received" and "Date Cleared." Then, we captured the descriptive details and generated an average time to clearance across the various location types and split these further by the level of urgency assigned to each case. The latter process occurred as it is known that different case urgency levels reflect different police responses and, therefore, will incur different policing costs. In sum, we employ a mixture of analyses to understand the implications of defunding the police on missing person police service calls. The results of these analyses are presented below, with the respective analytical approaches outlined in each section.

5. Results

Where Do Police Missing Person Service Calls Come From?

Table 11.1 presents a descriptive overview by way of frequency analysis of the different location types in which police missing persons calls for service originated. When comparing call figures across the different place types, the leading location from which missing person service calls were derived was private dwellings (n = 546; 26.9 per cent). That being said, concerning the whole sample, most service calls were from locations that were not private (n = 1487). Specifically, 73.1 per cent of missing person calls for service stemmed from social and health services or other public places – in essence, mission centres/shelters, group homes, mental health facilities, and hospitals. To expand on this, second to private dwellings was mission centres and homeless shelters, from which 23.5 per cent of, or 478, missing person service calls for police were initiated.

Group homes emerged third in the ranking of police missing person calls for service. This location type generated 451 calls for service throughout 2019, or 22.2 per cent of all missing person police reports. Group homes exist to support special populations that need a supervised living environment, including, but not limited to, children and youth in care, individuals with developmental or physical disabilities, and/or victims of domestic abuse. The purpose of group homes is essential to contextualize, as conversations surrounding defunding the police are centred on police not being involved in service calls involving such groups of people; yet, as it appears, these facilities are seeking assistance with persons they are safeguarding and who are under their care but are going missing.

Table 11.1. Descriptive Overview of the Location Types Reporting Missing Persons to the Police

Location Type	Total	%	Cumulative %
Private	546	26.9	26.9
Mission Centre/Shelter	478	23.5	50.4
Group Home	451	22.2	72.6
Mental Health Facility	205	10.1	82.7
Hospital Facility	122	6	88.7
Public	106	5.2	93.9
Retirement Home	65	3.2	97.1
Other	60	3	100.1
Total	**2033**	**100**	**100.1***

*Discrepancy in total percentage is likely due to the rounding procedure.

Making up 10.1 per cent of all police missing person service calls, or 205 reports, are mental health facilities for longer-term stays. Hospital facilities, including emergency mental health units and general hospital care facilities, comprised 6 per cent, or 122 calls for service. These are highlighted here as standard rhetoric regarding demands to defund the police, in that police should not be handling service calls involving persons in crisis and/or persons experiencing mental illness. Yet, other facilities existing to provide servicing and protection for these individuals appear to be locations that call the police to handle missing persons from their facility in this dataset. Lastly, public arenas (n = 106; 5.2 per cent), retirement homes (n = 65; 3.2 per cent), and other areas (n = 60; 3 per cent) are also calling the police to respond to persons who have gone missing, albeit they do so the least among location types that generate service calls.

In examining the general descriptive picture of the location types generating police missing person calls for service, we can understand that health and social services are primary callers for police services for missing persons in this dataset. Additionally, with mission centres and homeless shelters being the second key contributor to police calls for service, the third being group homes and the fourth being mental health facilities, it also becomes apparent that vulnerable populations in contact with institutional facilities and networks are frequently the focal population in police missing persons calls for service. Put another way, these individuals are already plugged into "upstream" institutional resources and networks. Yet, from our data, it appears as though these social and health care providers are, in fact, "offloading" responsibility onto the police as a means to locate missing people.

To What Extent Is Mental Health Implicated in Police Missing Persons Calls for Service?

Next, we inquired about how many of these calls for service implicated mental health–related issues in their reports. Table 11.2 presents the results of the cross-tabulation analysis. We can see that mental health was involved in 36 per cent of, or 731, police missing person calls for service. This means that most missing person service calls do not disclose mental health–related issues within the dispatcher's comments. To further assess this matter, we also conducted logistic regression. As documented in Table 11.2, we can see that mental health–related issues being involved in police missing person calls for service did not emerge as statistically significant (OR = 0.921, p > .05). Therefore, missing persons call for service: (1) often do not implicate mental health–related matters, but (2) are not significantly more or less likely to involve mental health.

To What Extent Is Mental Health Implicated in Police Missing Persons Calls for Service across the Location Types?

With the above in mind and our knowledge of the existing literature discussing the pervasiveness of mental health in police calls for service, we sought to conduct additional analyses to understand the extent of mental health being implicated in police missing persons calls for service across the location types reporting persons missing. Table 11.3 presents the results of this analysis. Unsurprisingly, across the calls that did implicate mental health–related issues, mental health facilities emerged as the highest group implicating such issues in their services calls related to missing persons (n = 205; 28 per cent). Closely following mental health facilities are group homes (n = 170; 23.3 per cent), mission centres and homeless shelters (n = 158; 21.6 per cent), and private dwellings (n = 138; 18.9 per cent). However, regarding the last location type, private dwellings also comprise the group in which the highest number of service calls did not implicate mental health (n = 408, 31.3 per cent). The main takeaway here is that this is a clear illustration of how complex missing persons cases can be, with a substantial number of missing persons eloping from facilities they are plugged into while having mental health–related concerns as an underlying issue.

Are Certain Location Types Significant Drivers of Police Missing Person Service Calls?

So far, our analyses have revealed that (1) social and health services make up the most substantial number of police service calls for missing persons across the location types; (2) mental health–related issues somewhat underlie missing person service calls; yet (3) missing person service calls across certain location

Table 11.2. Descriptive Overview and Logistic Regression Examining the Extent to Which Mental Health Is Implicated in Police Missing Person Service Calls

Mental Health?	Total	Percent	OR*
No	1302	74	–
Yes	731	36	0.921
			(0.017)
Total	**2033**	**100**	

*Odds ratio from logistic regression predicting mental health being implicated in missing person calls for service.

Standard error is in paratheses below OR.

"No" is the base category.

Weighted estimate by 95 per cent confidence interval.

Table 11.3. Cross-tabulation of Location Type and Mental Health (MH) Implications in Police Missing Persons Calls for Service

Location Type	MH – Yes (%)*	MH – No (%)*	Total (%)
Private	138 (18.9)	408 (31.3)	546 (26.9)
Mission Centre/Shelter	158 (21.6)	320 (24.6)	478 (23.5)
Group Home	170 (23.3)	281 (21.6)	451 (22.2)
Mental Health Facility	205 (28)	0 (0.0)	205 (10.1)
Hospital Facility	12 (1.6)	110 (8.5)	122 (6)
Public	38 (5.2)	68 (5.2)	106 (5.2)
Retirement Home	9 (1.2)	56 (4.3)	65 (3.2)
Other	1 (0.1)	59 (4.5)	60 (3)
Total	**731 (36)**	**1302 (74)**	**2033 (100)**

*Column percentages are in relation to the column totals. Row percentages are in relation to the final sample.

types implicate mental health substantially. To this end, we now present the results of two multinomial logistic regression models to predict service calls across the location types and predict mental health implications. Model 1 predicts which location types are the main drivers of police missing person service calls in comparison to private dwellings. Model 2 introduces mental health–related implications across the location types. These two models exist first to predict the extent to which each location type may contribute to missing person service calls and then extend this understanding by predicting mental-health implications across each location type; in other words, to see if location type and mental health calls compound such that they can significantly impact police missing person calls for service.

First, to discuss Model 1, several location types emerged as significantly more likely to generate police missing person calls for service than private dwellings. Specifically, retirement homes and hospital facilities emerged as over two times (2.505 times and 2.016 times, respectively) significantly more likely to generate police missing person service calls when compared to private dwellings. Mental health facilities emerged as 1.636 times significantly more likely to generate police missing persons calls for service, group homes as 1.441 times significantly more likely, and mission centres and homeless shelters as 1.474 times significantly more likely. This means that all of these location types are predicted to generate police missing person service calls more than private dwellings. In contrast, public areas, such as parks or malls, emerged as 0.153 times less likely to generate police missing person service calls than private dwellings. Other places did not appear as statistically significant.

Turning to Model 2, we can see some changes across the statistically significant covariates. Most notably, when implicating mental health in a service call, the effect size of mission centres and homeless shelters, group homes, and hospital facilities increased. To expand on this, mission centres and homeless shelters emerged as 1.589 times more likely to generate a missing person service call that implicates mental health in Model 2, compared to 1.475 times more likely without mental health implications in Model 1. Group homes emerged as 1.789 times more likely in Model 2, whereas these locations emerged as 1.441 times more likely in Model 1. The effect size of hospital facilities increased more substantially, with Model 2 reporting that these locations are 2.817 times significantly more likely to generate a service call when mental health–related issues are involved, in comparison to Model 1 recording 2.016 times more likely. Lastly, and expectedly, the mental health facilities' covariate effect size increased when interacting with mental health implications in police service calls. It increased to 2.011 times significantly more likely in Model 2 compared to 1.636 more likely in Model 1. The effect size of retirement homes decreased, although these locations still emerged as 1.523 more likely to generate a police missing person call for service than private dwellings when including mental health implications.

What do these findings mean? Ultimately, when a missing person service call involves mental health implications, mission centres and homeless shelters, group homes, and hospital facilities are around two times significantly more likely to generate such calls involving mental health–related issues in comparison to private dwellings. Therefore, in our dataset, health and social services offloading responsibilities to the police compound as a matter when recognizing that mental health–related issues can underlie missingness and exacerbate police missing person service calls.

Table 11.4. Multinomial Logistic Regression Predicting Calls for Service across Location Types

	Location Type	Location Type x Mental Health
Private (Base)		
Mission Centre/Shelter	1.475*	1.589***
	(0.027)	(0.097)
Group Home	1.441**	1.789**
	(0.028)	(0.033)
Mental Health Facility	1.636***	2.011***
	(0.088)	(0.194)
Hospital Facility	2.016***	2.817**
	(0.103)	(0.398)
Public	0.153*	0.355***
	(0.015)	(0.112)
Retirement Home	2.505***	1.523*
	(0.129)	(0.193)
Other	0.082	0.589
	(0.011)	(0.097)
Number of Observations	2033	2033

Standard errors are in parentheses below parameter estimates.

Model 1 = Location only, Model 2 = Location interacting with mental health implications.

Displayed in this table are the relative risk ratios from the multinomial logistic regression models.

*p < 0.05; **p < 0.01; *** p < 0.001.

Weighted estimates by 95 per cent CIs.

What Is the "Hidden Cost" for Policing Related to Health and Social Services "Offloading"?

Our results so far have shown that mental health–related service calls from social and health services are not only primary drivers of police reports but also are significantly more likely to occur in missing person reports compared to private dwellings. To this end, our final analysis involves introducing a cost analysis based on the variable "time to clearance" involving only those health and social service locations. As can be seen, the average time to clearance – which involves from the moment dispatch receives the service call until the call is cleared – is 456 minutes, or 7.6 hours. The range of clearance times is the minimum amount of time a call involved was 11.6 minutes, and the maximum amount of time taken up by a service call from these location types is 2,839.7 minutes, or 47.3 hours.

Table 11.5. Descriptive Statistics of "Time to Clearance" Variable

Variable	N	Mean (mins.)	Std. Dev.	Min (mins.)	Max (mins.)
Time to Clearance	731	456	395	11.6	2839.7

The average cost for a first-class constable in the police service from which these data are derived is $48.85 per hour. We have estimated that the typical call consumes about 7.6 hours (or 456 minutes) of police time for an average cost of approximately $371.26. There are certain caveats with this figure. First, clearance times do not tell us how the time was spent. It may be the case that an officer only spent two hours actually responding to the call, which would reduce the figure. It also does not tell us how many officers were involved in the call. We have estimated based on one officer, but it may be the case that for specific calls, as we noted above, multiple units may be involved, including a patrol sergeant. Multiple officers would increase the call costs. With these caveats in mind, our call costs for the 731 cases identified as originating from an institution or other facility are $271,391.06 per annum.

6. Discussion

In the preceding pages, we presented an analysis of police RMS data on missing person files from a municipal police service for the year 2019 to demonstrate the extent to which demands for police services related to absconding are generated by health care and social work facilities. Our point in offering this analysis is to highlight one aspect of police–civilian encounters with PMI that, to date, has received far too little attention. Whereas much of media and public attention has focused on police wellness checks,[35] or calls involving individuals in extreme emotional or psychological crises,[36] the more mundane but routine patterns of police interactions have escaped attention. What has also escaped attention is how many of the same institutional groups that are being held up as solutions to real or perceived crises in police encounters with PMI are, in fact, contributors to police workload in this area. The demands they generate arise through deliberate offloading of responsibilities for patients or clients who leave their premises. We have looked at this process here in the context of absconding, but it also occurs in relation to other call types.[37]

Recent calls to reimagine policing have employed economic arguments to shape policy and practice – namely, through reducing police budgets and reallocating funds to social and health care–based solutions ("defunding the police"). We believe that a similar argument could be made for reversing the trend of health care and social work institutions towards "dumping" aspects of their caseload responsibilities onto policing. One way to do this is to show the hidden costs associated with this offloading that are presently subsumed within police budgets. Based on our estimates, we believe that the one municipal police service is absorbing approximately $271,000–$272,000 per year in taking on this one task. Multiplying this cost for this one call type[38] over two hundred or so police agencies across Canada helps us start to understand the extent to which social and health care offloading is generating some of the costs associated with policing.

Our goal in highlighting both the problem of "offloading" and its costs is not to simply critique the present system, but rather to point out that shifts in policy and practice "upstream" – that is, by health care and social work organizations – could reduce police workload. Further, a more obvious solution – in terms of preventing the potential harm that critics of the police worry about, reducing the footprint of public policing and, from a purely economic standpoint, reducing costs of absconding – would be to focus on prevention efforts at the source.[39] However, many would-be reformers shy away from such efforts fearing the possibility of passive or active coercion being employed against institutionalized youth or adult mental health patients.[40] We believe that prevention is the key; however, we must begin to develop non-coercive strategies. If we don't, any long-term reform in this area will be stymied.

NOTES

1 Lorna Ferguson and Laura Huey, "Who Goes Missing from Canadian Hospitals and Mental Health Units?" *Policing: An International Journal* 43, no. 3 (2020): 525.
2 Thomas M. Green, "Police as Frontline Mental Health Workers: The Decision to Arrest or Refer to Mental Health Agencies," *International Journal of Law and Psychiatry* 20, no. 4 (1997): 469; Joel W. Godfredson, Stuart D.M. Thomas, James R.P. Ogloff, and Stefan Luebbers, "Police Perceptions of Their Encounters with Individuals Experiencing Mental Illness: A Victorian Survey," *Australian & New Zealand Journal of Criminology* 44, no. 2 (2011): 180; Tamsin Short, "Policing and the Mentally Ill: Victimisation and Offending in Severe Mental Illness," *Policing and the Mentally Ill* (2013): 176.
3 Laura Huey and Thomas Kemple, "'Let the Streets Take Care of Themselves': Making Sociological and Common Sense of Skid Row," *Urban Studies* 44, no. 12 (2007): 2305.
4 Darin Weinberg, *Of Others Inside: Insanity, Addiction, and Belonging in America* (Philadelphia: Temple University Press, 2005); Hanie Edalati, Tonia L. Nicholls, Anne G. Crocker, et al., "Adverse Childhood Experiences and the Risk of Criminal Justice Involvement and Victimization among Homeless Adults with Mental Illness," *Psychiatric Services* 68, no. 12 (2017): 1288.
5 Arthur J. Lurigio, "Comorbidity," in *Encyclopedia of Psychology and Mental Health*, edited by N. Piotrowski (Pasadena, CA: Salem Press, 2013), 439; Richard H. Lamb

and Linda E. Weinberger, "Understanding and Treating Offenders with Serious Mental Illness in Public Sector Mental Health," *Behavioral Sciences & the Law* 35, no. 4 (2017): 303.

6 Arthur J. Lurigio, "Forty Years after Abramson: Beliefs about the Criminalization of People with Serious Mental Illnesses," *International Journal of Offender Therapy and Comparative Criminology* 57, no. 7 (June 2013): 763; Jennifer Schulenberg, "Police Decision-Making in the Gray Zone: The Dynamics of Police–Citizen Encounters with Mentally Ill Persons," *Criminal Justice and Behavior* 43, no. 4 (2016): 459.

7 Robin Shepard Engel and Eric Silver, "Policing Mentally Disordered Suspects: A Reexamination of the Criminalization Hypothesis," *Criminology* 39, no. 2 (2001): 225–52.

8 Marc Abramson, "The Criminalization of Mentally Disordered Behavior: Possible Side-Effect of a New Mental Health Law," *Psychiatric Services* 23, no. 4 (1972): 101–5.

9 "Mental Health and Criminal Justice Policy Framework," Centre on Addiction and Mental Health, CAMH, 2013, accessed 17 November 2023, https://www.camh.ca/-/media/files/pdfs---public-policy-submissions/mh_criminal_justice_policy_framework-pdf.pdf; "It's Time to End the Criminalization of Mental Illness," Ben and Jerry's, accessed 7 December 2021 https://www.benjerry.com/whats-new/2019/10/mental-health-criminal-justice; "Criminalization of Mental Illness," Treatment Advocacy Center (TAC), accessed 7 December 2021, https://www.treatmentadvocacycenter.org/key-issues/criminalization-of-mental-illness; "Criminal Justice," Bazelon Center, accessed 7 December 2021, http://www.bazelon.org/our-work/criminal-justice-2/.

10 Laura Huey, Lorna Ferguson, and Adam D. Vaughan, "The Limits of Our Knowledge: Tracking the Size and Scope of Police Involvement with Persons with Mental Illness," *FACETS* 6, no. 1 (2021): 424–48.

11 Short, "Policing and the Mentally Ill," 176–91.

12 Egon Bittner, "The Police on Skid-Row: A Study of Peacekeeping," *American Sociological Review* 32, no. 5 (October 1967): 699–715.

13 Bittner, "The Police on Skid-Row."

14 Linda Teplin and Nancy S. Pruett, "Police as Streetcorner Psychiatrist: Managing the Mentally Ill," *International Journal of Law and Psychiatry* 15, no. 2 (1992): 139–56; Schulenberg, "Police Decision-Making," 459; Jennifer Wood, Amy C. Watson, and Anjali J. Fulambarker, "The "Gray Zone" of Police Work during Mental Health Encounters: Findings from an Observational Study in Chicago," *Police Quarterly* 20, no. 1 (2017): 81–105.

15 Jennifer Wood and Laura Beierschmitt, "Beyond Police Crisis Intervention: Moving "Upstream" to Manage Cases and Places of Behavioral Health Vulnerability," *International Journal of Law and Psychiatry* 37, no. 5 (2014): 439–47.

16 At the time of writing, Situation Tables and other similar models remain popular among the police some ten years after their adoption but have yet to be subjected to rigorous evaluation or evaluation that tracks case outcomes.
17 Colleen Reid and Maya Alonso, "Imagining Inclusion: Uncovering the Upstream Determinants of Mental Health through Photovoice," *Therapeutic Recreation Journal* 52, no. 1 (2018): 19–41.
18 "Addressing Law Enforcement Violence as a Public Health Issue," American Public Health Association (APHA), accessed 7 December 2021, https://www.apha.org/policies-and-advocacy/public-health-policy-statements/policy-database/2019/01/29/law-enforcement-violence.
19 CAMH, "Mental Health and Criminal Justice Policy Framework."
20 David Garland, "Strategies of Crime Control in Contemporary Society," *The British Journal of Criminology* 36, no. 4 (1996): 445–71.
21 "Background – 2020 Fast Fact Sheets," Canada's Missing, accessed 7 December 2021, https://www.canadasmissing.ca/pubs/2020/index-eng.htm.
22 David Hirschel and Steven P. Lab, "Who Is Missing? The Realities of the Missing Persons Problem," *Journal of Criminal Justice* 16, no. 1 (1988): 35–45; Claire Taylor, Penny S. Woolnough, and Geoffrey L. Dickens, "Adult Missing Persons: A Concept Analysis," *Psychology, Crime & Law* 25, no. 4 (2019): 396–419.
23 Ferguson and Huey, "Who Goes Missing," 525.
24 Lorna Ferguson, "Profiling Persons Reported Missing from Hospitals versus Mental Health Facilities," *International Journal of Police Science & Management* 23, no. 4 (2021): 372.
25 Laura Huey and Lorna Ferguson, "Did Not Return in Time for Curfew": A Descriptive Analysis of Homeless Missing Persons Cases," *International Criminal Justice Review* (2020).
26 Laura Huey and Lorna Ferguson, "Did Not Return in Time for Curfew."
27 S. Thompson, "Policing Vancouver's Mentally Ill: The Disturbing Truth beyond Lost in Transition, Report for the Vancouver Police Board," accessed 22 February 2022, https://vancouver.ca/police/assets/pdf/reports-policies/vpd-lost-in-transition-part-2-draft.pdf.
28 Eimear Muir-Cochrane, Candice Oster, Jessica Grotto, Adam Gerace, and Julia Jones, "The Inpatient Psychiatric Unit as Both a Safe and Unsafe Place: Implications for Absconding," *International Journal of Mental Health Nursing* 22, no. 4 (2013): 304–12; Treena Wilkie, Stephanie R. Penney, Stephanie Fernane, and Alexander I.F. Simpson, "Characteristics and Motivations of Absconders from Forensic Mental Health Services: A Case-Control Study," *BMC Psychiatry* 14, no. 1 (2014): 1–13; Gillian Mezey, Catherine Durkin, Liam Dodge, and Sarah White, "Never Ever? Characteristics, Outcomes and Motivations of Patients Who Abscond or Escape: A 5-Year Review of Escapes and Absconds from Two Medium and Low Secure Forensic Units," *Criminal Behaviour and Mental Health* 25, no. 5 (2015): 440–50; Isobel Voss and Ruth Bartlett, "Seeking Freedom: A Systematic Review and

Thematic Synthesis of the Literature on Patients' Experience of Absconding from Hospital," *Journal of Psychiatric and Mental Health Nursing* 26, nos. 9–10 (2019): 289–300.
29 Ben Andoh, "Hospital and Police Procedure When a patient Absconds from a Mental Hospital," *Medicine, Science and the Law* 34, no. 2 (1994): 130–6.
30 Laura Huey, Jennifer Schulenberg, and Jacek Koziarski, forthcoming.
31 Griffiths et al., "Improving Police Efficiency."
32 Amrita Ibrahim, "'Who Is a Bigger Terrorist Than the Police?' Photography as a Politics of Encounter in Delhi's Batla House," *South Asian Popular Culture* 11, no. 2 (2013): 133–44.
33 Margaret Heslin, Lynne Callaghan, Barbara Barrett, et al., "Costs of the Police Service and Mental Healthcare Pathways Experienced by Individuals with Enduring Mental Health Needs," *The British Journal of Psychiatry* 210, no. 2 (2017): 157–64; Carol Hayden and Karen Shalev-Greene, "The Blue Light Social Services? Responding to Repeat Reports to the Police of People Missing from Institutional Locations," *Policing and Society* 28, no. 1 (2018): 45–61.
34 Lisa Heslop, Larry Stitt, and Jeffrey S. Hoch, *Trends in Police Contact with Persons with Mental Illness* (London, ON: London Police Service, 2000).
35 Beatrice Britneff, "Police Wellness Checks: Why They're Ending Violently and What Experts Say Needs to Change," *Global News*, 24 June 2020, accessed 22 February 2022, https://globalnews.ca/news/7092621/police-wellness-checks-experts-change/; Vik Adhopia, "It's Time to Rethink Police Wellness Checks, Mental Health Advocates Say," CBC News, 4 July 2020, accessed 22 February 2022, https://www.cbc.ca/news/health/police-wellness-check-alternatives-1.5637169; Sahil Gupta, "Wellness Checks Are Broken," *Maclean's Magazine*, 17 August 2020, accessed 22 February 2022, https://www.macleans.ca/opinion/wellness-checks-are-broken/.
36 Shanifa Nasser, "Canada's Largest Mental Health Hospital Calls for Removal of Police from Front Lines for People in Crisis," CBC News, 23 June 2020, accessed 22 February 2022, https://www.cbc.ca/news/canada/toronto/police-mental-crisis-1.5623907.
37 Laura Huey, Jennifer Schulenberg, and Jacek Koziarski, *Policing Mental Health Public Safety and Crime Prevention in Canada*, SpringerBriefs in Criminology (Cham, Switzerland: Springer, 2022), accessed 22 February 2022, https://link.springer.com/book/10.1007/978-3-030-94313-4.
38 It is worth noting, for example, that police are also responsible for returning individuals to psychiatric facilities on involuntary admissions. Future research might consider looking at this role and associated costs.
39 Eimear Muir-Cochrane, Marie Van der Merwe, Henk Nijman, et al., "Investigation into the Acceptability of Door Locking to Staff, Patients, and Visitors on Acute Psychiatric Wards," *International Journal of Mental Health Nursing* 21, no. 1 (2012): 41–9.

40 Duncan Stewart and L. Bowers, "Absconding and Locking Ward Doors: Evidence from the Literature," *Journal of Psychiatric and Mental Health Nursing* 18, no. 1 (2011): 89–93; Trish Martin and Stuart D.M. Thomas, "Police Officers' Views of Absconding from Mental Health Units in Victoria, Australia," *International Journal of Mental Health Nursing* 23, no. 2 (2014): 145–52.

12 Engaging Evil? Conducting Research with and on Policing Organizations

KEVIN D. HAGGERTY, SANDRA M. BUCERIUS, AND DANIEL J. JONES

Introduction

In recent decades policing has become larger, more complex, and far more contentious. Ongoing efforts are consequently required to study and understand the evolving realities of police practice. As such, it is fitting that this volume is dedicated to Professor Margaret Beare, given her history of empirical research into policing Canada. As the first director of the Nathanson Centre at York University in Toronto, she established meaningful research collaborations relating to policing organized crime.

There can be concrete benefits to such research collaborations. Normally, this would be a trite truism. However, the political context of policing has shifted, stimulated most recently by a procession of high-profile incidents of police violence directed at Black Americans and Canadians. In response, a broad and vocal coalition is calling for meaningful and perhaps fundamental changes to police practices. One such demand is for policing scholars and academic institutions to sever research or institutional arrangements with the police. This call is not as prominent as other currently circulating demands for police reform. However, if academics widely embraced such divestment, it would have considerable consequences for the public and scholarly understandings of police practice and the prospect of introducing changes to policing informed by independently generated empirical evidence.

Our aim in this chapter is not to propose, support, or oppose any policy proposals for policing. Instead, we identify some of the conceptual roots of a particular disposition towards the police that we see as currently ascendant among a subset of advocates and academics. In particular, we suggest that the police are increasingly viewed as "evil," an orientation that contrasts with how the police have been conceived historically by large segments of society. We are concerned about this framing because if taken at face value as a policy orientation it limits the prospect of developing organizational relationships that could advance meaningful change.

We begin by briefly reviewing some contemporary concerns about collaborations between academics and the police that have been raised in Canada and the United States. We then trace some of the conceptual roots from which the evil frame appears to have grown. The majority of the chapter details the connections between this contemporary framing of the police and attributes characteristic of the secular relationship to evil, drawing prominently from the cultural sociology of Jeffrey Alexander and the philosophy of Adam Morton. We conclude by cautiously reaffirming the need for academics and universities to engage in research relationships with police organizations, fully cognizant that such arrangements are no panacea for the many challenges facing policing.

Two authors of this chapter (Bucerius and Haggerty) have conducted research involving the police and other criminal justice organizations. The third author (Jones) is a PhD candidate and also a retired inspector with twenty-five years of experience with the Edmonton Police Service (EPS) and three years of experience as a provincial and federal correctional officer. As a police officer, he established over thirty formal research arrangements between the police, academics, and community organizations. He is currently the Chair of Justice Studies at NorQuest College.

The Contemporary Situation

By any measure, the summer of 2020 was extraordinary. As the global COVID-19 pandemic rolled across North America, officials urged unsettled citizens to isolate themselves at home. At the same time, many of those same individuals felt compelled to take to the streets to demonstrate against shocking incidents involving police officers killing or assaulting Black Americans. In the United States, the murder of George Floyd, the killing of Breonna Taylor, and Jacob Blake's shooting were only the most recent high-profile examples of a lengthy history of such behaviour. In Canada, the deaths of Chantel Moore, Ejaz Choudry, Abdirahman Abdi, and Sammy Yatim at the hands of police officers in recent years also received considerable national and international attention. Instances of police corruption, fraud, and coerced confessions have garnered somewhat less coverage, but all these behaviours have combined to create a sense of crisis in policing.

In that context, demands for change gained wider circulation, typically under the "Defund the Police" banner. Community activists proposed various measures to reduce police involvement in certain aspects of social life, cut police budgets, and redirect funds to other forms of public safety or social service. A more extreme form of divestment involved calls to abolish the police entirely.[1] This sentiment initially gained traction in the United States with demands to abolish the Immigration and Customs Enforcement Agency in response to President Trump's policy of separating migrant children from the parents or guardians with whom they had entered the country illegally.

One manifestation of this growing divestment sentiment was a greater discomfort in some quarters with the relationships academic institutions and individual researchers have with police organizations. In Canada, many undergraduate degree programs offer students the opportunity to obtain credit for doing a placement with social service or criminal justice agencies, such as the police, substance misuse programs, halfway houses, governmental policy units, correctional institutions, and the like. In essence, these are a form of community service–learning designed to provide students with a grounded experiential understanding of the institutions, processes, and practices they are studying in the classroom.

Individual academics or research teams also have formal research arrangements with police organizations that facilitate research access to individual officers, confidential datasets, and specific units. Such agreements are similar to those that academics enter into when they study organizations such as health care, the military, or education. Although police openness to such arrangements has fluctuated over the years, there is an extremely long list of scholarly works that are the product of such agreements.

During the height of the 2020 protests, a subset of academics and activists singled out both of these situations as politically contentious. In statements, petitions, and policy proposals, these individuals sought to materially and symbolically distance universities and academics from the police. In Canada, the first of these was an editorial by Professors Hannem and Schneider in *Canadian Dimensions* that called for Canadian universities to "cease partnerships with police organizations and corporations that profit from police technologies."[2] Later that summer, a "ScholarStrike" petition was circulated online in the United States and Canada that, among other things, demanded that "All agreements between policing institutions and universities must be rescinded."[3] A second petition called on math professors not to work with the police to develop predictive policing measures.[4]

Soon afterwards, the Institute of Criminology and Criminal Justice at Carleton University in Ottawa garnered some attention when it announced it would no longer allow its students to do placements with police or correctional organizations.[5] Likewise, the criminology department at Toronto Metropolitan University[6] voted to pause their graduate placements with police agencies. Students and activists at several Canadian universities lobbied to eliminate on-campus police services. This call was aligned with numerous efforts to remove school resource officers from Canadian junior high and high schools.

Neither the public nor other academics uniformly embraced these proposals.[7] However, they did prompt an intriguing set of discussions and personal reflections among criminologists about the value or utility of arrangements with the police and the place of police organizations in academic practice.

Critical Criminological Approaches

Among academic criminologists, such de-affiliation proposals appear to have been embraced and championed most frequently by a subset of critical criminologists. Those who identify with this orientation contrast themselves with those they characterize as conventional or, more derisively, "administrative" criminologists. Traceable to foundational Marxist-inspired works published in the 1970s, most famously by Taylor Walton and Young's *The New Criminology*,[8] today critical criminology has firm institutional roots.

As the "critical" moniker has become more widely embraced, it has also come to encompass a more extensive and eclectic range of academics and scholarly approaches. It has also become a contested category, with much ink spilled debating the content, contours, and commitments of critical criminology. As such, it is hard to succinctly summarize.[9] Speaking in broad generalizations, Canadian critical criminologists tend to have a heavy leaning towards qualitative and interpretive methodologies. Theoretically, they have been profoundly influenced by feminism and European social theory, particularly (but not exclusively) variants of social thought coming out of France since 1968.[10] At its core, critical criminology has always involved a social justice orientation, with attention given to the dynamics of crime, victimization, and the operation of criminal justice institutions. Such studies and commentary have typically focused on the dynamics of power and the reproduction of different forms of inequality. While originally heavily influenced by Marxism, in recent years critical criminologists have been particularly attentive to injustices relating to race and gender and the intersections of such phenomena.[11] These works involve a critique of the constitutive role of legal apparatuses in the social production of crime and an indictment of these apparatuses for the harms that they inflict upon criminalized populations and victims.

Policing scholars aligned with this approach interpret police practice regularly through a hermeneutics of suspicion. In such an orientation, the focus and almost inevitable outcome of research and commentary are to censure the police for a vast assortment of failings. Prominent among those concerns have been the inability of the police to reduce crime,[12] the persistent patriarchal patterns of policing,[13] and intense scrutiny of the structural racism and colonizing practices of police organizations.[14]

These works have typically entailed a form of outsider critique, where scholars conduct research *on* the police as opposed to working in collaboration *with* the police to identify problems, develop pragmatic solutions, and empirically evaluate the successes and failures of existing programs and new initiatives. In recent years a subset of these critical criminologists, in solidarity with assorted social justice organizations, have embraced a view of the police that resembles how we conceive of evil individuals or institutions.

From Mundane to Evil

It was not many decades ago that the police, in the eyes of the vast majority of citizens, had a type of symbolic halo, with police organizations standing for justice and virtue.[15] In Canada, the Royal Canadian Mounted Police has served as a recurrent source of state symbolism and national myth-making.[16] A procession of policing scandals and highly publicized failings starting in the 1960s and arriving with some degree of regularity ever since have tarnished that halo. The result has been a diminution of the sacred status of the police, as they came to be seen, at root, as akin to any other large complex organizations, such as health care, educational systems, or the military. They were inefficient, often prejudiced, and routinely broken in several respects and in need of improvement on all of these measures. Nonetheless, the police were still generally understood to be a legitimate institution serving a defensible purpose (or purposes). Moreover, the police were understood as being amenable to reform to advance their diverse objectives, even if such reform was prolonged, uneven, and routinely resisted. Even in the immediate aftermath of a summer's-worth of protests against police violence, an Angus Reid poll published in October 2020 found that three-quarters of Canadians view the police favourably and that 72 per cent identify their local police as a source of pride (which includes two-thirds of Indigenous and visible minority respondents).[17]

Those assessments appear to have been fundamentally altered in the minds of a subset of Canadian academics and community activists. In particular, for these individuals, the police seem to have been transformed from what Everett Hughes would characterize as "good people doing dirty work"[18] into something closer to the embodiment of "evil" (through a process of normative mutation that we might call "evilization"). In this evil framing, the police are conceived of more along the lines of how one might relate to the brown shirts of 1930s Germany, the Ku Klux Klan, or Storm Troopers from the *Star Wars* franchise. Those who might doubt these analogies only need to attend a community meeting where police reform is being discussed or peruse the popular #ACAB (All Cops Are Bastards) Twitter hashtag. In these and other settings, one encounters vociferous totalizing condemnations of the police, often in the form of pointed assertions that the police are Nazis or an occupying force. It is this dispositional transformation that, in part, helps us to appreciate the current call for academics to divest from formal relationships with the police.

This evil characterization may initially seem forced, but if we situate this particular disposition to the police in the context of what we know about the contemporary social relationships with evil, numerous telling parallels emerge. First, however, a few points of clarification. To our knowledge, there is no campaign explicitly aiming to characterize the police as "evil." Instead, what appears to be occurring is something more along the lines of a shift in structures of feeling that is part of an evolving symbolic cultural undercurrent. The result among individuals who identify with this sensibility is a visceral and almost habitual cynicism about or hostility towards police practice and the police as an institution.

It is also the case that this "evil" disposition is not new. Slightly different versions have existed in other times and locations. In North America, the most prominent earlier manifestations occurred during the civil rights and countercultural movements of the 1960s. We will use the expression "evil adherents" as a normatively neutral term to denote individuals who alternatively vocalize this sentiment or who are sympathetic to such a framing. That said, even among the most strident, the term "evil" is not generally used to typify the police, although the now common characterization of the police as being systematically racist perhaps come closest to activating the same form of totalizing moral condemnation. Indeed, in his recent book *Woke Racism* Columbia University professor and *New York Times* columnist John McWhorter argues that the distinctive forms of anti-racist activism which often informs the current police/evil framing now amount to a religion among elements of the cultural left.[19]

The work of cultural sociologist Jeffrey Alexander is helpful in thinking about this cultural connection between police and evil.[20] In *The Civil Sphere*, Alexander posits a deep-rooted symbolic code that citizens habitually use to subconsciously demarcate the laudable "we" from the "they" who do not deserve respect or inclusion in civil society. This symbolic code operates as a set of normative homologies and antipathies that structure a society's symbolic order. Alexander demonstrates that people use such demarcations to tacitly differentiate motives, relations, and institutions.

Given our focus on the police, Alexander's comments about how the code operates in relation to institutions are particularly germane. As he stresses, institutions that are praised and supported for being "civil" are understood to have a set of admirable attributes. In contrast, anti-civil institutions are typified as having diametrically opposed characteristics. In this binary symbolic structure, we perceive institutions to be anti-civil if they are:

> arbitrary rather than rule regulated, that emphasize brute power rather than law and hierarchy rather than equality, that are exclusive rather than inclusive and promote personal loyalty over impersonal and contractual obligations, that are regulated by personalities rather than by office obligations, and that are organized by factions rather than by groups that are responsible to the needs of the community as a whole.[21]

Civil Institutions   Anti-civil Institutions

Rule regulated   Arbitrary
Law   Power
Equality   Hierarchy

Inclusive	Exclusive
Impersonal	Personal
Contracts	Bonds of loyalty
Groups	Factions
Office	Personality

This essentially pre-cognitive mental/cultural structure of diametrical opposites is arguably a universal way that people normatively demarcate aspects of civil society. What differs, however, are the precise specifics of what individuals, organizations, and processes are slotted into the left or the right side of the ledger. That process of typification is neither natural nor inevitable, but the result of agentic efforts of individuals operating in historically and spatially specific situations to alternatively claim a preferred civic status, defend themselves against the anti-civil designation, or characterize other agencies and individuals as anti-civil. This process is public and inherently political, where "[a]ctors struggle to taint one another with the brush of repression and to wrap themselves in the rhetoric of liberty."[22]

Where discussions of evil have historically had religious connotations or overtones,[23] today we have a mostly secular relationship to evil.[24] Following Alexander, when a process or institution is seen as embodying the most extreme anti-civil attributes, it represents "the 'worst' in the national community, *it embodies evil*" (emphasis added).[25] Rather than focus on demons or defilement, today, "evil centers on atrocity: death, pain, and humiliation imposed on others."[26] Common examples include genocides, slavery, or the murders committed by serial killers. Certain corporations have also found themselves strongly marked by the anti-civil side of this discourse of repression, perceived by many as evil for contributing to death and suffering[27] by virtue of such classically notorious activities as selling toxic products or callously producing life-threatening working conditions.

It is consequently instructive to scrutinize the right-hand side of the ledger above, where Alexander demarcates the anti-civil attributes of institutions. It is striking how neatly these anti-civil attributes of power, exclusivity, factions, hierarchy, arbitrariness, et cetera, correspond with how the police are portrayed in certain strands of the contemporary activist and academic discourse. This consistent pattern of public attributions repositions the police on what we might think of as a grid of symbolic associations ever closer to the embodiment of evil.

The process by which this occurs is much the same as when other problematic behaviours undergo such a normative transformation; via broad forms of signification and cultural messaging.[28] That said, we are not concerned here with undertaking the enormous project of tracing the genesis and fluctuations in these relevant representations. Instead, we aim to identify some of the connections with policing and reflect upon the more unfortunate implications of this framing. The work of the contemporary philosopher Adam Morton is instructive in this regard.[29]

As far as the evil frame is related to the police, it focuses almost exclusively on street level encounters involving violence, death, and/or racism. This is in keeping with the secular connection with evil noted above, which is concerned with the imposition of death, pain, and humiliation on others. Instances of such misdeeds by the police are plentiful and need to be denounced. However, it is also notable how such selective examples appear to semiotically overwhelm discussions of the police by evil adherents. By focusing on police (racist) violence and repression, the evil framing of "the police" pays scant scholarly attention to the wider range of police activities that do not self-evidently fit into such a characterization. Examples would include the specialized police units dedicated to investigating child abuse, vehicle theft, organized crime, hate crimes, human trafficking, break and entry, forensics, antiquities and cultural heritage, explosives, corporate crime, cybercrime, search and rescue, communications, marine, animal welfare, victim services, et cetera. This evilization portrait is therefore functionally akin to the process of stereotyping: it reduces a group to a constellation of selective traits that fit a dominant narrative that excludes aspects that contradict or complicate that narrative while also bolstering the moral legitimacy of those doing the stereotyping.[30] As such, evil thinking in relation to the police is essentializing. Operational and cultural differences within and across police organizations tend to be ignored or glossed over. By its very nature, we see evil as all-consuming; it represents the core of a person or organization. The evilization of policing has resulted in commentators treating the police in a homogenizing way that overlooks local specificity in a manner that would not be countenanced if scholars were speaking about a different social institution. This is a form of what Goldsmith and McLaughan refer to as "context collapse" in their analysis of the contemporary politics of the police, where "[c]ritical differences often disappear, to be replaced by a larger homogenized, imagined whole."[31] The upshot is that the evil framing of the police seems to be equally applicable to police organizations in Moose Jaw, Mississippi, or Manchester.

By implication, such an essentialist orientation lends itself to the conclusion that the police are beyond redemption or reform. The best one can do when encountering evil is condemn, isolate, and perhaps terminate. As Alexander notes, "those who are unfortunate enough to be constructed under the anti-civil, counter-democratic code – must be silenced, displaced, or repressed."[32] Again, this resonates with a notable strand of the evil frame concerning the police, with adherents to this approach increasingly treating the term and prospect of police reform with disdain.[33] In her *New York Times* article, Mariame Kaba[34] distilled this position to its essence: "We can't reform the police." In the notable recent (militarized) phrasing of two prominent activist/academics, police reform does not aim to improve policing but is a "strategy of destruction" or a form of "counter insurgency" aimed at further repressing Black individuals and marginalized groups. For individuals who advance such a framing, it is not that some aspect or attribute of the police is broken, unfair, or inequitable and therefore in need of reform. Instead, it is the police in toto that are the problem.

When conceived of as evil, people, organizations, and activities are lifted out of the realm of the commonplace and situated onto the terrain of the unique, the singular, or the exceptional. In the process, actions are placed "beyond the scope of ordinary understanding and into a category of wrongdoing that lies beyond any possibility of excuse."[35] By implication, there is no point in engaging with evil individuals or organizations to develop a sense of their motivations or the full range of situational, institutional, or biographical factors that might contribute to their actions. In popular culture, evil is not just a designation, it is an explanation – and often all the explanation required. Morton, writing about evil, posits that if "there is no possibility of understanding someone, then there is much less point in entering into a complex interaction with them. You don't do business with someone who is a complete mystery to you."[36] As this concerns the police, if the police are evil, they are beyond comprehension. As per the isolationist strategy, no good can come from academics associating with them.

Disengagement also limits or entirely forecloses the possibility of developing a subjective sense of police officers' actions and motivations and can make efforts to develop such an understanding appear repugnant. Subtle psychological factors can be at play in making people hesitant even to try to understand evil, as "we fear that if we succeed, we might not dislike the perpetrators enough. We might be in danger of forgiving them."[37] It is easier and more comfortable to treat evil as radically "Other" than risk the prospect of empathizing that can come with greater understanding.

As this pertains to criminology, the discipline has a long history of qualitative or ethnographic studies of different criminalized groups.[38] Examples are legion but would include studies of people who misuse substances, sex offenders, Mafiosi, white supremacists, soccer hooligans, and gang members – including accounts of torture and rape by such individuals.[39] It is also in the nature of such work that by spending extended periods of time with participants, researchers tend to produce a humanizing or empathetic portrait of the complexity of their lives and motivations.

This form of knowledge and insight is foreclosed by efforts to divest from research that involves collaborative arrangements with the police. Conducting prolonged research with police officers raises the possibility that rather than being seen as evil, they will appear most to be fallible human beings doing a challenging and often impossible job in an increasingly pressurized and polarized political environment.[40] As Morton continues, "[r]educe the imaginative distance between yourself and evil-doers and you might find yourself sympathizing with them,"[41] something that would seem to be out of step or even offensive as it pertains to certain strands of police research among groups of individuals where the evil frame is prevalent. People who engage in such research can also observe the profound variability within and across police organizations, which seems to inoculate them against essentialist claims about the police.

Another defining characteristic of evil is that it taints those who are in close proximity. Being close to evil is both uncomfortable and dangerous: "Not only can one's reputation be sullied and one's status endangered, but one's very security can be threatened. To have one's self or movement identified in terms of these objects causes anguish, disgust, and alarm."[42] Such an assessment again accords with current efforts to divest from the police and the evilization frame more generally. The material distance established by such measures appears to be appealing in part because of how it also provides a form of symbolic purification, ensuring that institutions and individuals are not tainted by being associated with what is seen as an evil organization.[43]

For criminologists, the increased prevalence of this discourse presents both gains and losses, with most of the gains resting on the activist side of the ledger. Conceiving the police as evil provides a degree of moral certainty that simplifies difficult issues and can motivate others to become politically active. It also operates as a type of symbolic boundary work[44] that helps forge social solidarity with other like-minded individuals. Lost or downgraded in such a framing, however, are many of the attributes that have historically been the hallmarks of interpretive research on the police, including an empirically grounded attention to nuance, humility in the face of complexity, and attention to irony, contradiction, countervailing tendencies, and local specificity.

It is impossible to fully detail how the sensibility informing this evilization approach is transforming scholarly practice and the culture of the academy, but eight brief anecdotes drawn from our recent professional experiences with different individuals are illustrative.

- A scholar on tenure track who was planning to commence an empirical study of certain aspects of police culture set that project aside, fearing it would be criticized by other Canadian criminologists for not being sufficiently denunciatory of the police.
- A master's student who was about to commence a study of the challenges relating to policing an impoverished urban neighbourhood arranged a meeting with her supervisor to ask, "Do my results have to criticize the police?" She had concluded from her readings that this was the overriding expectation of all such research.
- A community activist speaking at an academic conference condemned criminological research involving the police because "Police use academic data to enter communities all guns a blazing."

- A fourth-year criminology undergraduate student informed her instructor in confidence that she was concealing from the other students that she had previously been a civilian employee of a police service and would not mention in class any insights garnered from that experience. She had concluded that if she were to "come out of the closet" about this affiliation she would be ostracized or castigated by a group of students who had loudly condemned anyone associated with a police organization.
- A government-funded study that proposed to study police/civilian relationship will have to proceed without the police, as the activists working with the community groups have refused to participate if the police are involved.
- A scholar was denounced (to her face) by another Canadian criminologist as being "guilty by association" of police violence because she has ongoing research arrangements with the police.
- A professor had agreed to serve on the thesis committee for a master's student conducting research on a topic unrelated to policing. At the first committee meeting, the professor learned that the student had previously worked as a civilian analyst for a police organization. The faculty member declared that she could not work with such individuals, resigned from the committee, and left the room.
- A professor in one of Canada's large criminology departments tweeted the following: "As a criminology professor, may I just say, fuck the police."

All of these situations are, in part, real-world manifestations of the increasing prevalence of the evilization of policing and the attendant taint that some see as coming from being associated with such organizations. At the same time, there is a more abstract but perhaps more troubling concern about this trend. In particular, evil thinking "allows us to label others in a way that suspends our sense of their humanity."[45] One gets a sense of this Othering from a string of Tweets in the fall of 2020 from a Canadian criminologist. He starts by calling for a type of universal embrace of wrongdoers but then tellingly changes his tone to signal his discomfort with the possibility of including police officers in such a formulation:

> How we socially & individually respond when someone has done harm to others, is precisely the time when transformative justice work begins. We can't only support those who are considered "innocent" or have done no wrong. We must also support those who have done shitty things ... This is the hardest work, but the most vital work.
>
> This means not believing that people deserve poor or harsh treatment by the criminal justice system when we think they have done harm. This means standing up against such treatment & not accepting that as a natural outcome of doing harm. It means seeing beyond to something else.

> (*Of course, none of these comments apply to anyone deputized to enact state violence and harm, those people can suck it, joking, kind of*)
>
> (emphasis added)

This public statement by a professional criminologist resonates unsettlingly with Morton's assessment that the risk of evil thinking is that we start to reproduce the type of thing that we condemn, coming to think of such individuals as "worthless scum, inferior beings, or dangerously alien."[46] Indeed, in a widely viewed online presentation critical of the police in 2021, a professor used common hate speech tropes to explicitly advocate for hating the police (and also criminologists), and concluded by endorsing the "All Cops Are Bastards" (ACAB) slogan.

Discussion and Conclusion

Nothing we have said here defends the police either as an institution or in relation to specific instances of wrongdoing. Nor does it imply that police reform – even radical change – is not required. We unequivocally support the ultimate ambitions of the Movement for Black Lives, which is to eliminate racism and support marginalized people and communities. We also see it as the prerogative and sometimes the duty of citizens to call for change.

That said, it is also true that the public will continue to expect there to be some form of policing organization(s) to deal with prominent issues of crime and disorder. For example, in 2020, when public attention was focused on COVID, Black Lives Matter, and the imploding Trump presidency, one less commented upon reality were the 615 mass shootings that took place that year in the United States. These resulted in 521 deaths and 2,541 injuries, for a total of 3,062 victims – 181 more such incidents than in 2019.[47] Admittedly, mass shootings are an extreme (but crucial) example. Still, the point is that *no matter what* comes from current calls for policing reform, we will continue to require some kind of agency responsible for, responding to, and investigating both extreme events as well as the more quotidian aspects of violence, predatory behaviour, and disorder. Whether this agency is called "the police" or goes by some other name, members of that organization will be performing a policing function and will be called upon to deal with complicated and delicate situations that can be fraught with conflict, disruption, and violence.

Our concern here, however, is that when the discourse surrounding the police veers towards the type of evil framing we have identified above, it fosters a form of isolationist politics. Such a situation is counterproductive. It both draws upon and breeds an instinctual cynicism that limits the prospect of working collaboratively with the police (in whatever form the police may take) to conduct research, generate new knowledge, expose students to police practice, and introduce and empirically assess pragmatic reforms.[48]

Meaningful change will require smart, committed people working collaboratively to propose, introduce, and assess concrete measures for change. Isolationism, in contrast, would, unfortunately, relegate a subset of broadly progressive-minded academics to the margins of this process. Consider, for example, the call noted above for math professors not to work with police to institute predictive policing models. Such a development might be symbolically gratifying, but it will not prevent the rise of predictive policing. Instead, if implemented, it would ensure that the police alone would be responsible for creating and assessing such measures, which hardly seems like the preferred scenario.

It is also worth contemplating how police officials relate to this evil frame as well as the possible organizational or epistemological implications of their perceptions of this discourse. Anecdotally speaking, from discussion with both our personal and professional police contacts it is abundantly clear that officers are aware of instances when academics invoke the evil frame. Not surprisingly, when a professional criminologist tweets "Fuck the police," such messages circulate widely in policing circles. Officers then appear to generalize such an orientation to *all* (or almost all) academics, contributing to a situation where police officials are suspicious of the accuracy or impartiality of academic research findings. This situation culminates in police officials being reluctant to enter into research arrangements with academics as they (rightly or wrongly) anticipate these initiatives will produce findings that are biased or entirely politically preordained.[49] Such a situation is not beneficial for scholarship nor for the prospect of advancing police reform.

In some circles, there seems to be an assumption that academics who work collaboratively with the police will inevitably support contemporary police practices. This is a mischaracterization. Academics who have research agreements with the police need not be any more aligned with the structures of contemporary policing than are sociologists of insurance aligned with current actuarial arrangements or researchers who study the foster care system supportive of how foster care is organized. The job of policing scholars is not to habitually support the police but to honestly and accurately study policing institutions and practices. One of the more productive ways of doing so is to conduct research on and with such organizations. This will be true whether policing remains largely unchanged, if it undergoes significant reform, or if it is unrecognizably altered. Irrespective of what form policing takes into the future, academics working collaboratively with policing organizations can play a role in developing an accurate understanding of such structures and practices and proposing and assessing further changes.

NOTES

1 Mariame Kaba, "Yes, We Mean Literally Abolish the Police," *New York Times*, 12 June 2020, https://www.nytimes.com/2020/06/12/opinion/sunday/floyd-abolish-defund-police.html.
2 Stacey Hannem and Christopher Schneider, "Canadian Universities Should Divest from Policing Interests," *Canadian Dimensions*, 1 June 2020.
3 "About | Scholar Strike Canada," Scholar Strike Canada, accessed 27 May 2021, https://www.scholarstrikecanada.ca/about-us.
4 Courtney Linder, "Why Hundreds of Mathematicians Are Boycotting Predictive Policing," accessed 27 November 2021, https://www.popularmechanics.com/science/math/a32957375/mathematicians-boycott-predictive-policing.
5 Institute of Criminology & Criminal Justice, "ICCJ Statement: Actions to Address Issues Related to Settler Colonialism, White Supremacy, and Systemic Racism," accessed 27 November 2021, https://carleton.ca/criminology/wp-content/uploads/ICCJ-Statement_-Addressing-Systemic-Racism.pdf.
6 At the time this university was named "Ryerson."
7 Kevin Haggerty, "Carleton U, the Police and the New Academic Isolationism," *University Affairs*, 31 August 2020.
8 Ian Taylor, Paul Walton, and Jock Young, *The New Criminology: For a Social Theory of Deviance* (London: Routledge & Kegan Paul, 1973).
9 Walter DeKeseredy and Molly Dragiewicz, eds., "Introduction – Critical Criminology: Past, Present, and Future," in *Routledge Handbook of Critical Criminology*, 2nd ed., edited by Walter S. DeKeseredy and Molly Dragiewicz (New York: Routledge, 2018), 1–12; Pamela Ugwudike, *An Introduction to Critical Criminology* (Bristol: Policy Press, 2015); Kerry Carrington, "Feminism and Critical Criminology: Confronting Genealogies," *Critical Criminology: Issues, Debates, Challenges* (2002): 114–42.
10 Sylvère Lotringer and Sande Cohen, *French Theory in America* (New York: Routledge, 2013).
11 Katheryn K. Russell, "Development of a Black Criminology and the Role of the Black Criminologist," *Justice Quarterly* 9, no. 4 (1992): 667–83; James D. Unnever, Shaun L. Gabbidon, and Cecilia Chouhy, *Building a Black Criminology: Race, Theory, and Crime* (New York: Routledge, 2018), 24.
12 Peter K. Manning, *Police Work: The Social Organization of Policing* (Cambridge, MA: MIT Press, 1977).
13 Susan E. Martin, "'Outsider Within' the Station House: The Impact of Race and Gender on Black Women Police," *Social Problems* 41, no. 3 (1994): 383–400.
14 See, for example, Eugene A. Paoline, Jacinta Gau, and William Terrill, "Race and the Police Use of Force Encounter in the United States," *British Journal of Criminology* 58 (2018): 54–74; Martin, "'Outsider Within' the Station House," 1994; Charles Epp, Steven Maynard-Moody, and Donald Haider-Market, *Pulled Over: How Police Stops Define Race and Citizenship* (Chicago: University of Chicago Press, 2014).

15 Ian Loader and Aogán Mulcahy, *Policing and the Condition of England: Memory, Politics, and Culture* (New York: Oxford University Press, 2003).
16 Michael Dawson, *The Mountie: From Dime Novel to Disney* (Toronto: Between the Lines, 1998).
17 Angus Reid Institute, "Policing in Canada: Major Study Reveals Four Mindsets Driving Current Opinions and Future Policy Preferences," 9 October 2020. Accessed at https://angusreid.org/policing-perspectives-canada-rcmp/.
18 C. Everett Hughes, "Good People and Dirty Work," in *The Other Side: Perspectives on Deviance*, edited by Howard Becker (New York: The Free Press, 1964), 23–36. See also Eyal Press, *Dirty Work: Essential Jobs and the Hidden Toll of Inequality in America* (New York: Farrar, Strauss & Giroux, 2021).
19 John McWhorter, *Woke Racism: How a New Religion Has Betrayed Black America* (New York: Portfolio, 2021); for racism's relationship to evil, see Michel Wieviorka, *Evil* (Cambridge: Polity Press, 2012).
20 Jeffrey C. Alexander, *The Drama of Social Life* (Cambridge: Polity Press, 2017); Jeffrey C. Alexander, "Culture Trauma, Morality and Solidarity: The Social Construction of 'Holocaust' and Other Mass Murders," *Thesis Eleven* 132, no. 1 (2016): 3–16; Jeffrey C. Alexander, *The Civil Sphere* (New York: Oxford University Press, 2006).
21 Alexander, *Civil Sphere*, 59.
22 Alexander, *Civil Sphere*, 65.
23 Richard J. Bernstein, The Abuse of Evil: The Corruption of Politics and Religion since 9/11 (Malden: Polity Press, 2005); Richard J. Bernstein, Radical Evil: A Philosophical Interrogation (London: Polity Press, 2002); Susan Neiman, Evil in Modern Thought: An Alternative History of Philosophy (Princeton, NJ: Princeton University Press, 2015), 74; Alain Badiou, Ethics: An Essay on the Understanding of Evil (New York: Verso, 2002).
24 Wieviorka, *Evil*.
25 Alexander, *Civil Sphere*, 62.
26 Adam Morton, *On Evil* (New York: Routledge, 2004), 13.
27 Danny L. Balfour and Guy B. Adams, *Unmasking Administrative Evil*, 4th ed. (New York: Routledge, 2014).
28 See Alexander, "Culture Trauma, Morality and Solidarity," 2016.
29 Morton, *On Evil*.
30 Michael Pickering, *Stereotyping: The Politics of Representation* (New York: Palgrave, 2001).
31 Andrew Goldsmith and Eugene McLaghlan, "Policing's New Vulnerability Re-Envisioning Local Accountability in an Era of Global Outrage," *British Journal of Criminology* (2021): 3.
32 Alexander, *Civil Sphere*, 61.
33 Mychal Denzil Smith, "Incremental Change Is a Moral Failure," *The Atlantic*, September 2020.
34 Kaba, "Yes, We Mean Literally Abolish the Police."

35 Morton, *On Evil*, 5.
36 Morton, *On Evil*, 31.
37 Morton, *On Evil*, 21.
38 Sandra Bucerius, Kevin D. Haggerty, and Luca Berardi, eds., *Oxford University Press Handbook on Ethnographies of Crime and Criminal Justice* (New York and Oxford: Oxford University Press, 2021).
39 Dany Lacombe, "Consumed with Sex: The Treatment of Sex Offenders in Risk Society," *British Journal of Criminology* 48, no. 1 (2008): 55–74; Sandra Meike Bucerius, *Unwanted: Muslim Immigrants, Dignity, and Drug Dealing* (Oxford: Oxford University Press, 2014); James B. Waldram, *Hound Pound Narrative: Sexual Offender Habilitation and the Anthropology of Therapeutic Intervention* (Berkeley: University of California Press, 2012); Geoffrey Pearson, *Hooligan: A History of Respectable Fears* (London: Macmillan Press Limited, 1983); Randol Contreras, *The Stickup Kids: Race, Drugs, Violence, and the American Dream* (Berkeley: University of California Press, 2013); Philippe Bourgois, *In Search of Respect: Selling Crack in El Barrio* (Cambridge: Cambridge University Press, 2003).
40 For a recent example of this more nuanced approach, see Forrest Stuart, *Down, Out & Under Arrest: Policing and Everyday Life on Skid Row* (Chicago: University of Chicago Press, 2016).
41 Morton, *On Evil*, 21.
42 Alexander, *Civil Sphere*, 62.
43 Cynthia E. Devers, Todd Dewett, Yuri Mishina, and Carrie A. Belsito, "A General Theory of Organizational Stigma," *Organization Science* 20, no. 1 (2009): 154–71.
44 Michèle Lamont and Virág Molnár, "The Study of Boundaries in the Social Sciences," *Annual Review of Sociology* 28, no. 1 (2002): 167–95.
45 Morton, *On Evil*, 31.
46 Morton, *On Evil*, 6.
47 "List of Mass Shootings in the United States in 2020," Wikipedia, accessed 28 November 2021, https://en.wikipedia.org/wiki/List_of_mass_shootings_in_the_United_States_in_2020#List.
48 In some respects, former President Obama put his finger on the crux of one part of the current situation in an interview with *Vanity Fair* when discussing the political strategies used by Democrats in the United States to call for criminal justice reform: "The key is deciding, do you want to actually get something done, or do you want to feel good among the people you already agree with?"; Peter Hamby, "'Do You Want to Actually Get Something Done, or Do You Want to Feel Good?': Obama Urges Activists to Talk Reforming, Not Defunding, the Police," *Vanity Fair*, 1 December 2020, accessed 1 November 2023, https://www.vanityfair.com/news/2020/12/obama-urges-activists-to-talk-reforming-not-defunding-the-police.
49 Critical scholars tend to portray this situation as one where the police want to "control" research findings, while the police present it as wanting to ensure that any findings are "fair and objective."

13 Big Policing and Defunding: What's at Stake?

TONITA MURRAY

Introduction

Recently, a British financial researcher observed a shift from moral panic about crime to a financial panic over the cost and performance of police.[1] The same appears true for Canadian policing. Individually, the federal, provincial, and municipal governments attempt each year with only minimal success to trim or otherwise halt rising policing costs through the annual budgetary process. The concern is that Canadian police organizations are too big and too generously funded at the cost of other public programs. They are regarded as big not only in cost and personnel numbers, but in the range of their functions and their specialized support needs, which range from computerized information systems to helicopters, armoured personnel carriers, firearms, and tactical gear.[2]

Debates between police chiefs and municipal councils on annual policing budgets frequently make headlines;[3] the federal and provincial governments are preoccupied with the "economics of policing" and are cooperating on bringing down, or at least containing, costs.[4] At the same time, social activists incensed by police interventions that end in the deaths or injury of racialized and vulnerable people are demanding the defunding, if not the dismantling, of police and the diversion of the resources to other community agencies. A number of academics too have produced research results that support the call for lower police costs and less policing.[5] The arguments for limiting the police range from the neoliberal view that policing is a business, and a good part of its functions could be offloaded to private security companies, to the radical left view that policing oppresses the disadvantaged and privileges the already privileged so social justice would be better served by reducing funding and police numbers, if not abolishing the institution altogether. An argument common to all sides, however, is that the steep reduction in the Canadian crime rate since its high in 1991 should lead to a commensurate reduction in crime fighters.[6]

The costs that cause public concern are associated with the kind of policing Brodeur terms "low policing."[7] Low policing consists of such routine functions as order maintenance, crime prevention, criminal investigation, and traffic control. It is also largely visible policing. The public can see uniformed police on the street and associate them with the discussion of policing costs they read about in the newspaper or hear about on the local television or radio news. But in addition to low policing, police also engage in "high policing," which is concerned with the security of the nation and its institutions. This is less publicly visible and less structured police work undertaken with a variety of state partners, including national intelligence agencies. High policing activities are not normally conducted publicly, and their costs are not normally discussed in the media, so they attract less attention and avoid becoming targets for debate and criticism. But their invisibility also means that some important high policing activities do not receive the funding they need.

Brodeur observes that the original clear distinction between high and low policing has become blurred over time, particularly since 9/11 and the heightened concern with domestic terrorism, which necessarily includes public police.[8] An important strand of high policing that converges with low policing is responsibility for the control and investigation of money laundering and financial and corporate crime; in other words, the "big crime" that is examined in other chapters of this book. As the 2007–8 financial crisis demonstrated, malfeasance inside financial and business networks that can extend from the local to the international levels has the ability to destabilize national and global economies.[9] Public police at the federal, provincial, and municipal levels together with regulatory, law enforcement, and financial intelligence agencies such as provincial securities commissions, the Competition Bureau, Superintendent of Financial Institutions, Canada Border Services, or the Financial Transactions and Reports Analysis Centre of Canada (FINTRAC) therefore constitute a form of high policing that collectively works to protect Canadian business and banking and ultimately the Canadian economy and national security. This is what many argue is underfunded policing.

A compelling example of how high and low policing intersect and lead to the blurring Brodeur observes is the 2022 blockades of the Canadian parliamentary zone and selected Canadian–US border crossings by protesting truckers. The truckers positioned their giant rigs in strategic locations to form barriers to cross-border traffic and to movement around Parliament Hill and adjacent streets in Ottawa. While police were fighting a losing battle to maintain safety and public order, supporters of the protest both inside and outside the country were contributing funds electronically to enable the truckers to persist in their disruptive tactics to a point where the Canadian government believed there was a threat to the security of the national economy. The federal government eventually invoked the *Emergencies Act*, which provided special powers to police to end the blockades. To stem the flow of funds to the protesters, the government also enacted the *Emergency Economic Measures Order* under the *Emergencies Act*. This brought other agencies in the high policing system into play. The *Emergency Economic Measures Order* required financial institutions ranging from banks, securities dealers, and insurance companies to crowdfunding platforms to identify and cease dealing with designated persons and to report their suspicious transactions to FINTRAC.[10] Funding for the protest was thus frozen, the police were able to compel tow truck companies to move the rigs, and order was restored. On their own neither low nor high policing measures could have dealt with the situation, but the combination of the two allowed the expeditious resolution of a volatile situation that had affected social well-being in Ottawa and threatened the economy and international reputation of Canada.

The "high" policing cost to enforce the law against money laundering and financial and corporate crime is included in the general policing budgets that many believe are too generous. In contrast, the budgets of other agencies engaged in regulating and investigating corporations, banks, or financial markets are considered administrative rather than policing costs. Because the costs to the police of investigating such big crime are not published separately and other budgets fighting big crime are dispersed among different levels of government, and among different ministries and government agencies, the total cost of policing big crime is unknown. In recent years, the Canadian government has increased its investment in policing mechanisms against money laundering, partly to meet obligations under international agreements for protecting the integrity of global trade and financial markets. When police receive new funding for this purpose, there may be public announcements, but at budget time few connect the increase in the police budget with the earlier announcement. The result can be one group arguing that police are receiving more resources as crime is falling and another group lamenting the underfunding of big crime control because the police are driven by the low policing demands.[11]

To all appearances, governments are blindly steering between the Scylla and Charybdis of high and low policing, attempting to contain the costs of public policing on the one hand while expanding resources for big crime policing on the other, but without any strategic understanding of where the conflicting demands differ and where they intersect. Meanwhile, police seem similarly lacking in strategic management of resources. With or without new funding they take on new functions, while failing to drop or modify existing ones or adjust to meet the new responsibilities. As a result, resources are always under pressure and police are constantly managing competing demands. And while there is a considerable amount of transparency at government and policing levels on budgetary matters, it is often not sufficient, nor the right kind of information needed to understand where the resourcing pressures lie. Consequently, criticisms of over- or under-resourcing, over- or under-policing, or other police failures are often based on insufficient knowledge of how policing budgets are allocated and used. This may be one of the flaws of the defunding argument. While it may make sense to defunders to divert resources from policing to other agencies better able to deal with social problems, their awareness of what police budgets are actually spent on may not go much further than the policing functions that have their attention. The same applies to those who see policing solely as crime fighting and regard other activities as diversions from the core police function. Few understand that in fact the known "big money" spent on Canadian policing each year is leveraged in many directions to achieve far greater impacts than just the goals set out in police budgets across the country. Dismantling or radically restructuring policing and police funding according to recent suggestions could therefore do more harm than good by damaging settled arrangements that enable police to provide roughly equal standards of safety and security to Canadians despite social, economic, geographic, or jurisdictional differences.

One example of how police resources are leveraged is the RCMP contract policing services in 8 provinces, 3 territories, and 150 municipalities in Canada. Constitutionally, policing is a provincial responsibility, but when municipalities reach a certain population size they become responsible for their own policing under a provincial policing Act. With the exception of Ontario and Quebec, provinces contract out the provision of policing to the RCMP to obtain a standard of policing that would be more expensive and even unaffordable if self-provided. Municipalities in the contracting provinces can do likewise. An added incentive is that the federal government contributes to the RCMP contracted policing costs. Ontario and Quebec, which have their own provincial police, also contract with municipalities that choose to do municipal policing. As a result, outside of contract policing there are only 137 stand-alone police services and thirty-six self-administered First Nations police services in Canada.[12]

Criticism of the RCMP contract policing arrangements and recommendations for their elimination are frequent. Yet the contracts ensure that smaller provinces and municipalities without the tax base to sustain modern police services receive the same standard of policing as wealthier provinces and territories. In effect, contract policing provides Canada with a roughly equivalent level of cohesive national policing as the United Kingdom, Australia, New Zealand, or the European countries, despite its federal organization. In the United States, by contrast, there are over 17,500 state and local law enforcement agencies, apart from the FBI and numerous law enforcement agencies at the federal level. Of the state and local law enforcement agencies, 40 per cent employ nine or fewer sworn officers, 69 per cent employ twenty-four or fewer sworn officers,[13] and 80 per cent employ fewer than fifty sworn officers.[14] Only eighty law enforcement agencies at the state and local level in the whole of the United

States have 1,000 or more sworn officers. There are no national policing standards, and the small law enforcement agencies that are often maintained by impoverished local governments are unable to provide a full range of services or training for police. Small Canadian municipalities and provinces could face similar circumstances if it were not for the contracting police services of the RCMP, OPP, and QPF. The quality of Canadian police services is also superior to that of most state and local policing in the United States, and at a slightly lower cost. In 2017 US state and local law enforcement alone cost $351.54 per capita.[15] In comparison, in 2017 policing for all of Canada cost $315 per capita.[16] In 2022 the FBI had a budget of $10.25 billion and over 36,000 positions for its federal responsibilities.[17] By contrast, in 2022 the RCMP had a budget of roughly $4.2 billion and 31,500 positions for federal, provincial, and municipal policing and National Police Services.[18]

By virtue of contributing to the cost of provincial and local policing, the Canadian government is also able to participate in and influence general policing policy across Canada from which it would otherwise be constitutionally excluded. This contributes to uniform response to social problems across Canada, such as family violence or drug trafficking. In addition, the dispersal of RCMP members across the country filling federal, provincial, and municipal roles, and similar policing patterns in Ontario and Quebec, mean that policing resources are available to be deployed cheaply and quickly for major events, such as a G7 conference, an emergency, or supplementary resources when a policing partner requires them.

This cohesiveness is reinforced by the National Police Services (NPS), which is the second example of leveraging resources to achieve policing synergy. The services were first established under federal-provincial agreements in 1964. They are funded by the federal government and managed by the RCMP to provide technical support to police operations for the entire Canadian policing community. The services consist of the Canadian Police Information Centre (CPIC), the Criminal Intelligence Service Canada, the Canadian Police College, forensic and identification laboratories, firearms registration, licensing and investigation, and technical and specialized services for the support of cyber, multi-jurisdictional, or complex investigations. The services include a police information system enabling records checks from a desktop computer in a police station or a laptop in a patrol car anywhere in Canada, a computerized national fingerprint registry, a national DNA bank, a national firearms registry, forensics identification, and so on. While the federal government maintains and modernizes the services through the RCMP budget, it is mainly the provinces and municipalities that contribute the data to the systems in the form of motor vehicle licence plate ownership, fingerprints, DNA samples, or criminal records. These data have a public cost inherent in their collection and so are a valuable in-kind contribution not reflected in police budgets. NPS enables national economies of scale, provides services that would be prohibitively costly for individual provinces to maintain individually, and supports police operations at all jurisdictional levels.

Defunding, dismantling, or restructuring policing by eliminating contract policing could destroy what is a well-evolved and workable policing system based on consent and cooperation among the three levels of government that provides value for money. Without these arrangements, Canada would have a policing system more like that of the United States than of the professionalized centrally managed policing systems of the UK and Europe. But the system is not perfect. Current Canadian policing arrangements and funding do not come to grips with how to manage the conflicting demands of high and low policing and perhaps does not even recognize there are two layers of policing with different needs at different times that need continual balancing rather than attention only when one is in crisis. Just eliminating some services to provide others is not a strategic solution, but when attention turns to change or reform in policing there is a temptation to return to first principles and to start with the question "What do we want the police to do?"[19] Such questions are usually never answered and the strategic change, even if required, rarely occurs. But what people want the police to do was probably decided a thousand years ago in mediaeval English villages when inhabitants rotated responsibility among themselves to protect their communities. And the first principle may well have been flexibility to meet whatever threat to village life arose. Modern-day policing is still flexible and able to respond as circumstances change. Because big crime policing and general policing are both dynamic, requiring different policing configurations and different resources at different times, organic solutions may be more successful than rational solutions, which frequently have unintended consequences and fail to fit all purposes. Rather than asking what we want the police to do, the rest of this chapter explores what police do now, whether big policing should remain big, and whether there are other factors in the policing environment that if changed could improve the delivery of both high and low policing.

What Do Big Police Really Do?

The suggestion that the police could be whittled down now that the crime rate is low, ignores the general mandate of the police to keep the peace. Despite long-standing research having established that police spend less time on fighting crime than they do on restoring order and providing assistance,[20] the assumption is that police are first and foremost crime fighters, so if crime is declining fewer police are needed. For example, one Canadian study designed a calculator for measuring the cost of crime and the value of Canadian policing. The study recognized that over 40 per cent of its sample of crime statistics was non–*Criminal Code* or traffic enforcement activities but did not account for the 40 per cent in the analysis, thus producing an inflated figure for the cost of crime fighting.[21] Even among police themselves there is a view that any activity outside of crime control is accrued by default from other agencies, and therefore not a police responsibility. Yet, far from being incidental activity, keeping the peace is the principal function of the police and crime control is a subactivity of that function.

The *Criminal Code* affirms the common-law status of police officers as peace officers[22] and most provincial police Acts create police organizations first to preserve the peace and then to prevent and control crime.[23] This is commensurate with practice in other commonwealth jurisdictions.[24] According to Ceyssens, the common law created four principal duties: to preserve the peace; enforce the law; preserve life, protect against serious injury, and protect property; and execute warrants. In his view, the question of whether the duty to prevent crime is derived from the primary duty to keep the peace or is a separate but equal duty is "a minor conceptual debate."[25]

The notion of "peace" is an elastic concept that can be stretched in various directions. The Supreme Court of Saskatchewan accepted the definition of it as "the legal name of the normal state of society," a "state of repose or security" and "a state of public order and decorum." Canadian courts accept a definition of breach of the peace as the state where an actual assault is committed on an individual or public alarm and excitement is caused, or an act or actions which result in actual or threatened harm to someone.[26] Although a breach of the peace can result in detention or arrest, it may not be a criminal offence. In practice it is frequently police judgment and discretion that decide whether an act is a breach of the peace or a crime.

In social terms "the peace" includes community harmony, individual well-being, and freedom from harm. For a constable in the Middle Ages "peace" embraced both temporal and spiritual elements but in practical terms came down to monitoring the state of roads, ditches, and bridges; protecting the indigent; keeping vagrants out of the community; or settling quarrels among community members but little "crime fighting."[27] In nineteenth-century Canada the police responsibility for keeping the peace was not much different, although there was considerably more public disorder, violence, public drunkenness, prostitution, party political chicanery, poverty, and other disfunction in communities.[28] In the late twentieth century Bayley listed many situations to which police could be called to restore peace: noisy parties, teenagers drinking beer on a street corner, tenants refusing to be evicted from their apartment, slippery mud on a highway, truculent neighbours blocking driveways with their cars, or family disputes. Twenty-first-century Canada encompasses all of this and more: disputes between Indigenous and non-Indigenous lobster fishers, security for international political meetings, multiple-vehicle traffic collisions, terrorist and hostage-taking threats, order maintenance of militant demonstrations, drug overdoses and suicides, mental health crises, and enforcement of public health rulings for the recent COVID-19 pandemic. As Bayley observed, Bittner's description of keeping the peace perhaps best sums up what the police respond to: "something-that-ought-not-to-be-happening-and-about-which-someone-had-better-do-something-now."[29]

In a recent study of factors that impede police reform, Huey, Ferguson, and Schulenberg examine the police role in dealing with four "wicked" social problems.[30] Wicked problems are those such as poverty that elude solution despite all efforts. Huey et al. draw on twenty years of research, including interviews, surveys, field observations, and document analysis, to describe the operational experiences of police as the principal agents dealing with the manifestations of mental health, substance misuses, homelessness, and missing persons. In general, the research from the operational environment shows that police are resourceful, understanding, and persistent in interacting with people with mental illness, in finding services for people with crippling addictions, doing the rounds of the agencies to find resources for the homeless or developing innovative ways to manage missing children who frequently run away from group and foster homes and are reported as missing. The research also describes the offloading of responsibility by community agencies to the police; the "lack of resources, bureaucratic red-tape, and other barriers to service,"[31] that police encounter when trying to find help for people in crisis; the additional responsibilities governments delegate to police; and the frustration and sense of being overwhelmed that the police experience as a consequence. The picture suggests the police are the only available and constant agency in a community attempting to mitigate the effects of the four wicked problems on desperate people. Yet, in company with many others, Huey et al. do not regard such efforts as part of core police functions and daringly propose that police chiefs be given the independence to refuse government taskings that are not part of their mandate.[32] Yet these activities are keeping the peace at its most elemental. Moreover, the very characteristics of the police that are most criticized, such as their powers, their discretion, and their militarized structure, are what make them always available and able to act to "do-something-now-about-what-ought-not-to-be-happening-but-is."

With or without wicked problems, if police were not to keep the peace as part of their general duties, it is likely there would be less "public order and decorum" and more crime. Arguably, then, one of the reasons for the current low levels of crime and high public perceptions of safety,[33] even as population numbers, diversity, and urbanization rise and social and economic change accelerates, is because police are doing more to keep the peace and maintain order. And as governments create new policies and programs to meet new needs, much of the responsibility for enforcing the policies will fall to the police because they are already on the ground, which allows governments to avoid creating new single-mandate organizations with all the inherent costs and limitations.

Costs of Keeping the Peace

In 2021–2 there were 70,566 police officers in Canada, or 181 police for every 100,000 of the population. Despite an increase of 406 more officers from the previous year, police strength trended downward 1 per cent because of the growing population. The total policing budget for 2021–2 was $18.5 billion in current dollars, costing each Canadian $342 a year. This was an increase of 12 per cent from the previous fiscal year. Salaries and wages accounted for 67 per cent of the total, benefits for 17 per cent, and other operating expenditures for 16 per cent.[34]

Since the late 1980s, the concern of governments with cost containment, or efficiency, has replaced the frantic efforts of governments in the 1960s and 1970s when crime rates were rising rapidly, to recruit more and more police to stem the tide. That frenzy meant police organizations could depend on receiving whatever resources they asked for, no matter how high government deficit spending went. Resources for lengthy conspiracy investigations and prosecutions of organized crime, international drug trafficking or white-collar crime were also readily available.[35] Between 1962 and 1979 the reported crime rate rose by 176 per cent, and the police population by roughly 87.5 per cent.[36] In 1991 crimes reached a high of 10,342 per 100,000 of the population. By 2020 they had fallen to 5,301 per 100,000, or roughly the same rate as in 1971. Consequently, policing budgets are now hard fought. In Ontario, for example, the 2019 Ontario Provincial Police budget was cut by $19 million, in 2021 the Toronto Police Service achieved $400 million "savings" after having cut six hundred police positions between 2016 and 2018, and although the Ottawa Police Service received a 2 per cent increase ($11.45 million) for 2022, it was less than the requested 2.86 per cent increase. The foregone $2.65 million was reallocated to "social services and the development of a response system for lower-risk calls, including mental health and addiction crises."[37]

Demand to defund the police to reduce the negative impact of arbitrary and unaccountable police power on racialized and vulnerable people was sparked by the murder in 2020 of an African American man, George Floyd, by a white Minneapolis police officer.[38] The anger resonated with many in Canada who accused the Canadian police of similar systemic mistreatment of racialized and Indigenous peoples.[39] The logic behind defunding is that savings from reducing police budgets could be diverted to other social agencies better able to provide appropriate responses to vulnerable people in crisis, and fewer police would reduce racism. The target of social activists then seems to be social justice and better treatment for marginalized people rather than police financing.

Presumably, if they were satisfied with police services they would not be advocating cuts to police budgets; however, their approach links policing costs to the social impact of police and the functions they actually perform.[40]

Activities to keep the peace have cost implications that are not easily demonstrable; however, some indication of its consumption of police time, and therefore its cost, is measurable by counting police response to calls for service. Calls and outcomes are recorded, and the accumulated numbers occurring across Canada are reported annually by Statistics Canada. In 2021–2 Canadian police responded to 11.9 million calls for service, or an average of 1,356 calls an hour, an increase of 2.7 per cent from the previous year, when COVID-19 restrictions reduced movement.[41] It is mainly constable-level police who carry out general duty policing and respond to calls for service. Constables form 68 per cent of all police personnel in Canada, and their salary budget is about $9 billion a year, or about half of the 2021–2 Canadian policing budget.

Wuschke et al. shed further light on general duty or keeping the peace policing in their study of calls for service in the British Columbia city of Port Moody.[42] They organized all records of policing incidents that had occurred in Port Moody between 2001 and 2014 into eight categories: violent crime, property crime, other crime, public safety and welfare, traffic, by-laws, alcohol and drug incidents, and miscellaneous incidents. During the fourteen-year period, property crime and other crime incidents fell, as public safety and welfare incidents and violent crime rose, and the other categories remained the same. Significantly, there was a much higher number of public safety and welfare incidents than any other category. They accounted for 45–60 per cent of all police activity and in 2014 took 59.81 per cent of police time. Overall crime in the same period was responsible for 20–30 per cent of police time. Public safety and welfare incidents included alarm, civil and neighbour disputes, threats, suspicious persons or vehicles, maintenance of law and order, and although mentioned only in passing in the study, presumably mental health service and similar calls.

The same study also examined Port Moody policing costs from 1983 to 2014. As in other municipalities of British Columbia, it found that policing costs in Port Moody had increased but only in proportion to other social services. In the thirty years between 1980 and 2010 municipal policing expenses in British Columbia increased 2.5 times, schools 2.04 times, and health expenditures 2.86 times. The proportion of the Port Moody budget spent on policing ranged from 17 to 21 per cent between 1983 and 2014, but the fluctuation was a function of the municipal rather than the policing budget. Other municipalities in British Columbia spent slightly more or slightly less on policing. Overall, the range for the province was at or below 20 per cent of municipal budgets. In the budget year 2014–15, British Columbia expended 1 per cent of its total provincial budget on policing, compared to 4.16 per cent on children and family development,

7.76 per cent on social development and social innovation; 7.76 per cent on education, and 51.9 per cent on health.[43]

High police salaries and generous benefits are also blamed for rising policing costs. While over the years there has been a decline in the number of police officers in Canada, the proportion of police budgets spent on salaries and benefits has remained constant at about 81 per cent (in 2021–2 it was 84 per cent) because the number of civilian employees has risen as that of police officers has fallen. Although they are generally paid less and require less costly support, there are now more civilians in policing than formerly. In 1962 there were 26,129 police officers and 5,699, or 17.9 per cent, civilian employees. In 2021–2, there were 32,717, or 31.7 per cent, civilian employees in a total workforce of 103, 282.[44] Nor are the base salaries of police officers much higher than those at the same levels in comparable occupational groups. In 2020–1 for example, an RCMP constable with three years of service earned $74, 916.[45] A federal firefighter with comparable experience at the same level earned $77,401, a correctional officer $75,012, a nurse $75,723, and a specialist 1 in the armed forces $73,992.[46] Also, except for the Royal Newfoundland Constabulary and First Nations police services, the ratio of constables to higher ranks in the police has remained relatively steady since 1986. Constables account for 68 per cent of total police, non-commissioned ranks for 27 per cent and commissioned officers for 5 per cent of the total. Top-heavy police organizations therefore are not responsible for the continuing high cost of policing.

Where police pay starts to diverge is in the payment of overtime. Special duties such as security for international events held in Canada, large operations, or lengthy waits in courthouses to give evidence, mean police officers work extended hours for which they receive extra compensation. Mainly junior and non-commissioned police perform these duties, and most are unionized and are therefore well compensated for overtime work. Police services, as well as other components of the criminal justice system, are seeking better ways of managing the assignment of officers. Nevertheless, overtime pay may well be the most efficient way for dealing with non-routine demand because it is a way of acquiring extra police officers when needed.

An example is the Ottawa part of the 2022 Canadian trucker demonstration. The Ottawa Police Service has 1,480 police officers working on different shifts to provide 24/7 coverage to the city. The number was insufficient to deal with the problem, so the police chief requested 1,800 additional police officers, which were provided by the RCMP and the OPP. The exact cost of overtime and expenses for police during the three weeks of the demonstration is elusive, fluctuating from $800,000 a day for Ottawa police alone[47] to $14 million for the eighteen days of the demonstration to $35 million for costs of the Ottawa police and RCMP for the whole period. It may nevertheless have been a cost-efficient means of acquiring additional personnel, considering that even one hundred more permanently employed full-time Ottawa police officers would entail an increase to the Ottawa police salary budget of $11,800,000 a year, without considering the extra support costs, based on the Statistics Canada average cost of $118,000 per police officer.[48]

From the number of calls for service and variety of tasks performed, it is evident that general duty policing, or "keeping the peace," is an essential activity for the well-being of society. While firefighters, paramedics, utility workers, and others also have first response duties, they have narrower mandates than generalist police officers, and the police may well be called before other public workers because their generalist training and authority equips them to make initial assessments and decide on a course of action, including calling in specialists. Huey and Ferguson provide an example in their chapter of this book. They observe that community agencies frequently call the police to deal with missing people, who are often mentally ill or vulnerable in other ways. Although Huey and Ferguson see this as an extra charge on the police, it may also be regarded as a cost-effective division of labour. It could entail a greater cost and organizational burden for public agencies to manage at any time of the day or night different types of public disturbance for which they are not currently trained. Nor, given the variety of calls for police services, the amount of responsibility, and the need for instant decision-making, could most of the functions be contracted to lower-cost private security personnel with lower thresholds of empowerment, training, and accountability. The amount of public funding expended on the general duty function of the police may then be considered taxpayer money well spent as long as the police are providing the level of service expected of them and are not working contrary to constitutional, legal, or ethical norms.

Big Policing Coping with Big Crime

While common crime has fallen, big crime has grown to present greater challenges to the police. Fighting big crime differs in many respects from fighting crimes such as murder or housebreaking. In the latter case it is clear that a crime has been committed before the investigation begins and the aim of the police is to establish who did it. While financial investigations can be initiated by a complaint or evidence presented from another agency, often it begins with knowing the identity of one or more perpetrators, but it may take considerable time and resources before it can be established whether and what type of crime they have committed.

Financial crime fighting differs in other respects from general crime fighting or from keeping the peace. General policing is concerned with immediate human interaction, urgent or dynamic events in communities, and physical evidence. It requires officers to have general knowledge, instant access to necessary information, and quick decision-making skills. Financial crime investigation entails sustained pursuit of elusive paper and electronic trails and requires specialist knowledge and painstaking dissection to resolve. Property protection might be the focus in both approaches, but the property protected in public policing is usually tangible and in financial crime enforcement mainly intangible. Financial crime investigation is therefore difficult for police organizations structured for dynamic intervention. Police are trained as generalists and rotated frequently to ensure they gain a wide range of policing experience, but financial crime investigators take time to acquire the specialist skills and experience to be effective and then need to build on existing knowledge within their field to become experts.[49] This tension between different demands and requirements has not yet been resolved in police organizations.[50]

Only the best resourced and diversified police organizations, such as the RCMP, can accommodate prolonged, intensive financial crime investigations, and even those organizations have difficulties. This is evident in the periodic reconfiguring and reorganizing of police financial investigation and organized crime units. For example, since the RCMP established its first commercial crime unit in the 1960s, it has introduced, reorganized, or dismantled and reintroduced several different white-collar crime investigative groups, such as the Integrated Proceeds of Crime Sections (IPOC) and the Integrated Market Enforcement Teams (IMETs).[51] It most recently disbanded its financial crimes unit in Ontario and reassigned the 129 officers and eight civilian members to organized crime, anti-terrorism, and drugs investigations,[52] quite possibly in search of yet another way to control big crime. Recently, the Ontario government created the Ontario Serious Fraud Office jointly staffed by police and crown attorneys, which was a successor to other previous police organized crime and white-collar crime strategies. British Columbia too has had several different mechanisms for investigating organized and white-collar crimes. The search for a perfect organizational formula for effectively managing such offences seems almost as challenging as investigating the crimes themselves.

An acknowledged difficulty is the lack of police expertise for investigating complex financial and other white-collar crimes. There are plenty of university-educated police, so it is not a matter of intellectual capacity. In fact, some police are accountants and lawyers, and others become skilled financial crime investigators, but there are not enough of them. Also, white-collar crime crosses banking, securities investment, real estate, taxation, corporate or informal financial, and other sectoral lines, making it impossible for police or even civilian specialists to be competent in everything.

In the 1980s and 1990s, a switch in tactics for investigating big crime to focusing on the proceeds of crime and "following the money" brought increased realization of how much criminal money laundering through legitimate business was taking place.[53] Consequently, from the mid-1980s until 2000 the federal government created laws to deal with money laundering and financial crime and increased spending to develop a regulatory, preventive, and investigative framework to contain big crime. The government initiative was further stimulated to maintain tighter control over the big money system in Canada by its commitments to the G7 nations and the International Monetary Fund (IMF).

The current framework is governed by the *Proceeds of Crime (Money Laundering) and Terrorist Financing Act* (PCMLTFA) passed in 2000. The Act is administered and the activities of various agencies enforcing the regime under the Act are coordinated by the Department of Finance. The object of the Act is to detect and deter money laundering and the financing of terrorist activities, and to facilitate the investigation and prosecution of money laundering offences and terrorist financing offences. It requires all financial institutions, such as banks, and "designated non-financial businesses and professions," such as real estate agencies or casinos, to identify clients, keep records, and report suspicious financial transactions to FINTRAC. This agency operates under the Department of Finance with a mandate to collect and analyse financial information, to supply analysed intelligence to the RCMP, Canada Border Services Agency, Canada Revenue Agency, and the Federal Prosecution Service. Under prescribed conditions of mutual assistance, it also provides information to foreign law enforcement agencies. The framework helps Canada to control illegal domestic financial activity and to fulfil its obligation to contribute to the global control of money laundering and terrorist financing.

A 2016 evaluation by the international Financial Action Task Force (FATF)[54] found the Canadian framework for countering money laundering and terrorist financing was generally effective but identified weaknesses. Apart from Quebec, among several identified problems was law enforcement activity incompletely aligned with the magnitude of the identified money laundering risk, and a low level of proceeds of crime forfeitures. Agencies lacked some powers for effective investigation and did not make a general practice of "following the money." The evaluation, however, made no allowance for the protection of privacy and human rights, which is as much a concern for the Canadian government as prosecution of money laundering. In the 2018 five-year review of the PCMLTFA, the Canadian government reiterated its commitment to the protection of human rights and privacy, despite the comprehensive nature of the Act.[55,56] The matter of privacy, particularly in legal matters, remained an issue for Canada in the 2023 consultation on the PCMLTFA regime held prior to a parliamentary review later in the year and the next FATF evaluation in 2025. Since the last parliamentary review there have been improvements to the legislative and regulatory anti–money laundering and anti-terrorist finance framework, but there has been little operational progress.[57] The federal government was therefore at pains to introduce its beneficial ownership registry by late 2023 and to show progress on a plan to create a nationwide agency to investigate big crime. A centralized financial crime agency would mirror what a number of European and other countries have already created, and Canada seems to have realized that it must do the same to show FATF, G7, and other international trading partners that Canada is not a weak link in the global anti–money laundering network or a safe haven for money laundering. So far the Minister of Public Safety has been mandated and allocated $2 million to lead the development of a proposal and undertake initial work to develop and design the Canada Financial Crimes Agency.[58] There is the option in the consultation paper for the federal government to set up a separate investigative agency as in the United Kingdom, but another is to use RCMP, FINTRAC, CRA, and other law enforcement resources.[59] The second option would follow the usual Canadian pattern of combining existing resources into a new configuration. Whatever the structure of the new agency, it will be the resourcing, management, expertise, and investigative success of the agency that will determine if Canada is a strong contributor to the global partnership.

The Costs of Policing Big Crime

Information on the costs of policing big crime is patchier than that available for general policing. Until comparatively recently resources for investigating financial and related crime were not fenced or identified in police budgets, and budgets of regulatory or law enforcement agencies such as the Canada Border Services Agency similarly did not make a distinction. Moreover, the fine line between what is serious and what is minor financial crime, or what are regulatory and what are criminal offences means the budgetary line between what is spent on big crime and what is spent on the rest has also been hard to draw. As Canada has come to spend more on fighting big crime, the expenditures are becoming clearer.

In 2019 the federal government increased the RCMP budget for proceeds of crime, money laundering, and related investigations. It provided $68.9 million over five years; $20 million per year ongoing for enhanced federal policing capacity, including the identification and investigation of money laundering; and $10 million towards RCMP information technology for investigating complex financial crime.[60] The increases were in addition to an extra $22.5 million over five years and an extra $2.2 million a year thereafter allocated to FINTRAC in 2013, and an allocation in 2015 of $293 million over five years for additional intelligence and enforcement resources to strengthen national security.[61] In the 2021 federal budget FINTRAC received another increase, bringing its total budget to $60.2 million for fiscal year 2021–2.[62] At the same time, Innovation, Science and Economic Development Canada received $2.1 million over two years for the development and implementation of the corporate beneficial ownership registry. In 2021, the Liberal election platform included a promise of a further

$200 million over four years for the Canada Financial Crimes Agency.[63] Only $2 million of the amount promised is being spent on development costs of the proposed agency, but presumably the $198 million will be spent in due course. From 2013 to 2022, therefore, the federal government allocated roughly $490 million of new resources over two to five years to strengthen the protective framework against big crime; however, only about $25 million has been allotted as a permanent increase to departmental budgets.

Provincial securities commissions, particularly those of Ontario, Quebec, Alberta, and British Columbia, have also strengthened their oversight and investigative regimes, but their mandate is mainly regulation and prevention, and they are largely cost neutral since the commissions are supported by levies on market participants and fees for service. Following revelations of extensive money laundering through casinos, real estate, financial, and other services, the province of British Columbia appointed a commission of inquiry into money laundering. Its final report with recommendations was presented to the provincial government in June 2022. While it noted the insufficiency of both federal and provincial resources for dealing with money laundering, apart from urging adequate funding for an expanded British Columbia Financial Services Authority and a new provincial money laundering intelligence and investigation unit, it made no specific recommendation on funding levels for the control of money laundering or financial crime.[64]

The current comprehensiveness of the money laundering and terrorist financing regime suggests that the Canadian government in concert with allied foreign governments is prepared to support big policing to ensure confidence in domestic and international financial systems and consequent global economic stability, but there is still a question of whether Canada has gone far enough financially and organizationally to control big crime and the big money that creates the crime. While the police and regulatory agencies have received more resources for fighting big crime, financial support appears piecemeal and lacking in strategic vision. Given the constraints on the public purse it may not be possible to produce all the resources needed, but perhaps the greatest threat is that at some point in the future governments and police will again take their eyes off the ball, and the new measures will once more decline into empty observances or become victim to a "mission creep" that dissipates their strength and effectiveness.

Defunding, Professionalized Police, or Better Governance?

This exploration of general policing and big crime policing, or low and high policing, shows that while both fall short on delivery, both are responding to vital needs for the well-being, stability, and prosperity of Canada. Therefore, knee-jerk compression of general policing budgets while increasing funding to big crime policing, or vice versa, is not only self-defeating but puts the two strands of policing in unintended competition with each other. It is equivalent to robbing Peter to pay Paul and achieves little in the end because it fails to resolve the tension between the two and avoids the hard discussions needed to deal effectively with both.

While governments are accountable for spending money wisely and getting value for its policing dollars, curtailing spending on policing without taking present and future circumstances into account could ultimately entail greater costs in terms of social and economic instability. For example, the price of $18.5 billion for all policing services, combined with the few billion dollar cost of the regulatory agencies, is comparatively low in comparison to the up to $2 trillion laundered through the legitimate global money system each year,[65] or the potential for public disruption, infrastructure damage, or personal harm that the Canadian policing system generally curtails. Moreover, big policing may not be as costly as it seems when the returns on government investment in it are considered. A concrete example is the $583,643,289 in forfeited assets collected in the five years between April 2009 and March 2015, not including amounts and penalties recovered by the Canada Revenue Agency.[66] When both the economy and social stability are under threat, compression of policing budgets does not seem the best strategic move.

Ultimately, it may well be that the problem governments and society in general face is not the money invested in policing but the quality of the returns on the investment. Police racism and violation of human rights,[67] or police organizations allowing financial law enforcement programs to languish and fall short of intended objectives are examples of bad faith in delivering on the contract between the people, their governments, and the police. They may also be indications of a variety of other police shortcomings, from incompetent management to narrow training focused on tradecraft rather than intellectual stimulation, police organizations and culture still dominated by white masculine values, more familiarity with the streets than the suites, and a lack of openness to ideas and direction from outside.

The accepted convention that police are independent in operational matters to avoid political interference has in effect given them considerable independence from legitimate government direction. Much ink has been spilled over the question of governance of the police,[68] but at the end of the debate, police are created, empowered, and governed by laws passed by a legislative body and funded from the public purse. Independence therefore is limited, and current levels of what Roach terms "undergovernance"[69] perhaps has more to do with the failings of untrained, timid, or neglectful governing bodies than with an inherent right of the police to be independent of legal direction. As Beare points out in her chapter in this book, even a governing body as strong as the Toronto Police Services Board was too reticent to attend meetings on the organization of security for the 2010 G-20 summit where it legitimately had a place to ensure that Toronto municipal policing policies were known to all the different stakeholders in the security operation. Governments have also delegated much policing oversight to a multitude of arm's length agencies with specific mandates, making coherent and unified governance of the police virtually impossible. As a consequence, Canadian police governance is not strong.

In the 1970s, Canadian governments provided clear direction on police conduct through such mechanisms as new electronic surveillance law or clarification of police powers, and in the 1980s and 1990s brought changes to police performance through administrative and financial means. Since then, government interest in police reform appears to have waned and settled on achieving efficiencies in policing and some increase in the security of the big money system.

The 2013 Shared Forward Agenda is a national strategy on policing and community safety that emerged from consultations among federal and provincial governments on the economics of policing.[70] Its focus is efficiency.[71] While efficiency is a commendable management aim, it is an unpromising basis for visionary change to meet the challenges of public safety, protection of human rights, and big crime in a modern, rapidly growing, and diverse Canada. Such a minimalist agenda more than hints at a neoliberal approach to managing policing and could lead to less rather than more police governance and to poorer policing outcomes.

Canadians tend to follow the lead of the United States in social change, and Canadian policing is assumed to be very similar to American policing. Some of the more extreme Canadian defunding rhetoric, for example, links the origins of Canadian policing practices to Black slavery in the United States.[72] But as this chapter discusses, there are wide differences between policing in the two countries so, with some notable exceptions, the United States is not the best source of inspiration for Canadian policing. Better models for reform are Australia, New Zealand, the Republic of Ireland, and the United Kingdom where there have been moves to professionalize the police. Police professionalization is a means of compensating for the inability of governments to provide the degree of direction and oversight needed by delegating the responsibility to the police themselves.

There is a rhetoric of professional policing in Canada, but it means improved training and quality of service rather than creation of a profession of policing.[73] True professions have certain characteristics, such as a professional association, society, or college which is self-governing and has a state-recognized monopoly over practice. Since it is self-governing it is autonomous but accountable. It maintains standards of practice and a code of ethics, and registers, licenses, and disciplines members (such as removing a licence to practise). Entry into the profession requires self-funded higher education and a requirement for continuous learning. The professional body also possesses a body of specialized knowledge supported by ongoing research to ensure evidence-based standards and practices.[74] Transition to professional status is usually gradual. For example, the members of the "learned professions" of medicine and law were initially trained by serving apprenticeships.[75] More recently, nurses, teachers, and others have acquired many of the characteristics of a profession, such as the transition from in-service or college training to university degrees, and licensing by an independent professional body which has authority to set the standards of practice.[76]

The United Kingdom, Australia, the Republic of Ireland, and other countries in the European Union have introduced university education for all police, which means their police education and training is now measured in years rather than the months of Canadian and US policing. The United Kingdom has gone the furthest in professionalizing police by delegating to an independent college of policing some responsibilities formerly carried out by the Home Office.[77] The College of Policing[78] is an independent professional body. It is currently incorporated as an interim measure until legislation is passed to convert it to a statutory body. The College of Policing is authorized to set the framework for evidence-based operational practice and training, professional development, and ethics, and the development of a body of research. It is far from being a true professional body of independent members given its creation and majority funding by the UK government, but the innovation is that government has set the entry standard for policing as a university degree and divested both itself and individual police services of the responsibility and authority for setting and maintaining standards of practice, training curricula, and professional development, and given them to an independent professional body. The third innovation was the elimination of local police authorities in favour of fixing the responsibility in a single elected position (with appropriate management support) of police and crime commissioner for each of the forty-eight police services.[79] They serve four-year terms and are accountable to the Home Secretary, who in turn is accountable to Parliament for policing. The role of the commissioners is to hold the police accountable, and their principal functions are to set the police budget, ensure policing efficiency and effectiveness, hold the chief constable to account, and establish a police and crime plan. Remarkably, these three radical changes have been achieved without tinkering with the basic status and functions of the police, or of police organizations, which are the foundation of the policing system.

The professionalizing mechanisms of the United Kingdom could yield new ideas for reforming the weaknesses in the Canadian policing system and could significantly reduce costs of training and payment of recruits during training. Independent standards could mean separate evidence-based standards of practice for both general duty and specialized big crime policing. University educated police with practical training acquired at in-service training schools would have broader perspectives and a wider range of policing tools. As other professionals are, individual professional police could have professional mobility and be held to account by external professional standards as well as by the police organizations that employ them. It might even be possible to contemplate that an independent police standards-setting body could become a partner or at least consulted in strengthening the law enforcement component of the PCMLTFA regime.

Two barriers to true professionalization are provincial responsibility for policing and the police unions. Any police professionalization initiative would have to start at the provincial level, but contract policing, national police services, and even the Shared Forward Agenda are indications that the provinces and the federal government have a shared interest in policing and can work together. The prospect of professionalization would be threatening to police unions, but if they were partners in the process, their continuation assured and their core concerns met, they might possibly be won over. It might even be possible to contemplate that in time professionalization and unionization could converge into something new and uniquely Canadian.

Currently, Canadian policing appears to be adrift. It is under constant scrutiny and criticism, rightly castigated for mistakes and injustices but unrecognized for its basic institutional soundness and for what goes right. It does not have the attention of government for either its clear direction or its reform, even as other developments in Canadian society, such as the growth of big crime and accelerating social change, demand more effective policing. There is a need for new ideas and new solutions to push back on the more extreme of the defunding demands and to replace the somewhat tired, similar recommendations that numerous public inquiries and commissions have offered over the last twenty years, some of which if implemented would entail throwing the baby out with the bathwater. Perhaps police professionalization coupled with more "professional" police governance, in the sense of competence and quality, might offer some needed inspiration.

NOTES

1 Paul M. Collier, "Costing Police Services: The Politicization of Accounting," *Critical Perspectives on Accounting* 17, no. 1 (January 2006), https://doi.org/10.1016/j.cpa.2004.02.008.
2 Rebecca Hume, "'The Police Helicopter Is Not Going to Help Our Communities': A Q&A about Air1," WPG Police Cause Harm, 2021, https://winnipegpolicecauseharm.org/blog/air1-q-and-a; Jolson Lim and Victoria Gibson, "RCMP Plan to Buy More Armoured Vehicles amid New Scrutiny Over Policing Tactics," *iPolitics*, 22 June 2020, https://ipolitics.ca/2020/06/22/rcmp-plan-to-buy

-more-armoured-vehicles-amid-new-scrutiny-over-policing-tactics/; Dylan Short, "'For Public and Officer Safety': Edmonton City Police Mum on Possibility of Third Armoured Vehicle," *Edmonton Journal*, 16 August 2020, https://edmontonjournal.com/news/local-news/for-public-and-officer-safety-edmonton-city-police-mum-on-possibility-of-third-armoured-vehicle.

3 Dan Fumano, "Dan Fumano: Police Funding Shaping Up as Flashpoint in Vancouver Budget Debate," *Vancouver Sun*, 1 December 2020, https://vancouversun.com/news/local-news/dan-fumano-police-funding-shaping-up-as-flashpoint-in-vancouver-budget-debate; Dustin Cook, "Edmonton City Council to Consider Reducing 2021 Police Budget by $16.3 Million for Reallocation to Community Programs," *Edmonton Journal*, 10 June 2020, https://edmontonjournal.com/news/local-news/edmonton-city-council-meets-to-discuss-police-service-defunding-in-response-to-black-lives-matter-petition; Wendy Gillis, "Where Does the Money Go? How Toronto Police Planned to Spend More than $1 Billion in 2020," *Toronto Star*, 15 December 2020, https://www.thestar.com/news/gta/2020/12/15/where-does-the-money-go-how-toronto-police-planned-to-spend-more-than-1-billion-in-2020.html; Lindsay Nicholson, "Advocates Push City Council to Reconsider Increasing Montreal Police Budget," *APTN News*, 2 December 2020, https://www.aptnnews.ca/national-news/montreal-police-budget-defund-the-police/; Keith Doucette, "Report on 'Defunding' Halifax Police Recommends Reforms, No Specific Budget Cuts," *Peterborough Examiner*, 17 January 2022, https://www.thepeterboroughexaminer.com/ts/news/canada/2022/01/17/report-on-defunding-halifax-police-lists-reforms-includes-no-specific-budget-cuts.html.

4 Public Safety Canada, Economics of Policing and Community Safety, https://www.publicsafety.gc.ca/cnt/cntrng-crm/plcng/cnmcs-plcng/index-en.aspx.

5 Livio Di Matteo, *Police and Crime Rates in Canada: A Comparison of Resources and Outcomes* (Vancouver: Fraser Institute, 2014), https://www.fraserinstitute.org/research/police-and-crime-rates-canada; Christian Leuprecht, *The Blue Line or the Bottom Line of Police Services in Canada? Arresting Runaway Growth in Costs* (Ottawa: Macdonald-Laurier Institute, 2014), https://macdonaldlaurier.ca/mli-files/pdf/CostofPolicing_Final.pdf; Paul Brantingham et al., *How to Measure Efficiency, Effectiveness and Equity within the Complex Role of Police in a Democratic Society* (Vancouver: Simon Fraser University, Institute for Canadian Urban Research Studies, 2017), https://summit.sfu.ca/_flysystem/fedora/sfu_migrate/17722/econ_policing_2017_final.pdf; Kent Roach, *Canadian Policing: Why and How It Must Change* (Toronto: Delve Books, 2022); Brigitte Poirier, Étienne Charbonneau, and Rémi Boivin, "The Price Tag of Police Body-Worn Cameras: Officers' and Citizens' Perceptions about Costs," *Police Practice and Research*, 9 May 2023, https://doi.org/10.1080/15614263.2023.2210726.

6 Colin Perkel, "Communities Struggle to Rein in Budgets as Policing Costs Rise, While Crime Rates Fall," *Toronto Star*, 1 Apr 2016, https://www.thestar.com/news

/canada/2016/04/01/communities-struggle-to-rein-in-budgets-as-policing-costs-rise-while-crime-rates-fall.html.
7 Jean-Paul Brodeur, "High Policing and Low Policing: Remarks about the Policing of Political Activities," *Social Problems*, 30, no. 5 (June 1983): 507–20, https://doi.org/10.2307/800268.
8 Jean-Paul Brodeur, "High and Low Policing in Post-9/11 Times," *Policing: A Journal of Policy and Practice* 1, no. 1 (2007): 25–37, https://doi.org/10.1093/police/pam002.
9 See, for example, H.N. Pontell, W.K. Black, and G. Geis, "Too Big to Fail, Too Powerful to Jail? On the Absence of Criminal Prosecutions after the 2008 Financial Meltdown," *Crime, Law and Social Change* 61 (2014): 1–13, https://doi.org/10.1007/s10611-013-9476-4; Tomson H. Nguyen and Henry N. Pontell, "Mortgage Origination Fraud and the Global Economic Crisis: A Criminological Analysis," *Criminology and Public Policy* 9, no. 3 (2010), https://doi.org/10.1111/j.1745-9133.2010.00653.xC.
10 Commissioner the Honourable Mr. Justice Paul S. Rouleau, *Public Inquiry into the 2022 Public Order Emergency*, Vol. 1: *Overview* (Ottawa: Privy Council Office, 2023), 21–3.
11 CBC News, "Kemptville Broker Charged Years after Clients Lost Millions," 4 April 2007, https://www.cbc.ca/news/canada/ottawa/kemptville-broker-charged-years-after-clients-lost-millions-1.652054; House of Commons Standing Committee on Finance, *Meeting Pursuant to Standing Order 108(2), a Study of the Canada Revenue Agency's Efforts to Combat Tax Avoidance and Evasion*, Testimony of Prof. Arthur Cockfield, no. 027, 1st Session, 42nd Parliament,12.05 pm, 7 June 2016, https://www.ourcommons.ca/DocumentViewer/en/42-1/FINA/meeting-27/evidence.
12 Patricia Conor, Sophie Carrière, Suzanne Amey, et al., *Police Resources in Canada, 2019* (Ottawa: Canadian Centre for Justice and Community Safety Statistics, Statistics Canada, 2020), https://www150.statcan.gc.ca/n1/pub/85-002-x/2020001/article/00015-eng.htm.
13 Andrea M. Gardner and Kevin M. Scott, *Census of State and Local Law Enforcement Agencies, 2018 – Statistical Tables*, NCJ 302187 (Washington, DC: US Bureau of Justice Statistics, 2022), https://bjs.ojp.gov/sites/g/files/xyckuh236/files/media/document/csllea18st.pdf.
14 Audie Cornish, Ayen Bior, and Patrick Jarenwattananon, "The State of Police Training in The U.S.," interview with Chuck Wexler, Police Executive Research Forum, National Public Radio, 27 April 2021, https://www.npr.org/2021/04/27/991343004/the-state-of-police-training-in-the-us.
15 US Bureau of Justice Statistics, "State and Local Government Expenditures on Police Protection in the U.S., 2000–2017, Statistical Brief NCJ 254856," 2022, https://bjs.ojp.gov/content/pub/pdf/slgeppus0017.pdf.
16 Patricia Conor, *Police Resources in Canada, 2017* (Ottawa: Canadian Centre for Justice and Community Safety Statistics, Statistics Canada, 2018), https://www150.statcan.gc.ca/n1/pub/85-002-x/2018001/article/54912-eng.htm.

17 US Department of Justice, "Federal Bureau of Investigation (FBI): FY 2022 Budget Request," https://www.justice.gov/jmd/page/file/1399031/download.

18 Public Safety Canada, "Royal Canadian Mounted Police 2022-23: Departmental Plan," 2020, https://www.rcmp-grc.gc.ca/wam/media/5849/original/6e7d85ee00 cabe5bf76a0fde1b2d039d.pdf. Interestingly, the 2022 RCMP budget for federal policing alone was slightly over $1 billion, or about one-tenth the FBI amount for a comparable period. Given the relative population sizes of the two countries, it would suggest that they both spend about the same amount on federal law enforcement.

19 On the question of "What do we want the police to do?" an example is Laura Huey, Lorna Ferguson, and Jennifer L. Schulenberg, *The Wicked Problems of Police Reform in Canada* (New York and Abingdon: Oxon, Routledge, 2023), 13-15.

20 Egon Bittner, *The Functions of the Police in Modern Society* (Chevy Chase, MD: National Institute for Mental Health, 1970); David Bayley, *Police for the Future* (Oxford and New York: Oxford University Press, 1994), 19; Kathryn E. Wuschke, Martin A. Andresen, Paul J. Brantingham, et al., "What Do Police Do and Where Do They Do It?" *International Journal of Police Science & Management* 20, no. 1 (2018): 19-27, https://doi.org/10.1177%2F1461355717748973.

21 Rick Ruddell and Nicholas A. Jones, *The Economics of Canadian Policing Five Years into The Great Recession* (Regina, SK: University of Regina Collaborative Centre for Justice and Safety, 2014). The study was funded by the RCMP "F" Division, Saskatchewan.

22 *Criminal Code*, R.S.C., 1985, c. C-46, s.2.

23 See, for example, Ontario Police Services Act, Section 42(1); Alberta Police Act, Section 38(1); Quebec Loi sur la police, Section 48.

24 Paul Ceyssens, *Legal Aspects of Policing*, Vol. 1, chapter 2:1 (Saltspring Island, BC: Earlscourt Press, constant update).

25 Ceyssens, Legal Aspects of Policing.

26 Ceyssens, *Legal Aspects of Policing*, Vol. 1, chapter 2:19.

27 Robert Gardiner, *The Compleat Constable*, 2nd ed. (London, 1700), https://books.google.ca/books?hl=en&lr=&id=UINZAAAAYAAJ&oi=fnd&pg=PA1&ots=mHtTc4U8jn&sig=Cigkv3LJ_2XJUPj1vBRrZYVQ0xw&redir_esc=y#v=onepage&q&f=false; J. Kent, "The English Village Constable, 1580-1642: The Nature and Dilemmas of the Office," *Journal of British Studies* 20, no. 2 (1981): 26-49, https://doi.org/10.1086/385771; Clive Emsley, *The English Police: A Political and Social History*, 2nd ed. (London and New York: Routledge, 1991); Thomas Alan Critchley, *A History of Police in England and Wales, 900-1966* (London, Constable, 1967); Allan Silver, "On the Demand for Order in Civil Society: A Review of Some Themes in the History of Urban Crime, Police and Riot in England," Paper 11, Working Papers of the Center for Research on Social Organization, East Lansing: Michigan State University, Department of Sociology, 1965.

288 Tonita Murray

28 Greg Marquis, *The Vigilant Eye: Policing Canada from 1867 to 9/11* (Black Point, NS: Fernwood Publishing, 2016).
29 Bittner, The Functions of the Police in Modern Society; Bayley, Police for the Future, 19.
30 Huey, Ferguson, and Schulenberg, *Wicked Problems of Police Reform*.
31 Huey, Ferguson, and Schulenberg, *Wicked Problems of Police Reform*, 71.
32 Huey, Feguson, and Schulenberg, *Wicked Problems of Police Reform*, 24, 118.
33 Samuel Perreault, *Canadians' Perceptions of Personal Safety and Crime, 2014* (Ottawa: Statistics Canada, 2017), https://www150.statcan.gc.ca/n1/pub/85-002-x/2017001/article/54889-eng.htm.
34 Statistics Canada, "Decrease in the Rate of Police Strength in Canada in 2022," *The Daily*, 27 March 2023, 3.
35 Federal-provincial agreements signed in 1966 committed the federal government to provide several national policing services, such as the Canadian Police Information System (CPIC), the Canadian Police College, the Canadian Police Intelligence Service, and the national forensic laboratories for the collective benefit of all governments in Canada. It also created the first RCMP commercial crime units and provided grants for establishing criminology centres at six Canadian universities across the country to foster Canadian policing research. In their turn the provinces began the reform and upgrade of policing practices with new basic training institutions, the creation of police oversight commissions, and other programs. In particular, British Columbia instituted a $5 million justice reform commission including the Coordinated Law Enforcement Unit (CLEU), which was established to combat organized crime.
36 Conor et al., Police Resources in Canada, 24.
37 Craig Lord, "Ottawa Council Approves 2% Police Budget Hike in 2022," *Global News*, 8 December 2021, https://globalnews.ca/news/8434412/ottawa-police-2022-budget-increase-approved/.
38 NBC News, "Growing Calls to Defund the Police after Death of George Floyd," 8 June 2020, https://www.nbcnews.com/nightly-news/video/growing-calls-to-defund-the-police-after-death-of-george-floyd-84693573984.
39 Brooklyn Neustaeter, "One Year after George Floyd's Death, Where Does 'Defund the Police' Stand in Canada?" CTV News, 25 May 2021, https://www.ctvnews.ca/canada/one-year-after-george-floyd-s-death-where-does-defund-the-police-stand-in-canada-1.5441519.
40 An Angus Reid survey found there were four public attitudes towards police, which were labelled "True Blue," "Silent Supporters," "Ambivalent Observers," and "Defunders." Each group comprised roughly 25 per cent of the population, and attitudes were influenced by age and geographic location. "Defunders" tended to be younger and urbanized, and roughly half of them had had a positive experience with police, which challenges the assumption in the text above. David Korzinsky, "Policing in Canada: Major Study Reveals Four Mindsets

Driving Current Opinion and Future Policy Options," Angus Reid Institute (2020). https://angusreid.org/policing-perspectives-canada-rcmp/. See also Ipsos, "Canadians Divided," 2020-07/defundpolice-pressrelease-2020-07-27-v1 .pdf. The IPSOS survey of the Canadian public on defunding the police similarly showed divided opinions. See Factum, "Canadians Divided on Whether to Defund the Police: 51% Support the Idea, 49% Oppose It: Generations Divided on Issue," https://www.ipsos.com/sites/default/files/ct/news/documents/2020-07 /defundpolice-pressrelease-2020-07-27-v1.pdf.

41 Statistics Canada, "Decrease in the Rate of Police Strength in Canada in 2022," 3.
42 Wuschke, Andresen, Brantingham, et al., "What Do Police Do?"
43 Wuschke, Andresen, Brantingham, et al., "What Do Police Do?," 21–2.
44 Statistics Canada, "Decrease in the Rate of Police Strength in Canada in 2022," 3, 7.
45 Royal Canadian Mounted Police, Regular Member – Annual Rates of Pay, https://www.rcmp-grc.gc.ca/en/regular-member-annual-rates-pay. RCMP pay is influenced by the pay rates of other police services in Canada and is not the highest in the country.
46 Treasury Board of Canada, Pay Rates for Non-commissioned Members, https:// www.canada.ca/en/department-national-defence/services/benefits-military /pay-pension-benefits/pay/non-commissioned.html#private. Since 2020–1 RCMP members have signed their first collective agreement and there have been substantial salary increases, so there may not be the same close alignment among the occupational groups; however, in due course the other groups are likely to gain salary increases.
47 Joanne Chianello, "Protest Has Cost City of Ottawa More than $30M," CBC News, 23 February 2022, https://www.cbc.ca/news/canada/ottawa/ottawa-protest -demonstration-cost-city-1.6361367.
48 Conor et al., Police resources in Canada, 3.
49 Jonathan Legare, "The Never Ending RCMP White-Collar Crime Expertise Shortfall," LinkedIn, 14 June 2018, https://www.linkedin.com/pulse/never-ending -rcmp-white-collar-crime-expertise-jonathan-l%C3%A9gar%C3%A9-cfe/.
50 Legare, "RCMP White-Collar Crime Expertise Shortfall."
51 Royal Canadian Mounted Police, "Integrated Market Enforcement Team: 2018 Performance Improvement Action Plan," Ottawa: RCMP, 2018, https://ag-pssg -sharedservices-ex.objectstore.gov.bc.ca/ag-pssg-cc-exh-prod-bkt-ex/857%20 -%20Integrated%20Market%20Enforcement%20Team%20-%202018%20 Performance%20Improvement%20Action%20Plan%20RCMP%20-%20June%20 31%202018_Redacted.pdf.
52 Marco Chown Oved, "The RCMP Is Shutting Down Its Financial Crimes Unit in Ontario: Here's Why Former Top Mounties Says It's a Mistake," *Toronto Star*, 15 January 2020, https://www.thestar.com/news/investigations/2020/01/15/the-rcmp -is-shutting-down-its-financial-crimes-unit-in-ontario-heres-why-former-top -mounties-says-its-a-mistake.html.

290 Tonita Murray

53 As a result of a British Columbia government initiative, a federal-provincial task force developed various cooperative strategies, including seizure of criminal proceeds against organized crime. One result was a 1985 amendment to the *Criminal Code* (Sec. 312) to allow the confiscation of criminal proceeds. The author of this chapter and Margaret E. Beare, the author of another chapter in this volume, were both engaged in the research and policy development for the 1982–4 federal-provincial task force. In the 1990s the first money laundering Act was passed. A simple account of the organized crime concerns of the day can be found in James R. Dubro, Pierre De Champlain, and William L. MacAdam, "Organized Crime in Canada," *Canadian Encyclopedia* (published online 2006, updated by Andrew McIntosh, 2020), https://www.thecanadianencyclopedia.ca/en/article/organized-crime. An academic account of the evolution of organized crime in Canada from the late sixteenth to the early twenty-first century, and the evolution from following criminal activities to following the money can be found in Stephen Schneider, *Iced: The Story of Organized Crime in Canada* (Toronto: John Wiley & Sons Canada, 2009).
54 The Financial Action Task Force (FATF) is a body formed by the G-7 in 1989 for setting international standards and acting as the global money laundering and terrorist financing watchdog.
55 Ministry of Finance, *Reviewing Canada's Anti-Money Laundering and Anti-Terrorist Financing Regime*, Ottawa: 2018, https://www.canada.ca/en/department-finance/programs/consultations/2018/canadas-anti-money-laundering-anti-terrorist-financing-regime.html.
56 It is also worth noting that the Office of the Privacy Commissioner of Canada is aware of the potential of the Act to violate individual privacy; see Office of the Privacy Commissioner of Canada (2012), Privacy and the Proceeds of Crime (Money Laundering) and Terrorist Financing Act for Customer-Facing Employees, https://www.priv.gc.ca/en/privacy-topics/surveillance/police-and-public-safety/financial-transaction-reporting/faqs_pcmltfa_02/.
57 Department of Finance Canada, *Consultation on Strengthening Canada's Anti-Money Laundering and Anti-Terrorist Financing Regime* (Ottawa: Treasury Board of Canada, 2023), 6, 11, https://www.canada.ca/content/dam/fin/consultations/2023/Consultation-amlatfr-rclrpcfat-eng.pdf.
58 Finance Canada, *Consultation on Strengthening Canada's Anti-Money Laundering and Anti-Terrorist Financing Regime*, 35.
59 Liberal Party of Canada, "Forward for Everyone," 2021, 28, https://liberal.ca/wp-content/uploads/sites/292/2021/09/Platform-Forward-For-Everyone.pdf.
60 Peter Payne, "Money Laundering/Proceeds of Crime – RCMP Federal Policing Perspective," RCMP presentation to the Cullen Inquiry, April 2021, https://ag-pssg-sharedservices-ex.objectstore.gov.bc.ca/ag-pssg-cc-exh-prod-bkt-ex/868%20-%20Presentation%20-%20Money%20Laundering-Proceeds%20of%20Crime%20-%20RCMP%20Federal%20Policing%20Perspective%20April%202021.pdf.

61 Financial Action Task Force (FATF), *Anti-Money Laundering and Counter-Terrorist Financing Measures – Canada*, Fourth Round Mutual Evaluation Report (Paris: FATF, 2016), www.fatf-gafi.org/publications/mutualevaluations/documents/mer-canada-2016.html; Government of Canada, Ministry of Finance, "Strengthening Canada's Anti-Money Laundering and Anti-Terrorist Financing Regime," in *The Road to Balance: Creating Jobs and Opportunities*, Budget 2014, chapter 3.2:133, https://www.budget.gc.ca/2014/docs/plan/pdf/budget2014-eng.pdf.
62 FINTRAC, Annual Report 2019–20.
63 Liberal Party of Canada, "Forward for Everyone," 28.
64 Honourable Justice Austin F. Cullen Commissioner, *Report of the Commission of Inquiry into Money Laundering in the Province of British Columbia* (Victoria, BC: Attorney General of British Columbia, 2022), 6–7. A part of the mandate of the sole commissioner was to review and consider four research and investigative reports, two of which were the work of Peter M. German Q.C., who is the author of a chapter in this volume. German's reports were *Dirty Money: An Independent Review of Money Laundering in Lower Mainland Casinos, 2018*, and an independent review *Vancouver at Risk – Turning the Tide – An Independent Review of Money Laundering in B.C. Real Estate, Luxury Vehicle Sales & Horse Racing*, 2019.
65 United Nations Office on Drugs and Crime, "Money Laundering," https://www.unodc.org/unodc/en/money-laundering/overview.html.
66 FATF, Anti-Money Laundering and Counter-Terrorist Financing Measures – Canada, 56.
67 Scot Wortley and Akwasi Owusu-Bempah, "The Usual Suspects: Police Stop and Search Practices in Canada," *Policing & Society* 21, no. 4 (December 2011): 395–407; Scot Wortley, "Hidden Intersections: Research on Race, Crime, and Criminal Justice in Canada," *Canadian Ethnic Studies Journal* 35, no. 3 (Fall 2003): 99–117, http://link.gale.com/apps/doc/A116860854/AONE?u=anon~be02d815&sid=googleScholar&xid=ff07f976.
68 See, for example, the following studies, which are a very small sample of the literature on police independence and accountability: Geoffrey Marshall, *Police and Government: The Status and Accountability of the English Constable* (London: Methuen, 1965); Philip C. Stenning, ed., *Accountability for Criminal Justice: Selected Essays* (Toronto: University of Toronto Press, 1995); Margaret E. Beare and Tonita Murray, eds., *Police and Government Relations: Who's Calling the Shots?* (Toronto: University of Toronto Press, 2007); Kent Roach, *Canadian Policing: Why and How It Must Change* (Toronto: Delve Books, 2022).
69 Roach, Canadian Policing, 74.
70 Public Safety Canada, *Shared Forward Agenda*, https://www.publicsafety.gc.ca/cnt/cntrng-crm/plcng/cnmcs-plcng/shrd-frwrd-en.aspx.
71 While the focus is efficiency, some of the research conducted under the banner of efficiency has nevertheless brought some social issues into sharp focus. For example, the challenges and special needs associated with policing in northern and

remote communities is discussed in Curt T. Griffiths, Joshua J. Murphy, and Mark Tatz, *Improving Police Efficiency: Challenges and Opportunities*, Research Report 2015-R021 (Ottawa: Public Safety Canada, 2015).
72 Rinaldo Walcott, "Modern Policing Is an Invention of Slavery," *The Walrus*, 16 February 2021, https://thewalrus.ca/modern-policing-is-an-invention-of-slavery/.
73 Ruth Montgomery, "The Role of the Canadian Association of Chiefs of Police in Supporting the Professionalization of Police in Canada," *Policing: A Journal of Policy and Practice* 15, no. 1 (2019): 222–33, https://doi.org/10.1093/police/pay105.
74 Tracy Green and Alison Gates, "Understanding the Process of Professionalization in the Police Organization," *Police Journal: Theory, Practice and Principles* 87, no. 2 (2014): 75–91; Ian Lanyon, "Professionalization of Australasian Policing: It's Time for the Practitioners to Take the Lead…," *Australasian Policing* 1, no. 1 (2009); Milton Lewis and Roy Macleod, "Medical Politics and the Professionalization of Medicine in New South Wales 1850–1901," *Journal of Australian Studies* 12, no. 22 (1988): 69–82; Ivan Waddington, "The Movement towards the Professionalization of Medicine," *British Medical Journal* 301 no. 688 (1990), doi: https://doi.org/10.1136/bmj.301.6754.688.
75 Waddington, "Movement towards Professionalization of Medicine."
76 The College of Nurses of Ontario, which regulates nursing under the *Regulated Health Professions Act*, 1991 and the *Nursing Act*, 1991, is one such professional body.
77 Jennifer Brown, *Policing in the UK* (London: House of Commons Library, 2021), 14.
78 College of Policing, "About Us," https://www.college.police.uk/about.
79 Brown, *Policing in the UK*; His Majesty's Inspectorate of Constabulary and Fire & Rescue Services, "Role of Police and Crime Commissioners," https://www.justiceinspectorates.gov.uk/hmicfrs/police-forces/working-with-others/pcc/role-of-police-and-crime-commissioners/.

Contributors

Dr. Sanaa Ahmed teaches law at the University of Calgary. Her research interests include financial crime, money laundering, financial regulation, and human rights and surveillance.

Margaret E. Beare the late Professor Beare had a cross-appointment with the Department of Sociology and Osgoode Hall Law School at York University and was the founding director of the Nathanson Centre for the Study of Organized Crime & Corruption. Her research interests were social control, policing, crime and delinquency, organized crime, women and justice issues, criminology and corrections, and sociology.

Sandra M. Bucerius received her PhD from the University of Frankfurt, Germany and is a Henry Marshall Tory Chair and Professor for Sociology and Criminology at the University of Alberta. She is the Director of its Centre for Criminological Research and of the University of Alberta Prison Project and co-edits the *Oxford Handbook Series of Criminology* (with M. Tonry).

Lorna Ferguson is a PhD(c) at the University of Western Ontario, Canada and is the Founder of the Missing Persons Research Hub. Lorna has a broad interest in policing research and developing evidence-based approaches to policing and crime prevention, including issues related to crime concentration, cybercrime, and responses to missing persons.

Peter M. German, KC is a former Deputy Commissioner of the RCMP and of Correctional Service Canada. A lawyer and member of the BC and Ontario Bars, he specializes in criminal justice matters.

Andrew Goldsmith LLB Adelaide; LLM London (LSE); MA Toronto (Criminology); MA Social Theory (Monash); SJD Toronto; LLD London (LSE) is

Emeritus Professor, Flinders University, Australia. His research interests are corruption and anti-corruption, crime prevention and crime policy, organized crime, police governance and accountability, and transnational crime.

Professor Kevin D. Haggerty is a Killam Research Laureate and Canada Research Chair. He is co-director of the University of Alberta Prison Project and has published on topics relating to prisons, opioids, surveillance, governance, research ethics, policing, and risk.

Laura Huey is a Professor of Sociology, Editor of the journal *Police Practice & Research*, and a member of the College of New Scholars of the Royal Society of Canada.

Daniel J. Jones is the Chair of Justice Studies at NorQuest College. A graduate of the applied criminology program at the University of Cambridge, he spent three years as a correctional officer and twenty-five years as a police officer, retiring as an inspector.

Elizabeth Kirley teaches in the Master of Laws program at Osgoode Hall Law School, York University, Toronto, for which she was awarded the 2021 Excellence in Teaching Award. She holds JD (Western), LLM, and PhD degrees (Osgoode), has served as Assistant Crown Attorney and Children's Lawyer for Ontario's Attorney General, and has managed a criminal defence practice for over fifteen years. As research scholar at Osgoode's Nathanson Centre, Dr. Kirley examines the challenges to our perceptions of crime, security, and human rights posed by emerging digital technologies.

Peter K. Manning PhD (Duke), is a Senior Fellow at the Garfinkel Archive, and a Fellow of the Yale Urban Ethnography Project. He has taught at Michigan State, the University of Michigan, York University, MIT, and Oxford. His research interests are in qualitative methods, social theory, and police studies.

Tonita Murray is a former director general of the Canadian Police College and an independent researcher and police reform practitioner. Her research interests include organized and financial crime, police leadership, and human rights and gender reform in policing, particularly in the Global South.

Stephen Schneider is a professor of criminology at Saint Mary's University in Halifax. His areas of research include organized and corporate crime, and he is the author of five books, including the bestselling *Iced: The Story of Organized Crime in Canada*.

James W.E. Sheptycki was born in Regina, Saskatchewan, and was educated at the University of Saskatchewan, Essex University, the London School of Economics, and the School of Law at Edinburgh University. He subsequently taught and researched topics related to transnational crime and policing for thirty years, first at Durham University in the United Kingdom and, from 2003, at York University, Toronto.

Laureen Snider is an Emerita Professor of Sociology at Queen's University, Kingston, Ontario. She has written extensively on corporate crime, crimes of the powerful, surveillance/technology, punishment, and the criminalization of women.

Anna Willats (she/they) has been a Toronto-based social justice activist, organizer, and educator for over forty years. She is a founding member of the Toronto Police Accountability Coalition and the Groundswell Community Justice Trust Fund, and she taught with the Assaulted Women's and Children's Counsellor/Advocate program at George Brown College for twenty-three years.

Stephen C. Wilks is an Associate Professor at Michigan State University College of Law, where he teaches commercial law. His research interests focus on governance and regulation.

Index

2SLGBTQI+, 208–9, 213; First Nations, 219. *See also* LGBTQ
5G networks, 105, 112; projects, 111
9/11, 15, 42, 266

ABN Amro Holding, 41
Aboriginal peoples, 22, 195. *See also* First Nations; Indigenous peoples
absconding, 232–3, 242–3
accountability: in the art market, 123, 139n16; of large complex financial institutions, 45; and neoliberalism, 152; police, 22, 179–80, 196, 213, 214, 215, 217; police accountability strategies, 215: and police financing, 3; and police governance, 168; and police independence, 191; of private security, 276; and state crime, 67–8, 70–1; systems of, 220
agenda(s): Agenda 2030, 66; neoliberal, 7, 150, 215, 282; Shared Forward, 282, 284
AIG (American International Group), 44
Airbus Affair, 193
Alberta, 59, 89, 280
algorithm(s), 131, 177, 78, 180; art recognition, 132; method, 132; tools, 102, 134–5
Al Rajhi Bank, 42
Al Zarooni Exchange, 42

American Express, 46
American International Group (AIG), 44
AML. *See* anti-money laundering
An Garda Siochana, 171
anti-money laundering (AML), 24–5, 35–8, 92, 135–6, 140n23; agencies, 82n88; *Bank Secrecy Act* (US), 140n27; European Union directive, 140n24; laws, 35; police investigative teams, 24; policies, 47; policy and program deficiencies, 35; program, 78, 136; regime, 92; and terrorist financing 74–5n24, 139–40n23, 278
anti-money laundering framework, current 91–3, 278–9; former framework, 89–91, 277; future framework, 94
Anton Pillar orders, 92, 97n35
APEC Summit (1997), 26
Arab Bank, 42
Argentinian government, 39
art: Art Basel, 123, 135; authenticity 125–6, 131; collectors, 121, 124, 131, 133, 137; commodities, 121; conservation, 26; Courtauld Institute of Art, 123; crime(s), 121, 130, 134, 137; criminals, 121, 133, 137; definition, 138n2; detection 134; detectives, 121, 123, 132–4; in the

digital age, 5; forger (s), 100, 131, 137; forgery, 126, 130, 135, 139n8; fraud, 101, 102, 122, 131–3; ID-art app, 133; identification, 125; 132, 134; investment, 100, 122, 123; museums, 122, 123, 124, 130, 136; recognition algorithm, 132
artificial intelligence (AI), 122, 132–4, 136, 137; ChatGPT, 133; DALL-E, 132; OpenAI, 132; recurrent neural networks (RNN), 132; role of in policing art crime, 13, 131; training, 133, 134
artwork, computer-generated, 102
auction(s), 122–3, 124, 125, 127; auction firms, 131; Christie's, 122–3, 125, 126, 127, 131; houses, 136; online, 131; Sotheby's, 127, 131
Australia, 111, 178, 268, 281, 283
automobile manufacturers, 12

Bahamas, 159
Bangladesh, 35, 41–2
bank(s): ABN Amro Holding, 41; accounts, 25; Al Rajhi Bank, 42; Arab Bank, 42; Bank of America, 38, 46; Bank of New York Mellon, 37; *Bank Secrecy Act* (US), 35, 123; Barclays, 38, 41, 43, 44; BNP Paribus, 41; Canadian, 25, 59; card fraud, 25; central, 18; chartered, 25; Citibank, 38; clients, 42; Commerzbank, 41; correspondent, 36, 41; Credit Suisse, 40, 41, 46; Deutsche Bank, 37, 38, 41, 44, 46, 47, 48; digital currency, 27; employees, 25, 39; European, 135; exchange rate manipulation, 43–4; extremist groups links, 36, 41; financial crime prevention 92, 169; global, 25, 36, 38, 41; Goldman Sachs, 46; ING Direct, 37; Iranian-based, 101; Islami Bank Bangladesh, 42; JPMorgan Chase Bank, 43, 46; LIBOR scandal, 43–4; Lloyds, 44; malfeasance, 48; managers, 36; Mitsubishi UFJ Financial Group, 43; money laundering, 12, 36–7; mortgages, 152; national DNA, 269; People's Bank of China, 27; phantom accounts, 40; private, 39; profits, 4; Royal Bank of Scotland, 41, 43, 44; Social Islami Bank, 42; Société Générale, 44; Standard Chartered Bank, 37, 41, 42; stripping information, 40–1; suspicious transaction reporting, 24, 36–7; Swiss, 39, 40; Swiss accounts, 38, 39, 124, 140n27, 153; terrorist financing, 35; UBS, 37, 44; Wells Fargo, 38, 46, 47; World Bank, 26, 153
Bank of America, 38, 46
Bank of New York Mellon, 37
Bank Secrecy Act (US), 35, 123
banking: Canadian, 266, 277; cross-border, 40; fraud, 99, 101, 106; global system, 15; offshore 18; secrecy, 25; self-service technologies, 25; services 25, 41
Barclays, 38, 41, 43, 44
Belgium, 168; Government of, 111
Bell Telephone Manufacturing Company (BTM), 111
beneficial ownership, 68, 70, 73n10; register, 278, 279
Bermuda, 156, 159
Biden, US President Joe, 66, 155; infrastructure plan, 66
"big crime," 1–8, 61, 99; big crimes, 35
"Big Four" transnational accounting firms, 156
"big policing," 61, 101, 150, 169, 266; aspects of, 6; big policing versus big crime, 276–9; costs of, 260, 279–81; definition, 2–3;
billionaires, 158, 159
Black Action Defense Committee, 213

Black Lives Matter, 180, 260
Black women, 213, 217
Black Women's Collective, 213
blockchain: accounting systems, 136; non-fungible tokens (NFTs), 18, 123, 136; technology, 18
BNP Paribus, 41
Board of Commissioners of Police, Toronto, 198
boiler rooms, 85
Breaking Isolation project, 214
bribery, 88, 89, 137, 157, 158. *See also* corruption
British Columbia (BC), 232, 274, 277; attorney general, 23; *Business Corporations Act* and regulations, 73n11; casinos, 12, 24, 59; Civil Liberties Association, 24; Financial Services Authority, 280; Government of, 60, 91, 290n53; Lottery Corporation (BCLC), 24; Missing and Murdered Indigenous Women and Girls Inquiry, 218; money laundering, 12, 24, 59, 91, 280; policing costs, 274–5; real estate inquiry, 23
British Institute of Art and Law, 135
British Virgin Islands, 39, 159
broken windows, 173, 174, 175, 187
BTM (Bell Telephone Manufacturing Company), 111
budget(s): Canada Border Services Agency, 279; federal, 76n31, 83, 279–80; FINTRAC, 279; municipal, 83, 274–5; other agencies, 267; public service,152; regulatory and law enforcement agencies, 279; Science and Economic Development, 279
Burma, 40

Cairn Energy, 42
calls for service: mental illness, 229; police, 177, 185n58, 274, 276; police missing persons, 233–4, 235, 236, 237–8, 239–40
Canada: attraction for criminal organizations, 12; business investor programme, 65, 68; Canada Revenue Agency (CRA), 24, 160, 278, 279, 281; Competition Bureau, 91, 266; Confederation, 88, 89; *Constitution*, 22, 88, 93; *Criminal Code*, 88, 89, 93, 271; Dominion Police, 89; Federal Prosecution Service, 278; Finance, Department of, 13, 278; frontier(s) 22, 23; Innovation, Science and Economic Development, 279; Justice, Department of, 194; Solicitor General, 194, 197; Supreme Court, 214
Canada Anti-Fraud Centre, 91, 95n8
Canada Infrastructure Bank, 66
Canada Revenue Agency (CRA), 24, 160, 278, 279, 281
Canadian government, 64, 65, 66, 70; failure to penalize corporate crime, 13; financial contributions to policing, 268; financial crime laws, creation of, 278; position *vis à vis* Meng affair, 114; use of high and low policing against truckers, 266–7; use of police against anti-capitalist protestors, 26
Canadian Panel on Violence against Women, 216
Canadian policing, 187, 265, 267, 284; community, 269; funding, 268, 270, 274; system, 88, 281, 283
capital, 153, 155, 160, 161; accumulation, 68, 70; cultural, 124; capital flight, 39, 62, 63, 158; facilitation of capital flight, 36, 38, 39; foreign, 64–5; gains, 26; investment, 63, 156; markets, 13, 49, 107, 124; state accumulation of, 68, 70
Capital One Financial Corp, 46
capitalism, 7, 69, 151, 155; "casino," 17; consumer, 21; criminogenic, 5, 157;

crony, 49; disaster, 19; finance, 48; global, 26, 100, 151, 153, 160; late, 157; lifestyle of the rich under, 121; neoliberal, 150, 154; surveillance, 16, 19

carding, 188, 200n3

cartels, 36, 38, 84, 89

casinos, 4, 91; British Columbia, 12, 24, 59; Canadian, 4; money laundering in, 90, 280; regulation of, 60; reporting to FINTRAC, 278

Cayman Islands, 25, 156, 159; Special Trusts Alternative Regime (STAR), 159

Charbonneau, Quebec Commission of Inquiry, 23, 71n2, 154; Mme Justice France, 91; report, 154

Charter of Rights and Freedoms, 93

ChatGPT, 132–3

China, People's Republic of, 5, 27, 77n38; Canadian difficulties with, 113–14; Communist Party, 101, 106, 110; economic interventionism, 108; geopolitical influence, 105; green energy strategy, 112; industrial espionage, 110; labour force, 105; Ministry of Posts and Telecommunications, 111; People's Bank of China, 27; recession 2007–9, 108; reforms, 106; relations with Trump administration, 101, 105, 109; relations with the US, 107–8, 113; rent seeking, 112; rising financial power, 27; subsidies, 113; tariffs, 110; technology transfer strategies, 109–10; telecommunications joint venture, 111–12; telecommunications research and development, 112; trade dispute, 110, 113; trade practices, 108, 109. 112, 113; trade relations with US, 107–8; 109–10, 113, 116n29; trade talks with US, 110; trade war, 5, 101; World Trade Organization, 105, 106, 108. *See also* Chinese government

China Mobile, 112

Chinese government, 111, 112; forced technology transfer, 109–10; Huawei links to, 110–11; joint ventures support to Huawei, 106; recession stimulus package, 108; US perspectives on, 101. *See also* China, People's Republic of

Christie's auction house, 122–3, 125, 126, 127, 131, 137

cigarette manufacturers, 12. *See* tobacco companies

Citibank, 38

Citizen Independent Review of Police Actions, 197

City of London, 159

Clearview, 134

coerced confessions, 250

Cold War, 19

Commerzbank, 41

commission(s): Charbonneau, 23, 71n2; Commodity Futures Trading Commission (US), 48; Cullen commission of inquiry into money laundering, 280; International Trade Commission (US), 107; Missing Women Commission of Inquiry, 218; National Commission on the Causes of the Financial and Economic Crisis (US), 44, 50; Ontario Civilian Commission on Police Services, 211; Ontario Human Rights Commission, 208; President's Crime Commission 1967 (US), 172; Rouleau Public Order Emergency Commission, 25; royal commissions, 190; securities commissions, 91, 92, 266, 280; Securities and Exchange Commission (US), 45–6, 155

commissioners: appointment of, 191; role of, 283: Toronto Board of Commissioners of Police, 198

Commodity Futures Trading
  Commission, 48
common law, 89, 91, 202n33, 271
communism, 19, 151
communist party of China, 106
community agencies, 6, 168, 265, 272, 276
community safety, 23, 231, 282
community safety, 23, 282, "community safety and well-being" model, 231
Competition Bureau, 91, 266
Compstat, 167, 175
Confederation, 88, 89
conspiracy, 40, 41, 43; investigations and prosecutions, 273, of silence, 137, 211
constable(s), police, 185n55, 284; average cost of; 242; chief, 283; general-duty policing, 274; in Middle Ages, 271; percentage of all police personnel, 274; ratio to higher ranks, 275; salaries, 275; sexual assault training, 209
Constitution, Canada, 22, 88, 93
construction industry, 23, 59, 60, 66, 154
corruption, 5, 13, 94, 95n16, 152; administrative, 60; anti-, 91, 153; anti-corruption laws, 160; arms, 62; big crime element, 2; bribery and, 88, 89; business, 150; Charbonneau inquiry, 59; in construction, 23, 66, 154; corporate, 87–8, 100, 149, 150, 154; *Corruption of Foreign Officials Act,* 153; definition of, 153; elite corruption, 100, 149, 153–5; grand, 87; impunity of, 102, 154; inquiries, 66; interface between licit and illicit economies, 26; International Anti-Corruption Unit, 153; neoliberal influences on, 150; normalization of, 66, 87, 149; pandemic, 87, 135–6; police, 191, 250; in politics, 4 15, 90; private sector, 154; public sector, 153; reforms from corruption, 171; standard for courts, 66. *See also* bribery

Corruption of Foreign Public Officials Act, 153
cost(s), 1, 6, 151, 265; analysis, 229, 236, 241; anti-money laundering compliance, 135; benefit, 233; borrowing, 63; call 242; containment, 273; corruption, 162n26; crime, 93, 270, 271; cultural, 153, cutting, 152; debt servicing, 63; dirty money, 137; doing business 94; efficient, 275, fraud, 25; hidden, 229; 233, 236, 241, 243; labour, 105; low, 105; neutral, 280; no-cost recommendations, 212; production, 113; public, 231, 269; public service, 23; regulatory agencies, 281; resettlement, 65. *See also* police costs
Courtauld Institute of Art, 123
COVID-19, 260; cornering the health equipment market, 151; dip in art market, 123; police enforcement of pandemic rulings, 272
credit card(s), 17, 46, 47, 92
Credit Suisse Bank, 40, 41, 46
crime: commercial crime units/sections, 90, 91, 277, 288n35; commercial fraud sections, 90; cost of, 93, 270, 271; crypto, 136; economic, 61; enterprise crime units, 90; governmental, 67; institutional, 3; rate, 265, 270, 273; root causes of, 50, 217, 231; state, 4, 67, 68, 69; transnational, 8, 23, 67
crime, art, 5, 134, 137; barriers to prosecution, 121, digital detection in money laundering, 135–6; digital detection tools, 122, 130–5; risk, 100; traditional expert detection, 125–30
crime control, 21, 167, 181, 275; aims of, 21; crime focus, 181, 271; fads, 167; finance, 1; mission, 172; police data for, 178; police role, 173, 175; reversion to crime control model, 168,

187; in streets, 21; underfunding of big crime control, 267
crime, corporate, 3, 50; criminalized corporate actors, 13–14; criminogenic culture, 50; low fines for, 13; parallels with organized crime, 11; state facilitation, 68, 160; threat to Western economies, 169, underfunding of high policing for 266–7
crime, cyber, 25, 90, 135, 180, 256,
crime, financial, 11, 83–5, 96n29, 137; in Canada, 84, 89–91; control, 1; cost of investigation, 93; extent of, 84; funding for control of, 279–80; global, 87–8; increase in, 83; laws for, 271–8; nature of financial crime investigation, 276–7; police difficulties in curbing, 59, 71, 92–3, 197, 277; private sector policing of, 92, 94; reporting, 37; requirements or responding to financial crime, 2; social harms of, 94; state sanctions of, 70
crime, organized, 21, 134, 191, 290n53; changing mechanisms against, 277; earlier strategies against, 90–2; groups, 11, 26, 86, 90; money-laundering, 12, 137, 160; national strategy for, 94; networks, 85; organized crime units, 277; parallels with corporate crime, 11–13; persistence of, 24; police resources for controlling, 273; policing of, 249, 256, 277, 288n35; prosecution of, 273; in Quebec construction, 12, 23, 154; receiving more attention than financial crime, 12–13, 26, 160; state-organized crime, 68, 69, 70; teams, 91; telemarketing, 85–6; transnational, 83, 85, 86
crime, white-collar, 1, 12, 13, 21, 273; evolution of, 62; extent, 23; investigative groups, 277, prosecution, 155; strategies, 77

Criminal Code, 88, 89, 93, 271
critical criminologists, 252
crown attorneys, 277
"crypto exchanges," 18
cryptocurrency, 18, 136
Cuba, 40
currency traders, 18

DALL-E, 132
deferred prosecution agreements, 49
defunding, 230, 280; argument, 268; contract policing, 270; demands, 284; logic, 273; movement, 220; police, 180, 229, 236, 242, 265; politics of, 23; rhetoric, 282; in US, 3
Delaware, 124, 160
Deloitte, 156
deregulation, 150
Deutsche Bank, 37, 38, 41, 44; amount processed in suspicious transactions, 47; fines for transgressions, 47; marketing mortgage-backed securities, 46
digital currency (E-RMB), 27
digital payment systems, 122
digital telephone switch, HJD-04, 112
Discover Financial Services, 46
discretion: bank, 39, community, 198; legal, 196, 197; police, 168, 192, 195, 196–7, 271–2; political, 195, 197; power of, 198, 199
DNA, national bank, 269; samples, 269
Doe, Jane, 210, 211–12, 216, 222nn7,12
donations, political, 156
drug trafficking, 1, 35, 269; international, 273; proceeds of, 12, 13, 36; rings, 86
"due process of law," 196, restrictions, 21; safeguards, 24

economy, Canadian, 61, 62, 6, 68, 70; global, 5, 7, 113

elite(s), 49, 69, 94, 158, 189; Anglo-Saxon, 158; artworld, 122; attitudes, 157; autonomy, 69; business, 101; corrupt, 26, 153; criminality, 26, 153; cultures, 20, 149, 154; deviance, 70; economic, 126, 99, 192; financial, 21; groups, 67; monetary, 18–19, 27; moneyed 13, 15, 28; organizations, 178; patriarchal, 151; transnational, 21
e-RMB (digital currency), 27
Ernst and Young, 156
espionage, 101; commercial, 105, 110; counter, 89; industrial, 110; military, 105, 110
ethics, 5, 45, 283; code of, 283; of tax avoidance, 156
Europe, 11, 110, 155, 270; transnational police networks, 19
European Community, 94
European Union, 43, 140n24, 160, 283
"evil," 249, 250, 253–60; "evilization," 253, 254, 256, 258; frame, 250, 253, 256, 258, 260–1; individuals, 252; police, 253, 254, 256–8, 260–1
Executive Order 13771 (US), 154
extradition, 5; Meng, 102, 106; treaty, 114
extremist groups link with banks, 36, 41–2

facial recognition: technologies, 134; tools, 134
Fannie Mae, 108
FATF, 278, 279. *See also* Financial Action Task Force
FBI (Federal Bureau of Investigations), 111, 268, 269
Federal Prosecution Service, Canada, 278
Finance, Department of, Canada, 13, 278
Financial Action Task Force, 26, 74n24, 135, 277, 290n54. *See also* FATF
Financial Crimes Enforcement Centre (FINCEN), 37, 38, 42, 47
financial crimes unit, RCMP, 71, 277

financial crisis (2007–8), 36, 44–6, 49, 160, 266; contribution to, 47; global, 4, 108; in wake of, 43; role in, 13, 48
financial institutions. *See* large complex financial institutions (LCFI)
financial system(s), 14, 44; Canada, 24; global, 13, 18, 43; international, 280; legitimate, 2, 87; surveillance, 25; US, 36, 41, 42, 45
Financial Transactions and Reports Analysis Centre of Canada. *See* FINTRAC
FINCEN. *See* Financial Crimes Enforcement Centre
FINTRAC (Financial Transactions and Reports Analysis Centre of Canada), 24, 82n88, 135, 266; funding, 279; suspicious transactions, 267, 278
firearms manufacturers, 12
First Nations, 268, 275; girls, trans, two spirit, women, 219; Kettle and Stony Point Ojibway First Nation, 21–2; policing, 22, 268, 275. *See also* Aboriginal peoples; Indigenous peoples
Floyd, George, 171, 250, 273
"following the money," 277, 278, 290n53
Foreign Accounts Tax Compliance Act (US), 160
forgery: art, 100–1, 122, 130, 135, 137; artificial intelligence (AI), 130–1, 132–4, 136; detection 125, 129–30; legal question of, 127; policing, 121; proof of, 131; provenance, 126; reporting, 133
France, 38, 127, 252; Government of, 39; Revolution, 19; tax evasion, 38
fraud, 11, 13–14, 21, 137; accounting fraud, 13; art, 101, 102, 122, 131–3; bank(s), 25, 46, 48, 101, 106; bank clients, 42; bankruptcy, 90; business and consumer fraud, 150; Canada Anti-Fraud Centre, 95n8; consumer

protection agencies, 92; cost of, 25; cost of doing business, 94; cryptocurrency, 18; detection, 136; enforcement, 197; gambling fraud, 155; historical offence, 89; internet, 84; investigative bodies, 90–1; investment, 49, 135; justification for, 157; mass marketing, 84; neoliberal, 155; Ontario Serious Fraud Office, 277; police, 250; Ponzi, 38, 47, 49; private sector prevention, 92; securities frauds, 13; syndicates, 85; tax fraud, 13, 155; telemarketing, 85; wire fraud, 101, 106
Freddie Mac, 108
free markets, 5, 149, 152, 157
freeports, 122–5; advantages of, 124; difficulties of investigation, 125; government-approved, 5; origin, 123; policing of, 124–5

G8 meetings, Ottawa (2002), 26
G8 summit, Toronto (2010), 192
G20 summit, Toronto (2010), 26, 193; demonstrations, 192; Morden Inquiry, 193; police responsibility, 193
GATT (General Agreement on Tariffs and Trade), 106
genealogy software 134
General Agreement on Tariffs and Trade (GATT), 106
globalization, 1, 5, 109, 153; of financial markets, 83; protest, 26
Golden decision, 214
Goldman Sachs, 46
Google Ireland Holdings, 156
governance, 27, 183, 280, 281; apparatus of, 27; behavioural, 16, 19; breakdowns, 45; corporate, 44; democratic, 22, 23; global, 19, 27, 28: institutions of 27; neoliberal, 152; police, 168, 170, 282, 284; state, 18; under-governance, 281

government, 3, 5, 7, 23, 24; authority, lack of, 125; bail out, 49, 108, 135; borrowing, 63; commitment to G7 countries, 278–9; constitutional responsibility, 88; corrupt practices, 87; cost-benefits for policing, 268–70, 273; costs for big crime, 267, 279–81; decision-making, 8; democratic, 5; direct funding, 112; direction of police, 281–2, 284; extradition, use of, 5; French, 39; and gender-based violent crime, 215; global, 7, 109; Harris government, 215, 216–17; historical development in Canada, 89; inaction, 83; incompetence, 4; intervention, 7; municipal, 23, 88, 93, 159, 265; neoliberal, 5; and police politics, 195–6; power to control police, 7; priorities, 6, 71; privacy and human rights concerns, 278; protectionism, 5; provincial, 22, 24; relationship to police, 191–3; response to crime, 86, 90–4, 176; reticence in penalizing big crime, 4; revenue, 63; role in inquiries, 190–1; social programs, 215; spending, 100, 157; stolen funds, 38; technology, use of, 134; Thatcher, 17; UK, 283; US, 5, 35, 42, 108, 111
group homes, 229; mental health service calls, 240; missing persons calls for police service, 236, 237, 238, 240
Guernsey, 159

Harris, government of, 215, 216–17
"high" and "low" policing: conflicting demands, 270; distinction between, 20; intersection of, 266; spending on 7, 267; tension between, 2
homelessness, 215, 230, 231, 272
Hong Kong Shanghai Banking Corporation. *See* HSBC

HSBC (Hong Kong Shanghai Banking Corporation), 4, 35, 47, 48; facilitation of capital flight and tax evasion, 38–42; HBMX, 36, 37; HBUS, 36–7, 38, 40, 42; Middle East, 40; money laundering and lack of compliance, 36–7; polluted culture and organizational pathology, 49–50

Huawei, 5, 105, 106; allegations against, 106; C&C08 system, 112; communication with Iran, 101, 106; connection to Chinese government, 110–11; HJD-04 digital telephone switch, 112; HSBC loan, 106; origins, 106; subsidies, 113; technology transfer, 111–12; US national security concerns, 110–11. *See also* Skycom Tech. Co. Ltd.

human rights: Ontario Human Rights Commission, 208; police protection of, 6, 213, 278, 282; principles of, 70; training, 178; violations of, 67, 281

ID-Art app, 133
illicit financial flows, 62, 68, 70
IMF (International Monetary Fund), 153, 278
immigration, Canadian, 64, 109, 189; business, 64, 65, 66, 68; enforcement, 218, officials, 189; status, 218; targets, 65
immigration, Québec business, 64
Immigration Act (1952), Canada, 64
independence, police, 191–194, 272, 281
Indigenous peoples: anti-Indigenous bias, 219; genocide of, 208; lobster fishers, 271; men, 214; missing and murdered Indigenous women and girls, 22, 219; patients, 232; police treatment of, 171, 209, 214, 217, 273; poll respondents, 253; rural communities, 22; women, 209, 214, 217. *See also* Aboriginal peoples, First Nations

ING Direct (International Netherlands Group), 37
Innovation, Science and Economic Development, 279
inquests, 190, 211
inquiries, 22, 167, 189, 190–1; Charbonneau inquiry on contracts in the Quebec construction industry, 23, 71n2; Cullen commission of inquiry into money laundering in the province of British Columbia, 280; independent review of money laundering in British Columbia real estate, 23–4; Ipperwash, 22, 190, 191, 192–3; Junger/Whitehead inquiry, 211; McDonald commission of inquiry (1984), 193; missing and murdered Indigenous women and girls, 22, 218–19; Morden independent review, 193, 194; on police, 191; recommendations, 190, 191, 199, 211; reports, 191; US permanent subcommittee on investigations report on HSBC, 35, 40; witness, 191
insider trading, 13, 84, 126
integrated market enforcement teams (IMETs), 277
integrated proceeds of crime sections (IPOC), 277
Internal Revenue Service (IRS), 40, 160
International Emergency Economic Powers Act (US), 35
International Monetary Fund (IMF), 153, 278
International Trade Commission (ITC), 107
Ipperwash Inquiry, 22, 190, 191, 192–3
Iran, 40, 41, 47, 48, 101
Ireland, Republic of: An Garda, 171; Dublin Metropolitan Police, 171; human rights training; 177, police

reform, 282; university education for police, 283
IRS (Internal Revenue Service), 40, 160
Islami Bank Bangladesh, 42
Isle of Man, 159
ITC (International Trade Commission), 107

Japan: World Trade Organization complaint, 112
Jersey, 39, 156, 159
JPMorgan Chase Bank, 43, 46
J.P. Morgan Securities, 46
Justice, Department of, Canada, 194
Justice, Department of, United States, 106; investigation of LIBOR abuse, 44; Meng deferred prosecution, 101; plea agreement with Credit Suisse, 41; settlement with Wells Fargo, 46–7

keeping the peace, 2, 230, 272, 274, 276; Bittner's description of 272; costs of, 273–6; in nineteenth century Canada, 271; primary police role, 169, 271
Kelling, George, 173, 174
"kettling," 193, 202n35
Kleptocracy: grand corruption, 87; kleptocrats, 87; Russia, 38
KPMG, 156

land ownership: schemes, 66; source of wealth, 155; transfer of, 155; transparency in 60
large complex financial institutions (LCFI), 4, 27, 25, 37–8; activities of, 49; bailing out, 108; Bangladesh, 41; breakdown of ethics, 45, 47; businesses and corporations, 63; coffers of, 13; conspiracy to manipulate LIBOR, 43; contribution to financial crisis, 44; criminogenic, 48, 49; *Emergency Measures Order*, 267; facilitation of money laundering, 37; foreign, 160; Iran, 47; largest, 35; lenient penalties against, 48; Libya, 47; Mexican, 36; multinational, 44; polluted culture, 36; role in financial crisis, 45–6, 48; Saudi Arabia, 41; Sudan, 47; Superintendent of Financial Institutions, 266; Syria, 47; transgressions, 35; US, 40, 44–5, 160
large language models (LLMs): crime detection with, 132
LCFI. *See* large complex financial institutions
Lehman Brothers, 44
Leonardo da Vinci, 122, 127, 129, 130, 132
LGBTQ 178, First Nations, 219. *See also* 2SLGBTQI+
LIBOR (London interbank offered rate), 36, 43; abuse of, 44; investigations, 44; scandal, 43–4
Libya, 40, 47
Lichtenstein, 156
Liquor Licence Act (Ontario), 208
LLMs. *See* large language models
Lloyds, 44
London, 39, 41; banks in, 43; City of, 159; "London Whale: trader, 47, Metropolitan Police, 50; new police, 191; Stock Exchange, 17
London interbank offered rate. *See* LIBOR
Lottery Corporation, British Columbia (BCLC), 24
"low" and "high" policing: conflicting demands, 270; distinction between, 20; intersection of, 266; spending on 7, 267; tension between, 2
Lucent, 111
Luxembourg, Findel airport, 124; freeport, 125; free trade zone, 124; tax haven, 156, 160

Madoff, Bernard, 47
Manulife, 60, 72n4
Mareva injunctions, 92, 97n35
market(s): analyses, 133; black, 11, 12; black and grey, 125; capital, 13, 49, 107, 124; capitalization, 36; Chinese, 107, 110, 112; commodities, 124; competitiveness, 5, 48; construction, 66; consumer, 105; credit, 44; criminogenic, 69; currencies, 43; digital, 136; distinction between licit and illicit, 11; distorted by criminogenic money system, 26; drugs, 15, 60; external audit, 157; financial, 13, 83, 121, 267; foreign, 108; fraud, 13; free, 149, 150, 152, 157; futures, 46; FX Shot Market, 43; global, 105; global art, 5; globalization of, 1; integrated market enforcement teams, 277; liberalization, 150; manipulation, 13, 90; money, 100; mortgage, 49; new, 153; participants, 280; policies, 23; real estate, 23, 59, 66; relations, 18; retail, 16; share, 85, 110; stock, 44, 90; technology exchange for market access, 111; telecommunications, 110; Wachovia Capital Markets, 46; Western, 107
markets, art, 140n23; amount generated in 2018, 135; Chinese and UK share of, 123; dip in during COVID-19, 123; ease of access to 121, 122; effect of heightened control on, 125; global, 5; hidden nature of, 123; lightness of regulation of, 123; luxury commodities markets and freeports, 124; money launderers in, 137 promise of digital artworks for, 136; thinly regulated, 99
Mauritius, 159
McDonald Commission of Inquiry (1984), 193

mental health, 231, 232, 235; apprehensions (MHAs), 230, 232, 233; calls for police service, 229, 233, 238, 239; costs, 23, 236; crises, 169, 231; crisis, 23; disabilities, 217; facilities, 229, 232, 234, 236–7, 238; missing persons, 229, 235, 238–9; police services for, 231; as research category, 234–5; resources, 231
Merrill Lynch, 46
Metro Toronto Police Force, *see* Toronto Police Service
Metro Toronto Police Services Board. *See* Toronto Police Services Board
Mexico, 36, 110, 159; Mexico City, 106
Milken, Michael, 155
Missing and Murdered Indigenous Women and Girls Inquiry, 22, 218–19
missing person(s), 168, 229, 232, 242, 272; calls for service, 233, 234, 235–41; complexity of cases, 238; data sets, 234, 237; location types, 237, 238–40; mental health, 238–41; reports, 232, 236, 241
Mitsubishi UFJ Financial Group, 43
MLAT (mutual legal assistance treaty), 194
Modestini, Diane, 126, 127, 132, 137
Monaco, freeport, 125
money: electronic, 17, 25; evolution of, 3, 19, 27
money laundering, 4, 47, 49, 94, 160; banks and large complex financial institutions, 36–42, 50; in capital markets, 13; costs, 135; definition, 84, 87; "dirty money," 15, 61, 86; Financial Action Task Force (FATF), 26, 74n24, 135, 277, 290n54; financial elites, 127; global control of, 278; in global money system, 12; harm done by, 137; international scandals, 36, 37, 38; process, 86–7; lack of prosecution, 13; risk assessment, 37; schemes, 12

money laundering in the art market, 5, 122, 123, 126; AI tools for detection, 130; policing of, 135

money laundering in Canada, 12, 23–5; 59, 70, 87; commission of inquiry into money laundering in BC, 280; costs of policing, 267, 279–80; counter measures, 91–2; anti-money laundering investigative teams, 24; as economic actor, 61–3; high-policing responsibility, 266–7; independent review of money laundering in BC real estate, 23–4; *Proceeds of Crime (Money Laundering) and Terrorist Financing Act* (PCMLTFA), 92, 278; RCMP role in, 90–1; "snow-washing," 59–60, 62; state, role in, 67, 71

money system, 1, 3, 4, 6, 7; big money, 278, 282; Canadian money system and policing, 21–7, 278; criminal opportunity structure, 12, 16; global money system and policing, 16–21; high policing and the money system, 20; licit, 25, 26; Moloch, 16; and transnational policing, 16; US dominance of, 27

Morden Inquiry, 193, 194

Morellian analysis, 130

mortgage(s): credit collapse, 152; "garbage mortgages," 152; losses, 44; mortgage-backed securities, 47, 49; mortgage-related securities, 44, 45, 46, rates, 63; residential (home, house), 43, 63, 152; risk, 44, 46, 152; rules, 64; subprime, 49, 157; toxic, 44, 47

Mossack Fonseca, 26, 160

Motorola, 111

municipal government, 23, 88, 93, 159, 265

mutual legal assistance treaty (MLAT), 194

Myanmar, 47

National Commission on the Causes of the Financial and Economic Crisis (US), 44, 50

National Inquiry into Missing and Murdered Indigenous Women and Girls. *See* Missing and Murdered Indigenous Women and Girls Inquiry

NEC, 111

Neoliberalism, 5, 23, 27, 149; age of, 17; agendas, 7, 149–50, 214; capitalism, 150, 153, 160; competitiveness, 150; corruption justification 149–50, 153, 154; decision-making, 152; free markets, 23, 149, 152; moral imperative, 149–51, 160; neoliberal states, 150; New Public Management, 152; policies, 100, 150, 154 155; policing, 27, 265, 282; transnational money flows, 26

Netherlands, 160

neural networks, 130, convolutional, 132; recurrent, 132

Nevada: tax haven, 160

New Criminology, The, 252

New Public Management, 152

New York City Transit Police, 175

New York Police Department (NYPD), 174, 175

New York State Department of Financial Services, 41, 47

New Zealand, 91, 111, 152, 268, 282

non-fungible digital tokens, 18, 123, 136

Nortel, 111

North America, 152, 155, 173, 174; anti-police demonstrations in, 234; civil rights demonstrations, 234; origins of police in, 208; police in, 177; police negotiation in, 198; police violence in, 176

North Korea, 40

Northern Ireland: police 167, 179, Patten report, 180

NYPD (New York Police Department). 174, 175

Obama, Barack: China trade 108; white-collar crime penalties, 155
OECD, 94, 153, 160
offloading, 229; hidden cost, 236, 241, 243; to police, 231, 237, 240, 242, 272
Ontario, 89, 215, 216, 268; civil forfeiture, 92; Civilian Commission on Police Services, 211; Coalition of Rape Crisis Centres, 210; Government of, 231; Human Rights Commission, 208: Ipperwash inquiry, 22, 190, 191, 192–3; policing arrangement, 269; prosecution service, 92; provincial police, 22, 90, 91, 191, 215; provincial police budget, 273; *Public Works Protection Act*, 193; Serious Fraud Office, 91, 277
Ontario Association of Chiefs of Police (OACP), 231
Ontario Provincial Police (OPP), 22, 90, 91, 191, 215, Anti-Rackets Squad, 90; budget, 273
Ontario Serious Fraud Office, 277
OpenAI, 132
OPP, see Ontario Provincial Police
Organization for Economic Co-operation and Development. *See* OECD
Ottawa Police Service, 273
oversight: banking transactions, 36; civilian, 280; financial institutions, 49; police, 213, 282; regimes, 280; regulatory, 59, 60, 136; state, 192

P3s. *See* public-private partnerships
Panama, 39, 160; Mossack Fonseca, 26, 160
Panama Papers, 26, 99, global banking exposure, 15; incentive for policing freeports, 125; "snow-washing" revealed, 62

Pandemic, 15, 18, 27, 66, 250; closure of businesses, 135; economy, 65, 76n31; keeping the peace during, 272; money laundering during, 135, 136; plummeting art sales, 133; profiteering during, 151, 135
Paradise Papers, 15, 59, 65
Patten report, 180
peacekeeping. *See* keeping the peace
People's Bank of China, 27
persons with mental illness (PMI), 168, 231, 232, 233, 242; calls for service, 229; mass shootings, 179; police interactions with, 230, 237, 272
police: civilian employees, 275; corruption, 191, 250; data, 175–6, 177, 178, 229, 234; "evilization," 253, 254, 256–8, 260–1; First Nations 22, 268, 275; funeral, 188–9; gender bias, 167; governance, 168, 170, 282, 284; governing bodies, 281; human rights protection, 6, 213, 278, 282; human rights training, 178; human rights violations, 178, 180, 281; independence, 191–4, 272, 281; interventions, 168, 174, 177, 230, 265; legitimacy, 23, 168, 198, 199; mental health calls, 25, 238; militarization, 3, 6, 169, 180, 272; municipal, 23, 89, 229, 232, 242; municipal police resources, 2, 83, 90, 243; patrol, 174–5, 177, 178, 216, 233; politics, 175, 194, 197; provincial, 88, 90, 190, 268, 273; provincial police Acts, 271; provincial police budgets, 83, 269, 274; provincial responsibility for, 284; salaries, 90, 175, 273, 275; Toronto Police Accountability Coalition, 220; professionalization, 282–4; trust, 22, 168, 179; violence, 6, 179, 213–14, 215, 249; wait times, 233; workload, 242, 243

police accountability, 3, 22, 196, 214, 217; behaviour, 167, 190, 199, 209, 250; conduct, 176, 189, 210, 211, 282; misconduct, 190, 211; obstacles to reform and accountability, 179–80; oversight, 213, 282; strategies, 215; systems, 220

police budget(s), 90, 181, 233, 265, 280–1; FBI, 269; fenced budgets, 279; hidden social service costs, 229, 233, 242–3; Ontario Provincial Police, 273; Ottawa Police Service, 273, 276; Port M4; provincial police budgets, 83, 269, 274; RCMP, 269–70, 279; reductions, 175, 242–3, 250, 273–4; transfers to social services, 231; Toronto Police Service, 273; value for money Canadian policing, 267–70. *See also* budgets; police costs

police calls for service, 276; data, 233; facilities making mental-health related, 237; mental-health related, 169; methodology for analysis of 233–6, results, 236–42

police costs, 176; calls for service, 242; cost-benefit of RCMP contracts, 268–70; keeping the peace, 273–6; policing big crime, 279–81; training cost reduction through professionalization, 283. *See also* costs; defunding; police budgets; policing costs

police culture, 100, 173, 188, 258, 287

police discretion, 168, 195, 271, 272; in applying the law, 192; negotiation and political priorities, 196–9

police racism, 209, 256, 281, 273; anti-Black, 213; RCMP, 219; statistically generated, 175; structural and systemic, 169, 252; UK police, 178; Women's Coalition Against Racism and Police Violence, 213

police reform, 3, 6, 167–8; early reform and variations of community policing, 171–2; reform based on computers and data, 175, 176

police training, 169, 177–8, 181, 276, 281; training on sexual violence, 209, 212, 215

policing: Anglo-American, 167, 171–2, 177–8; 180, 181n5; big crime policing, 61, 280–1; big data, 176; "big policing," 2–3, 6, 7–8, 276–9; big policing and state interests, 61; democratic, 28, 178; economics of, 23, 265, 282; elite organizations, 178; fads, 167, 174, 175, 176; general duty, 274, 276, 280, 283; global, 7, 16, 20, 27; intersection of high and low policing, 266–7; politics of 8, 16, 19, 20, 213, 256; private, 7; public, 22, 23, 26, 169, 266; reform, 213, 260; self-policing, 2; system(s), 88, 267, 270, 281, 283; transnational, 16, 19, 135; wicked problem, 169

policing, costs, 3, 170, 267–8, 275; for big crime, 260, 279–80; British Columbia, 274; contract policing, 268; cost-benefits to government, 268–70, 273; high policing, 7, 267; mental health service calls, 236, 243; municipal policing 274; Port Moody policing, 274. *See also* budgets; police budgets, police costs

policing, high, 2, 7, 27; convergence of high and low policing, 266; costs, 7, 267; crisis conditions for, 20; distinction from low policing, 2, 20, 266; lack of funding, 266–7, 280; protection of moneyed elites, 28

policing, low, 2, 6, 7, 28; blurring between high and low policing, 266; costs causing public concern, 7, 266; distinction from low policing, 2, 20, 266; with vulnerable groups, 168

political economy, 59, 61–6, 68, 70, 71

politics of policing, 8, 16, 19, 20, 256
Ponzi scheme, 38, 47, 49
Port Moody policing costs, 274
predatory product marketing, 13
Pricewaterhouse Coopers, 156
private security: accountability, 276; companies, 265; guards, 26
proceeds of crime, 24, 86, 87, 100, 279; from bribery, embezzlements, and drugs, 137; from drug trafficking, 12, 36; forfeitures, 278; fraud-related, 14; integrated proceeds of crime sections, 277; laws, 13; legislation, 90; and money laundering, 91, 93; *Proceeds of Crime (Money Laundering) and Terrorist Financing Act*, 92, 278; of tax fraud, 13
Proceeds of Crime (Money Laundering) and Terrorist Financing Act, 92, 278
professionalization, police, 282–4
profiling, racial, 214
public order, 2, 23, 26, 84, 272; police management of, 6; state of, 271; supporters, 266
public-private partnerships, 65–6

Quebec: beneficial ownership registry, 73n10; Charbonneau commission of inquiry, 23, 71n2, 154; construction industry, 23, 59, 60, 154; government of, 64; immigration program, 64; Summit of the Americas 2001, 26; Sûreté du Quebec, 90

racial profiling, 214
racism, 109, 214, 230, 273; anti-Black, 217; politicians embracing, 175
rape, 207, 209, 219, 257; crisis centres, 210; Ontario Coalition of Rape Crisis Centres, 210; persistence of myths about, 209; police, 210; rape within marriage, 209; rate of dismissal, 209; Slut Walk, 219; Toronto Rape Crisis Centre, 208, 209, 213
RBS Securities, 46
RCMP. *See* Royal Canadian Mounted Police
real estate, 61, 66, 91, 277, 280; agencies, 278; brokers, 24; Canadian, 23; investment in, 4; markets, 59, rentals, 64; sector, 24, 64
recession (2007–9), 44, 108, 65; global, 63; great, 66
recurrent neural networks (RNN), 132
regulation, 44, 69, 280; anti-regulation, 100, 154; art market, 123; banking, 105; casinos, 60; of laundering, 62; moral, 151; self-regulation, 157; state, 11; weak, 161
regulations, 13, 36, 67, 70, 99; cuts, 100, 154; technology, 110; US financial, 101
regulatory agencies, 36, 92, 169; federal, 91; resources, 280, 281; role of, 69; weakened, 154
regulatory systems, 4, 99
Rekognition software, 134
risk(s), 45, 46, 100; artificial intelligence (AI), 133; cybersecurity, 20, 25; institutional, 20; management, 45, 47, 48; money laundering, 37; mortgage-related, 46; national security, 110; privacy, 20, 25; security, 25; systemic, 25; taking, 13, 36; tax avoidance, 160
Rouleau Public Order Emergency Commission, 25
Royal Bank of Scotland, 41, 43, 44
Royal Canadian Mounted Police (RCMP): anti-corruption unit, 91, 153; budget, 422; commercial crime branch, 153; commercial fraud sections, 90; integrated market enforcement teams (IMETs), 277; integrated proceeds of crime sections (IPOC), 277

rule of law, 22, 27, 86, 87, 137
Russia: tainted funds, 38

Safra Republic Holdings, 39
Salvator Mundi, 122, 137; attribution, 125; authenticity, 125–30, 132; chronology of ownership, 125, 127; description, 122; price, 122; provenance, 126, 129; sale, 123; storage, 124
Saskatchewan: Ministry of Corrections, Policing and Public Safety, 231; Supreme Court of, 271
Saudi Arabia, 35, 41
savings and loan crisis, 48
Scandinavia, tax evasion, 158
"ScholarStrike" petition, 383
secrecy, 26, 101, 123; art forgery, 11; bank, 25; *Bank Secrecy Act* (US), 35, 123; cryptocurrency payment systems, 136; culture, 122; freeport storage, 122, 125; offshore companies, 39, 99; art provenance, 122; "secrecy jurisdictions,"124; tax, 99, 101, 156
securities commissions, provincial, 91, 92, 266, 280
Securities and Exchange Commission, US, 45, 155
self-service banking technologies, 25
sexual assault, 207, 212, 214, 217, 220; community engagement with police, 216; dismissal rate, 209; investigation, 212, 218; police training, 209; Toronto Auditor's Review of Sexual Assault Investigation by Toronto Police, 212; survivors, 212
Seychelles, 156
Shanghai Bell, 111
Shared Forward Agenda, 282, 284
shell companies, 26, 39–9, 60, 63, 154
Shock doctrine, 19
Siemens, 111

Skycom Tech. Co. Ltd., 106. *See also* Huawei
Slut Walk movement, 219
"snow-washing," 59–60, 62
social class, 18, 23, 187
Social Islami Bank, 42
Société Générale, 44
Society of Trust and Estate Practitioners (STEP), 156
Society for Worldwide Interbank Financial Telecommunication. *See* SWIFT
Solicitor General Canada, 194, 197
Sotheby's, 127, 131
South Africa, policing in, 167
South Dakota, tax haven, 160
South-East Asia, art markets, 123
sovereign bonds, 63
sovereign debt, 63
sovereign wealth funds, 18
Special Trusts Alternative Regime (STAR), 159
Standard Chartered Bank, 37, 41, 42
STAR (Special Trusts Alternative Regime), 159
STEP (Society of Trust and Estate Practitioners), 156
"stripping," 40–1
Sudan, 40, 47
Summit of the Americas, Quebec City, 26
Superintendent of Financial Institutions, 266
Supreme Court (Canada), 214
Supreme Court, Saskatchewan, 271
Sûreté du Quebec, 90
suspicious activity reports, 37
suspicious transactions reporting, 24
Sweden, 152
SWIFT (Society for Worldwide Interbank Financial Telecommunication), 17

Switzerland, 39, 132, 156, 160
Syria, 47
systemic racism, 169, 219

tax(es), 18, 100; abuse, 62, 66; advantages, 124; avoidance, 62, 99, 149, 155, 160; and big crime, 101; breaks, 100; Canada for minimizing taxes, 26; Canada Revenue Agency, 24; Canada Revenue Agency losses, 63; European Union losses, 160; fraud, 13, 155; grabs, 157; havens, 39, 99, 100, 156, 159–60; income, 156; introduction of income tax, 155; lowering, 5, 23; policies, 156; rate, 5, 156, 160; revenue losses, 65, 159; payers, 45, 48; relief, 112; scams, 123; secrecy, 99, 101, 156; shrinking tax bases, 105, 109; status of City of London, 159; *Tax Cuts and Jobs Act* (US), 158; tax exempt vehicles, 155; Tax Justice Network, 26, 65; taxable "big crime," 61; toll taxes, 65; Trump tax cuts effects, 158–59; US *Foreign Accounts Tax Compliance Act*, 160; US tax loophole 501(C) 4, 156

Tax Cuts and Jobs Act (US), 158

tax evasion, 46, 62, 99–100, 125, 149; bank facilitation of, 35–6, 39–40; Canada Revenue Agency evasion cases, 160; by Canadians, 160; corruption through, 154; elite attitudes to, 157–8; evasion and money laundering, 38–9; wealth managers, 155–6

Tax Justice Network, 26, 65

taxation, 100, 124, 157, 231, 277; strategists, 99

TD Ameritrade, 46

technologies, 123, 134; emerging, 136; facial recognition, 134; information, surveillance and communications, 2, 16, 20, 134; Huawei Technologies, 106; identification, 102; LLM (large language models), 134, 135; police, 251; restriction of sales, 111; self-service banking technologies, 25; transfer, 111

telecommunications: 5G, 105; China-Western joint ventures in, 111; Huawei, 5, 101, 105, 106, 110–13; infrastructure, 105; market, 110; Ministry of Posts and Telecommunications, China, 111; networks, 106; pricing effects on, 113; western expertise, 112; western firms, 111, 113

telemarketing, 85

terrorist financing, 15, 35, 37, 42, 280; al-Qaida and other terrorist groups, 41; evaluation of Canadian framework against terrorist finance, 278; offences, 278; *Proceeds of Crime (Money Laundering) and Terrorist Financing Act,* 92, 278

time to clearance, 236, 242, 242

tobacco companies, 12. *See* cigarette manufacturers

"too big to fail," 4, 35, 44, 49

Toronto: Anti-Violence Intervention Strategy, 16; Board of Commissioners of Police, 198; City Auditor's Review of the Investigation of Sexual Assaults by Toronto Police, 212; city council, 215; community action policing, 216; Police Accountability Coalition, 220; police chief, 193, 194, 198, 219; Police Service, 23, 187, 208, 214–15, 273; Police Services Board, 23, 193, 213, 215, 281; Rape Crisis Centre, 208, 209, 213; real estate, 59; sex crimes unit, 212; sexual assault squad, 209, 212; Women's Bathhouse Committee, 208 trade: art, 124; conflict, 106–10; deficits, 105; disputes, 109, 110, 113; free trade zone, 124; General Agreement on Tariffs and Trade (GATT), 107; global, 5, 267; liberalization, 108, 109; practices, 105, 107, 108, 109, 112; rules, 107, 110, 112, sanctions, 35, 40–1, 47, 48, 109; source of wealth; Trans-Pacific Partnership, (TPP), 108; US-China talks, 110; US International Trade Commission, 107; US Trade Representative, 108

Trade Act (US), 107, 109

Trading with the Enemy Act (US), 35

Trans-Pacific Partnership (TPP), 108

trucker protests, 233; Freedom Convoy, 25

Trump presidency, 260; anti-regulatory policies, 100, 154; impact on Canada, 113; pardons for corporate criminals, 155; protectionism, 5; state-enabled corruption, 154; trade tensions with China, 101, 105, 109, 113

trusts, 155, 159, tax avoidance/evasion, 160; use of tax havens, 160, 161

Turkey, 159

UBS, 37, 44

UBS Securities, 46

United Kingdom: art market, 123; ban on Huawei contracts, 111; Compstat, 175; financial crime prosecution model, 91, 279; human rights training, 177–8; lost corporate taxes, 160; neoliberal practice in public service, 152; New Public Management, 152; police finances, 3; police professionalization, 282–3; Police racism and gender bias, 178; "scandal-based reform,"167–8; stability of policing mandate, 177; telemarketing fraud, 85; unitary government, 88

United Nations, 94; eleventh crime congress, 84; Office on Drugs and Crime (UNODC), 135

United States, 5, 42, 108, 111; Capitol building, 84, 179; Commodity Futures Trading Commission, 48; Congress, 123; Consumer Financial Protection Bureau, 46, 47; defunding the police, 3; Financial Crimes Enforcement Centre (FINCEN), 37; *Foreign Accounts Tax Compliance Act*, 160; Immigration and Customs Enforcement Agency, 250; International Trade Commission, 107; invasion of Iraq, 19; Justice, Department of, 44, 46, 47, 101, 106; National Commission on the Causes of the Financial and Economic Crisis, 44, 50; National Institute of Standards and Technology, 134; Office of Foreign Assets Control, 40; Permanent Subcommittee on Investigations report on HSBC, 35, 40; President's Crime Commission, 1967, 172; rising protectionism, 101; Secret Service, 193; *Tax Cuts and Jobs Act* (2017), 158; *Trade Act* (US), 107, 109; Trade Representative, 107; Treasury Department, 48, 123

UNODC. *See* United Nations Office on Drugs and Crime

upstreaming, 229, 230

Vancouver: area hospitals, 232; fentanyl peddlers, 63; housing prices, 68; police, 218; real estate, 59; "Vancouver model," 59, 123

victims of crime, 195; Justice for Victims of Crime initiative, 195–6

Vienna Convention, 90

Virgin Islands Special Trusts Act (VISTA), 159

Wachovia Capital Markets, 46
wealth management, 156; culture, 157; professionals, 156
Wells Fargo, 38, 46, 47
Women's Coalition Against Racism and Police Violence, 213
World Bank, 26, 153
World Trade Organization. *See* WTO
World Values Survey data, 157

WTO (World Trade Organization), 105, 106–7, 109, 112, 115n13; China-WTO relationship, 105, 116n29; Chinese membership, 108; complaints, 107; compliance, 113; countries, 108; dispute resolution mechanisms, 109; enforcement, 112; rulings 108; trade rules, 110
Wyoming, tax haven, 160

Printed and bound by CPI Group (UK) Ltd, Croydon, CR0 4YY
31/08/2025
14727216-0002